FIFTH EDITION

PLANNING LOCAL ECONOMIC DEVELOPMENT

For Ralph Warren Hajosy, husband of Nancey Green Leigh

In memory of Edward J. Blakely's uncle, Charles A. Carter, who dedicated his life to creating economic and social equity.

FIFTH EDITION

PLANNING LOCAL ECONOMIC DEVELOPMENT

THEORY AND PRACTICE

NANCEY GREEN LEIGH | EDWARD J. BLAKELY

Georgia Institute of Technology   *The University of Sydney*

Los Angeles | London | New Delhi
Singapore | Washington DC

Los Angeles | London | New Delhi
Singapore | Washington DC

FOR INFORMATION:

SAGE Publications, Inc.
2455 Teller Road
Thousand Oaks, California 91320
E-mail: order@sagepub.com

SAGE Publications Ltd.
1 Oliver's Yard
55 City Road
London EC1Y 1SP
United Kingdom

SAGE Publications India Pvt. Ltd.
B 1/I 1 Mohan Cooperative Industrial Area
Mathura Road, New Delhi 110 044
India

SAGE Publications Asia-Pacific Pte. Ltd.
3 Church Street
#10-04 Samsung Hub
Singapore 049483

Printed in the United States of America

Library of Congress Cataloging-in-Publication Data

Blakely, Edward J. (Edward James), 1938-
Planning local economic development: theory and practice / Nancey Green Leigh, Georgia Institute of Technology & Edward J. Blakely, University of Sydney.—Fifth edition.

pages cm
Includes bibliographical references and index.

ISBN 978-1-4522-4259-0 (pbk.: alk. paper)

1. Industrial promotion—United States. 2. Community development—United States. 3. Economic development. I. Leigh, Nancey Green. II. Title.

HC110.I53B56 2013
338.973—dc23   2013008145

This book is printed on acid-free paper.

Acquisitions Editor: Patricia Quinlin
Editorial Assistant: Katie Guarino
Production Editor: Brittany Bauhaus
Copy Editor: Kim Husband
Typesetter: C&M Digitals (P) Ltd.
Proofreader: Jennifer Gritt
Indexer: Ellen Slavitz
Cover Designer: Gail Buschman
Marketing Manager: Liz Thornton
Permissions Editor: Jennifer Barron

Certified Chain of Custody
SUSTAINABLE Promoting Sustainable Forestry
FORESTRY
INITIATIVE www.sfiprogram.org
SFI-01268
SFI label applies to text stock

14 15 16 17 18 10 9 8 7 6 5 4 3 2

Brief Contents

Detailed Contents

Preface

Planning Local Economic Development is now in its fifth edition. As coauthors, we continue to respond to the needs of planners and academics, carefully considering their feedback as we undertake our revisions. Each edition of the book evolves due to this feedback, as well as in response to what the authors have learned from their research and practice. Each edition of the book also strives to reflect how the context for economic development planning and practice is changing.

The intervening years between the fourth and fifth editions of this book officially encompass the recovery from the Great Recession. However, the weakness of this recovery overall has meant that many localities haven't seen any signs of recovery, and most other economies have not returned to their prerecession states. We have worked hard in this edition to respond to the difficult fact that the challenge to local economic development planning has never been greater. Accordingly, we deepen efforts to incorporate sustainability and resiliency into local economic development planning that were introduced in the previous edition.

We revised Chapter 6, "Introduction to Analytical Methods for Local Economic Development Planning," to reflect evolving North American industrial and occupation classification systems, as well as U.S. efforts to measure the green economy. In this chapter, we also introduce social network analysis as a method for understanding local economic development planning capacity.

Added to Chapter 8, "Locality Development," is a discussion of the important influence of urban design for self-renewing economies. Further discussion of the importance of urban design is added to Chapter 11, "Community Economic Development," with a section on LEED-ND (Leadership in Energy Efficient Design-Neighborhood Development). Chapter 12, "Building the Implementation Plan," is substantially revised to provide a more in-depth focus on public–private partnerships and to highlight marketing efforts of different kinds of community.

Added to the last chapter (14) is a discussion of advanced manufacturing and other technologies as a critical component of "Local Economic Development Planning's Response to the Flatter and Climate-Challenged World." Finally, the fifth edition continues to include a number of the composite case studies introduced in the previous edition and augments them with several actual case studies.

Many individuals generously granted us permission to use material that we include in order to enrich our understanding of local economic development planning. We are most grateful for the research assistance and contributions to this book made by Dana King, economic development researcher and planner par excellence. Georgia Tech students Patrick Terranova, Nathanael Hoelzel, and Jeong-Il Park also contributed valuable research assistance.

We remain indebted to our many colleagues, and especially Michael Teitz, whose comments, criticisms, and own writings helped us to articulate our view of planning local economic development.

Nancey Green Leigh

Edward J. Blakely

Reference

Fitzgerald, Joan, and Nancey Green Leigh. 2002. *Economic Revitalization: Cases and Strategies for City and Suburb.* Thousand Oaks, CA: Sage.

Overview

In the Overview to the third edition of *Planning Local Economic Development*, we observed that local issues had been put aside for the nation's needs because of September 11, 2001. Localities and citizens largely accepted the notion that response to a common danger required focusing on broader international concerns. In 2009, we observed that the fourth edition was going to press after nearly a decade of putting aside local needs with severe consequences. Localities and economic development planning had suffered significantly, and we expressed our concern that the foreseeable future posed even greater challenges for economic development planning. This stemmed from the burdens imposed on local economies as a result of the national crisis that destroyed credit markets and imperiled national assets. Because of the financial sector's misdeeds in this country, every locality, citizen, and honest business ended up bearing a portion of this burden, but a significant part of the global economy will be affected as well. We have rapidly descended into the worst economic conditions since the Great Depression of the 1930s. While it is too soon to tell whether the degree of economic dislocation, job loss, and housing foreclosures will match or exceed that dark period, the pace of economic deterioration feels like a main artery of the economy was cut and no one can stop the bleeding.

Thus, as we alluded to in the Preface, fully comprehending the context for planning future local economic development is now more challenging than ever. The Bush administration, with Congressional approval, launched the largest national direct funding scheme for banks in history with $700 billion (as of January 2009) that offered little for state and local government or economic development agencies. Instead, it was aimed at those financial institutions whose mismanagement caused the economic crisis but whose survival is seemingly critical to the intertwined domestic and global economies. The Obama administration took over in late January of 2009 in an economy that continued to deteriorate. New economic stimulus measures are being aimed at states and localities, but the impact they may have will not be known for a very long time.

The domestic economy was not performing well for many Americans before the crisis of 2008, and there was growing concern over rising inequality and unemployment. In response, local government and community groups increasingly pursued opportunities to improve economic, wealth, and employment bases in ways that promoted sustainability and equity. They became much more aware of how the global economy impacts their local economy. But, through the normal zoning and permitting process or through public–private partnerships undertaken for the best of reasons, many localities were unwittingly caught up in facilitating the subprime mortgage-backed home building spree that has now left abandoned neighborhoods and unfinished suburban developments throughout the nation.

However, starting with the impetus given to local government initiatives as far back as the Clinton administration, localities do have a foundation from which to navigate the road to sustainable economic recovery and planning. Depressed neighborhoods and rural unincorporated areas have learned to develop their own approaches for local business creation, including creating new institutions such as community development finance institutions to generate capital or stabilize the community's economic base. In some instances, local governments and groups have acted on their own; in other instances, they have cooperated with other communities and government levels to create new economic development activities. While there has been great diversity in organizational structures and initiatives, the common goal has been to provide the neighborhood, locality, or region with greater capacity to contribute to determining its own economic destiny.

Local institutional involvement in economic development is always a complex process that admittedly became a lot harder in 2009. For the nation to thrive, communities will have to do more to build human capacity and innovation so we can produce competitive products and services while reducing energy and raw material consumption. This requires increased knowledge and cooperation on the part of government officials, businesses, unions, professional leaders, and community groups. Therefore, community organizations or local government officials must consider carefully whether they possess the necessary institutional resources as well as economic development opportunities before they embark on any activities. Economic development may not be useful or reasonable for every situation. Nonetheless, irrespective of their size or location, communities must consider their economic destiny as a major component of their political agenda. One thing is very clear: The forces of economic change do not respect national, regional, local community, or neighborhood boundaries.

This book is aimed primarily at students studying to become professional planners or practitioners of local economic development at the regional, agency, city or county government, or neighborhood levels. We hope that the updated edition, which strives to reflect the evolving field, will also continue to be a reference for economic development professionals as they carry out their responsibilities. Economic development specialists and planners should find the resource materials included in the text useful for their work.

This book continues to provide guidance for community-based organizations and their client groups engaged in the struggle to find viable means to develop the economic base of their communities. The book is also designed to serve as primary material or as an adjunct to other materials used in teaching economic development. Both the reference materials and case examples are arranged in a manner suitable for teaching. Sample resource materials are included to facilitate its use in this manner. The sample materials are also intended to support analytical efforts designed to determine community economic and employment requirements, as well as to develop project or program strategies.

Policymakers at either the local government or the community level may find the book useful in exploring the roles that private enterprise, unions, community groups, and other institutions can play in local economic and workforce development activities. In addition, the book can aid private citizens interested in local economic development and employment issues to determine ways they might assist government bodies or community groups in meeting their economic development objectives. Community groups may find the illustrations and case examples discussed in the text valuable for networking with those in similar circumstances throughout the country. While the book is written for a U.S. audience because it is difficult to fashion both methods and policies across national legal structures, it has fundamental principles for local or community-based institutions around the world.

Local economic development and workforce initiatives are continually evolving. There are no hard and fast rules or long-proven experiences upon which to draw. We ground this book in the needs, issues, and options available at the local level and encourage readers to contribute ideas for future editions.

This book strives to place the basic tenets of local economic development planning in one volume. It explicitly broadens the view of local economic development from one that emphasizes real estate development and industrial recruitment to one that encompasses workforce development and community-determined processes. It explicitly incorporates the notions of equity and sustainability. It distinguishes itself from all other texts on economic development planning by explicitly asserting that authentic economic development incorporates the basic principles of sustainability.

It is clear that the job of the economic development planner and the work of the community in achieving sustainable economic development have become much harder because of the national and global economic crisis. But it is also crystal clear that the role of local economic development planning has never been more important. This book surveys the full range of activities that constitute the planning of local economic development. If all localities were to systematically undertake this full range of activities, they would be competitively positioned to weather economic crises created by forces beyond their control, or to thrive in more benign economic conditions. However, the next few years will provide an important opportunity to chronicle and reflect on local economic development planning that communities use to respond to our current crisis. We look forward to including their case studies in the next edition.

Acknowledgments

The authors and SAGE would like to acknowledge the contributions of the following reviewers:

John Accordino, *Virginia Commonwealth University*

Sharmistha Bagchi-Sen, *State University of New York–Buffalo*

Susan L. Bower, *Blue Mountain Community College*

Jeffrey Doshna, *Temple University*

Derek Eysenbach, *University of Arizona*

Carl Grodach, *University of Texas at Arlington*

Jan Kircher, *St. Cloud State University*

Ric Kolenda, *Georgia State University*

Lee Pugalis, *Northumbria University, UK*

Henry Renski, *University of Massachusetts Amherst*

Dr. Nicholas J. Swartz, *James Madison University*

Dr. Stacey Sutton, *Columbia University*

1

The Enduring Argument for Local Economic Development Planning

C ities, towns, counties, and all local entities in a global economy have the challenge and opportunity of crafting their own economic destinies. This is true for the poorest as well as the wealthiest localities. In reality, the forces of nature, demography, technology, and industry are such that no local economy can ever count on an achieved position of stability and security. This has always been true, but the contemporary context for local economic development planning is severely challenged by the two trends of rising inequality and global warming. It is also challenged by the increasingly transitory nature of any given local economy in the face of overwhelming forces of globalization. These forces flatten the world in such a way that few, if any, local economies are exempt from globalizing forces that can bring growth and development or decline and increased poverty (Friedman, 2005).

Local Economic Development Planning in the Face of Globalization

The globalizing economy—until the recession that began in at the end of 2007—was truly a case of the whole being greater than the sum of its parts. The integration of national and local economies into one global economy accelerated growth in the gross world product. The International Monetary Fund (2007) calculated that the world economy had grown at a rate of 3.2% from 1988 to 1997 and 4.4% from 1998 through 2007. This was accompanied by continued growth in the share of world income that went to individuals (gross domestic product per capita), with persons in the newly industrializing and emerging market countries gaining at a higher rate.

1

Unfortunately, the other side of the coin of an increasingly integrated global economy is that economic downturn in one major nation can spread across the globe, as happened from the second half of 2008. The global economy experienced the worst recession since the Great Depression of the 1930s. And while the recession was officially declared to have ended in the United States in mid 2009, the U.S. and the rest of the global economy have yet to recover, nor are they expected to do so for years to come. We provide a brief explanation of the Great Recession below.

The U.S. financial crisis had at its core the subprime housing market. Home loans were made to unqualified buyers in violation of prudent lending practices and regulations. The banks making the loans did not hold on to them. Instead, they sold them to secondary mortgage consolidators, who then packaged them into derivative financial instruments. These, in turn, were sold to investors across the globe, who suffered severe losses when the loans went into default. There followed a major credit crisis as many banks and investing houses failed.

Some 70% of the U.S. economy is consumer based. Without access to credit, because of bank failures and decreased lender ability, as well as willingness to provide credit even to financially sound businesses and individuals, consumer spending severely declined. Consequently, all the businesses that sell to them have suffered. At first, the businesses selling big-ticket items such as autos were especially hard hit. But as the effects of the Great Recession have lingered, many small businesses were unable to hold on. The small business failure rate increased 40% between 2007 and 2010, with retailers and manufacturers experiencing the highest rates of failure (Dunn and Bradstreet, 2011).

The U.S. auto industry is one of the most globalized in terms of its production systems, sourcing parts from around the globe. Further, a large proportion of the goods sold in stores within the United States are imported. Thus, countries around the globe experienced the backlash of the U.S. economic crisis with associated declines in foreign trade, number of firms, and employment.

What does increased global integration mean for the local economies that we focus on in this book? We answer this question within the context of three phases of globalization that Thomas L. Friedman (2005) has described. Long before the Great Recession that began in 2008, the United States' globalizing and sending of goods abroad, or what Friedman calls Globalization 1.0, brought significant prosperity to many local economies making manufactured goods, growing crops, and producing services and entertainment. As U.S. companies globalized in the 2.0 phase, accessing overseas markets and employing labor in other nations, U.S. local economies experienced plant closings on an accelerating scale. Local economies overly dependent on the industry sectors that found it most profitable to move their operations overseas experienced the greatest devastation. Many of the companies in these industry sectors simply were unable to compete with cheaper imports and thus moved overseas to take advantage of lower labor and other production costs. At the same time, companies from other nations have located in local economies across the United States to gain access to our consumer market, and in the case of certain industry sectors, to less expensive labor and other costs of production. On balance, however, there was legitimate concern that the process of globalization could leave behind many local economies, and demographic groups within those economies, if they continued to pursue "business as usual."

Globalization 3.0 is the most recent phase, according to Friedman (2005). This phase shifted the drivers of globalization away from U.S. and European companies to individuals and non-Western nations. Further, even before the Great Recession, Globalization 3.0 created major new challenges for local economic development planning and practice in the United States. The solutions, as Friedman (2005) astutely observed, called for an orientation away from traditional business development and recruitment toward ensuring all participants in a local economy have adequate preparation to make maximum contributions. Recovering from the Great Recession and creating a new path for prosperity requires a shift from "business as usual." It also requires an economy focused on reinventing itself through new technologies, innovations, and renewed commitments to ethical leadership. The challenges to local economic development are the greatest they have been since the establishment of the formal field. More than ever, local economic development planners and policymakers will need to have a sophisticated and comprehensive set of tools and strategies to remake their economies.

Prior to the Great Recession, new immigrants' increasing labor force contributions and the problem of longtime residents with weak attachment to the labor market was of growing importance because of the aging population of the United States and the rest of the "rich world." Most of Europe, as well as Japan, will experience sharp drops in population over the next three to four decades due to declining birth rates. The resulting aging of the population signals increased expenditures for health care and other government-provided services and places real strain on the future prosperity of these important global European partners of the United States. It is possible, however, that an aging labor force will now no longer be able to retire at the normal age due to the impact that the stock and housing market declines have had on retirement investment portfolios.

Historically, the United States has been in an enviable demographic position compared with its advanced nation allies. As a result, international capital flowed to the United States at a record pace. The United States also has had one of the most liberal and desirable immigration programs in the world. Thus, we should have an adequate *number* of workers to meet demand once there is a full recovery from the recession. However, the local economic development challenge is to ensure that this labor force is fully prepared to meet the demands of employers facing heightened global competition. One of the most encouraging economic development trends in the aftermath of the Great Recession has been that of in-shoring, or bringing back production to the United States. However, many employers (especially in manufacturing) are complaining that they can not find the skilled workers they need.

It will be critical for the United States to retain its high rate of economic productivity. In most industries, the combination of American workers and technology has created higher productivity than anywhere else in the world. However, the average U.S. worker has not benefited from productivity increases, as once was the case. In fact, one of the most important explanations for rising inequality and threats to the American (read middle-class) standard of living is that earnings from work have grown much more unequal over the last 25 years. Princeton Professor Allan Blinder (2007) cites evidence from IRS data that the average taxpayer in the top one tenth of 1% of all wage and salary earners had earnings amounting to that of 44 average taxpayers in the bottom half in the year 1979, but by 2001, this earnings disparity had increased almost fourfold, equating to that of 160 earners. The gap between the average American worker and the executive class is increasingly polarizing the nation.

The Influence of Outsourcing and Insourcing

Workers and communities across the United States have been losing control over their destinies as the nation has increasingly become tied to global rather than national and local forces. Globalization is altering the locus of firms and work for all nations, rich and poor. The growing dominance of multinational firms within and outside of the United States is one of the most important trends accompanying globalization. There were approximately 40,000 multinational companies in the United States prior to the Great Recession, up from 7,000 in 1975 (Atkinson and Correa, 2007). Sassen (2006) suggests that the multinational firm has evolved to supersede much of national authority, elevating the significance of global cities and the connections between them in the globalization process.

The negative impacts on manufacturing employment from globalization have been felt for more than two decades. More recently, significant concern has been voiced over the offshoring of service jobs. A review of the evidence, however, suggests fewer than a million service jobs had been lost to offshoring prior to the Great Recession, which is less than one month's normal turnover in the labor force (Blinder, 2007).

However, this may be just the tip of the iceberg, according to Blinder, who suggests "the key labor-market divide in the Information Age will not be between high-skilled and low-skilled workers, as it has been in the recent past, but rather between services that can be delivered electronically with little loss of quality and those that cannot be" (Blinder, 2007, p. 3). This can just as easily impact high-skill jobs such as software engineers and financial analysts as it does low-skill jobs such as assembly workers. As information technology continues its global diffusion, Blinder estimates that 22% to 29% of American jobs today could be offshored, though he expects this will actually occur to only a fraction of them. Nevertheless, job displacement will be a growing problem across a wide range of the labor market, and local economic development planning will be greatly needed:

> [W]e must take steps to ensure that our labor force and our businesses supply and demand the types of skills and jobs that are going to remain in America rather than move offshore. Among other things, that may require substantial changes in our educational system—all the way from kindergarten through college. And it will certainly entail a variety of steps to ensure that the U.S. remains the home of innovation and invention, for we will never compete on the basis of cheap labor. Nor do we want to. (Blinder, 2007, p. 4)

It is important to appreciate that globalization also brought employment to the United States. Many law, advertising, and other firms in the United States have provided value-added services and products to the developed and developing world alike. Further, the United States gained new jobs as foreign corporations invested here. It has been estimated that 21.1 million jobs in the United States come from foreign direct investment (FDI), with the largest number occurring in Manufacturing (12.2 million). FDI also contributes 2.3 million jobs to the Wholesale and Retail sector, .5 million to the Finance, Insurance and Real Estate sector, 1 million to the Information sector, and 800,000 jobs to Professional, Scientific and Technical Services (PWC 2012).

Networks

The competitive advantage of firms in the new economy has been greater specialization. However, this results in more interdependency with other firms, organizations, and suppliers. Business is no longer conducted by companies working alone. When leading-edge firms need specialized skills, they outsource to another organization in a related field or even in the same field. Many companies hire partner companies and form "virtual corporations" that combine for one product and then recombine with entirely different sets of collaborators for another product.

The concept of "Blue Ocean," coined by Kim and Mauborgne (2004), is based on the notion that innovation comes from "reinvention" as well as new invention. They cite Cirque du Soleil as a prime illustration of reinventing within the template of an existing industrial category to generate a new product for new buyers. Some people and places seem to generate more of this sort of intellectual ware for reasons that Florida (2002), along with Kim and Mauborgne, cites as conducive to collaborative activities or launchpads for new ideas. Bradshaw and Blakely (1999) provide a spatial dimension to this argument in their work on Third Wave Economic Development approaches.

Thus, it is no longer feasible for a firm located in one place to be unconcerned with the network of institutions and suppliers that can provide its materials and talent. Firms with well-developed networks are flexible, able to identify and select strong suppliers, as well as to penetrate new markets. The implication for workforce development is clear. In a networked economy, the skills of suppliers are as important as the skills within the firms.

The enduring challenge for local economic development planning is that the loss and gain of firms and jobs is never a one-for-one match, for either the community or the worker. When an auto job is lost in Detroit, its replacement in the American economy is more likely to be in financial services and located elsewhere. Even when another auto job from a foreign-owned firm appears in the U.S. economy, it does not do so in Detroit. Instead, it is located in the new Auto Alley running through the Southeastern states. A classic explanation for this is found in Schumpeter's (1947) notion of "creative destruction." That is, capitalism and market economies only survive and grow through a process that destroys old ways and creates new ways of doing business. Cities, regions, and nations are affected by this process because they are the hosts to economic activities that experience birth and decline. Some of the new and key characteristics associated with evolving capitalism's manifestation in the economy are discussed below.

The Geography of the New Economy

What came to be called the New Economy has been with us since 1990. Atkinson and Correa (2007) describe the transformation to the New Economy as "equivalent in scope and depth to the emergence of the factory economy in the 1890s and the mass production, corporate economy in the 1940s and 1950s" (2007, p. 3). They identify five major areas by which the transformation can be defined and measured: knowledge dependent, global, entrepreneurial, rooted in information technology, and innovation (see Box 1.1 for a more detailed description). Using 26 indicators to capture transformation in the five areas, Atkinson and Correa have examined recent economic activity in the United States and concluded that transformation to the New Economy has been uneven: It is most strongly in evidence within the Northeast, mid-Atlantic, Mountain West, and Pacific regions. The lagging regions are the Midwest, Great Plains, and South. When viewing the transformation through a metropolitan lens, Atkinson and Gottlieb (2001) observed a shift from the largest metro areas to mid-sized metro areas (between 250,000 and one million people). Within metro areas, the shift to the New Economy is associated with decentralization of activity away from the central city. Unfortunately for rural counties not adjacent to metro areas, Atkinson and Correa (2007) observe that they have been left out of the New Economy and have lost job share.

Jobs have been far more mobile than people. Over the past three decades, the Northeast and Midwest "Snow/Rust Belts" have shed manufacturing and related jobs. In the 1990s, these areas regained some of this type of employment but added a significant segment to the service employment base, particularly in new technology areas and in transportation and goods movement sectors. Old factories have been restored as logistic centers, moving freight by air and rail. Expansions in international trade have created new jobs for heartland workers importing and exporting goods to Latin America and Canada. The South and West have added new technology and trade jobs, too, as well as construction and food production employment. Although the North lost manufacturing jobs during the 1980s and 1990s, the Southeast added some manufacturing jobs in the auto sector as European automakers came to the South seeking cheap skilled labor during the same period.

Box 1.1   The New Economy

So what exactly is the New Economy? The term refers to a set of qualitative and quantitative changes that in the last 15 years have transformed the structure, functioning and rules of the economy . . . The New Economy is a global, entrepreneurial and knowledge-based economy in which the keys to success lie in the extent to which knowledge, technology, and innovation are embedded in products and services.

Today's economy is *knowledge dependent*. Of course, managers and "knowledge workers" have always been part of the economy, but by the 1990s, they had become the largest occupational category. Managerial and professional jobs increased as a share of total employment from 22 percent in 1979 to 28.4 percent in 1995 and to 34.8 percent in 2003. In contrast, about one in seven workers is employed as a production worker in manufacturing, and even there, knowledge and continual skills enhancement is becoming more important.

Today's economy is *global*. While it is true that some firms have long had global links, today's globalization is pervasive, as more nations join the global marketplace, as more goods and services are traded, and as more of the production process is interconnected in a global supply web. Since 1980, global trade has grown 2.5 times faster than global gross domestic

(Continued)

(Continued)

product (GDP). World exports are now at $12.5 trillion, nearly 20 percent of world GDP.

Today's economy is entrepreneurial. While it is true that entrepreneurial growth, market dynamism, economic "churning" and competition have been features of the American economy since the colonial days, the center of gravity seemed to shift to entrepreneurial activity after the 1990s. At the same time, the underlying operation of the economy accelerated to a new speed and became more customized and innovative. For example, in the 60 years after 1917, it took an average of 30 years to replace half of the 100 largest public companies. Between 1977 and 1998, it took an average of 12 years. Moreover, from 1980 to 2001, all of the net U.S. job growth was from firms less than five years old, while older firms actually lost jobs.

Today's economy is *rooted in information technology.* While it is also true that information technology has played a role in the economy since the invention of the telegraph, something happened in the 1990s when semiconductors, computers, software, and telecommunications became cheap enough, fast enough, and networked enough to become so ubiquitous as to power a surge in productivity growth. Indeed, information technology is now the key technology driving the economy, not just in the IT industry itself—which continues to see high-wage job growth—but also in the use of IT in virtually all sectors to boost productivity, quality and innovation.

Today's economy is driven by *innovation*—the development and adoption of new products, processes, and business models. Nations, states, regions, firms, and even individuals compete on their ability to accumulate, aggregate, and apply their assets to create value in new ways for increasingly diverse customers all over the world.

Source: Reprinted with permission from Atkinson and Correa (2007).

Atkinson and Gottlieb (2001) argue that the most appropriate way to view the New Economy is through the "lens" of metropolitan areas, observing that America is "neither an urban nor a rural nation, but rather a metropolitan nation where the majority of the population lives and works in large metropolitan areas that include both historic central cities and dispersed suburban development" (p. 3). Contrary to common perception, the movement of jobs has not been confined to North–South or East–West shifts. Some northern metropolitan regions that lost population and employment during the 1980s and 1990s are now rebounding with new technologies and reinventing themselves as part of the new economy by acting as springboards of industries like publishing and printing as well as other communications firms. For example, many academic presses are now in New England in old picturesque mill towns that can compete with New York City because they have digital printing capacities and can be reached on the Internet.

Beyond major metropolitan areas, the United States has continued to become more urbanized—or, more accurately, suburbanized, as we will discuss later. The population and employment picture for rural or nonmetropolitan areas has not been as steady as that in urban areas (Kusmin, 2003; Pigg, 1991). Many have suffered from the continued losses of manufacturing and farm employment. However, between 2005 and 2006, the 2 years before the Great Recession, rural counties actually experienced net domestic migration (where the number of in-migrants exceeded the number of out-migrants). This trend was greatest in Western locations that combined scenic attributes with tourism, recreation, second-home development, and retirement migration. Parts of the rural South (Texas Hill Country, southern Appalachia, the Florida coast, and northern Virginia) experienced rapid growth due to the amenities they provided in conjunction with their proximity to metro employment (Kusmin, 2003).

Correspondingly, in some locations, the skill level of rural dwellers has increased to a degree that is competitive with urban and suburban areas. Extending the work on the creative class begun by Richard Florida (e.g., 2002), McGranahan and Wojan (2007) found that particularly high-amenity rural areas are competitive with urban areas in attracting the creative class. Their research provides an important contribution to understanding current economic development trends. The creative class is composed of people in highly creative occupations such as artists, architects, engineers, design, entertainment, and science. Florida argues that economic growth is driven by the creation of knowledge and ideas that primarily come from those in occupations that involve high levels of creativity. This creative class seeks a high quality of life as well as rewarding work. McGranahan and Wojan (2007) observe, "While developed with major metropolitan areas in mind, the creative-class thesis seems particularly relevant to rural areas, which lose much of their young talent as high school graduates leave, usually for highly urban environments" (p. 18). McGranahan and Wojan found that, between 1990 and 2004, rural counties with high proportions of creative-class workers experienced a 44% growth in jobs, while metro counties experienced a 39% job growth. Whether in rural or urban areas, the activities associated with the creative class bring new jobs and growth, and the message for all localities is to carefully preserve their natural amenities as well as to nurture their cultural resources.

People and Places Left Out of the New Economy

Growing Income and Earnings Inequality

One way of understanding the changing economy is to see how growth is shared between its component parts—labor and capital. While labor

Figure 1.1   Shares of Income After Transfers and Federal Taxes, 1979 and 2007

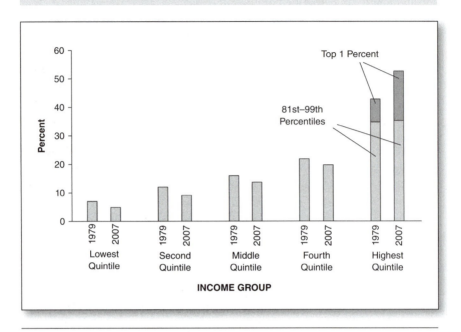

Source: U.S. Congressional Budget Office, Trends in the Distribution of Household Income Between 1979 and 2007, http://cbo.gov/sites/default/files/cbofiles/new/homepage_graphic_large .png; accessed May 20, 2012.

productivity has been increasing, this has not translated into increasing wages (DeNavas-Walt, Proctor, and Lee, 2006). The share of national income going to wages and salaries is the lowest ever recorded and fell below 50% for the first time in 2010, while the 14.15 share going to corporate profits was the highest ever recorded (Norris, 2011). Therefore, the common perception that all boats rise and fall as the overall economy cannot be assumed. Instead, more of the real gains are transferred to capital that may reside outside of the United States, and to small segments of wealth-capturing groups with strong stock and other capital asset portfolios.

Not only has labor generally not shared in the increasing national prosperity, there has been a shift in the distribution of earnings within labor segments. The top of the economic pyramid has fared far better in the distribution of income than the bottom portion. The real improvements have been for those who receive income from capital flows rather than labor (Willis and Wroblewski, 2007). Between 1979 and 2007, the U.S. Congressional Budget Office (2011) found that after-tax income for the highest-income households grew more than it did for any other group. Specifically, income increased

275% for the top 1% of households, 65% for the next 19%, just under 40% for the next 60%, and only 18% for the bottom 20%.

Gaps in opportunity have also increased across all spectra of the economy. The high-tech and finance, as well as athletic, superstars who represent a very small segment of the nation have gained immensely relative to others. Decline in unions and manufacturing employment has pushed many less-educated and computer-illiterate workers into lower-wage jobs where they compete with international labor pools. The continuing high level of unemployment after the Great Recession ended has eroded household savings and decreased wages as higher numbers of job seekers compete for few openings.

Debate over whether the middle class was shrinking or merely moving into the growing upper middle class has been an ongoing accompaniment to the shift to the New Economy (see Box 1.2). But the Great Recession and its lingering effects have shifted the debate's focus to the overall decline in the middle class, the top 1%, and to those whose education should have prepared them for a place in the middle class. A 2012 analysis estimated half of new college graduates were unemployed or underemployed (Yen, 2012). Boushy and Hersh (2012) make the case that a strong middle class is essential to a strong economy for four reasons. It promotes the development of human capital and a well-educated population; creates a stable source of demand for goods and services; incubates the next generation of entrepreneurs; and "supports inclusive political and economic institutions, which underpin economic growth" (p. 3).

Box 1.2   What Is Happening to the Middle Class?

The "plight of the middle class," as it is subjected to forces transforming the U.S. economy has become a major topic of interest among economists, political analysts, policymakers and politicians. Economic development planners should understand the debate as the middle class is the backbone of the U.S. economy and American society. The middle class standard of living is a benchmark by which economic development progress is measured. Historically, the mass market has been oriented towards satisfying the middle class consumer. A position in the middle class is generally considered the development goal of the lower classes and of many of those who aspired to assist the lower classes.

The debate over what is happening to the middle class is intertwined with two other major economic debates: that of the U.S.'s industrial

(Continued)

(Continued)

transformation, and that of the effects of changing demographics (aging baby boomers, immigration . . .). How the middle class is defined can make a significant difference in the trends observed and conclusions drawn. Various trend analyses have focused on earned income or total income, as well as household income or individual earnings. They have used different definitions of the middle (a range around the median level, or dividing the earnings or income distribution into quintiles and focusing on the three middle segments). Using household or family income enables one to look more at the total income picture. If the main concern is with impacts on standard of living, then household or family income may be the most appropriate variable for analysis. If the primary concern is what effect the declining middle has on employment and earning opportunities, then individual earnings is the appropriate variable. Both are important from an economic development perspective. Today, the two-earner household increasingly makes up the family income unit while there are also growing numbers of single earner/occupant households. How has the possibility for attaining a middle class standard of living changed in concert? Does it now take more than one earner in most households to achieve a middle standard of living? If so, does this represent economic development advancement if it takes two or more earners to maintain a middle standard where one could do so previously?

Source: Leigh, N.G. (1994). Stemming Middle-Class Decline. New Brunswick: Center for Urban Policy Research, © 1994 by Rutgers, The State University of New Jersey.

The loss in middle-income families has had a corresponding impact on working middle-class neighborhoods. Middle-income neighborhoods have declined by 58% since 1970, according to a recent Brookings Institution study (Booza, Cutsinger, and Galster, 2006). This dramatic decline far outpaced the corresponding drop in the proportion of metropolitan families earning middle incomes, from 28% in 1970 to 22% in 2000. Of the nation's 12 largest metropolitan areas, only 23% of their central city neighborhoods were middle class in 2000 (Booza et al., 2006). The Great Recession has worsened these trends.

Growing Racial Inequality

Income growth has been largely stagnant, with growing inequality between races. The median household income for all races was $49,445 in 2010, an increase of less than 2.6% since 2006 (U.S. Census Bureau, 2006). The median White household income was 105% of that for all households, while it was 130% for Asians, 76% for Hispanics, and only 65% for Blacks. Hispanic household income actually declined slightly during the 4-year period, the only group to experience a decline. This growing racial inequality is reinforced by the fact that the Black poverty rate was the highest of all racial groups. At 27.4%, it was more than double that of Whites and Asians and 0.8% higher than for Hispanics (see Table 1.1).

In part, these discrepancies are attributable to racial differences in educational attainment and in single-earner versus dual-earner households. Additionally, foreign-born workers can remain trapped in various forms of domestic service work in which they have low wages and no bargaining power without better language skills. From an economic development perspective, the link between high rates of poverty and low educational attainment is clear. Consequently, the success of the local education system is a necessary foundation for local economic development.

Welfare reform introduced by President Clinton in 1994 was aimed at moving welfare recipients—particularly Black single-headed households—from poverty to work. It is clear that welfare rolls have declined substantially as a result of this law. While states now spend less on welfare *per se,* they spend a good deal more on job training, education, and programs designed to lower teenage pregnancy and other factors that cause intergenerational poverty (Haskins, Sawhill, and Weaver, 2001).

Table 1.1 Household Income Poverty by Race, 2006–2010

	Household Income 2006	*Household Income 2010*	*Change (percent)*	*Median Household Income as Percent of Total Median Household Income 2010*	*Poverty Rate 2010*
All Races	$48,201	$49,445	2.58%	100%	15.1%
White	$50,673	$51,846	2.31%	105%	13.0%
Black	$31,969	$32,068	0.31%	65%	27.4%
Asian	$64,238	$64,308	0.11%	130%	12.1%
Hispanic	$37,781	$37,759	−0.06%	76%	26.6%

Sources: U.S. Census Bureau, Income, Poverty, and Health Insurance Coverage in the United States: 2006, Tables A-1 and B-2; U.S. Census Bureau, Income, Poverty, and Health Insurance Coverage in the United States: 2010, Tables 1 and 2.

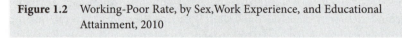

Figure 1.2   Working-Poor Rate, by Sex, Work Experience, and Educational
Attainment, 2010

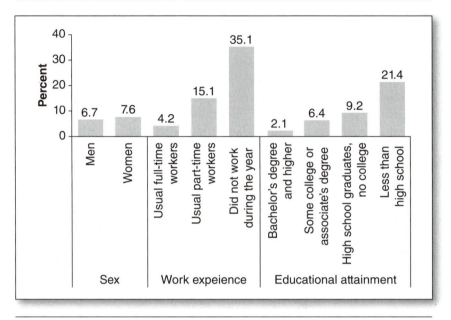

Source: U.S. Bureau of Labor Statistics 2012. "The Editor's Desk," April 5, http://www.bls.gov/
opub/ted/2012/ted_20120405.htm. Accessed May 20, 2012.

However, there is mounting evidence that the work welfare recipients find
is low wage and often only part time. Thus, those formerly dependent on welfare are increasingly working for wages at or below the poverty line, thereby
requiring other forms of support, such as food stamps, to make ends meet.

The Working Poor

Former welfare recipients may be part of a larger group known as the
working poor: persons who are in the labor force (at least 27 weeks) but still do
not earn enough to have an income above the poverty level.

The working poor have increased since the start of the Great Recession. For
the overall American labor force, the working poor grew from 6.5% to 7.0%
between 2007 and 2010. The Black (12.6%) and Hispanic (14.1%) rates of working poor were significantly higher than those for Whites (6.5%) and Asians
(4.8%). Further, 24% of those who worked part-time involuntarily (because they
wanted full-time work but could not obtain it) were also working poor. Being a
member of the working poor is correlated with one's occupation and educational

level. Those without a high school education are most likely to be working poor, as are those who work in service, natural resources, construction, and maintenance jobs (U.S. Department of Labor, 2007). However, unequal access to quality education is also correlated with race and income levels.

For families, those with children under 18 years were about 4 times more likely to be working poor and those with female heads were more likely to be in poverty (U.S. Department of Labor, 2012).

As can be seen in Table 1.2, while about a quarter of the workforce is low wage (average hourly wage of $8.31 in 2009), nearly three-fifths of this low-wage workforce is female.

Part-time low-wage work is no longer a short-lived interlude until a better full-time job is found. Few of the skills developed in low-wage work are transferable to higher-order jobs. In fact, many part-time jobs are deskilling. For example, the worker becomes more of a watcher than a technical aid for the work performed. Store clerks no longer need to add and subtract, or indeed do any high-order functions, since the computer calculates and analyzes. Few part-time jobs offer any training or require much skill, so they are not ladders to anything better.

While globalization has increased the competition for lower-skilled workers in many countries, the fact is most of the United States' lowest-paid part-time work cannot go overseas to sell hamburgers or make beds. This form of work is infiltrating sectors that once provided job ladders like custodial services and that served for many new immigrants as the way into government and other work. These civil-service job-ladder opportunities are now closed because the work is now performed by contractors. Low-skilled minorities, especially women, are caught in a vicious cycle of low-wage employment that is time consuming but not skill enhancing, and too often they lack the resources or support systems to further their educations so they can move to higher wage occupations.

Table 1.2   The Low-Wage Workforce

Characteristic	Low-Wage Workforce	Total Workforce
Percentage of workforce	26%	100%
Average hourly wage (2009)	$8.31	$20.65
Gender		
Female	58%	49%
Male	43%	51%

(Continued)

Table 1.2 (Continued)

Characteristic	Low-Wage Workforce	Total Workforce
Race		
White	57%	68%
Hispanic	23%	15%
Black	14%	11%
Asian/other	5%	7%
Education		
Less than high school	19%	9%
High school grad	36%	29%
Some college	34%	30%
College grad+	10%	33%
Age		
18–24	32%	13%
25–34	24%	24%
35+	44%	63%
Occupation		
Services	55%	28%
Operations	19%	21%
Clerical	13%	14%
Managers	11%	37%
Others	2%	1%

Source: Economic Policy Institute (2009).

The Decline in Good Jobs

The picture of a deeply dividing labor force that Bennett Harrison (1978) painted more than three decades ago is still with us today. The picture of this labor force presented in Figure 1.1 is only slightly modified from what Harrison originally conceived. At the core of the current labor market are the primary

(or good) jobs. Primary employment consists of career professional and technical positions with good wages and benefits, career mobility, and additional training opportunities. These jobs have historically been unionized or had some
degree of employment security based on the ability of the workers holding these
jobs to bargain, since they possessed skills and technical knowledge needed in
the productive economy. In addition, jobs in the primary sector are generally
more rewarding than other positions because they tend to be "knowledge intensive." That is, individuals' intellectual skills are more likely to be used in the work.

Surrounding the core primary jobs are more marginal employment activities, which have increasingly come to be seen as "bad" jobs. The principal real

Figure 1.3   The Structure of Urban Labor Markets

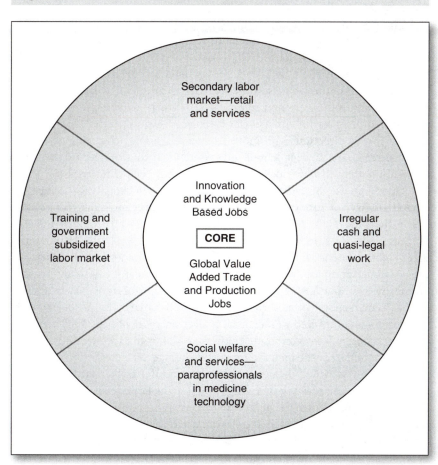

Source: Modified from Harrison (1978).

employment in this segment lies in what has been called the secondary labor market: low-wage, unstable employment in personal consumer services areas or in firms that are footloose. The secondary labor market includes many occupational categories, ranging from manufacturing to clerical. Individuals in this market seldom have any job security and enjoy few benefits from their employers. As a consequence of the low wages paid in the jobs, individuals and families in most urban areas are forced to send more members of the family to work, including working-age children. At the top of the figure are the increasingly part-time retail jobs. To the left of the core are public-sector job-training programs for welfare-to-work transitions and displaced and hard-to-employ legal workers. To the right of the core is the segment of workers who are legal and illegal. The alegal portion is made up of individuals and some small firms that do all their business in cash and pay few or no taxes. A portion of this sector is engaged in illicit activities.

The government sector, at the bottom of Figure 1.1, was larger when Harrison (1978) first depicted the labor market. The jobs it shed have been replaced by those in the social welfare sector and by paraprofessional jobs in medicine, social services, and other arenas filled by contract employees. The latter work without benefits, so they are dependent on a new form of government handout from grants and contracts. This is a growing sector that has less power than the government agencies it replaces. Even the education sector is moving in this direction, with more and more schools privatizing as charter schools. While the charter schools give more local control over teachers and curriculum, they also provide less job security than the public system.

Good jobs are those that provide, at a minimum, a living wage so that, if a person works year-round, full time, his or her earnings will take him or her above the poverty level. These jobs also have employer-provided benefits such as health care, retirement plans, and opportunities for job training and career advancement. As more work becomes part time and small employers replace larger ones, job quality is suffering. In particular, health-care benefits are nearly as important as wages, for without health insurance, even a small medical emergency can push a household into bankruptcy. Since the only resource for an uninsured worker is the emergency room of a local government-supported hospital, the community suffers as well from excessive and unreimbursed use of the most expensive form of health care.

Employer-provided health insurance is more associated with larger employers who can realize cost savings from buying large group policies. However, large employers see the aging and unhealthy workforce as a future liability, particularly given the increasing incidence of type 2 diabetes, asthma, and other largely preventable diseases. This, in combination with soaring health-care costs, has caused the major employers to cut back on health-care coverage. As Figure 1.3 shows, the incidence of private-sector employer-provided health insurance coverage has been on the decline since the late 1970s and throughout the period. But, while health insurance provision is typically associated with the largest private employers, the largest employer of all, Wal-Mart, developed a reputation for stinginess due to the high cost and minimal coverage of the health care it made available to its employees. Indeed, less than half of its 1.4 million U.S. employees were insured in 2007. Responding to national- and local-level pressures, however, Wal-Mart is now providing better benefits for full- and part-time workers (Barbaro and Abelson, 2007).

Corporate downsizing, offshoring of jobs, the decline of unionized jobs, and the rising use of temporary help agencies to meet firm employment needs, are just some of the factors that have contributed to an eroding Good Jobs base. Some states and communities have tried to preserve and grow their Good Jobs base by tying job quality to the provision of economic development incentives.

Figure 1.4   Health Insurance Coverage Declining for Workers

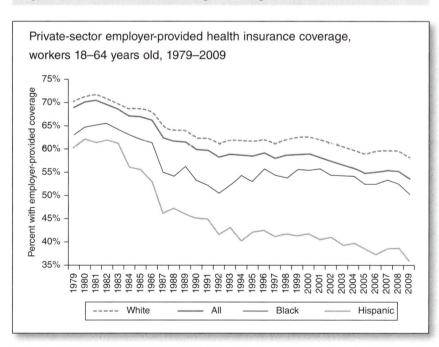

Source: EPI's analysis of the Current Population Survey, Annual Social and Economic Supplement.

Note: Sample is of private wage-and-salary earners ages 18-64 who worked at least 20 hours per week and 26 weeks per year. Coverage is defined as being included in an employer-provided plan where the employer paid for at least some of the coverage.

Overall, the U.S. labor market faces substantial challenges in continuing to be the vehicle through which the majority of Americans, newcomers and old-timers, achieve the American Way of Life. Beyond corporate restructuring and offshoring, two trends represent particular challenges for marrying local economic development efforts with workforce development efforts. The first is incorporation of the foreign-born population, and the second is the rehabilitation of a growing and largely Black male prison population.

The Rise of the Foreign-Born Population

Foreign immigration has increased over the last three decades, particularly augmented by the wave of Vietnamese immigrants since the 1970s. Unlike previous generations, new immigrants from all regions of the world are able to keep many of their linguistic and other traditions, since international communications such as satellite television, radio, and the Internet make it easier to maintain contact with their homelands. As the new immigrants settle, they also become important assets to communities in a variety of ways, from providing needed labor to purchasing local goods and services.

On the other hand, new immigrants are seen as competing for jobs at the low end of the scale, thereby depriving local workers of these jobs. Immigrants are also producing increasing numbers of children due to higher fertility rates than the locally born or domestic population. Immigrants work and do pay taxes, but in areas with high concentrations of low-skilled, low-paid immigrants, they impose net costs on U.S.-born workers. The reason for the so-called "immigrant burden" is that illegal immigrants receive services like education and health care for which they may not pay directly, since they seldom pay property and income taxes. Furthermore, the vast majority of legal immigrants are in the lowest income groups and thus have higher welfare or other public supports. Yet, as we will discuss later in this book, immigrants have the potential to be strong forces for local economic development.

Prison Populations

Prisons are new "employers" for many of the nation's minority males, as a consequence of their first job choice: drug dealing. Prisons have become the disproportionate home for many young Black males, generating incarceration role models that are even celebrated in song. In 2005, there were 3,145 inmates per 100,000 Black males in the United States, compared with 1,244 inmates per 100,000 Hispanic males and only 471 inmates per 100,000 White males (Harrison and Beck, 2006). The tragically higher rate of Black males in prison is a symptom of household and community dysfunction that has generated deep despair among policymakers of all colors who are unable to find successful corrective courses of action. Post-release from prison, few ex-convicts can find living-wage work. Moreover, state lawmakers eager to show toughness on crime have extended sentences, thereby reducing the possibility of successful rehabilitation to community life. What is clear from Table 1.3 is that the low attachment rates to the educational system significantly increase the likelihood that Blacks, Hispanics, and Whites will become incarcerated and diminish their chances for fully participating in the legal economy.

Table 1.3   Educational Attainment of Males, Ages 20 Through 39, by Race/Hispanic Origin, for State Prison Inmates and the General Population

	White		Black		Hispanic	
Educational Attainment	General Population	State Prison Inmates	General Population	State Prison Inmates	General Population	State Prison Inmates
8th grade or less	4.30%	9.90%	2.30%	9.90%	20.90%	24.10%
Some high school	9.6%	17.8%	13.3%	34.0%	20.4%	27.7%
High school diploma	32.1%	61.0%	40.5%	47.9%	27.0%	41.6%
Postsecondary/ some college	30.7%	9.3%	32.4%	7.1%	22.8%	5.3%
College graduate or more	23.4%	1.9%	11.5%	1.1%	8.9%	1.4%

Sources: U.S. Bureau of Justice Statistics, Survey of Inmates in State and Federal Correctional Facilities, 1997: Bureau of Labor Statistics, Current Population Survey, March supplement, 1997.

Note: Probationers excluded from general population. Percentages may not add to 100% due to rounding.

Growing Spatial Inequality

Two primary ways to examine trends in spatial or regional inequality in the United States are through the categories of major regions (Northeast, Midwest, South, and West) and the metro/nonmetro regions (treated as synonymous with urban/rural). From Table 1.4, we see that there are significant differences in income levels, incidences of poverty, and lack of health insurance coverage between the four major regions and within metro regions as well as between metro and nonmetro regions. Despite the high population and employment growth rates the South has experienced for many decades, its income levels continue to lag behind the other regions of the United States, while the proportion of persons in poverty and lacking health insurance is highest. Even though the West had the highest income in 2010, the proportion of Westerners lacking health insurance was almost as high as the South's. The Northeast and Midwest rank second and third, respectively, for the three standard of living indicators: income, percentage below poverty, and percentage without health insurance. Although both regions have suffered significant losses in good jobs over the last several decades due to manufacturing decline in the industrial heartland, the stronger labor agreements that are the legacy of unionization have helped to stabilize their standards of living. However, the Midwest had the greatest jump in population without health insurance coverage.

Within each of the four regions, there is significant diversion in standards of living and economic development at the state and substate levels. As discussed previously, much of this diversion is attributable to whether a location within a region has natural amenities such as mountains and coastlines that make logical resort choices or whether it is part of a metropolitan area. Indeed, it is not regions or states but metropolitan areas that are the true drivers of U.S. development. Around four-fifths of the U.S. population lives in metropolitan areas, and half of the U.S. population lives in their suburbs. Even more significant is that U.S. population and economic activity are concentrated in only one-third of all our metro areas:

> The 100 largest U.S. metropolitan areas contain 65 percent of the nation's population and 68 percent of its jobs, but gather even larger shares of innovative activity (78 percent of U.S. patent activity), educated workers (75 percent of graduate degree holders), and critical infrastructure (79 percent of U.S. air cargo). As such, they generate three-quarters of U.S. gross domestic product. (Berube, 2007, p. 7)

Dabson (2007) has detailed the key connections between the nation's metro and rural economies, noting that the major metro economies "draw strength from, and provide benefits to, smaller places throughout the nation . . . " (n.p.). Indeed, more than half of the population living in rural areas, defined as low-density areas and towns, are in counties within metropolitan areas (Dabson, 2007). Dabson notes that firms in major metropolitan areas depend on the lower cost labor in these rural areas, which are either part of their commuter sheds or may be hundreds of miles away and provide business process services made possible by information technology advances.

Table 1.4 Spatial Inequality in Income, Poverty, and Health Insurance

Area	Income			Percentage Below Poverty			Percentage With No Health Insurance		
Region	*2006*	*2010*	*% Change*	*2006*	*2010*	*% Change*	*2006*	*2010*	*% Change*
Northeast	$52,057	$53,283	2.4%	11.5%	12.8%	11.3%	12.3%	12.4%	0.8%
Midwest	$47,836	$48,445	1.3%	11.2%	13.9%	24.1%	11.4%	13.0%	14.0%
South	$43,884	$45,492	3.7%	13.8%	16.9%	22.5%	19.0%	19.1%	0.5%
West	$52,249	$53,142	1.7%	11.6%	15.3%	31.9%	17.9%	17.9%	0.0%
Metro Status									
Inside Metro	$50,616	$51,244	1 2%	11.8%	14.9%	26.3%	15.8%	16.3%	3.2%
Inside Central City	$42,627	$44,049	3 3%	16.1%	19.7%	22.4%	19.0%	19.4%	2.1%
Outside Central City	$55,775	$56,140	0 7%	9.1%	11.8%	29.7%	13.8%	14.4%	4.3%
Outside Metro	$38,293	$40,287	5.2%	15.2%	16.5%	8.6%	16.0%	16.2%	1.3%

Sources: DeNavas-Walt et al., 2006; DeNavas-Walt et al., 2011.

Increasing Metropolitan Inequality

Despite metropolitan America—particularly its top 100 cities—being the geographic focal point of U.S. economic growth, there are a number of concerns raised by recent patterns. First, there is a twin set of increasing bifurcation occurring within metro areas. This is associated with the significant suburbanization within U.S. metropolitan areas that has transformed metropolitan spatial structure from the dichotomous form of central city-suburbs to one of a multiring polycentric structure with suburban rings and subcenters (see Figure 1.4). The resulting metropolitan region is an interactive system of downtown, inner city, inner-ring suburbs, outer-ring suburbs, subcenters, and exurbs. Within this system, downtowns are experiencing gentrification and revitalization in reaction to the long commutes associated with metropolitan sprawl, while the minority-populated inner-city portion of the central city continues to suffer from high crime rates, disinvestment, poor schools, and poverty concentration. At the same time, the suburbs are becoming increasingly differentiated, and the inner-ring suburbs have been experiencing declining household incomes. Their aging housing stock is being occupied by new immigrants and the traditional poverty population that is being displaced by "back to the downtown" movements (Lee and Leigh, 2007).

Figure 1.5   The Emergence of Suburban Rings and Subcenters in the
Metropolitan Areas

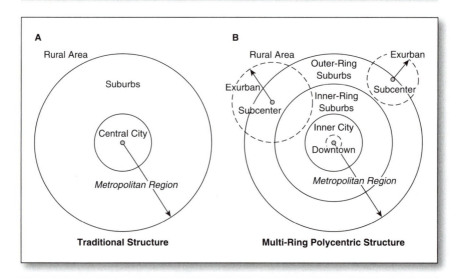

Source: Lee and Leigh (2004).

The signs of suburban decline are clear, including homeless people in shopping malls in many close-in suburban and even some affluent areas. Affordable housing, which was a code word in the 1980s for low-income housing, is now a concern of suburban police officers and schoolteachers as well as the poor. The suburbs have also witnessed a rise in crime and in the number of new social problems in their midst, with many families experiencing stress and rising levels of child abuse and family dysfunction. Suburban schools, once thought to be sanctuaries, have experienced violence of unimaginable scale and horror across the nation. In April of 2007, Blacksburg, Virginia—a small picturesque college town with no history of violence—rocked the nation with 32 unprovoked killings by a psychotic student. Less than a decade earlier, Columbine High School in Colorado Springs experienced a similar incident. Although some have blamed television for these horrific acts, many sociologists blame the suburban living arrangements that isolate youth from a larger network of social settings, which fosters good communal life. At the same time, participation has been declining in community institutions that formed the backbone of civic life for 50 years, such as PTAs, 4-H Clubs, and Lions Clubs; even attendance in traditional churches has been in long-term decline (Putnam, 2000).

Increasing Rural Inequality

The bifurcation in economic fortunes within rural areas and small towns is just as significant as that which has occurred within our metro areas. Those who prosper, as previously discussed, have significant natural amenities and/or are close to a thriving metropolitan area. Those with an employment base in farming continue to experience net job and population loss.

Farmland speculation, global competition, and overproduction have severely taxed many rural communities. As farms collapse, mines close, and other natural resource operations diminish, the dwindling employment base in agriculture and extractive areas declines even more swiftly. The loss in farm, timber, and mining income has a disastrous ripple effect through an entire community. In fact, many single-crop and single-firm nonmetropolitan communities have been extremely vulnerable due to their narrow economies. Further, manufacturing branch plant closings have had a more marked impact on rural than urban communities. As branch plant economies, these communities exercise little control over the corporate decision-making process. When international commodity prices fluctuate, the actions of other suppliers of raw materials influence the base economy. In a sense, some rural communities have been trapped by their own success in attracting firms and expanding foreign trade. They will need to reformulate their economic development strategies to achieve more resilient economies.

Shaping Global Warming: The U.S. Economic Engine

The year 2007 was a watershed for the debate over global warming and climate change. Only a small minority of scientists and policy advocates refuse to recognize the significance of climate change for the U.S. and global economies. The United States has only 4% of the world's population but produces more than 23% of the CO_2 gases that threaten the global atmosphere. Our American lifestyle is not without cost to the rest of the world. Americans consume more than half the world's natural resources to maintain an increasingly fragile form of consumption-oriented living. Americans transport, consume, and produce debris in greater quantities than almost all of the rest of the world combined. We are running out of landfills for our waste and reducing our own fresh water supply by wasteful practices.

The International Panel on Climate Change report indicates global temperatures may rise as much as 6 degrees Celsius (11 degrees Fahrenheit) by the turn of the next century. Such a rise in temperature could inundate more than 70% of the world's largest metropolitan areas, since they border on the oceans. Cities like New York, Sydney, and Mumbai are equally threatened by sea level rises of as much as 3 to 6 feet. While the sea is rising, we are also witnessing the spread of deserts in Africa and Asia and the diminishing rainfall that feeds the rivers of Australia.

The economic consequences of global warming are far from trivial, yet the actions needed to deal with climate change may still be within our grasp. But how proactively nations will confront this impending disaster is not certain. The largest CO_2 producer, the United States, sees reductions in the production of greenhouse gases to be hostile to economies. Meanwhile, large and rapidly growing nations like China and India are adopting U.S.-style living patterns as their growing middle classes urbanize and adopt automobile-based economic and cultural systems. As their combined population is several billion compared with more than 310 million for the United States, adoption of U.S. consumption and auto-dependent lifestyles by these nations could greatly accelerate global warming.

The only real course is for a new economy to emerge that is less dependent on fossil fuels and more oriented toward the production of low-energy and low-waste lifestyles. Some policymakers and scientists see the new economy as one that uses substitutes for fossil fuels and for materials that alter the form but not the content of the current lifestyles—that is, substituting wind or corn for fossil fuels might be a way around the current energy-production system. Others view climate change as the call to drastically change our way of life— to produce communities that are less dependent on fuels for survival and that produce more of their own food to be consumed locally rather than transported nationally or globally. This latter approach takes people out of their cars and does not just substitute for the automobile. Switching to a non–auto-based and low-energy American way of life is a major challenge that some see as insurmountable for the United States and the rest of the world. So new techniques for lowering fuel consumption and better using existing resources are the preferred alternatives. This means a vastly different economic engine will have to be produced in very short order to prevent massive dislocations of people and the starvation of many.

While the national governments of the largest CO_2 producers are slow to acknowledge and respond to the challenge of global warming, there is a growing local level response that was initiated when Seattle's Mayor Greg Nickels became the first to adopt the Kyoto Protocol in May 2005. The Kyoto Protocol sets target greenhouse gas emission reductions for industrialized nations. Two years later, at Nickels' request, the U.S. Conference of Mayors endorsed his Climate Protection Agreement and, as of May 2012, 1,054 U.S. mayors from all 50 states, Washington, DC, and Puerto Rico had signed on to it. This agreement requires mayors to (1) strive to meet or beat the Kyoto Protocol targets in their own communities, through actions ranging from antisprawl land-use policies to urban forest restoration projects to public information campaigns; (2) urge their state governments and the federal government to enact policies and programs to meet or beat the greenhouse gas emission reduction target suggested for the United States in the Kyoto Protocol—7% reduction from 1990 levels by 2012; and (3) urge the U.S. Congress to pass the bipartisan greenhouse gas reduction legislation, which would establish a national emission trading system.

Additionally, nonprofit organizations such as KyotoUSA and ICLEI's Local Governments for Sustainability are providing assistance to community groups as well as local governments seeking to protect our climate (see www .kyotoUSA.org and www.ICLEI.org). Over 600 U.S. cities had measured their greenhouse gas emissions and adopted reduction plans with ICLEI's assistance by 2012.

The Future of Local Economic Development Planning

The United States is enmeshed in the global market system as leader, follower, and participant. No American firm of any size remains solely within the domestic market system, and consequently neither does any American community. American firms and labor once shielded from international competition are now subject to the vagaries of international finance. The traditional system of economic development planning and practice has not only been ineffective in responding to a market system that itself has undergone globalizing structural shifts, but it is also actually contributing to structural shifts in environmental and social systems that are significant cause for concern. Growing recognition of evidence of these shifts in the form of widening inequality and global warming increasingly appears to be a tipping point from which we may be able to look back one day and see a transformation of the traditional system of economic development planning and practice. In addition to the mayors who have signed on to the Climate Protection Agreement and the cities that have already measured their greenhouse gas emissions, other key actors are taking major steps. For example, the International City/County Management Association (ICMA) adopted a formal resolution on sustainability in October 2007 that requires recognition of the interdependence between environmental stewardship, economic development, social equity, and financial viability. The Brookings Institution has formulated a Blueprint for American Prosperity that calls for "productive, inclusive, and sustainable growth that helps the United States maintain its economic leadership, fosters a strong and diverse middle class, and advances U.S. efforts to address climate change and achieve energy independence" (Berube, 2007, p. 22). Lastly, the economic stimulus package of the Obama administration aimed at bringing the United States out of recession incorporated major provisions for creating green jobs and economic activities.

American communities can no longer depend—if they ever could—on an industry base that pledges long-term loyalty to a community or its workers. Silicon Valley is only slightly better positioned to handle the new economy than Peoria, Illinois. And any such advantage is temporary. Therefore, communities must obtain more control over their economic directions and destinies. The task may be difficult, but it is not impossible. Local economic and political decision makers need not surrender their communities' fates to chance, the marketplace, or unsupportive federal policies. Policymakers in local economic development must confront many crucial questions. Can anything meaningful be done to incorporate the unemployed and underemployed into the employment system? Are there enough jobs? Are there enough "good" jobs? Are there sufficient energy and natural resources to support the local economy? Can a single community tackle the problems of joblessness, homelessness, or climate change by itself? Can a politically and economically divided nation meet its goals of providing for all?

There are, of course, no clear answers to these questions. But it is clear that communities must have a better perspective on the problems affecting the global economy and their consequences for citizens in general and for specific groups. Local economic development and employment creation can be designed more effectively to deal with these problems. Adopting strategies that promote the green economy, foster entrepreneurship and local cultural assets, and substitute locally produced goods and services for those imported into the community and for export to the global economy are a few of the possibilities. The central thesis of this book is that locally based economic development and employment generation are more likely to be successful if initiated at the community and local level than elsewhere. Each of the factors influencing the economy has unique manifestations and slightly different causes in each local area. Solutions to community problems will not succeed if they are not targeted to specific groups and linked to the total regional economic system. Although this book is written for a U.S. audience, we are mindful of the growing international audience adopting the same strategies. Previous book editions have been translated into Korean, Arabic, Spanish, Dutch, German, and Russian in whole or in part, with a special edition for India.

Local economies the world over can translate these circumstances into their own settings. We hope that everyone who reads this book, whether in urban or rural areas, and whether in the United States or elsewhere, develops a new concept of how to solve local dilemmas for now and for many years to come.

Community leaders can assess their community's situation and place it in a larger context. Similarly, they can assess affected groups to determine how these will respond to different courses of action. In this way, local solutions can be found for national problems. The next chapter explores the dimensions of national policy that currently serve as a basis for local economic development.

References and Suggested Readings

Aron-Dine, Aviva, and Isaac Shapiro. 2007. *Share of National Income Going to Wages and Salaries at Record Low in 2006: Share of Income Going to Corporate Profits at Record High.* Washington, DC: Center on Budget and Policy Priorities. Accessed February 19, 2009 from http://www.cbpp.org/8-31-06inc.htm

Atkinson, Robert D., and Daniel K. Correa. 2007. *The 2007 State New Economy Index.* Washington, DC: The Information Technology and Innovation Foundation.

Atkinson, Robert D., and Paul D. Gottlieb. 2001. *The Metropolitan New Economy Index.* Washington, DC: The Public Policy Institute. Accessed February 19, 2009 from Accessed August 18, 2012 from http://opensource.telkomspeedy.com/repo/abba/v01/DLL/NewEconomyIndex/2001-04-metropolitan.pdf.

Barbaro, Michael, and Reed Abelson. 2007. A Health Plan for Wal-Mart: Less Stinginess. *The New York Times*, November 13.

Berube, Alan. 2007. *MetroNation: How U.S. Metropolitan Areas Fuel American Prosperity.* Washington, DC: Brookings Institution, Metropolitan Policy Program.

Blinder, Allan. 2007. *Will the Middle Hold? Two Problems of American Labor.* Testimony to the Joint Economic Committee, January 31.

Booza, Jason C., Jackie Cutsinger, and George Galster. 2006. *Where Did They Go? The Decline of Middle-Income Neighborhoods in Metropolitan America.* Washington, DC: Brookings Institution.

Boushy, Heather and Adam S. Hersh, "The American Middle Class, Income Inequality and the Strength of Our Economy," May 2012, www.AmericanProgress.org; Accessed May 20 2012.

Bradshaw, Ted K., and Edward J. Blakely. 1999. What are "Third-Wave" State Economic Development Efforts? From Incentives to Industrial Policy. *Economic Development Quarterly* 13(3): 229–244.

Camarota, Steven A. 2007. *100 Million More: Projecting the Impact of Immigration on the U.S. Population, 2007 to 2060.* Washington, DC: Center for Immigration Studies. Accessed November 6, 2007 from http://www.cis.org/articles/2007/back707.html

Dabson, Brian. 2007. *Rural–Urban Interdependence: Why Metropolitan and Rural America Need Each Other.* A background paper prepared for the Blueprint for American Prosperity Metropolitan Policy Program, Brookings Institution, November.

DeNavas-Walt, Carmen, Bernadette D. Proctor, and Cheryl Hill Lee. 2006. *Income, Poverty, and Health Insurance Coverage in the United States: 2005.* Washington, DC: U.S. Census Bureau, Current Population Reports.

DeNavas-Walt, Carmen, Bernadette D. Proctor, and Jessica C. Smith. 2011. *Income, Poverty, and Health Insurance Coverage in the United States: 2010.* Washington, DC: U.S. Census Bureau, Current Population Reports.

Dunn and Bradstreet, "The State of Small Businesses Post Great Recession *An Analysis of Small Businesses between 2007 and 2011,*" May 2011, http://www.dnbgov.com/pdf/DNB_SMB_Report_May2011.pdf. Accessed May 20, 2012.

Economic Policy Institute. 2009. Data accessed October 3, 2011 from http://www.epi.org

Florida, Richard. 2002. *The Rise of the Creative Class: And How It's Transforming Work, Leisure, Community, and Everyday Life.* New York: Basic Books.

Friedman, Thomas. 2005. It's a Flattened World, After All. *New York Times,* April 3.

Harrison, Bennett. 1978. *Job! What Kind, for Whom, and Where?* Cambridge: MIT Press.

Harrison, Paige M., and Allen J. Beck. 2006, May. *Prison and Jail Inmates at Midyear 2005.* Washington, DC: U.S. Department of Justice, Bureau of Justice Statistics.

Haskins, Ron, Isabel V. Sawhill, and R. Kent Weaver. 2001. *Welfare Reform: An Overview of Effects to Date.* Washington, DC: Brookings Institution.

International Monetary Fund. 2007. *World Economic Outlook: Globalization and Inequality.* October. Accessed February 19, 2009 from http://www.imf.org/external/pubs/ft/weo/2007/02/index.htm

Kim, Chan, and Renee Mauborgne. 2004. Blue Ocean Strategy. *Harvard Business Review* 82(10): 79–88.

Kusmin, Lorin D. 2003. *Rural America at a Glance.* U.S. Department of Agriculture Economic Research Service, *Economic Information Bulletin* 31.

Lee, Sugie, and Nancey Green Leigh. 2004. Philadelphia's Space in Between: Inner-Ring Suburbs Evolution. *Opolis: An International Journal of Suburban and Metropolitan Studies* 1(1): 13–32.

——. 2005. The Role of Inner Ring Suburbs in Metropolitan Smart Growth Strategies. *Journal of Planning Literature* 19(3): 330–346.

——. 2007, Winter. Intrametropolitan Spatial Differentiation and Decline of Inner-Ring Suburbs: A Comparison of Four U.S. Metropolitan Areas. *Journal of Planning Education and Research* 27(2): 146–164.

Leigh, Nancey Green. 1994. *Stemming Middle Class Decline: The Challenge to Economic Development.* New Brunswick, NJ: Center of Urban Policy Research.

McGranahan, David A., and Timothy R. Wojan. 2007. The Creative Class: A Key to Rural Growth. *Amber Waves,* U.S. Department of Agriculture Economic Research Service, April.

McNeil, Lawrence R. June, 2007. Foreign Direct Investment in the United States: New Investment in 2006. *Survey of Current Business,* pp. 44–51. Accessed February 19, 2009 from http://www.bea.gov/scb/index.htm

Norris, Floyd. 2011. "As Profits Rise, Workers' Income Declines," *New York Times,* August 5.

Pigg, Kenneth. 1991. *The Future of Rural America: Anticipating Policies for Constructive Change.* Boulder, CO: Westview.

Putnam, Robert D. 2000. *Bowling Alone: The Collapse and Revival of American Community.* New York: Simon & Schuster.

PWC (Price Waterhouse Cooper). 2012. "Economic Impact of U.S. Subsidiaries: Prepared for the Organization for International Investment." Accessed May 10, 2012 from http://www.ofii.org/docs/OFII_Report_May_2012_PwC.pdf

Sassen, Saskia. 2006. *Territory, Authority, Rights: From Medieval to Global Assemblages.* Princeton, NJ: Princeton University Press.

Schumpeter, Joseph. 1947. *Capitalism, Socialism, and Democracy.* New York: Harper.

U.S. Bureau of Justice Statistics. 1997. *Survey of Inmates in State and Federal Correctional Facilities, 1997*: Bureau of Labor Statistics, Current Population Survey, March supplement.

U.S. Bureau of Labor Statistics. 2012. "The Editor's Desk," April 5, http://www.bls.gov/opub/ted/2012/ted_20120405.htm. Accessed May 20, 2012.

U.S. Congressional Budget Office. October 2011. *Trends in the Distribution of Household Income Between 1979 and 2007.* http://www.cbo.gov/sites/default/files/cbofiles/attachments/10-25-HouseholdIncome.pdf. Accessed August 19, 2012.

U.S. Department of Labor, U.S. Bureau of Labor Statistics. 2007. *A Profile of the Working Poor, 2005.* Report 1001, September. Washington, DC: Author.

U.S. Department of Labor, U.S. Bureau of Labor Statistics. 2012. *A Profile of the Working Poor, 2010.* Report 1035, September. Washington, DC: Author.

Willis, Jonathan, and Julie Wroblewski. 2007. What Happens to Gains, From Strong Productivity Growth? *Federal Reserve of Kansas City Quarterly*, first quarter.

Yen, Hope. 2012. "1 in 2 new graduates are jobless or underemployed." *SFGATE,* April 22, http://www.sfgate.com/cgibin/article.cgi?f=/n/a/2012/04/22/national/w070232D21.DTL#ixzz1vQY62lHo.

2

The Influence of National and State Policies on Local Economic Development

The use of national industrial and social policies to stimulate and sustain the economy has a long history in the United States. The Louisiana Purchase in 1803, the later development of the railroads, the creation of the land grant college system after the Civil War, and the Depression-era New Deal were all national policies. They were pursued with vigor, and they used whatever national resources were necessary to obtain the desired economic results. Many of these programs, like the New Deal, were controversial when they were introduced. Nevertheless, stimulating the national economy by using federal government tax, financial, regulatory, and monetary policy is "as American as apple pie."

Though many American economists do not like government intervention to affect the course of national or local economies, the United States has a crazy quilt of de facto or ad hoc industrial policies. The substance of these national policies ranges from farm supports to tax advantages for certain investments. States and cities in the United States have added their own taxes, land subsidies, and similar incentives to national efforts. The net effect is bewildering and sometimes counterproductive. Nevertheless, this collection of perspectives makes up the current national economic policy—or nonpolicy.

Three Approaches to National Economic Policy

Since 1990, three general approaches have dominated the economic development debate. The first approach invokes past traditions with regard to economic planning and advocates nationwide reindustrialization. It seeks to rebuild the nation's industrial stock through a new set of targeted tax incentives and national financing of infrastructure development. This approach also supports deregulation of labor to limit the power of unions to shape industrial actions, especially regarding international trade and firm outsourcing to overseas lower-wage areas. It refocuses economic development programs on rebuilding the nation's economy in the sectors where the nation must remain internationally competitive (Cohen and Zysman, 1987). As part of this approach, the transformation from old to new industrial and commercial activities should be accelerated through federal intervention that would identify "sunrise" industries—those producing new jobs that compete in a global market—as soon as possible, and encourage them with appropriate investments and tax incentives (e.g., see Reich, 1991). This approach has taken on new life as part of the Obama administration's post–Great Recession efforts to strengthen the national economy and its global competitiveness. The administration established the Advanced Manufacturing Partnership of industry, government, and universities to invent and deploy new manufacturing technology, processes, and products. It also set a goal of doubling U.S. exports overall and created the Renewable Energy and Energy Efficiency Export Initiative for increasing U.S. capacity in clean energy manufacturing, exports of renewable energy and energy-efficient manufactured goods and services, and reducing waste.

The second approach takes a dim view of incentives and dedicated taxes. It favors less rather than more government involvement in economic development and industry. Those advocating less government claim that the more interventionist groups have essentially made the nation a victim of regulations, special support systems, and inconsistent, often contradictory industrial and commercial policies that restrict trade and make the nation less competitive. Instead, they support a move to a fundamentally free market. In the American market economy, the best can and will survive, and the nation will be better served.

Some free-market economists would like to see the labor market further deregulated and the minimum wage either abolished or floated like the currency to absorb unemployed groups in the nation. These economists claim that if wages found their natural level, many more jobs would be available for those genuinely willing and able to work. The George W. Bush administration favored this policy approach in sharp contrast to the Clinton policies, which were more interventionist. Additionally, the George W. Bush administration favored major tax cuts as a means to stimulate the economy. Many advocates suggest these cuts stimulated spending and investment. Dissenters countered that tax cuts have distorted the gap between the rich and poor and placed a greater burden on the middle class to pay larger shares of the tax burden. Meanwhile, the nation's deficit soared, creating a new burden for future generations. In fact, the third richest man in the world, the American billionaire Warren Buffett, publicly stated his concerns about the inequity of the U.S. tax system in an interview with major television network broadcaster Tom Brokaw:

> The degree to which . . . the taxation system has tilted toward the rich and away from the middle class in the last ten years is . . . dramatic . . . and should be addressed. (Cripppen, 2007)

Buffett used his own firm as an example, noting that while he had no tax planning and just paid what the U.S. Congress specified, the total taxes he paid were only 17.7% of his income, while the average for 15 of his office staff was 32.9%. Buffet noted that even his office receptionist paid a higher rate of tax than he did (Crippen, 2007).

Concern over the decline of the middle class has become a major focus of national dialogue. Growing inequality between the top 1% and the other 99% of income distribution has spawned national protests, in particular the long-running Occupy Wall Street Movement (OWM). The Obama administration's efforts to address the beleaguered middle and lower income classes have been confounded by the need to recover from the global financial crisis and by a gridlocked Congress.

A third group of planners and economists suggests that both free-market and regulated industrial policy perspectives aiming at firms alone are misconceived. This is because they are based on the long-held but increasingly false premise that what is good for business is good for communities and workers. As Sloan Foundation president Ralph Gomory (2007) observes, the origins of this premise come from Senate testimony by the Chair of General Motors in 1953 that what was good for General Motors was good for the country and vice versa. While the premise explains much about why national policies have engendered the growing power of multinational corporations, it has become increasingly false with the advent and growth of globalization. Firms like General Motors found that what was good for them was not to be "good" to a community or even a nation of origin, but rather to move their facilities to where production costs were perceived to be lower.

This job-exporting trend of U.S. businesses shows small signs of reversing for three reasons:

1. as a patriotic response to the Great Recession's lingering impacts and concerns over the eroding standing of the United States in the global economy;

2. because labor and material costs have been rising substantially in international competitor economies (e.g., China); and

3. because in advanced manufacturing as well as other key U.S. industry sectors, labor compensation has been stagnant while productivity levels have significantly increased.

One of the enduring postwar trends of U.S. capitalism has been increasing industry concentration (see Adams and Brock, 2005). Consequently, the firms in these concentrated or oligopolistically organized industry sectors have become so large that if they were to fail, there would be severe impacts on the overall economy. The global recession brought about by failures in the large firms of the U.S. financial sector that, in turn, threatened the auto industry and beyond led to unprecedented moves on the part of the government to stabilize or bail out firms considered too large to fail. This has led to renewed debate over what is the proper role for government intervention in the private sector.

Going forward, while there may be circumstances under which assisting firm expansion is warranted, our fundamental view is that national economic and industrial policy must have a local dimension. Thus, we need national policies that (1) increase community control over corporate investment policies, (2) allow communities a greater role in determining their economic stability and quality of life, and (3) give workers increased control and certainty over their livelihoods.

Because of the increasing impacts of globalization, the means to reach these ends must come from the national, state, and local levels. They include national policies that restrict tax write-offs for nonproductive investments, provide government assistance in local economic development planning, including loans to achieve both ownership and development of industrial space at the community level, and provide worker retraining credits and/or educational incentives as well as more portable retirement and benefits. In essence, each worker could have an employer-supported transportable retirement account outside of social security, to which any employer could contribute and to which the worker could also make contributions. Effective national support for local development should target resources and efforts to create a more "level playing field" across state and local jurisdictions so that all participants in the economy have an opportunity to realize their full potential.

States and localities are severely challenged by reductions in revenue and government personnel due to the prolonged effects of the Great Recession. At this time, reassertion of "a real role for the federal government at the community level, ending decades of retreat and delegation of social and economic problems to the states and cities" (O'Connor, 1999) may be welcomed. States and localities need help in maintaining and strengthening all levels of education to maximize their economic development potential. They need help in correcting the long-deferred maintenance of infrastructure (mass transit, highways, railways and bridges, power grids, water and sewer systems) that is critical for economic development.

The Organization for Economic Cooperation and Development (OECD) (1986) has long advocated that national economic policy must incorporate regional and local economic development in order to both moderate the impact of rapid economic change on firms, localities, and individuals and revitalize local economies and facilitate their adjustment to the transformation of the national economy.

Specific objectives of regional and local economic development should include the following:

- strengthening the competitive position of regions and localities within regions by developing otherwise underutilized human and natural resource potential
- realizing opportunities for indigenous economic growth by recognizing the opportunities available for locally produced products and services
- improving employment levels and long-term career options for local residents
- increasing the participation of disadvantaged and minority groups in the local economy
- improving the physical environment as a necessary component of improving the climate for business development and of enhancing the quality of life of residents

Policies to accomplish these aims include sustained investment, medium- and long-term job creation, and the building of local institutions capable of sustaining an area's economic vitality.

Monetary and Tax Policy

In the 1970s, the Federal Reserve Board began promoting a set of economic management approaches based on controlling interest rates. These policies have led to a relatively high cost of borrowing for the nation's business. They are designed to combat inflation and deal with a high-consumption/ low-production economy, which has succeeded for some and failed for others. For new small businesses, these policies have meant that money has been tight. For others, however, the reduction in the inflation rate and the economic stability have increased business confidence and stabilized both wages and prices. Overall, federal policies have achieved the basic mission of controlling rapid economic growth. For several decades, the United States was in good shape compared with its leading international competitors. The nation's economic strength up through 2007 led to strong job growth and created a wave of industrial production. But it did not arrest plant closings or inner-city neighborhood disinvestments. In large measure, the nation's basic industries and weak industrial base could not be restored by fiscal policy alone. Indeed, economist Robert Kuttner (2007) presciently argued that there had been a failed 30-year unnatural experiment in financial deregulation. The goal of the experiment had been the "deliberate dismantling of the mixed economy" (p. 1). Kuttner observes:

> globalization of capital and commerce makes the project of managed capitalism far more difficult, institutionally and politically. It was the nation state that balanced pure capitalism with regulation and social investment. There is no global government, and financial interests have far more influence than ordinary citizens in transnational rule-setting bodies such as the World Trade Organization and the International Monetary Fund. "Free trade" versus "protectionism" is not a helpful distinction. The real issue is *laissez faire* versus a mixed, balanced economy. (p. 1)

Despite the global recession, demand for U.S. goods and services abroad remained high ($2.1 trillion in 2011), but the U.S. demand for foreign goods and services was even higher ($2.7 trillion). Thus, the United States has one of the world's largest trade deficits: approximately $56 billion in 2011. The reason for this is simply that many foreign goods remain relatively cheap and superior in quality compared with domestic counterparts. Monetary policy alone will not address this situation. The global recession has made it even more imperative that management in the United States become sensitive to customers' demands both here and abroad in order to compete successfully.

Tax policy has always been a major component of economic development policy. Federal taxes are sophisticated instruments designed to steer private investment capital. Tax write-offs and loopholes are the primary motivators for short-term investments. Numerous targeted tax credits in the new technologies have been implemented in recent years and have stimulated some good and many poor investments. A prime example of the benefits of this strategy has been strong support by Congress for the development of the Internet without tax interference or government controls or regulations.

More recently, a bevy of tax incentives was put in place for the Gulf Coast areas devastated in 2005 and 2006 by Hurricanes Katrina and Rita. These GO Zone incentives, as they are known, along with other incentives, provide more than 50% tax credits through rapid depreciation allowances in areas devastated by the hurricanes. But even these measures do not bring back customers, so the incentives are not being acted on very quickly by national firms interested in the Gulf region. These firms need to wait until their customer base is in the region before making significant long-term investments.

Foreign investments have long been a source of pretax dollars. The United States has embarked on a set of new policies designed to find better ways to tax foreigners so that they pay their fair share. These tax policies, combined with a slow market, may positively influence capital flows to the United States.

Whatever the direction in which capital moves, communities must help businesses by planning carefully and aggressively to assist new firms, to rebuild old ones, and to meet the needs of firms seeking new markets or developing new products. In other words, capital has to be captured—it will not necessarily seek investment.

Trade Policy

As noted above, the United States continues to experience one of the worst balances of payments (incoming goods versus outgoing goods) in the history of the nation. At one time, the demand for U.S. products was so great that we could scarcely keep pace with it. At that time, we were champions of "free trade." The general belief was that the best producers could and would maintain their markets and that tariff protection served only to protect weak industries and underpinned weak economies.

Now, however, the proverbial shoe is on the other foot. U.S. goods are not penetrating foreign markets as expected. To some extent, the trade policies of the European Common Market, Japan, and other major trading partners are not as open as those of the U.S. market. Until 2007, the U.S. dollar, as the world currency, was maintained at such artificially high levels that it was difficult for U.S. manufacturers to compete in overseas marketplaces. However, the significant fall in the dollar that occurred in 2007, and which has caused concern among nations that peg their currency to the U.S. dollar, has resulted in greater exports for the United States. Further, while it would be expected that imports become more expensive, the degree to which they have done so appears to have been held down by foreign countries trying to maintain U.S. markets (Andrews, 2007b). The North American Free Trade Agreement (NAFTA, enacted in 1994), provided a new platform for the United States in international trade competition. NAFTA supporters argued that increased free trade would eventually bring more jobs to both the United States and Mexico, although in the short term there would be dramatic alterations in the location of employment centers and wage rates in both of these countries.

At the same time, U.S. labor unions, farmers, and even some businesses call for the protection of American firms from unfair international competition. Sometimes this is a retaliatory move against the other country's own import quotas and duties on U.S. goods, as in the case of Japan or China. In other instances, the desire for higher tariffs is a response from an inferior competitive position. Unions and some communities view high tariffs and import quotas as the only mechanism for saving jobs. While some see a protectionist approach as shortsighted, others see it as an important current remedy for workers and firms, as well as for the members of Congress who represent the communities, that are being adversely affected in the global economy. A companion policy to the creation of shelters for domestic industry is the creation of export subsidies for agriculture. The rationale for this is that U.S. agriculture is in global competition with more heavily subsidized farmers in Europe, Australia, and Asia. The General Agreement on Trade and Tariffs (GATT) Accord on agriculture was almost killed by very highly subsidized French farmers. Whether or not the subsidy arguments have an economic rationale, they are politically volatile. Congress has yielded to protectionist sentiments by creating large export subsidies for agriculture.

A substantial body of recent research indicates that the most heavily protected manufacturing firms have been the least competitive internationally. Clearly, the use of tariff protection and subsidies will mean some short-term improvement in various communities. As Ohlsson (1984) has noted, however, "It is well established in economic literature that tariffs or quotas are not the best policies to achieve goals related to national or sectoral production and employment . . . [and] are even less preferable for achieving regional employment goals" (p. 14).

For these reasons, some economists contend that protection-oriented trade policies cannot discriminate sufficiently to protect a nation's competitive enterprises from less productive firms still in existence due to tariffs. Furthermore, tariff protection as a leading economic policy merely locks dying, uncompetitive firms and industries into certain regions, which only undermines long-term economic viability by discouraging community-initiated diversification into more competitive sectors of the national and international economy.

Welfare to Workfare Policy

The literature on social welfare has generally been critical of both the goal and the result of this program. Some opponents of welfare have suggested that welfare itself created the underclass. Certainly, poverty has not decreased under the welfare policies of the past several decades—indeed, it has increased. In 1961, more than 65% of African Americans below the poverty line were engaged in some form of work. Moreover, most were in intact family situations despite their poverty. By 1971, only 31% of African Americans below the poverty line were engaged in any form of legitimate employment. Most of the African Americans below the poverty line were in irregular family situations and rapidly drifting toward underclass status. By 1985, the total central city population living in poverty reached 20.9 million, almost double the 1970 poverty population (Goldsmith and Blakely, 1992).

National welfare policy was always intended to be temporary. Its evolution into a permanent feature of American life surprised and confounded policymakers and social workers. Welfare recipients increasingly did not move into employment. Many of the nation's welfare recipients are from welfare homes (Gottschalk, 2001).

The general public, including many poor people, came to view welfare in contempt and recipients as principally lazy and licentious persons (Gottschalk, 2001). This loss of public sympathy combined with a shrinking employment structure has led national and state policymakers to experiment with welfare, combined with education and work, as a path to employment. A number of schemes have been put into effect with the aim of introducing welfare recipients into the work world, some focusing on the prevention or correction of bad work habits that contributed to "unemployability."

Workfare, as this approach is called, aims at requiring welfare recipients to increase their employable skills in exchange for public assistance. This can involve nonprofit agencies employing welfare-eligible people to work in community-serving enterprises. The agency receives the welfare payment plus a premium to provide social services and in turn places the welfare-eligible person on the payroll of a regular but highly subsidized job. It can also involve profit-making firms' hiring welfare-eligible workers at subsidized rates while they develop their skills and work habits.

The results of these approaches have been mixed. Nevertheless, they constitute an alternative to being locked into the underclass. As economic development policy tools, they offer the potential to increase human capital in the urban population, thereby making it more possible for urban areas to attract or retain an economic base.

Health-Care Policy

Over recent years, fewer and fewer of the new jobs being created have provided any health benefits. The percentage of the population under 65 years of age with no health insurance coverage was more than 18% in 2010 (DeNavas-Walt et al., 2011). More than 85% of this group were in the prime working age group of 18 to 44 years.

One health tragedy has become enough to send many families into economic shock. Employee health coverage has diminished both because of the costs and because health policies and practices like managed care have decreased the number and quality of health-care providers. Health-maintenance organizations (HMOs), originally thought to be the salvation of the American worker, have turned out not to be as capable of meeting the diverse health needs of the nation as presumed. Many HMOs have been consolidated, and others have gone out of business. While the health status of the poor has long made them unacceptable risks for many insurers, even middle-class families and self-employed individuals are now finding themselves blacklisted from reasonably priced private insurance just for taking cholesterol-lowering medicine (Consumer Reports, 2007).

To date, there is no consensus on a national policy of health-care reforms to deal with these problems. But it is clear that a strong attachment to the labor force is no guarantee of access to quality health insurance and care.

Employment Policy

Through much of the 1960s, employment and training plans were designed to improve the employability of the "hard-core" unemployed, or to improve the ability of certain areas of the country or segments of the population to enter the job market. The problem was perceived as a deficiency of skills in an abundant job market. Training would and could solve the skills dilemma. This was only partially true at the time the program was conceived. Discrimination, lack of social skills, and poor aggregate job formation in lagging regions of the country or inner-city areas prevented most people from entering the job market. Nevertheless, the investments in human capital formation were appropriate for the time.

By contrast, the introduction of the Comprehensive Employment and Training Act (CETA) during the Nixon administration initiated a new wave of employment policies driven by economic development. It was recognized that training programs could not solve unemployment problems because there were not enough jobs, and clearly not enough "good" jobs. As a result, training had only marginal impacts on the very poor. Therefore, employment planners became concerned with increasing the number of jobs above the poverty line that would pay decent wages and offer some form of benefits. The CETA program and its successor, the Jobs Training Partnership Act, built expressly on the notion that investments in the workforce must be matched by investments in job creation and retention. More recent policies to reduce unemployment and retrain workers for new enterprises, such as the Workforce Investment Act and Clinton's Jobs Programs, have continued this emphasis.

However, the "jobs crisis" today shows a clear spatial distribution inequity that presents difficulties for national policymakers: Depressed rural farms, factory towns, and inner cities with abandoned industrial sites are in sharp contrast to affluent, predominantly White suburbs with strong employment rates. Macroeconomic solutions are inadequate to address these disparities. Thus, the need for federal policy to be coordinated with local development efforts has increasingly been recognized.

National Policy Targeting Local Economic Development

The national government has always played a role in local economic development planning, though the level of its engagement has varied over time. The federal influence can stem from legislation, policies, or programs for which federal budget expenditures are made. In 2009, *explicit* economic development activities constituted less than 3% of total federal expenditures.[1] This suggests a low level of engagement, but there are other federal programs and policies that strongly impact economic development. For example, the U.S. government is pursuing key science and technology initiatives and recently drafted the National Nanotechnology Initiative Strategic Plan (see www.nano.gov).

The U.S. Economic Development Administration (EDA), located within the Department of Commerce, is charged with leading the federal economic development agenda to promote innovation and competitiveness, as well as to prepare regions for growth and success in the global economy. EDA has numerous Memoranda of Agreement with other federal agencies, most of which are listed in Table 2.1, to leverage its economic development initiatives. As can be seen in the table, there is a very wide array of activities that receive economic development funding, and they take place in every type of location, including Indian reservations, rural areas, inner cities, downtowns, and suburbs.

Although national economic policy is important, it is limited in its ability to meet the twin needs of economic sectoral adjustments and regional or local employment requirements. Furthermore, few effective national policy tools will assist in basic job formation. Many economic stimulators that the federal government uses are designed to facilitate overall economic growth rather than to address specific population groups or localities. National policies with real employment consequences must improve the ability of firms to compete and increase the capacity of communities to build employment.

For this reason, the federal government has been adopting more regionally and locally targeted economic development strategies, including such measures as regional economic policies, neighborhood revitalization, and community development banks. However, national economic development policies targeting localities are not new. Development policies for lagging areas were the cornerstone of the New Deal. The development of the Tennessee Valley Authority, Rural Electrification, Cooperative Extension, and a plethora of other programs aimed at underdeveloped rural areas are now an important part of the pattern of American life. In the1960s, Presidents Kennedy and Johnson merely extended these good ideas to the inner cities to stimulate internal development of urban neighborhoods and central business districts hard hit by the development of the suburbs. The federal government enticed many local governments to embark on a set of social and economic development experiments in an attempt to aid communities and individuals who were not benefiting from economic expansion. Neighborhood and central-city revitalization was proposed through the Model Cities Program, along with a new urban focus for the Economic Development Administration, which had previously served a rural constituency. Urban renewal activities, as well as other

Table 2.1 Federal Economic Development Spending (in thousands) by Program Fiscal Years 2001, 2005, and 2009 (2005 Dollars)

Department	Program	FY 2001	FY 2005	FY 2009	9-Year Change
Agriculture	Forestry Incentives Program	$4,760	$7	n/a	n/a
	Small Business Innovation Research	$23,129	$14,756	$264,173	1,042.2%
	National Rural Development Partnership	n/a	n/a	n/a	n/a
	Rural Housing Site Loans and Self-Help Housing Land Development Loans	$4,481	$450	$30,518	581.%
	Rural Community Development Initiative	n/a	n/a	n/a	n/a
	Emerging Markets Program	n/a	$11,404	$14,801	n/a
	Cooperative Forestry Assistance	$165,888	$38,793	$148	−99.9%
	Schools and Roads Grants to States	$410,902	$1,453,627	$81	−100.%
	Schools and Roads Grants to Counties	$11,801	$12,973	$67	−99.4%
	National Forest-Dependent Rural Communities	$333	$428	$14,406	4,226.2%
	Rural Development, Forests and Communities	$3,504	$2,341	$4,122	17.6%
	Wood in Transportation Program	n/a	$42	n/a	n/a

(Continued)

Table 2.1 (Continued)

Department	Program	FY 2001	FY 2005	FY 2009	9-Year Change
	Forest Products Lab: Technology Marketing Unit	n/a	n/a	$240,431	n/a
	Water and Waste Disposal System for Rural Communities	$670,327	$453,123	$4,131	−99.4%
	Emergency Community Water Assistance Grants	$26,207	$10,677	$57,539	119.6%
	Community Facilities Loans and Grants	$87,909	$52,107	$40,922	−53.4%
	Intermediary Relending Program	$48,451	$33,657	$1,078,842	2,126.7%
	Business and Industry Loans	$61,442	$877,811	$5,862,918	9,442.2%
	Rural Enterprise Business Grants	$61,718	$43,288	$36,214	−41.3%
	Water and Waste Disposal Loans and Grants	$42,260	$44,482	$8,724	−79.4%
	Rural Cooperative Development Grants	$44,326	$9,913	$7,398	−83.3%
	Empowerment Zones Program	$3,789	$250	$5,152	36. %
	Rural Business Opportunity Grants	$11,474	$3,075	$9,022	−21.4%
	Rural Electrification Loans and Loan Guarantees	$2,723,370	$3,652,428	$622,776	−77.1%
	Rural Telephone Loans and Loan Guarantees	$814,115	$1,364,592	n/a	n/a
	Rural Telephone Bank Loans	n/a	$683,819	n/a	n/a

Department	Program	FY 2001	FY 2005	FY 2009	9-Year Change
	Rural Economic Development Loans and Grants	$655	$8,120	$33,251	4,976.5%
	Distance Learning and Telemedicine Loans and Grants	n/a	n/a	$8,798	n/a
	Assistance to High Energy Cost/Rural Communities	$24,322	n/a	$545	−97.8%
Commerce	Grants for Public Works and Economic Development Facilities	$351,526	$177,183	$137,974	−60.7%
	Economic Development Support for Planning Organizations	$28,891	$27,509	$27,017	−6.5%
	Economic Development Technical Assistance	$11,841	$10,302	$8,805	−25.6%
	Economic Adjustment Assistance	$202,746	$78,221	$354,832	75. %
	Trade Adjustment Assistance	$12,962	$12,006	$12,653	−2.4%
	Manufacturing Extension Partnership	$98,954	$88,250	$83,972	−15.1%
	Congressionally Identified Projects	n/a	$51,884	$63,233	n/a
Defense	Procurement Technical Assistance for Business Firms	$438,459	$426,093	$361	−99.9%
	Community Economic Adjustment Planning Assistance	$5,114	$4,629	$46,886	816.8%

(Continued)

Table 2.1 (Continued)

Department	Program	FY 2001	FY 2005	FY 2009	9-Year Change
Housing and Urban Development	Community Development Block Grants	$5,637,344	$4,702,000	$6,112,473	8.4%
	Empowerment Zones Program	n/a	$47,687	n/a	n/a
	Rural Housing and Economic Development	n/a	$24,071	n/a	n/a
Interior	Road Maintenance-Indian Roads	$8,937	$12,075	$15,441	72.8%
	Minerals and Mining on Indian Lands	$179	$506	$813	354. %
	Fish, Wildlife, and Parks Programs on Indian Lands	$34,001	$59,738	$26,173	−23. %
	Bureau of Indian Affairs Facilities-Operations and Maintenance	n/a	$29,534	$29,509	n/a
	Construction and Repair of Indian Detention Facilities	n/a	$725	$658	n/a
	Indian Loans Economic Development	n/a	$4,143	$7,444	n/a
	Recreation Resource Management	$3,943	$57	$6,484	64.4%
	Urban Interface Community and Rural Fire Assistance	$3,755	$29,629	$1,774	−52.8%

Department	Program	FY 2001	FY 2005	FY 2009	9-Year Change
	Outdoor Recreation-Acquisition, Development and Planning	$8,468	$49,276	$34,375	305.9%
Labor	Employment Service	$963,970	$824,504	$1,042,563	8.2%
Transportation	Airport Improvement Program	$3,442,155	$2,048,398	$4,337,567	26. %
	Highway Planning and Construction	$32,810,227	$34,682,247	$53,497,402	63.1%
	Recreational Trails Program	$2	$642	$73,827	3,691,269.5%
	Formula Grants for Non-Urbanized Areas	$268,317	$139,094	$954,229	255.6%
	Transit Planning and Research	$33,432	$20,692	$48,157	44. %
	Job Access-Reverse Commute	$102,551	$69,037	$123,696	20.6%
	Payments for Essential Air Service	$61,527	$0	n/a	n/a
	Minority Business Resource Center	$7,719	$6,000	n/a	n/a
	Small Community Air Service Development	n/a	$16,764	n/a	n/a
Health and Human Services	Community Services Block Grants Discretionary Awards	$740,670	$677,179	$38,281	−94.8%

(Continued)

Table 2.1 (Continued)

Department	Program	FY 2001	FY 2005	FY 2009	9-Year Change
	Job Opportunities for Low-Income Individuals	$5,850	$4,936	$4,012	−31.4%
	Native American Program	$49,447	$37,189	$34,763	−29.7%
	Medicaid Infrastructure Grants to Support the Competitive Employment of People With Disabilities	n/a	$25,040	$67,416	n/a
	Health Care and Other Facilities	$302,241	$423,173	$236,408	−21.8%
Small Business Administration	Technical Assistance	n/a	n/a	n/a	n/a
	Small Business Investment Companies	$3,334,544	$363,290	$635,444	−80.9%
	Small Business Loans	$9,384,164	$10,675,778	$5,925,274	−36.9%
	Certified Development Company Loans (504 Loans)	$2,952,785	$5,055,487	$3,348,307	13.4%
	Microloan Demonstration Program	$4,119	$13,329	$17,833	333. %
Environmental Protection Agency	Capitalization Grants for State Revolving Rounds	$1,597,481	$1,033,812	$4,196,284	162.7%
	Capitalization Grants for Drinking Water State Revolving Fund	$896,177	$779,596	$2,478,730	176.6%

Department	Program	FY 2001	FY 2005	FY 2009	9-Year Change
	Brownfields Training, Research, and Tech Assistance Grants and Cooperative Agreements	n/a	$4,066	$4,706	n/a
	Brownfields Job Training Cooperative Agreements	n/a	$1,576	$7,053	n/a
	State and Tribal Response Program Grants	n/a	$44,655	$42,682	n/a
	Brownfields Assessment and Cleanup Cooperative Agreements	n/a	$76,959	$145,166	n/a
Appalachian Regional Commission	Appalachian Area Development	n/a	$46,660	$56,563	n/a
	Appalachian Regional Commission	$88	$70	n/a	n/a
Denali	Denali Commission	$61	$128	n/a	n/a
Delta	Delta Area Economic Development	$0	$3	$20,174	n/a
Total Federal Spending in Millions		$69,725	$72,153	$92,654	32.9%
Inter-period Change			3.5%	28.4%	

Source: Consolidated Federal Funds Reports (2001, 2005, 2009), U.S. Census Bureau.

Note: Funding estimates based on available program-level funding data. Determinations as to which programs are relevant to economic development are based on the February 2006 Government Accountability Office (GAO) report *Rural Economic Development: More Assurance Is Needed That Grant Reporting Is Accurate.*

government programs, provided local governments with the first impetus to plan for the local economy in a systematic way.

During the Reagan–Bush era (1980–1992), however, many economic development programs to assist localities with physical improvements or industrial support were drastically reduced or simply eliminated. In the 1970s, for example, the federal government had poured nearly $60 billion a year into urban aid projects ranging from community revitalization projects to schools and job training. It had spent more than $5 billion on public service job training alone (Ferguson and Dickens, 1999). These funds almost disappeared in the 1980s, and as a result, the hope and spirit associated with urban recovery seemed to fade as well.

But in the 1990s, local economic development—particularly of urban communities—once again moved to the forefront of national policy. It was becoming clear that the challenges of the cities and the suburbs were linked and that the inner cities could no longer be written off. Over the previous decade, urban economists had painted a grim picture of what could happen to the national economy if the human and economic resources of the cities remained untapped. Finally, the message was heard, not just in cities but in the suburbs as well. Civic leaders in cities and suburbs began to see across their borders that they had a common economic agenda. Furthermore, it became more generally recognized that the economic and social problems of both the cities and the suburbs threatened the country's ability to invest in productive enterprise. As a result, the national administration was free for the first time in three decades to call for regional and metropolitan redevelopment. When the Clinton administration took office in 1992, it found allies for a national metropolitan policy among state governors of both parties. Henry Cisneros, Secretary of the U.S. Department of Housing and Urban Development (HUD), began to fashion a new agenda for urban America aimed at rebuilding community with social capital–forming citizens at its core.

The idea was to create economically and socially integrated communities as the backbone of the national economy. The White House and Congress have worked together to build both physical and human capital through programs of various loosely linked federal agencies, such as programs to end housing discrimination in lending, establish urban empowerment zones, increase aid to inner-city schools, and offer tax credits for jobs, housing, and economic development (U.S. Department of Housing and Urban Development, 2000). The newest federal programs attempt to build human capital into new enterprise formation: investing in new businesses that start up in low-income communities rather than trying to persuade firms to move into those communities. This approach is designed to rebuild communities and the local skill base by combining the establishment of enterprise zones with welfare reforms, rebuilding of inner-city infrastructure, and school improvements. For example, the Labor Department has introduced a variety of demonstration programs targeting youth employment that are aimed at linking job formation with skill building and new enterprise creation. Some of these programs show young people how to start businesses; others have strong mentorship components, connecting large and small firms with local schools to work more directly.

The George W. Bush administration, like the Clinton administration, pushed for ending housing discrimination in lending, increasing aid to inner-city schools, and offering tax credits for jobs, housing, and economic development. Policies endorsed by President Bush had a place-organizational emphasis, but they were less concerned with increasing social welfare supports than with using market forces and community institutions like churches to revitalize communities and strengthen their social structure.

The Obama administration's economic platform (2008–2012), responding first to the downward spiral that the nation found itself in due to the Great Recession, had to focus on strengthening the social safety net and the market simultaneously. After saving the U.S. auto and banking industries from collapse, its economic platform has been focused on job creation, reform and fiscal responsibility, and increasing security for the middle class. The American Recovery and Reinvestment Act created a number of supports for urban communities. Among these were Neighborhood Stabilization Funds, increased spending for disadvantaged school systems, and broadband access to underserved areas. In particular, the administration's policy reflects a "new metropolitan reality—that strong cities are the building blocks of strong regions, which in turn, are essential for a strong America" (The White House, 2012).

The Obama administration is particularly focused on boosting manufacturing, energy production, and entrepreneurship for job creation. It is focused on regulatory, health care, and tax reform as well as deficit reduction and eliminating federal government waste. While these areas are practically an automatic focus of each administration, their explicit tie to middle-class security is unique. For example, the administration linked the reform of the financial industry to a law that created the Consumer Financial Protection Bureau to protect consumers and homeowners from exploitive mortgage and payday lending practices.[i] President Obama also passed comprehensive health insurance reform that allows adult children to stay on their parents' health care plans until

---

[i] The Consumer Financial Protection Bureau (2012) defines these loans as follows:

Payday loans are typically marketed to bridge a cash flow shortage between pay or benefits checks. They generally have three features: the loans are small dollar amounts; borrowers must repay the loan quickly; and they require that a borrower give lenders access to repayment through a claim on the borrower's deposit account. Most loans are for several hundred dollars and have finance charges of $15 or $20 for each $100 borrowed. For the two-week term typical of a payday loan, these fees equate to an Annual Percentage Rate ranging from 391 percent to 521 percent.

they are 26, prevents coverage denial for pre-existing conditions, and provides tax credits to small business, among other provisions.

The George W. Bush administration was particularly proactive in promoting brownfield redevelopment activity through market-based activity. While the U.S. Environmental Protection Agency (EPA) is the lead agency for brownfield redevelopment, other federal agencies, in particular Housing and Urban Development (HUD), have been active as well. The EPA's role began with its 1995 Brownfield Action Agenda that included brownfield pilot grants to communities, clarification of liability issues for brownfield property owners, partnerships between federal, state, and local agencies to promote brownfield redevelopment, and job development and training for brownfield remediation. Its proactive stance was significantly enhanced with the Small Business Liability Relief and Brownfields Revitalization Act in 2002. HUD administers the Brownfield Economic Development Initiative (BEDI) to promote the return of brownfields to productive economic use. It provides financial assistance to public entities in the redevelopment of brownfields. The Brownfields National Partnership Action Agenda, begun in 1997, brings together more than 20 federal agencies to address brownfield cleanup and redevelopment issues in a more coordinated approach and to link environmental protection with economic development and community revitalization.

National policy can have unintended and negative consequences for economic development. In fact, the need for federal action to spur brownfield redevelopment stemmed from an unintended consequence of the 1980 passage of the Comprehensive Environmental Response, Compensation, and Liability Act (CERCLA). This act was the federal government's attempt to address the environmental contamination that was the legacy of more than a century of industrial and commercial activity. Its initial intent was to promote cleanup of contaminated land and to provide opportunities for EPA to recover cleanup costs from all potentially responsible parties (PRPs), including past and present property owners as well as lending institutions. However, it had the effect of steering potential investors and developers away from previously developed properties for fear of becoming liable for the contamination on brownfield sites. The subsequent federal brownfield initiatives have been aimed at eliminating this unintended consequence as well as providing market stimulation.

Two recent issues are also demonstrative of the unintended consequences that national-level decisions can have for local economic development. The first was the Supreme Court case *Kelo v. New London, Connecticut*, which was about the taking of private property by eminent domain for local economic development purposes. The second was the Federal Reserve Bank's focus, during the George W. Bush administration, on increasing home ownership as a means for improving economic opportunity. Traditionally, the power of eminent domain— the right of the government to take ownership of private property for a "public purpose" without the owner's consent—has been limited to the specific needs of public infrastructure development (i.e., utilities, highways, railroads, etc.). The

City of New London sought to use the power of eminent domain to acquire the property of Julie Kelo and several private owners who did not want to sell for a redevelopment initiative that would put these properties into other private parties' hands. Kelo sued and the case went all the way to the Supreme Court. In the June 2005 *Kelo v. City of New London* decision, the Supreme Court expanded the definition of "public purpose" to include economic development considerations, thereby giving New London permission to condemn Kelo's and others' properties and transfer them to another private party. There was a significant outcry over the decision at the state and local levels throughout the country. Within 2 years of the court's decision, in an effort to make sure it could not happen in their location, 35 states had enacted reform and the voting public in 10 states had passed ballot measures limiting or prohibiting the use of eminent domain or regulatory takings for economic development purposes (Shigley, 2007). *Regulatory taking* refers to land for which the use has been so heavily regulated that it effectively becomes a form of eminent domain. The intent of much of the property-rights backlash to the *Kelo* decision was to limit the use of eminent domain as an economic development tool to areas of blight. Further, the definition of what constitutes a blighted area was narrowed in many states.

Key economic development organizations around the country have tried to stop the backlash against using eminent domain for economic development purposes. For example, the International Economic Development Council (IEDC) argued that judicious use of eminent domain was critical to local economic growth and development: its use to assemble land helps to revitalize local economies, create much-needed jobs, and generate city revenues. The council argued that, "[If] eminent domain for economic development is prohibited, one person could veto the redevelopment of an *entire distressed community*. This would have the practical effect of making such projects *virtually impossible*" (IEDC, n.d.).

The subprime mortgage lending crisis that began in 2007 created economic shocks throughout the economy (and affected foreign countries, which have been large investors in the U.S. mortgage market). By the end of 2008, it was clear that the economy had entered into the most severe downturn since the Great Depression: it was in a "Great Recession" from which recovery has been very slow.

The subprime crisis has its roots in the Federal Reserve and the George W. Bush administration placing a high priority on "promoting 'financial innovation' and what President Bush has called the 'ownership society'" (Andrews, 2007a). In essence, the traditional criteria for mortgage lending were significantly loosened (for example, requiring a down payment). The subprime lending was focused on individuals with weak credit who are most often found among the poor. Aggressive financial institutions targeted minority communities. Subprime lenders offered adjustable-rate mortgages (ARMs). Borrowers were qualified for the loans based on their initial low teaser interest rates rather than the significantly higher rates that they would have to subsequently pay and that many had no realistic chance of meeting. Mortgage delinquency rates, as well as foreclosures, rose dramatically in 2007, and lenders and home builders have gone into bankruptcy. Dan Immergluck, a national expert on the housing market, observes that the federal role in promoting the subprime crisis, which disproportionately affected minority communities, stemmed in part from a lack of enforcement of the Community Reinvestment Act (CRA) and fair lending laws (personal correspondence, 2007). Further, foreclosures affect not only the homeowner but also the surrounding neighborhood and community. For example, Immergluck and Smith's (2006) research found that a foreclosure on a home lowered the price of other nearby single-family homes, on average, by 0.9%. They also reported that the downward pressure on housing prices extended to houses that sold within 2 years of the foreclosure. Further, this negative impact was cumulative—that is, each additional foreclosure on the block lowered values an additional 0.9%. The impact was even higher in lower-income neighborhoods, where each foreclosure dropped home values by an average of 1.44%.

Large portions of cities have been affected by the subprime mortgage crisis, to the extent that some entire cities are now in crisis (see Box 2.1). The crisis affected inner cities in older areas, but it also affected fast-growth suburban areas in the country, particularly in places like California with high levels of minority population.

Box 2.1	Cleveland Sues 21 Lenders Over Subprime Mortgages

Cleveland is suing 21 of the nation's largest banks and financial institutions, accusing them of knowingly plunging the city into a financial crisis by flooding the local housing market with subprime mortgage loans to people who could never repay.

The city is seeking "at least" hundreds of millions of dollars in damages, Cleveland's law director, Robert J. Triozzi, said Friday. The list of defendants includes some of the most prominent firms on Wall Street, like Citigroup, Bank of America, Wells Fargo, Merrill Lynch, and Countrywide Financial.

Mayor Frank G. Jackson said in an interview on Friday that the companies would be "held accountable for what they've done."

"We're going after them to get the resources we need to rebuild our city," Mr. Jackson said.

The financial crisis has hit Cleveland especially hard, with more than 7,000 foreclosures in each of the last two years, Mr. Jackson said. Entire city blocks have been abandoned. The city's budget has been strained by the effort to maintain thousands of boarded-up homes, and by the cost of responding to a rise in violent crime and arson.

The major banks involved did not return calls about the lawsuit. A spokesman for Merrill Lynch, Mark Herr, said, "We're declining to comment right now."

The Cleveland suit is separate from one filed Tuesday in federal court by the City of Baltimore against Wells Fargo, accusing it of violating fair-housing laws by singling out African-Americans for high-interest mortgages.

The Cleveland suit, filed Thursday in Cuyahoga County Common Pleas Court under the state's public nuisance law, asserts that the financial institutions created nuisances across broad swaths of Cleveland because their loans led to widespread abandonment of homes. "We've torn down 1,000 abandoned houses, and haven't even made a dent," Mr. Jackson said.

The drop in homeownership, and a steep decline in population—to 444,000 residents in 2007 from almost a million in 1950, according to census figures—has drained Cleveland's budget. In December, Mr. Jackson announced that the city was unable to borrow money and would be forced to postpone or permanently shelve millions of dollars in public works projects.

"The strain on our budget is too much," Mr. Jackson said. "These companies have knowingly created a public nuisance by exploiting the city of Cleveland."

Several Cleveland suburbs have expressed interest in joining the case as a class-action suit, Mr. Triozzi said. Because the city is suing under a state statute, cities outside Ohio could not join. "This case is about what these Wall Street bankers did to Cleveland," Mr. Triozzi said.

Instead of aiming at the banks that originally made subprime mortgage loans in the city, the lawsuit is against those firms that bundled the loans into securities to be divided into shares and sold on the stock exchange. This process, and the large fees the firms generated from the work, Mr. Triozzi said, drove their effort to make as many loans as possible during an era of low interest rates and a prolonged housing boom.

Coordination of Local and National Development Efforts

Communities across the nation develop their own industrial and broader economic development policies using various approaches. If a national policy, for example, one to promote advanced manufacturing or to increase exports, is adopted at the national level, it will have little effect unless there is companion policy at the local level to take advantage of available federal resources as well as to muster local resources.

In general, almost all federal *development* efforts have had a "bricks and mortar" orientation. The role of the federal government in stimulating economic development in the poorest regions has been to provide the physical conditions and infrastructure to induce development rather than direct intervention in the private sector (except for the War on Poverty). Some marginal interventions have been companions to these physical programs, like the location of military facilities and government offices.

Both the federal government and local officials have tacitly agreed that federal government should remain in the background, using its money but not its muscle to bring about economic change. But now federal funds available for local use are diminishing, and although local officials have more need for federal assistance, less is forthcoming. For example, military base closures have affected hundreds of communities over the years. As a result of smaller budgets, local and state governments are hard pressed both to meet social commitments to the unemployed and to stimulate development. The liberal use of economic incentives has to be reconsidered given shrinking state and local government revenues.

The federal government's response to the need to curtail the growth of public programs and subsidies has been to reduce the red tape and strings attached to its funding as a means of increasing positive impacts. Essentially, the national government has given local officials more authority to deal with the fewer resources they receive for their locality. This gives many local residents the impression that local policymakers have more discretion over federal funds and more options to cure local problems. But the simple truth is that there are more problems than there is money. Local officials have to use the funds they have as investments in the future, not as temporary aids to meet current emergencies. This is why local economic development is both necessary and difficult.

The federal government's response to the needs of communities and individuals has been and will continue to be under significant revision since the War on Poverty era. But whatever the federal government response, communities faced with plant closures and other business failures, high unemployment, labor skills shortages, environmental degradation and climate change impacts, growing inequality, and public assistance burdens, simply cannot afford to risk a *laissez-faire* approach to their own destiny.

State Economic Development Approaches

Although the national government has been somewhat reluctant to develop active economic development policies, our federalist system gives states great powers to do so. Almost every state in the union has an explicit or at least a discernible implicit economic development policy. State policies range from a statewide tax or incentive plan to more complicated programs that provide targeted incentives for specific industries. In fact, the states offer a bewildering array of policies. For example, several states have abolished certain taxes as implicit development incentives. Some, like Oregon, have no state sales tax; others, like Texas and Florida, have no income tax. Nevada has almost no taxes on residents and builds its state budgets on tourism and hotels, along with gambling revenues. This policy has induced a number of durable goods and transportation firms to relocate from California to Nevada.

Most states have a state development plan and a state economic development office. In some states, the economic development office is in the same location as the governor's office. In many other states, it is a major state department with responsibility for recruiting businesses, as well as creating and retaining jobs in the state. State economic development offices do everything from coordinating other state agencies to promoting the state via glossy brochures and a long list of incentives. Bradshaw and Blakely's (1999) early in-depth study of state economic development policies and programs found that those concentrating on business retention, human skill development, and infrastructure building, showed the best overall economic development results (see Table 2.2).

Table 2.2   Characteristics of Innovative State Economic Development Programs

Leadership

Emphasis by governor on economic development

Business "welcome" events

Business councils, industrial associations

Worker compensation and tort reform

Environmental ombudspersons

Lotteries

Building community capacity to do attraction and retention

Information

Technical assistance and standards

University outreach programs

Electronic bulletin boards

Site information

Partnerships to do planning and promotion

(Continued)

Table 2.2 (Continued)

Brokering

Permit one-stop shops

Coordination of economic development with other programs (e.g., housing)

Interstate regional cooperation

Marketing

Source: Bradshaw and Blakely (1999, p. 241).

Phases of Economic Development

There has been an increasing array of services and inducements offered by states, as well as sophistication of state policy and program tools for promoting economic development. In general, the evolution of these tools follows the pattern of what can be seen as five waves of economic development practice at the state and local levels (see Fitzgerald and Leigh, 2002). The transition from business attraction to broader perspectives on economic development is a predominant theme of the descriptions of these phases (Bradshaw and Blakely, 1999; Fitzgerald and Leigh, 2002). The phases are both chronological and overlapping. That is, while their emergence may be associated with a particular point in time, the predominant practices associated with each have not disappeared. Instead, state and local economic development agencies typically engage in practices from more than one of the phases.

The first phase, that of industrial recruitment, began in the 1930s. Economic development practice was concentrated on creating a good business climate through tax abatements, loan packages, infrastructure, and land development. While its beginning is often associated with the post-Depression period, in reality the Southern states were actively recruiting industry from the end of the Civil War onward (e.g., see McMath, 1991). This phase was informed by two theoretical perspectives: a regional and community development perspective drawing on international development theory and an industrial location perspective drawing from firm behavior theory. Both perspectives sought to identify the causes of regional growth and development and how local efforts can alter this path. Further, economic development potential was seen to be predicated on the local area's export base. The directing of public funds to private-sector firms to influence their location in this phase marked the beginning of what later came to be labeled "corporate welfare" (Bartlett and Steele, 1998).

After World War II, Southern states with declining agricultural bases were particularly aggressive in using inducements to attract manufacturing plants to their low-wage and low-union environments. Millions of jobs moved into Southern states due to these strategies. Ultimately, virtually all states were competing for jobs that were moving around the country, professional industrial relocation agencies were established in all major cities, and incentives became expected costs of obtaining a factory for any of the many regional industrial parks that were being established with federal funds. Not surprisingly, this strategy was termed "smokestack chasing."

Civic leaders viewed the industrial attraction concept and methods positively during the long wave of economic growth because there were generally enough new firms and growth for all communities to share. Though spirited competition existed among different localities, the general view was that the economy was dynamic enough to accommodate any reasonable bidder.

However, as growth subsided and as most states became involved in business attraction, the price of the incentives needed to induce a plant skyrocketed, and businesses learned to play one location against another to extract more costly incentive packages. The National Governors' Association became concerned that states were losing money and gaining few new jobs from this reckless activity. Moreover, existing businesses saw that their out-of-state competitors were receiving benefits that placed older, loyal, local firms at a distinct disadvantage compared with the newcomers.

The second phase was characterized by political critiques of local economic development practices that began in the late 1960s and were spurred by factors such as manufacturing decline and failure of urban redevelopment efforts. Economic development analysis shifted its focus from implementation of various techniques and strategies to identifying the participants in the economic development process and their motives, as well as the beneficiaries of the process. Political economist Molotch's (1976) classic article, "The City as a Growth Machine," argued economic development activity was led by landholding elites interested in increasing the value of their property. He argued that job creation, one of the main justifications of local economic development practice, was not increased by the activities of economic development practitioners; instead, jobs were merely transferred between locations. By the late 1970s, rising global competition along with a stagnant world economy led some to dismiss business attraction efforts as smokestack chasing of footloose industry that did not provide the jobs and wealth creation promised. The interests of cities and states, and the businesses within them, were not mutual: cities and states sought stability of employment and tax base, while firms sought mobility to produce in the place of lowest costs or highest profits. Approaches in the second phase retained a component of business attraction but added strategies to retain and expand existing businesses and incubate new enterprises. The tools of the second phase included offering incentives to businesses that were losing their competitive edge and providing expansion loans and grants to firms with new markets that could expand locally or globally, such as firms in new technologies. They also included the establishment of small business units to assist small business formation and growth.

Two more strategies, both in reaction to the failure of the first two traditional strategies, were introduced in the third phase of local economic development. First, the entrepreneurial strategy represented a shift from supply-side industrial attraction to developing new business and industry, particularly in sectors perceived to be high tech. Other entrepreneurial strategies included international trade promotion, venture capital funds, and small business development (Eisinger, 1995). More recently, creative class attraction and development schemes (Florida, 2002) can be seen to be an extension of the entrepreneurial strategy. Second, the equity strategy emerged in the late 1970s and early 1980s to confront growing issues of inequality. It advocates place-based strategies that focus on issues of equity and redistribution. It also expands the notion of who participates in local economic development decision making to include neighborhood organizations, civic groups, and labor unions, and it introduces new ways of examining old problems (i.e., identifying race and gender implications). The third-phase programs that emerged in the 1990s focus on using regional resources to support the growth of specified industrial clusters of related firms, as well as providing new emphasis on building local capacity through education and training of the local workforce.[2] They attempt to link technology, human resources, and capital in such a way as to give networked firms a global competitive advantage. These programs are based on the recognition that the skill of the labor force is essential to the ability of new-economy firms to compete, so they strengthen the links between schools and colleges and industry— for example, by establishing specialized certificate programs. They also emphasize local participation in industrial associations, collaborative product-testing facilities, and the like. Third-phase programs, unlike their predecessors, offer few direct investments or gifts to businesses. Instead, they help businesses to finance expansions and respond to technological change by a variety of funding options that involve access to credit or low-cost lending. Rather than simply assuming that communities will benefit from individual firm decisions, current programs attempt to create the context in which locational advantages and industrial bases can be used to the advantage of the region.

Numerous states have now developed third-wave initiatives based on increasing the real competitive advantages of the state in national and international terms. As Fosler (1991) notes, they are interested in "achieving high levels of productivity and competitiveness that increase income and provide a high standard of living and quality of life for all residents . . . They are concerned with the ways in which workers and businesses interact in networks and clusters" (p. 5). To this end, states on an international border, such as Texas and Washington, are even creating cross-border economic development strategies.

Many states now have international offices to coordinate goods, services, and people exchanges as a bridge to long-term economic partnerships across international cultural boundaries.

Bradshaw and Blakely (1999) found that the most progressive states (e.g., Washington, Nevada, and Florida) had designed well-thought-out plans that included the active participation of state stakeholders, including nonprofits, community groups, and business. That is, economic development policy had moved beyond the sole province of the private sector. State officials recognized that important actors like schools and churches had to be included in any attempt to rebuild a civic agenda that would induce new business and keep existing firms. State strategies, like California's, have built on successful public–private collaborations, such as the joint venture Silicon Valley. This recognition complements the widening of professional focus during the third phase to confront issues of socioeconomic inequality and to become advocates for those passed over in the development process. The introduction of equity planning into economic development necessitated a different set of questions in creating and evaluating economic development strategies and particularly focuses on who benefits and who pays in the development process. As Fitzgerald and Leigh (2002) observe, "In addition to expanding participation in the planning process, equity planning introduces new ways of examining old problems such as identifying the race and gender implications of economic development strategies and programs" (p. 17). They go on to note that equity planners still represent only a minority voice in economic development practice.

The fourth phase can be characterized as sustainable economic development. Economic development was called on to be environmentally sensitive and responsible to the equity criterion of the third phase. Campbell (1996) argues that economic development planning was required "to 'grow' the economy, distribute this growth fairly, and in the process not degrade the ecosystem" (p. 297). Jepson and Haines (2003) interpret sustainable economic development to be that which emphasized self-sufficiency over an export-based economy and development over growth. Newby (1999) argues that sustainable local economic development (SLED) should be the vehicle by which to achieve sustainable improvements in quality of life. She observes that it is too often "assumed that what is 'good for the economy' is automatically good for society." Further, how economic development is implemented has profound positive or negative impacts on society and the environment. Consequently, the practice of sustainable local economic development considers the entire range of economic development and regeneration options available, appraises their individual impacts, and prioritizes "those approaches that yield social, economic and environmental benefits together, rather than one benefit at the expense of another" (p. 68).

The fifth phase of economic development, beginning in the 1990s, was originally characterized by two approaches, the first relying on market solutions, and the second promoting metropolitan or regional strategies. Porter's (1998) work on competitive advantage has been highly influential in this stage. Economic developers are called on to identify unmet demand, provide government facilitation and financing, and encourage public–private partnerships for minority firms and market developments. In recognition of the negative consequences of urban sprawl and associated traffic congestion on local economies, economic developers and other development officials have been taking steps to revitalize obsolete or underperforming areas. The approaches first pursued in major metropolitan areas have diffused to smaller metro regions and even small towns as the high auto and truck dependency of U.S. local economies of all sizes has resulted in pervasive sprawl. The market emphasis of this stage can be seen as akin to the viewpoint Newby (1999) critiques in the quote, "what is good for the economy is good for society." Without explicit commitment to larger sustainability principles, the phase has the potential to yield unintended consequences such as new gentrification trends whereby the higher-income residents of a region are returning to enjoy newly revitalized downtowns and urban life, and the poor are displaced to declining suburbs that lack necessary support systems and public transportation needed to give them access to the economy. While the spatial focus of this phase is regional or local, states have played a significant role in fostering its implementation.

As was noted at the outset of this section, the five phases that have been described are overlapping. We can continue to observe the dominant characteristic of each phase in economic development practice today. The continued implementation of strategies associated with different phases rests on the explicit or implicit definition of local economic development held by the practitioner and the economic development.

Challenges and Opportunities Inherent in Economic Development Policy Making

To implement strategies appropriate to economic development, states will need, more than ever, to strengthen ties with policymakers in specific regions and localities within their purview. Simultaneously, community policymakers taking up the challenges of local economic development will be well served if they maintain a broad, realistic view of their available alternatives. To implement the most effective, most integrated policies, whether state or local, almost all U.S. communities will have to come to terms with the following:

- Economic development will be much less about a community having lower costs of production than about a high quality of life and community assets that attract and retain knowledge-intensive and innovative firms and their workers. This means that communities must provide for quality housing and neighborhoods, educational systems, mobility, health, and cultural facilities.

- *Attracting* new manufacturing firms continues to fade as a viable strategy for communities seeking to increase local employment opportunities. As a result, our nation's communities and regions need to become directly involved in cultivating firms from the advanced information and service sectors mentioned earlier, or from other areas of activity, as their new base employers. However, communities should not overlook the possibility that existing manufacturers may continue to be competitive and offer jobs and that there may be opportunities for the development of small and medium-sized advanced manufacturers. Communities must look to human capital as the critical engine for economic development. Thus, job creation is now based on talent pools that create new economic activity rather than competing to move existing firms around the nation or the world.

- American communities could once rely exclusively on their regional and national market positions to determine local economic stability, but this is no longer the case. Today, a global economic system predominates. In many instances, as in the cases of Los Angeles, New York, San Francisco, and Miami, regional ties to the international economy are more significant than their ties to the domestic economy. Numerous programs are showing that, because of the major changes in the international economy—rather than in spite of them— local communities can pursue development policies that complement national economic objectives. Clearly, larger metropolitan export-oriented economies can take advantage of international development options more readily than can smaller rural communities. Nonetheless, it is important that every community pursue economic policies that enhance or facilitate local industries with international potential, and that meet the employment needs of all community residents.

- Communities based on a single industry (such as agriculture or mining) or a few major employers will be more vulnerable than those with a more diverse economic base. As a result, communities with narrow or declining economic bases will have to develop more sophisticated economic strategies to remain economically and socially desirable places.

- All American communities have increased pressure to develop programs that deal with adult long-term unemployment. In addition, new (young) entrants to the labor market, particularly teenagers, will have location-specific employment problems related to job access as well as to undereducation and undertraining. Poor job access can be due to inadequate transportation, lack of informal information networks that connect people in all communities to new opportunities, or lack of knowledge regarding positions created with unfamiliar names and opaque skills requirements in new, small, fast-growing firms— or, as is increasingly the case, a mismatch between jobs and the social attributes and language skills of the job seekers.

- Comparative geographic or transportation advantage is no longer determined entirely by the availability of natural resources. Increasingly, location *per se*, as that term relates to proximity to markets, natural resources, or transportation, is less important in today's economic circumstances than the availability of specialized technology-oriented infrastructures, such as research facilities, higher education services, high-quality up-to-date telecommunications, and special financial assistance to accommodate business startups or expansions.

The quality of support services in a locality directly determines the potential for new economic activity. Thus, irrespective of their geographic location, localities may be able to construct alternative economic futures by carefully assessing and achieving the best match between their physical, natural, and human resources.

- As the first decade of the 21st century made clear, local economies and major portions of state economies can be devastated by acts of terrorism or nature. Box 2.2 recounts the economic costs of several recent natural disasters. The extent to which communities can recover their economic development positions and move forward will depend on how well they anticipate and prepare for disasters. Resiliency planning should be seen as a fundamental component of long-term economic development policy and planning.

Box 2.2	Natural Disasters' Impacts on Economic Development

The 2007 Georgia drought has repeatedly been called one of the most severe in the state's recorded history. Even before the drought intensified in the fall, the University of Georgia Center for Agribusiness and Economic Development estimated $787 million in agricultural losses alone (estimate as of July 2007). The landscaping industry's early estimated financial losses were $1.2 billion and the industry's estimated job losses were around 12,000. Not included in these early estimates are the recreational establishments, hardware stores, feed stores, and others that depend on rain and the health of Georgia's Lake Lanier. It will be years before the state's sizable forestry industry can estimate its losses due to drought-induced slowed growth or premature death of trees, or economists can comprehensively determine the drought's secondary economic impacts to farm equipment and supply dealers and retailers, and others that agricultural businesses (and their employees) regularly utilize. The economic losses incurred were a major factor in Georgia drafting its first Comprehensive Statewide Water Management Plan, despite calls for such a plan for many years. Key economic development and industry representatives in the state were involved in drafting the plan.

The year 2007 also marked one of the most devastating and costly series of wildfires in California. In October 2007, a series of 23 fires ravaged Southern California, with San Diego County's "Witch Fire" being the most significantly destructive. Seven deaths have been attributed to the fires, and early estimates are that the fires' economic impact will be well above $1 billion when all insurance, job, and income losses, and other measurable losses are considered. Some estimate the impact in San Diego County alone will be $1 billion. California's farm and tourism industries experienced unrecoverable losses, government budgets were stretched by the necessary emergency services expenses and infrastructure cleanup in the aftermath, and homeowners will experience as of yet unknown losses in property values and increased insurance rates. Early estimates from the State's Labor Market Information Division were that the fires directly impacted 3,135 businesses, 41,394 jobs, and $512 million in wages. Add to that the as of yet unknown estimate of losses in sales, and the direct impact to businesses and wage earners was significant.

The 2007 Georgia drought and California wildfires—projected to be the "most costly" drought and fire events in U.S. history—follow just two years after what has been determined to be the most expensive natural disaster in U.S. history: the 2005 ravaging of the Gulf Coast by Hurricane Katrina. The U.S. Department of Commerce National Climatic Data Center reports that Hurricane Katrina's preliminary cost estimate was $125 billion as of March 2007. Much of the comparatively high cost can be attributed to the foreseeable break in New Orleans' levee system, which caused significant flooding, deaths (approximately 1,833), and devastating economic losses to the City of New Orleans.

These increasingly costly natural disasters raise the question of what factors are within local economic development professionals' control to curtail the cost of these events to people, businesses, and governments. Could the costs of Georgia's drought have been less severe—or even avoidable—if state governments had previously negotiated a more favorable water sharing agreement? Would the losses in Southern California have been measurably less if land-use patterns had been more sensitive to potential wildfire patterns? And few, if any, can argue that New Orleans' losses would have been much less if the city's levees had originally been built to sustain the impact of a category five hurricane. Pre-Katrina, engineers agreed that the levees would break and water would flood New Orleans should a hurricane of that magnitude hit the city. All levels of government failed to address this known threat to the city in time to save it from Katrina. The Katrina disaster can be said to have catalysed a movement of resiliency planning which will be discussed later in this book. The federal government has played a key role in helping communities become better prepared for such disasters.

Georgia Drought Source: Shearer (2007).

California Fires Sources: "Economic Impact of the 2007 Southern California Wildfires" (2007); Schoen (2007); Veiga (2007).

Hurricane Katrina Source: "Billion Dollar U.S. Weather Disasters" (2007).

Conclusion

From the national government point of view, the rationale for state and local economic development policies is to bring about a more equitable distribution of development and to take advantage of the enormous capacity of localities to promote and sustain the development process. The underlying assumption is that local economic adjustment is a vital component of facilitating sustained national economic performance.

In our evolving economy, economic development at the local level is set within the context of national and international forces that inevitably affect local opportunities and create local economic development opportunities, as well as challenges. Globalization provides significant benefits to local firms in terms of expanded markets, production efficiency, and sources of innovation and personal talent. But it also means that local companies are players in a global economy whether or not they want to be, and as such are influenced by a wider array of forces outside their control than ever before.

From an economic development perspective, localities cannot control what happens in the global economic system, and neither can their state government, or even the federal government. However, this does not mean that local economies must simply be victims of unknown forces. Communities need to learn about the external economic forces shaping them and work to position themselves to take advantage of opportunities and to avoid threats from outside their reach. They must be entrepreneurial in seizing opportunities, cutting losses, investing in strategic programs, and leveraging their assets to compete in the new economy. No matter what actions they take, local communities will have to stretch current resources and find ways to increase public and private productivity.

Local communities cannot expect to succeed in the global economy either by looking for handouts, whether from the federal government or from corporate saviors, or by working independently. First, they must know the rules of federal economic development policy and understand how trade policy, money, labor, and technology are affecting the industries that are of central importance to them. They must also identify what their assets are and mobilize them to respond to the changes occurring in the global economy without waiting for a federal program to assist them. If such a program or funding source exists, by all means the local community should take advantage of it, but that should be a supplement to the local initiative and not the whole package. Moreover, now that businesses are so mobile, big businesses and industries are not the core resource for local economic development that they once were. Thus, a broader strategy to increase employment is needed than just the attraction of large firms. Businesses and other resources flow toward communities that are successful and away from communities that are declining. But even the most destitute community has resources that can be leveraged to start business growth, and this will then attract other resources that are needed.

Second, communities in the global economy cannot work alone. This counters all the old "wisdom" about how communities are in competition with each other for a limited number of factories moving around, so that either your community or another gets the factory. In an economy characterized by knowledge resources, specialization, and rapid change, local communities rarely can compete by themselves for an edge. Development is likely to come not in the form of a factory but in the form of a set of interrelated firms. Employees are drawn from a wide region, and specialized services in the area benefit several firms. Training facilities, transportation, information, and marketing in the area give local firms additional advantages. Thus, a network of communities joined by an effective collaboration to provide collective economic development resources will be more attractive than any single community by itself. Consequently, while national policy sets the context for successful local economic development, communities prosper by replacing competition with collaboration.

Notes

1. This was calculated by dividing the total expenditures in Table 2.1 ($92.654 billion) by the total federal expenditures for FY2009 of $3,238 billion.
2. See Blakely (2001) for a full discussion of these relations.

References and Suggested Readings

Adams, Walter, and James Brock. 2005. *The Structure of American Industry* (11th ed.). Upper Saddle River, NJ: Pearson Prentice Hall.

Andrews, Edmund L. 2007a. Fed and Regulators Shrugged as the Subprime Crisis Spread. *New York Times,* December 18.

———. 2007b. Strong Silence from U.S. on Dollar's Weakness. *International Herald Tribune,* October 10.

Bartlett, Donald L., and James B. Steele. 1998. What Corporate Welfare Costs You. *Time Magazine,* November 9, 16, 23, 30.

Billion Dollar U.S. Weather Disasters. 2007. NOAA Satellite and Information Service, National Environmental Satellite, Data, and Information Service (NESDIS), National Climatic Data Center, U.S. Department of Commerce. Accessed November 4, 2007 from http://www.ncdc.noaa.gov/oa/reports/billionz.html#chron

Blakely, Edward J. 2001. Competitive Advantage for the 21st-Century City: Can a Place-Based Approach to Economic Development Survive in a Cyberspace Age? *Journal of the American Planning Association* 67(2): 133–140.

Blakely, Edward J., and Philip Shapira. 1984. Industrial Restructuring: Public Policies for Investment in Advanced Industrial Society. *Annals of the American Academy of Political and Social Science* 475: 96.

Bradford, C. L. Finney, S. Hallet, and J. Knight. 1981. *Structural Disinvestment: A Problem in Search of a Policy.* Evanston, IL: Northwestern University, Center for Urban Affairs.

Bradshaw, Ted K., and Edward J. Blakely. 1999. What are "Third Wave" State Economic Development Efforts? From Incentives to Industrial Policy. *Economic Development Quarterly* 13(3): 229–244.

Campbell, Scott. 1996. Green Cities, Growing Cities, Just Cities? Urban Planning and the Contradictions of Sustainable Development. *Journal of the American Planning Association* 62: 296–312.

Carter, Robert. 1984. The Spatial Basis for Economic Development and Adjustment Policies. In *Regions in Transition,* edited by R. Stimson. Canberra, Australia: Department of Local Government and Administrative Services.

Cohen, Steven S., and John Zysman. 1987. *Manufacturing Matters.* New York: Basic Books.

Consumer Financial Protection Bureau. "Consumer Financial Protection Bureau examins payday lending," January 19, 2012, http://www.consumerfinance.gov/pressreleases/consumer-financial-protection-bureau-examines-payday-lending/

Consumer Reports. 2007. Are You Really Covered? *Yonkers* 72(9): 16–22.

Crippen, Alex. 2007. NBC's Tom Brokaw Puts Spotlight on Warren Buffet's call to "Tax the Rich!" CNBC post of October 30. Accessed February 12, 2007 from http://www.cnbc.com/id/21543506/site/14081545

DeNavas-Walt, Carmen, Bernadette D. Proctor, and Jessica C. Smith, U.S. Census Bureau, Current Population Reports, P60-239, Income, Poverty, and Health Insurance Coverage in the United States: 2010, U.S. Government Printing Office, Washington, DC, 2011.

Drucker, Peter. 1991. The Changed World Economy. In *Local Economic Development,* edited by R. Scott Fosler. Washington, DC: International City/County Management Association.

Economic Impact of the 2007 Southern California Wildfires. 2007. State of California Employment Development Department, Labor Market Information Division, October 30. Accessed November 4, 2007 from http://www.labormarketinfo.edd.ca.gov/article.asp?ARTICLEID=706&PAGEID=&SUBID=

Economic Indicators. 2000. *The Economist,* June, p. 106.

Eisinger, Peter. 1995. State Economic Development in the 1990s: Politics and Policy Learning. *Economic Development Quarterly* 9: 146–158.

Ferguson, Ronald F., and William T. Dickens, eds. 1999. *Urban Problems and Community Development.* Washington, DC: Brookings Institution.

Fitzgerald, Joan, and Nancey Green Leigh. 2002. *Economic Revitalization: Cases and Strategies for City and Suburb.* Thousand Oaks, CA: Sage.

Florida, Richard. 2002. *The Rise of the Creative Class: And How It's Transforming Work, Leisure, Community, and Everyday Life.* New York: Basic Books.

Fosler, R. Scott. 1991. *Local Economic Development.* Washington, DC: International City/County Management Association.

Goldsmith, William, and Edward J. Blakely. 1992. *Separate Societies: Poverty and Inequality in U.S. Cities.* Philadelphia: Temple University Press.

Goldstein, Harvey A., and Edward M. Bergman. 1986. Institutional Arrangements for State and Local Industrial Policy. *Journal of the American Planning Association* 53: 266.

Gomory, Ralph E. 2007. Testimony of Ralph E. Gomory, President, the Alfred P. Sloan Foundation to the Committee on Science and Technology, U.S. House of Representatives, June 12.

Gottschalk, Peter T. 2001. Ethnic and Racial Differences in Welfare Receipt in the United States (with Robert A. Moffitt). In *America Becoming: Racial Trends and Their Consequences Vol. II* edited by Neil J. Smelser, William Julius Wilson, and Faith Mitchell. Washington, DC: National Academy Press.

Government Steering the Economy. 1999. *The Economist,* September 11, p. 21.

Hanson, Burt E., Richard A. Cohen, and Edith P. Swanson. 1979. *Small Town and Small Towners.* Beverly Hills, CA: Sage.

Harrison, Bennett, and Barry Bluestone. 1988. *The Great U-Turn: Corporate Restructuring and the Polarization of America.* New York: Basic Books.

Herbers, John 1990. A Third Wave of Economic Development. *Governing* 9(3): 43–50.

The Hollow Corporation: A Special Report. 1986. *Business Week,* March 6.

Immergluck, Dan, and Geoff Smith. 2006. The External Costs of Foreclosure: The Impact of Single-Family Mortgage Foreclosures on Property Values. *Housing Policy Debate,* 17(1): 57–80.

International Economic Development Council (IEDC). n.d. *Eminent Domain Tool Kit.* Washington, DC: Author. Accessed February 5, 2009 from http://www.iedconline .org/Downloads/Eminent_Domain_Kit.pdf

Jacobs, Jane. 1969. *The Economy of Cities.* New York: Random House.

Jarboe, Kennan Patrick. 1985. A Reader's Guide to the Industrial Policy Debate. *California Management Review* 27: n.p.

Jepson, Edward J., and Anna L. Haines. 2003. Under Sustainability: Rebuilding the Local Economic Development Toolbox. *Economic Development Journal* 2(3): 45–53.

Kuttner, Robert. 2007. Prosperity Squandered. Comment in Kuttner, Robert and Robert B. Reich, Who's to Blame for the Brave New Economy? *The American Prospect,* November 5, pp. 1–6.

McMath, Robert C., Jr. 1991. Variations on a Theme by Henry Grady: Technology, Modernization, and Social Change. In *The Future South: A Historical Perspective for the Twenty-first Century,* edited by Joe P. Dunn and Howard L. Preston. Urbana: University of Illinois Press.

Molotch, Harvey. 1976. The City as a Growth Machine: Toward a Political Economy of Place. *American Journal of Sociology* 82(2): 309–332.

National Center for Health Statistics (NCHS). 2007. *Chartbook on Trends in the Health of Americans.* Hyattsville, MD: Author.

Newby, Les. 1999. Sustainable Local Economic Development: A New Agenda for Action? *Local Environment* 4(1): 67–72.

O'Connor, Alice. Swimming Against the Tide: A Brief History of Federal Policies in Poor Communities. In *Urban Problems and Community Development,* edited by R. Ferguson and W. Dickens. Washington, DC: Brookings Institution. 1999.

Ohlsson, Lennart. 1984. *International and Regional Specialization of Australian Manufacturing: Historical Developments and Implications for National and Regional Adjustment Policies.* Bureau of Economics Contributed Paper no. 1. Canberra: Australian Government Printing Service.

Orfield, Myron. 1996. *Metropolitics.* Washington, DC: Brookings Institution.

Organization for Economic Cooperation and Development (OECD). 1986. *The Revitalization of Urban Economies.* Paris: Author.

Porter, Michael E. 1998. Clusters and the New Economics of Competition. *Harvard Business Review* 76(6): 77.

Reich, R. 2007. Who's to Blame for the Brave New Economy? *The American Prospect*, November 5, pp. 1–6.

Reich, Robert. 1991. The Real Economy. *Atlantic Monthly*, February, pp. 124–143.

Ross, Doug, and Robert E. Friedman. 1990. The Emerging Third Wave: New Economic Development Strategies. *Entrepreneurial Economy Review* 90: 3–11.

Schoen, John W. 2007. California Adds Up the Cost of Wildfire Damages. MSNBC, October 26. Accessed November 4, 2007 from http://www.msnbc.msn.com/id/21492649/page/2

Shearer, Lee. 2007. Economic Impact to Last Many Years, Experts Say. *Morris News Service*, October 28. Accessed November 4, 2007 from http://chronicle.augusta.com/stories/102807/met_149572.shtml

Shigley, Paul. 2007. Round 3 for Eminent Domain: An Update on Post-Kelo Battles. *Planning*, March, pp. 11–15.

Silver, Hilary, and Dudley Burton. 1986. The Politics of State-Level Industrial Policy. *Journal of the American Planning Association* 52: 277.

The White House, "Urban Policy," http://www.whitehouse.gov/issues/urban-policy. Accessed September 6, 2012.

U.S. Department of Housing and Urban Development. 2000. *New Markets: The Untapped Retail Buying Power in America's Cities*. Washington, DC: Author.

Veiga, Alex. 2007. Economic Impact Will Rise Through Rebuilding Phase. *Associated Press*, October 24. Accessed November 4, 2007 from http://www.pasadenastarnews.com/news/ci_7273693

3

Concepts and Theory of Local Economic Development

The predominant definition that has undergirded traditional economic development practice is increasingly recognized as insufficient. Even in the most prosperous economies, time and again it has been shown that the major economic development problems cannot be solved using this definition. Indeed, the legacies of this definition are global warming and growing inequality. These two trends are at the forefront of contemporary U.S. concerns precisely because inadequate attention has been paid to the distributional aspects and environmental impacts of economic growth in the past.

Defining Local Economic Development

What drives the diffusion of the phases of economic development discussed in Chapter 2 is the definition of economic development upon which they are based. The traditional and most widely referenced definition of economic development has long been that of wealth creation. This definition is the driver of the first and second economic development phases exclusively, and the entrepreneurial strategy of the third phase. Increasing the tax base and creating jobs are the fundamental objectives of this definition that equates economic development with economic growth (Fitzgerald and Leigh, 2002; Malizia and Feser, 1999). There is nothing wrong with creating wealth and jobs and increasing the tax base. But it is a great mistake to equate economic growth with economic development. The blind pursuit of economic growth can destroy the foundation for economic development. For example, if an economy's growth is based on an exhaustible natural resource supply (e.g., timber, seafood, coal), then it will eventually come to a halt. The workers will be unemployed and, without proper attention to the education and skill development of the labor force or to the development of a more diversified industry structure, the community can enter a death spiral. The same scenario applies in the case of one-industry or one-factory towns. Shifts in the global economy or in technology can negate the community's desirability to its sole industry. The industry may move, or its owners may exit the industry and the town, taking their capital with them. These are the simplest of examples, and it should be understood that a town with more than one industry but with a narrow industrial base can be just as vulnerable.

At least in the public and nonprofit sectors, blind pursuit of economic growth simply to create more wealth and jobs needs to be rejected if it is likely to lead to increases in income inequality, irrevocably harm the environment, or worsen the plight of marginalized groups. Economic growth that is based on exploitation of workers with few or no alternative employment options is not only unethical but may violate fair labor standards and other laws. Growing inequality can ultimately destabilize the economy and society and result in clashes between the "haves" and "have nots." Such clashes can result in community-destroying violence.

The sources of growing inequality are multiple but often reflect a failure in economic development leadership—for example, a failure to provide a skilled labor force that is attractive to advanced industries, thereby replacing the previous source of good jobs in industries that have declined; or to support entrepreneurs who create new jobs and might even grow into large local firms; or to judiciously provide economic incentives such that their costs do not undermine the ability to maintain quality schools and infrastructure that are foundations of real economic development. Perhaps one day the field of economic development planning will have progressed to the point where it is no longer necessary to state that economic development does not automatically equal economic growth. Nor will the use of the term *development* need to be qualified by sustainability; instead, it will be integral to the concept. Likewise, it will not be necessary to say *sustainable* and *equitable*; instead, it will be understood that the two terms have significant areas of mutuality. But for the foreseeable future, it will be necessary to do so to counter trends in global warming and growing inequality, and to push local economic development practice to create the impetus for the fourth phase—sustainable local economic development—to more widely permeate practice.

We offer here a three-part definition of sustainable local economic development that focuses on the desired end state rather than growth-defined objectives:[1]

> Local economic development is achieved when a community's standard of living can be preserved and increased through a process of human and physical development that is based on principles of equity and sustainability.

There are three essential elements in this definition, detailed below:

First, economic development establishes a minimum standard of living for all and increases the standard over time.

Recognition of the need for a minimum standard of living in economic development translates into not just job creation but also job creation that provides *living wages* (earnings for full-time work that are high enough to lift individuals and families out of poverty). A rising standard of living is associated with consumption of better goods and services and quality housing, as well as increasing the number of households receiving paid health care plans, being able to save for retirement, and being able to provide vocational or collegiate education for their children.

Second, economic development reduces inequality.

While the "economic development as economic growth" approach can mean that there is more wealth and assets, it does not try to ensure that everyone benefits from the additions to the economy. Consequently, certain groups and certain places are not only left behind but can have a harder time securing the standard of living they once knew because economic growth has driven up the costs of living for all. Thus, economic *development* reduces inequality between demographic groups (age, gender, race, and ethnicity) as well as spatially defined groups such as indigenous populations versus in-migrants, or old-timers versus newcomers. Likewise, it reduces inequality between different kinds of economic and political units (small towns versus large cities, inner city and suburbs, rural and urban areas).

Third, economic development promotes and encourages sustainable resource use and production.

If economic development does not incorporate sustainability goals, then its process can create inequality between the present and future generations. Economic development requires recycling the goods cast off by an increasingly affluent and consumer-oriented society, as well as greater controls on growth to stem greenfield consumption and sprawl proliferation. Rising standards of living that are attained through sustainable resource use and production require different approaches to economic development (increasingly characterized as green development). They also create demand for new kinds of products, markets, jobs, firms, and industries that do not harm the environment and may even help it.

Theories of Growth and Development

Local economic development is an evolving field and, as we contend above, should be distinguished from economic growth. Most of the body of theory that historically has sought to explain regional or local economic development has not made this distinction. However, students of local economic development planning should be familiar with this work and its continuing influence on the field. Table 3.1 presents Malizia and Feser's (1999) summary of all the significant economic development theories through to the end of the last century. It describes each theory's underlying definition of development, strengths and weaknesses, and applications.

Further, Malizia and Feser (1999) do make a distinction between whether the theories actually focus on growth or development. Unlike the above distinction between growth and development, which clearly has normative elements, their distinction is simply descriptive (see Malizia and Feser, 1999, Chapter 11). They categorize growth theories as those that focus on the near-term expansion of the local economy and include, among others, economic base and neoclassical economic theory. Development theories are those that focus on the long-term process of evolutionary and structural change of an economy and include, among others, staple and entrepreneurship theories. But as Malizia and Feser (1999) state, "theory offers the underlying principles that explain the relationships we observe and thereby motivates and informs our action" (p. 16). Thus, if we find that growing inequality and global warming are problems that require action, then our theory of economic development will identify the causes of these problems and the principles by which to address them.

In this chapter, we focus on five of the theories in Table 3.1,[2] then discuss some developments since 2000, as well as the new directions economic development theory will need to take to explicitly incorporate sustainability.

There are several partial theories that point to the historical underlying rationale of local economic development. The sum of these theories may be expressed as:

Local and regional development = $c \times r$, where c equals an area's capacity (economic, social, technological, and political capacity) and r equals its resources (natural resource availability, location, labor, capital investment, entrepreneurial climate, transport, communication, industrial composition, technology, size, export market, international economic situation, and national and state government spending). A c value equaling 1 represents a neutral capacity that neither adds to nor detracts from the resources of a community. A c value greater than 1 represents a strong capacity that, when applied to (multiplied by) resources, increases them. Strong organizations that can form effective partnerships to meet the needs of the local economy can multiply resources. And a c value less than 1 represents weak community capacity (low-functioning social, political, and organizational leadership), whether due to cronyism, corruption, self-interest, disorganization, or ineptitude, that, when applied to resources, decreases them and hampers development.

Table 3.1 Summary of Economic Development Theories

Theory	Basic Categories	Definition of Development	Essential Dynamic	Strengths and Weaknesses	Applications
Economic Base Theory	Export or basic and nonbasic, local or residentiary sectors	Increasing rate of growth in output, income, or employment.	Response to external changes in demand; economic base multiplier effects.	Most popular understanding of economic development in the United States and a simple tool for short-term prediction. Inadequate theory for understanding long-term development.	Industrial recruitment and promotion for export expansion and diversification, expansion of existing basic industries, import substitution by strengthening connections between basic and nonbasic industries, and infrastructure development for export expansion.
Staple Theory	Exporting industries	Export-led economic growth.	Successful production and marketing of the export staple in world markets. External investment in and demand for the export staple.	Historical perspective on economic development. Descriptive theory, difficult to apply.	Build on export specializations. State does everything possible to increase competitive advantage. Character of economic base shapes political and cultural superstructure.

(Continued)

Table 3.1 (Continued)

Theory	Basic Categories	Definition of Development	Essential Dynamic	Strengths and Weaknesses	Applications
Sector Theory	Primary, secondary, and tertiary sectors	Greater sectoral diversity and higher productivity per worker.	Income elasticity of demand and labor productivity in primary and secondary sectors.	Empirical analysis possible. Categories are too general.	Promote sectoral shifts. Attract and retain producers of income elastic products.
Growth Pole	Industries	Propulsive industry growth leads to structural change.	Propulsive industries are the poles of growth.	General theory of initiation and diffusion of development based on the domination effect.	Growth center strategies.
Regional Concentration and Diffusion Theories	Commodities and factors (Myrdal) or industries (Hirschman)	Higher income per capita.	Spread and backwash effects (Myrdal) or trickle-down and polarization effects (Hirschman).	Address the dynamics of development.	Active government to mitigate backwash effects and reduce inequality (Myrdal). Location of public investments spurs development (Hirschman).
Neoclassical Growth Theory	Aggregate (macro) or two-sector regional economy	Increasing rate of economic growth per capita.	Rate of saving that supports investment and capital formation.	Supply-side model.	Government should promote free trade and economic integration and tolerate social inequality and spatial dualism.

Theory	Basic Categories	Definition of Development	Essential Dynamic	Strengths and Weaknesses	Applications
Interregional Trade Theory	Prices and quantities of commodities and factors	Economic growth that leads to greater consumer welfare.	Price adjustments that result in equilibrium terms of trade; price-quantity-effects.	Unique emphasis on consumer welfare and price effects. Ignores the dynamics of development.	Government intervention should promote free trade. Infrastructure development, efficient local government.
Product Cycle Theory	Products: new, maturing, or standardized	Continual creation and diffusion of new products.	New product development; innovation.	Popular basis for understanding development among researchers.	Development strategies promote product innovation and subsequent diffusion.
Entrepreneurship Theories	Entrepreneurs or the entrepreneurial function	Resilience and diversity.	Innovation process; new combinations.	Mediated theory.	Support industrial milieu or ecology for development.
Flexible Specialization Theories	Production regimes, industrial organization	Sustained growth through agile production, innovation, and specialization.	Changes in demand requiring flexibility among producers.	Detailed analysis of firm/industry organization; aggregate outcomes and relationships seldom specified.	Encourage flexibility through adoption of advanced technologies, networks among small firms, and industry cluster strategies.

Source: From Malizia and Feser, *Understanding Local Economic Development*, 1999. Copyright © 1999, Rutgers, The State University of New Jersey, Center for Urban Policy Research. Reprinted with permission of the publisher.

Resource capacities are measured in many ways, and different theories give pre-eminence to different resources, including raw materials, infrastructure, government spending and markets, size of markets, access to money, and access to communications.

Theories of economic development have traditionally focused mainly on the r part of the equation (resources), neglecting the c part (capacity). For example, location theories emphasize the advantages that come from being close to markets. But central cities, though close to markets, are economically lagging because they lack the social and political capacity to take advantage of their geographical advantages. Other theories focus primarily on infrastructure and the need to invest in any number of programs, such as building industrial parks, roads, airports, baseball stadiums, or telecommunications hubs. But these resources, in the absence of fully developed programs to utilize them, do not add to the community capacity: Witness the thousands of rural industrial parks that have failed to attract businesses and remain empty. Thus, any theory of local economic development must consider resources and capacity together.

More community capacity can make up for limited resources in local economic development. A community lagging in the amount and variety of resources must work harder to use the resources available most effectively. Of most obvious benefit for local economic development are natural resources, such as iron ore, coal, forests, water, and agricultural land. However, natural resources are not enough for a strong economy, and they often shape the economy in ways that rely on excessive primary processing, which historically has led to unstable and low-paying jobs. Most strong economies find their advantages in features other than natural resources. Labor, capital, infrastructure, proximity to new technologies, access to trade, federal government spending, and other factors are even more advantageous inputs to economic activity, and local areas that have ample and easy access to these resources can create better economic opportunities.

However, from a development perspective, resources are often underused, and this is where local capacity comes in. The more varied types of capacity a local community has, the greater its ability to turn resources into development opportunities. For example, communities need an economic development organization (e.g., a business association, chamber of commerce, economic development corporation, or government agency for economic development) to effectively address the issues and problems of a lagging economy and enhance available resources.

Neoclassical Economic Theory

Neoclassical theory offers two major concepts for regional and local development: *equilibrium* of economic systems and *mobility* of capital. It asserts that all economic systems will reach a natural equilibrium if capital can flow without restriction. That is, capital will flow from high-wage/cost to low-wage/cost areas because the latter offer a higher return on investment. In local development terms, this would mean that ghettos would draw capital because prices for property and sometimes labor are lower than in the overall market. If the model worked perfectly, then all areas would gradually reach a state of equal status in the economic system. Much of this rationale has under-laid the recent wave of deregulation of banking, airlines, utilities, and similar services. In theory, all areas can compete in a deregulated market.

Neoclassical economic theorists like Nobel Prize winner Milton Friedman oppose any form of government or community regulations on the movement of firms from one area of the nation to another or even to other countries. They also oppose any restrictions on firms, such as those requiring minority or local equity participation, that could make it less advantageous for firms to locate in an area. They suggest that such regulation is doomed to fail and disrupt the normal and necessary movement of capital. Moreover, they argue that there should be no attempts to save dying or uncompetitive firms. Workers who lose their jobs should move to new employment areas as a further stimulus to development in such places.

These theories have been tested both in the United States and abroad. In developing nations, the International Monetary Fund (IMF), which oversees international emergency loans to nations, has required national governments to divest themselves of controls of assets and to reduce market and currency controls. The immediate impacts on these economies have been very severe—though in many instances, like that of Mexico, the national economy has rebounded and is now making enormous strides. Detractors of IMF policy, for example, point to the increasing gap between the rich and poor in countries with deregulated economies to suggest that the market is not evenhanded in allocating resources and that some government controls and interventions are essential to deal with inequities.

Many regional and local economic development advocates reject neoclas-sical theories and the policies derived from them. Blair (1995), for example, points out that the development promoted by such theories "should not mask the fact that there are often some groups that will benefit from growth more than others" (p. 170). Furthermore, the neoclassical framework is generally viewed as antagonistic to the interests of communities as places with a *raison d'être* beyond their economic utility. Finally, classical models tell us little about the real reasons why some areas are competitive while others fail.

Nevertheless, some useful concepts can be derived from the neoclassical economic theory. First, in a market society, all communities must ensure that they use their resources in a manner that attracts capital. Artificial barriers, low-functioning governmental bureaucracy, and a poor business climate are barriers to economic development. Second, communities or disadvantaged neighborhoods can and should attempt to gain the resources necessary to assist them to reach an equilibrium status with surrounding areas. This can partially be accomplished by upgrading commercial properties through local government loans and grants, as well as by offering training and other programs that enhance the value of local labor. These measures can act as inducements to equalize the value of inner-city neighborhoods and other disadvantaged areas with more prosperous places.

Economic Base Theory

Economic base theory proposes that a community's economic growth is directly related to the demand for its goods, services, and products from areas outside its local economic boundaries. The growth of industries that use local resources (including labor and materials) to produce goods and services to be exported elsewhere will generate local wealth and jobs.

The local economic development strategies that emerge from this theory emphasize the priority of aid to and recruitment of businesses that have a national or international market over aid to local service or nonexporting firms. Implementation of this model would include measures that reduce barriers to the establishment of export-based firms in an area, such as tax relief and subsidy of transport facilities and telecommunications or establishment of free-trade zones.

Many of the current entrepreneurial and high-technology strategies aimed at attracting or generating new firms draw on economic base models. The rationale is that nonexporting firms or local service-providing businesses will develop automatically to supply export firms or those who work in them. Moreover, it is argued that export industries have higher job multipliers than local service firms. Thus, every job created in an export firm will generate— depending on the sector—several jobs elsewhere in the economy. There are regional economic methods that will test and measure such impacts of firms on the local economy.

It is important to understand that economic base theory is applicable in the short run only because its export sectors and economic structure—its primary focus—change over time. Staple theory is an extension of export base theory that has a long-run view. It seeks to explain a local economy's evolution based on how its export specialization changes over time. The staple of the economy is defined as an internationally marketable commodity (such as a natural resource or agricultural product) that generates related manufacturing activity (to process the staple), which generates supplying industries and attracts outside industries seeking to take advantage of a growing market (Malizia and Feser, 1999).

A key weakness of the economic base model is that it relies on satisfying external rather than internal demands. Thus, it ignores opportunities for import substitution that can provide another means of generating jobs and income in the local economy (and stop the leakage of income outside the economy in the purchase of imports). Overzealous application of the economic base model can lead to a skewed economy almost entirely dependent upon external, global, or national market forces. This model is, however, useful in understanding how a local economy grows or declines from changes in external demand for the goods and services it sells to the outside world. It is also useful for proactive industry sector targeting aimed for achieving economic growth, development, and stability. In Chapter 6, we discuss the methodology for determining the export base of a local economy.

Product Cycle Theory

One aspect of economic base theory involves understanding industry product cycles that explain the fate of regions and localities through the innovation and diffusion process. Product cycle theory was first proposed by Raymond Vernon (1966), who showed how product development must take place in areas with greater wealth and capital to invest in the process of inventing and developing new products, supported by local markets that can pay higher prices for products that have not yet become standardized. For example, new electronic products are likely to find first markets in areas where there are affluent and educated persons, not in areas lacking the income and skills with which to purchase and use these items. Over time, the product becomes standardized, and it enters mass production and markets. Its production process becomes so routine that it no longer needs to be done by specialized labor, and thus there is a decline in the wages and skills (or good jobs) it generates. At that point, production can move to less developed economies, where firms compete not on the basis of unique products, but rather on price (Figure 3.1).

As Malizia and Feser (1999) describe the theory,

> economic development is defined as the creation of new products and the diffusion of standardized products. Development originates in the more developed region and is exported to the less-developed region through trade and then investment. Establishing a new industry in the less-developed region creates a progressive force that can help eliminate the barriers to interregional equality. Yet product cycle theory does not predict convergence of regional incomes; the development process can be convergent or divergent. (p. 177)

The firms in a region and their prospects are both shaped by their place in the product cycle. Some industries have fast-changing product cycles in which

Figure 3.1   The Product Cycle

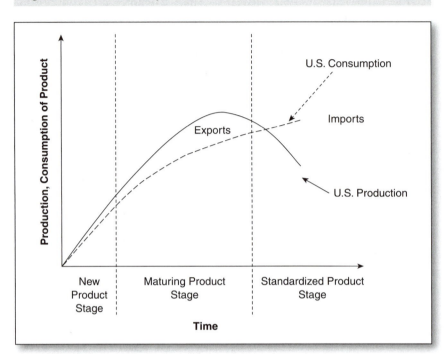

Source: Adapted from Vernon (1966).

new products are rapidly introduced, whereas other industries are relatively stable. For example, high-technology electronics industries are almost by definition rapidly changing, with diffusion of one product after another to cheap production elsewhere. Other industries are more tightly bound to their central location, and product innovation is not a factor. In investment banking, for example, each decision is so specialized that there is little potential to standardize.

Location Theories

Location theories seek to explain how firms choose their locations, and thus they also provide explanations for how local economies grow (or decline). Firms maximize profits by selecting locations that minimize their costs of production and of transporting goods to market. Early location theory focused on whether the product a firm created gained or lost weight in its production process, thereby either increasing or decreasing the transport costs of the final product relative to the inputs from which it was created. To minimize transport costs, a firm with a final product that weighs less than its inputs will locate at the source of the inputs and ship the final product to market. Such firms are labeled weight losing or input oriented in standard economics, and some classic examples of products they produce are listed in Table 3.2. If the final product created by a firm weighs more than its inputs, then the firm will locate at its markets, transporting the inputs required for production. Such firms are market oriented or weight gaining.

Location theory also considers other factors besides transportation costs that influence a firm's location. With the significant advances in efficiencies in the last three decades in trucking and ocean and air cargo transport, the influence of transportation costs on firms' location decisions has declined significantly. Today, it is more appropriate to think in terms of logistics rather than

Table 3.2   Locational Orientation of Firms

Orientation	Relevant Characteristic	Example
Transport-cost oriented	Transport costs relatively more important	
Input oriented	Inputs weigh more than outputs Inputs bulkier than outputs Inputs more perishable than outputs	Ore refining Steel Fruit canning
Market oriented	Outputs weigh more than inputs Outputs bulkier than inputs Outputs more perishable than inputs	Bottling Auto assembly Baking
Production-cost oriented	Local input costs relatively more important	
Energy	Energy-intensive production	Aluminum
Labor	Labor-intensive production	Textiles
Intermediate inputs		
Specialized inputs	Localization economies of scale	Software
Business services	Urbanization economies of scale	Corporate HQ
Amenity	Weather, recreation, taxes, etc.	R&D, tourism

Source: Bogart, William Thomas, *Economics of Cities and Suburbs, The,* 1st Edition, ©1998, p. 61. Reprinted by permission of Pearson Education, Inc., Upper Saddle River, NJ.

simply transportation costs. The logistics industry encompasses a range of activities for planning, storing, and controlling the flow of goods, services, and related information from point of origin to point of consumption. This includes not only transportation but also warehouse and distribution activities. Advances in information technology applications for logistics have played a key role in the development of our global production and market network.

Beyond transportation and logistics, other factors that affect the quality or suitability of a location are labor costs, the cost of energy, availability of suppliers, communications, education and training facilities, local government quality and responsiveness, and waste management. Different firms require differing mixes of these factors to be competitive. Therefore, communities generally attempt to manipulate the cost of several of these factors to become attractive to industrial firms. All of these actions are taken to enhance a location beyond its natural attributes.

In Table 3.2, we also see reference to localization and urbanization economies of scale. These two concepts are variations of a key concept in the study of urban and regional economics—agglomeration economies—which refers to the cost savings that arise from spatial proximity. In other words, a local or regional economy generates particular production cost savings that a firm would not realize if it were located in an undeveloped area. Localization economies of scale mean that firms benefit from locating near other firms because they may use the same type of labor or inputs, or there is better access to information about competitors, suppliers, new technologies, and so on. Urbanization economies of scale mean that the larger the local economy (that is, the bigger the city), the greater the production cost savings and other benefits to the firm. These can derive from access to larger markets, to more specialized services (for example, industrial designers, advertisers, venture capitalists), or to the transfer of knowledge and technologies between one industry sector and another in the larger economy.

The location of firms in overall economic space has long been of interest to economic developers (Malizia and Feser, 1999). Some of the early theorists who dealt with the issue of location during the 1950s include François Perroux (1983), who described "growth poles," Gunnar Myrdal (1957), who produced a theory of cumulative causation, and Friedmann and Weaver (1979), who offered a core–periphery model.

Perroux's (1983) growth pole theory hypothesizes that growth is stimulated by cutting-edge industries, firms, or other actors who are dominant in their field. Perroux wanted to refute the claim of classical theorists that growth would flow to less costly areas. In fact, the opposite often occurs with "propulsive industries" that have an edge in technology, wealth, and political influence. Perroux argued that these growth poles were linked to other growth poles but not necessarily to the periphery area of the central growth node. This helps explain why not every community in Silicon Valley, like Oakland or East Palo Alto, benefits from rapid economic growth in a nearby fast-growing area.

Myrdal's (1957) theory of cumulative causation sought to explain why some areas are increasingly advantaged while others are disproportionately disadvantaged. Market forces, by their nature, pull capital, skill, and expertise to certain areas. These areas accumulate a large-scale competitive advantage over the rest of the system. Casual observation of the decay of urban neighborhoods demonstrates the basic concept of cumulative causation: The interplay of market forces increases rather than decreases the inequality between areas, so that a divergence in regional income is a predictable result. Myrdal gave the following example of cumulative causation:

> Suppose accidental change occurs in a community, and it is not immediately canceled out in a stream of events; for example a factory employing a large part of the population burns down . . . and cannot be rebuilt economically, at least not at that locality. The immediate effect is that the firm owning it goes out of business and its workers become unemployed. This will decrease income and demand. In its turn, the decreased demand will lower incomes and cause unemployment in all sorts of other businesses in the community which sold to or served the firm and its employees . . . If there are no exogenous changes, the community will be less tempting for outside businesses and workers who had contemplated moving in. As the process gathers momentum, businesses established in the community and workers living there will increasingly find reasons for moving out in order to seek better markets somewhere else. This will again decrease income and demand. (p. 23)

Advanced technology and telecommunications have altered the significance of specific locations for the production and distribution of goods that early location theory sought to explain. Communities of significantly smaller sizes can compete with large cities for certain firms and industries because information technology and reduction in transport costs have reduced the significance of distance in location decisions. Less tangible variables, such as the quality of community life, cultural and natural amenities, and reasonable cost of living, can now assume greater weight in the firm's location decision based on the preferences of the owners or the workers required by the firm. Rather than local economic developers being limited by the natural attributes or original features of a location for encouraging firm location, they now have the opportunity to improve the factors in location decisions that have surpassed the importance of minimizing transportation costs or physical proximity to markets for many firms.

Central Place Theory

Central place theory is a variant of location theory that is most applicable to retail activity. According to this theory, each urban center is supported by a series of smaller places that provide resources (industries and raw materials) to the central place, which is more specialized and productive. These smaller places are in turn surrounded by even smaller places that supply and are markets for the larger places. The urban center contains specialized retail stores that serve the entire region; professional specialists such as corporate lawyers, investment bankers, and heart surgeons; and headquarters for corporations as well as nonprofit organizations. When inhabitants of a very small place need a specialized product or service, they must go to the central place, though they can find many less specialized products and services in their own community. For example, residents of a small place do not need to go to the central city for groceries or car repair, though they must leave home to hear a performance by a world-class symphony orchestra.

Regional development models for rural areas have relied heavily on central place theory to guide resource allocations on the assumption that the development of a central place will improve the economic well-being of the entire region. The application of central place theory can be observed in rural service bureaucracies like the Tennessee Valley Authority (TVA), Rural Electrification, and the Economic Development Administration (EDA). Each of these organizations attempted to develop a regional economic plan with one or two communities either designated or emerging as regional nodes for development.

However, as Bradshaw and Blakely (1979) observed three decades ago, rural communities in advanced industrial society are increasingly able to take advantage of specialization that once was limited to urban areas. While lacking some of the advantages that are available in urban settings, such as proximity to other specialists, rural communities are competing for advanced manufacturing, professional services, sophisticated communications, and other types of businesses because people value the rural environment and are willing to use electronic linkages to minimize the disadvantages of being located in a small place. The Internet and the mega-mall have greatly altered the commercial relations of central and peripheral places. Today, several billion dollars a year are spent by consumers in Internet transactions with both existing retailers and new "e-tailers."

Central place theory has relevant applications for both urban and rural local economic development. It is necessary, for example, to differentiate the functions of various neighborhood areas so that they can remain viable centers. Some areas will become regional core cities serving an entire region; others will be smaller villages or towns that serve only the local resident community. Local economic development specialists can assist communities or neighborhoods to develop their functional role in the regional economic place hierarchy and electronic hierarchy.

At the same time, central place theory is unable to explain why, within major market areas, individual neighborhoods can be seriously lacking in retail services. This is particularly the case in low-income and minority neighborhoods and has been the focus of economic development attention since the late 1990s, leading to the development of the "new markets" strategy discussed below.

Translating Theory Into Practice

Economic development theory has influenced practice, as the following sections demonstrate.

Attraction Models

Models of community attraction are based on location theory and employed widely by communities seeking economic development. Communities across the globe have initiated policies and programs to make their area more attractive to investors, firms, new migrants, entrepreneurs, and others, and thereby to gain a competitive advantage over other areas with similar resource endowments.

The basic assumption of attraction models is that a community can alter its market position with industrialists by offering incentives and subsidies. This assumes that new activity will generate taxes and increased economic wealth to replace the initial public and private subsidies. A more cynical view, supported by considerable evidence, is that the cost of such efforts is, in fact, paid by the workers and taxpayers of the community while the benefits go largely to landowners and firms (Bluestone, Harrison, and Baker, 1981). Consequently, inequality can increase.

A new approach in attraction is the change in emphasis from attracting factories to attracting entrepreneurial populations, particularly certain socioeconomic groups, to a community or area. New middle-class young retirees to an area bring both buying power and the capability to attract employers. In addition, recent migrants are more likely to start new firms. As a result, many communities have reassessed their firm attraction efforts and reoriented them toward "people" attraction. This approach has been particularly effective in rural areas where the quality-of-life factor can attract new populations—leading to increased economic growth as a response to both internal demand and new export enterprises created by the new migrants. Furthermore, it has been suggested that some localities can offer special "knowledge networks" to act as incubators for high-technology firms or inventors. These areas are natural entrepreneurial centers because they develop a certain style or *esprit de corps*. Route 128 in Massachusetts, the Silicon Valley, and the North Carolina Triangle, as well as some areas of Florida, have gained reputations as innovation centers, for example.

In attraction models, communities are products. As such, they must be "packaged" and appropriately displayed. The objective evidence of this packaging can be observed in magazine and newspaper advertisements extolling the virtues of certain places over other communities. Anecdotal evidence suggests that community promotion works and that failure to use it may be a political liability. No city or neighborhood should hide its virtues "under a bushel basket." Some form of marketing is necessary, though the means and the rationale are as important as the desired result in undertaking this mode of development planning, since the ends have not always justified the means in the past. Communities have also learned from the past, and a growing number are adding restrictions or conditions to the public incentives they offer to attract firms. These are intended to recoup the public investment made if the firm does not stay in the community long enough to generate taxes and wages that meet or exceed the investment. The conditions imposed can also specify that the jobs created by the firm go to local residents and pay living wages.

New Markets Model

According to the U.S. Department of Housing and Urban Development (HUD), in the year 2000, America's inner-city neighborhoods possessed an unrealized potential purchasing power of $331 million, or nearly one third of the retail capacity of the nation's urban cities. Rural areas containing new migrants also have large unrealized market potential—for example, the counties that make up the Kentucky highlands in Appalachia are estimated to have more than $1.3 billion in retail purchasing power (Cuomo, 1999). The reason these communities are underserved relates to misperceptions and poor information regarding these markets. Retailers have either left these communities or resisted serving them because of the belief that incomes were too low and crime too high to make such markets valuable. But as the national economy has prospered, crime in these communities has fallen to levels that have not been observed for more than three decades. Further, while inner-city household incomes may be lower than those of the suburbs, the greater population density creates higher foot traffic and strong buying power. Moreover, employment participation in both the inner city and rural areas has increased. Finally, the Internet has equalized opportunities for many rural areas to draw service jobs.

According to Michael Porter (1995), inner-city areas have features that place them in the forefront of the new economy. Not only do they have proximity to a large downtown area with concentrated activity, making them prime markets for retailing, but more important, they have proximity to crucial competitive clusters:

> The most exciting prospects for the future of inner city economic development lie in capitalizing on nearby regional clusters: those include close-to-a-region collections of related companies that are competitive nationally and even globally. For example, Boston's inner city is next door to world class

financial services and health care clusters. South Central Los Angeles is close to an enormous entertainment cluster and a large logistical-service whole-saling complex. (p. 60)

In the new markets model, ghettos and declining rural areas are economic opportunity zones that are not being utilized appropriately. Economic develop-ment of these areas, according to James Carr (1999, p. 20), requires:

- understanding the value of community assets
- creating or matching financing tools to these assets
- designing value-recapture mechanisms to recycle the new wealth generated by these assets back into the communities from which they originated so that these resources can stimulate more new economic activity in the community, from new businesses and housing to social and community services
- determining ways in which the wealth generated can be shared by a wide range of community members
- developing methods to evaluate the long-term benefits of these investments

Although these concepts increase the opportunity for new investment and reinvestment in inner-city and low-income areas, they also require some form of subsidy to get started. New forms of economic finance, such as community development finance institutions (CDFIs), have been created to enhance both equity and debt finance targeted to low-income areas. The creation of these new financing vehicles, combined with a new infusion of capital from the fed-eral treasury in the form of $26 billion in loan guarantees, acts as a stimulus for larger firms to take the risk of investing in low-income areas. But an even greater stimulus for brand-name firms like Gap and Starbucks to invest in the inner city is the need to find new consumers via bricks-and-mortar retailing. Furthermore, the influx of immigrants to formerly low-income, predominantly Black neighborhoods has altered the market opportunities for retailers in these communities. The new markets model is the creative realization of old market economics in a new economy.

Theories, Models, and Fads in Local Economic Development Planning

In this chapter, we have covered five of the most significant theories that have been employed to explain local economic development outcomes and to shape planning for economic development (albeit where development is equated with growth). Economic development is not an academic discipline per se, but rather a field or subfield in which scholars specialize from a number of disciplines, including business, city and regional planning, demography, education, economics, geography, political science, public policy, regional science, and sociology. Theories of economic development, consequently, can be influenced by any of these disciplines. We noted at the beginning of this chapter that local economic development is an evolving field. Further, as we will discuss in Chapter 4, those working in the field come from a wide variety and range of levels of academic and professional experiences.

Overall, economic development professionals are action oriented. Indeed, their jobs often depend on producing results. They are drawn to new ideas and theories to help them do so for their localities. While their motivations are laudable, past experience has shown that they sometimes latch onto unproven ideas and theories to which the always limited resources of time, personnel, and dollars are committed. A particularly notable example occurred during the 1980s, when David L. Birch put forward the theory that small business is the true engine of the economy and job creation, and the true source of innovation (1979). This was based on findings from his analysis of Dun & Bradstreet data that 80% of the jobs created between 1969 and 1976 were produced by businesses with fewer than 100 workers, and nearly two thirds by firms with fewer than 20. However, his methodology was subsequently faulted (White and Osterman, 1991), and it was ultimately concluded that "the largest business organizations continue to account for the great majority of jobs, to pay the highest wages and benefits, and to dominate the coordination of production among networks of firms, the control of finance, and the adoption and implementation of new technology" (Harrison, 1994). By this time, however, localities throughout the country were already on the "small business bandwagon," using their resources to create new centers and programs to foster small business. Encouraging small business development is not a bad economic development idea, but it was also not the panacea for economic development problems brought on by restructuring and employment shedding of the U.S. manufacturing industry during the 1980s and beyond. Economic development professionals needed to maintain focus and assistance to manufacturing plants and other large firms that formed the economic base of their communities.

We introduced two recent and very popular theories in Chapter 1 that are currently garnering a lot of economic development attention: Kim and Mauborgne's (2004) Blue Ocean theory and Richard Florida's (2002) concept of the Creative Class. Blue Ocean is focused on firms that create new markets, which in turn will bring substantial economic development to localities in which they are located. In contrast, the Creative Class theory focuses on people as drivers of economic development. Each concept has garnered substantial attention and generated private- and public-sector initiatives for economic development. But each is receiving substantial criticism for claims of originality, the analysis used to prove its theses, and the validity of its theories.

On the Creative Class, Jamie Peck (2005) observes,

> [The thesis] that urban fortunes increasingly turn on the capacity to attract, retain and even pamper a mobile and finicky class of "creatives," whose aggregate efforts have become the primary drivers of economic development—has proved to be a hugely seductive one for civic leaders around the world, competition amongst whom has subsequently worked to inflate Florida's speaking fees well into the five-figure range. From Singapore to London, Dublin to Auckland, Memphis to Amsterdam; indeed, all the way to Providence, RI, and Green Bay, WI, cities have paid handsomely to hear about the new credo of creativity, to learn how to attract and nurture creative workers, and to evaluate the latest "hipsterization strategies" of established creative capitals like Austin, TX or wannabes like Tampa Bay, FL: "civic leaders are seizing on the argument that they need to compete not with the plain old tax breaks and redevelopment schemes, but on the playing fields of what Florida calls 'the three Ts [of] Technology, Talent, and Tolerance'" (Shea, 2004: D1). According to this increasingly pervasive urban-development script, the dawn of a "new kind of capitalism based on human creativity" calls for funky forms of supply-side intervention, since cities now find themselves in a high-stakes "war for talent," one that can only be won by developing the kind of "people climates" valued by creatives—urban environments that are open, diverse, dynamic and cool (Florida, 2003c: 27). Hailed in many quarters as a cool-cities guru, assailed in others as a new-economy huckster, Florida has made real waves in the brackish backwaters of urban economic development policy. (p. 740)

Returning to our distinction between growth and development, the Creative Class thesis has been criticized for prescribing strategies that do not address issues of inequality, gentrification, and the working poor, and for focusing on a narrow concept of diversity as an enabler of economic development (e.g., gays only). Thus, even if its premise about what causes economic growth is correct (and at least one author—Malanga (2004)—has published data that claims the so-called Creative Class cities have underperformed the traditional corporate and working-class cities), a wholesale adoption of Creative Class development strategies could exacerbate the enduring economic development problems of inequality and improving the standard of living for the poor. As was the case with the small business development fad, economic developers need to critically assess the Creative Class thesis before devoting substantial community resources to its pursuit.

The Continued Evolution of Economic Development Theory Into Local Practice

Existing development theories must evolve in order to reflect changing economic structures and maintain relevance for local economic development activities. In Table 3.3, we have reformulated the concepts emphasized by various theories—locality, business and economic base, employment resources, community resources—to create a new foundation for local economic development.

Locality

Technology has shattered the traditional view of physical location as the major determinant of development. Firms, even large-scale manufacturing operations, are not as tied to a specific location as they used to be, especially as they reduce dependence on natural resources and substitute the more mobile resource of knowledge as their critical input. Firms increasingly have the ability to be footloose. And even those firms that choose to stay put have the ability to outsource increasingly advanced tasks due to the globalized information and production network. What is known is that firms consistently value a place in which physical and social or organizational factors cooperate to make a quality environment in which to live and do business. Thus, the traditional view that the availability of transportation and market systems determines a community's economic viability is outmoded.

Table 3.3 A Reformulation of the Components of Local Economic Development

Component	Old Concept	New Concept
Locality	Physical location (near natural resources, transportation, markets) enhances economic options.	A quality environment and strong community capacity multiply natural advantages for economic growth.
Business and economic base	Export base industries and firms create jobs and stimulate increased local business.	Clusters of competitive industries linked in a regional network of all types of firms create new growth and income.
Employment resources	More firms create more jobs, even if many are minimum wage.	Comprehensive skill development and technological innovation lead to quality jobs and higher wages.
Community resources	Single-purpose organizations can enhance economic opportunities in the community.	Collaborative partnerships of many community groups are needed to establish a broad foundation for competitive industries.

The new location logic is most clearly seen in the changing opportunities for rural economic development. Whereas rural communities previously spent most of their energy attempting to acquire roads, industrial parks, and related infrastructure to promote manufacturing development, they now find this strategy less productive. Fewer footloose firms are finding remote rural areas attractive at any cost, regardless of services, especially when they can relocate to Mexico, Asia, or many other places across the globe that provide cheap labor to produce goods that can be inexpensively shipped to markets due to logistics advances. Instead, growth in rural areas seems to follow from a pristine natural environment for recreation and ambiance and a quality social infrastructure, including civic organizations, cultural opportunities, and business networks. Thus, some rural areas are growing even without such large-scale investment in infrastructure. It does not seem to matter whether a rural community is a designated population growth center or a target area for increased industrial development or resource exploitation. A rural area's economic opportunities are determined by the quality of the available human resource base and preservation, rather than exploitation, of its natural resources.

Location, by itself, is no longer a "pull" factor. But the new local economic development model suggests that there are locational development-inducing factors. These factors apply more to the quality of the local physical and social environment than to larger-scale geographic considerations. Moreover, the development of a community's recreational, housing, and social institutions can determine economic viability. When a community concentrates on building a social and institutional network, it creates an *inviting environment* for a firm to develop or locate there. If the structure is organized properly, economic activity will ensue—it will not have to be pursued.

Business and the Economic Base

The economic base model relies heavily on a sectoral approach to economic development. The approach concentrates on transactions within the economic system rather than the failures and inadequacies of the system in which the transactions are taking place. This approach is based on the notion that the local economy must maximize its internal institutional linkages in the public and private sectors.

Local economic development theory builds on the premise that the institutional base must form a major component of both finding the problems in the local economy and altering institutional arrangements. Building new institutional relationships is the new substance of economic development. Communities can take control of their destiny when and if they assemble the resources and information necessary to build their own future. This is not a closed political process but an open one that places local citizens in a position to plan and manage their own economic destiny.

In the new economy, business remains important to the economic development agenda, but the focus has shifted from individual firms to networks of firms or clusters of interdependent firms in industries in which human, natural, and technological linkage advantages are present. Rather than providing special incentives to individual firms, economic development involves brokering among firms to explore how they can benefit from each other. It also involves shifting business practices to those that are environmentally benign and helping firms create new sustainable products and processes that may well use as their inputs the wastes of other firms.

Employment Resources

Boosting local employment has been the major and sometimes the sole rationale for communities to engage in active development efforts. In the neoclassical model, lower wage rates and cheaper costs are sufficient to create employment. This model thus suggests that areas benefit from having low-cost labor, which often is linked to low taxes and limited education and training opportunities. Firms are recruited on the basis of how many jobs they can provide, regardless of the skill level or wages paid. Too often, firms enter areas seeking low wages and generate many minimum-wage jobs that leave residents of the local community in poverty. This does not raise the community's standard of living, reduce its level of inequality, or provide a foundation for sustained development.

Firms in our advanced economy need highly skilled labor and are willing to pay for it. Highly competitive firms recognize that the firm and the community must continuously invest in assuring a highly skilled workforce. The myriad job training and job development schemes in this country are testimony to the importance of transforming the existing labor force into a more productive resource for existing and new employers.

The quality of an area's human resource base is a major inducement to all industries. If the local human resource base is substantial, either new firms will be created by it regardless of location or existing firms will migrate there. Therefore, communities must not only build jobs to fit the existing populace but also build institutions that expand the capability of this population. Rural communities and inner-city neighborhoods seldom have higher education or research institutions that serve them. Indeed, rural communities and urban neighborhoods seldom consider the need for such resources beyond the teaching function or community problem-solving requirement.

Local economic development, however—both now and in the near future—will be dependent on the ability of communities to use the resources of higher education and research-related institutions. Rather than attracting a new factory that may initially employ thousands, a community may be better served by attracting and retaining a few small, related research labs in leading-edge technologies that could eventually create jobs and stability for the total region.

The goal of local economic development is to enhance the value of people and places. Thus, the community builds economic opportunities to "fit" the human resources and utilize or maximize the existing natural and institutional resource base. In essence, the emphasis shifts from the demand (firm) side of the equation to the supply side of labor and natural resources.

Community Resources

In the classical model, the economy is developed by a business-oriented organization that can advocate for the interests of the firms in the region. In the new economy, the community has many organizations representing diverse interests, and only through a collaboration among the organizations is economic development possible. For example, government, business organizations (such as chambers of commerce), workforce development organizations, and community-based organizations must work in partnership to ensure that the necessary preconditions for economic development are present. The entity responsible for delivering economic development is no longer one organization but a virtual organization made up of all the organizations that can contribute to the success of a particular economic development project and then, when that project is completed, disband, to be replaced by a different network of organizations that are appropriate for the next project.

Conclusion

The conceptual and theoretical framework for economic development shown in Table 3.3 defines the changing context for economic development in our advanced economy. It suggests that local economic development is not as "spatially free" as the market and that old efforts focused on single-minded expansion of firms and jobs will not generate local well-being in the economy. In the changing economy, specific locations must be tied to specific people. In local economic development, we are concerned with both people and place. Therefore, local economic development is a process that emphasizes the full use of existing human and natural resources to preserve and increase a community's standard of living that is based on principles of equity and sustainability.

Old theories are not necessarily incompatible with the definition of economic development we put forth in this chapter. But this definition does ask for a careful consideration of the impacts of uncritical application of strategies based on these theories. In an increasingly technological age, the old emphasis on employment generation actually has increasing merit. But it must be qualified to focus on good jobs and to prepare workers and their communities for more dynamic labor markets and ongoing skill development to be relevant in these labor markets.

Thus, economic development theory must evolve to meet the challenge of explaining how communities create strong foundations for sustainable economic development that counters trends in global warming and growing inequality, as well as preserves natural resources while raising standards of living. In turn, the public and private sectors must work together to identify and support sustainable economic development strategies. Government is responsible for reducing economic and social disparities while protecting natural resources. It uses its power and resources to foster a strong business sector that increases rather than diminishes sustainable local economic development. Among other things, this requires reshaping existing strategies such as "New Markets," as well as removing barriers in existing regulations and programs.

Notes

1. This version of the definition of sustainable local economic development was published originally in Fitzgerald and Leigh (2002). It is a refinement of a definition that Leigh originally developed in 1985.

2. The serious student of local economic development planning is encouraged to read Malizia and Feser's (1999) comprehensive discussion of economic development theories.

References and Suggested Readings

Alonso, William. 1972. Location Theory. In *Regional Analysis,* edited by L. Needham. Harmondsworth, UK: Penguin.

Birch, David L. 1979. *The Job Generation Process.* Cambridge: MIT Program on Neighborhood and Regional Change.

Blair, John P. 1995. *Local Economic Development: Analysis and Practice.* Thousand Oaks, CA: Sage.

Blakely, Edward J. 2001. Competitive Advantage for the 21st Century: Can a Place-Based Approach to Economic Development Survive in a Cyberspace Age? *Journal of the American Planning Association* 67(2): 133–140.

Bluestone, Barry, Bennett Harrison, and Lawrence Baker. 1981. *Corporate Flight: The Causes and Consequences of Economic Dislocation.* Washington, DC: Progressive Alliance Books.

Bradshaw, Ted K., and Edward J. Blakely. 1979. *Rural Communities in Advanced Industrial Society.* New York: Praeger.

Carr, James. 1999. Community, Capital, and Markets: A New Paradigm for Community Reinvestment. *NeighborWorks* (Summer): 20–23.

Corporation for Enterprise Development. 1982. *Investing in Poor Communities.* Washington, DC: Author.

Cuomo, Andrew. 1999. *New Markets: The Untapped Retail Buying Power in America's Inner Cities.* Washington, DC: Government Printing Office.

Czamanski, Stanislaw. 1972. *Regional Science Techniques in Practice.* Lexington, MA: D. C. Heath.

Daniels, Belden, and Chris Tilly. 1985. Community Economic Development: Seven Guiding Principles. *Resources* 3(11): n.p.

Eisinger, Peter K. 1988. *The Rise of the Entrepreneurial State: State and Local Economic Development Policies in the United States.* Madison: University of Wisconsin Press.

Fitzgerald, Joan, and Nancey Green Leigh. 2002. *Economic Revitalization: Cases and Strategies for City and Suburb.* Thousand Oaks, CA: Sage.

Florida, Richard. 2002. *The Rise of the Creative Class: And How It's Transforming Work, Leisure, Community, and Everyday Life.* New York: Basic Books.

Friedmann, John, and Clyde Weaver. 1979. *Territory and Function: The Evolution of Regional Planning.* Berkeley: University of California Press.

Giloth, Robert, and Robert Meier. 1989. Spatial Change and Social Justice: Alternative Economic Development in Chicago. In *Restructuring and Political Response,* edited by Robert Beauregard. Newbury Park, CA: Sage.

Goldstein, William A. 1979. *Planning for Community Economic Development: Some Structural Considerations.* Paper prepared for the Planning Theory and Practice conference, Cornell University, Ithaca, NY.

Hackett, Steven C. 2006. *Environmental and Natural Resources Economics: Theory, Policy, and the Sustainable Society,* 3rd ed. New York: M. E. Sharpe.

Hanson, Niles M. 1970. How Regional Policy Can Benefit From Economic Theory. *Growth and Change* (January): n.p.

Harrison, Bennett. 1994. The Myth of Small Firms as Predominant Job Generators. *Economic Development Quarterly* 8(1): 13–18.

Hirschman, Albert O. 1958. *The Strategy of Economic Development.* New Haven, CT: Yale University Press.

Hoover, Edgar M. 1971. *An Introduction to Regional Economics.* New York: Knopf.

Isard, Walter, and Stanislaw Czamanski. 1981. Techniques for Estimating Local and Regional Multiplier Effects of Change in the Level of Government Programs. In *Regional Economics,* edited by G. J. Butler and P. D. Mandeville. Brisbane: University of Queensland Press.

Kim, Chan, and Renee Mauborgne. 2004. Blue Ocean Strategy. *Harvard Business Review* 82(10): 79–88.

Leigh-Preston, Nancey. 1985. *Industrial Transformation, Economic Development, and Regional Planning.* Chicago: Council of Planning Librarians Bibliography 154.

Malanga, Steven. 2004. The Curse of the Creative Class. *City Journal* (Winter). Accessed September 15, 2008 from http://www.city-journal.org/hteml/14_1_the_curse_.html

Malizia, Emil, and John Feser. 1999. *Understanding Local Economic Development.* New Brunswick, NJ: Rutgers University, Center for Urban Planning Research.

Myrdal, Gunnar. 1957. *Economic Theory and Underdeveloped Regions.* London: Duckworth.

Peck, Jamie. 2005. Struggling With the Creative Class. *International Journal of Urban and Regional Research* 29(4): 740–770.

Perroux, François. 1983. *A New Concept of Development.* Paris: UNESCO/Universite du Paris IX.

Porter, Michael. 1995. The Competitive Advantage of the Inner City. *Harvard Business Review* May–June: 55–71.

Richardson, Harry W. 1971. *Urban Economics.* Harmondsworth, UK: Penguin.

———. 1973. *Regional Growth Theory.* New York: John Wiley.

Robinson, Carla Jean. 1989. Municipal Approaches to Economic Development. *Journal of the American Planning Association* 55(3): 283–295.

Rubin, Herbert. 2000. *Renewing Hope Within Neighborhoods of Despair.* Albany: State University of New York Press.

Shragge, Eric. 1997. *Community Economic Development.* Buffalo, NY: Black Rose.

Vernon, Raymond. 1966. May. International Investment and International Trade in the Product Cycle. *The Quarterly Journal of Economics,* 80(2): 190–207.

White, Sammis B., and Jeffery D. Osterman. 1991. Is Employment Growth Really Coming From Small Establishments? *Economic Development Quarterly* 5(3): 241–257.

Williams, S. 1986. *Local Employment Generation: The Need for Innovation, Information and Suitable Technology.* Paris: Organization for Economic Cooperation and Development.

Wolman, Harold, and Gerry Stoker. 1992. Understanding Local Economic Development in a Comparative Context. *Economic Development Quarterly* 6(4): 415.

4

The Local Economic Development Profession and Professionals

Ask one hundred economic developers how they got into the field, the old adage goes, and ninety-five will tell you: by accident. . . . For many working in the field, this was not their profession, vocation or intended career—it was merely a job. . . . Further, local-level politicians, who are responsible for much of the hiring (read: political appointment) of economic developers across the country, have historically not realized that the skills of their economic developers should be similar to those of their town planners and city engineers. The times, they are a-changing.

—Waterhouse (1997, p. 84)

Economic development practitioners and planners now belong to a recognized profession. However, as the above quote suggests, this recognition is relatively recent, even though the practice of economic development has been with us since the first individual tried to influence the location of business.

The economic development field has a number of formal associations, and the author of this quote was president of what was once the American Economic Development Council but has since experienced a merger that increases its stature. Within the economic development profession, there are state associations of economic developers found across the United States, as well as national and international associations. These associations are distinct from economic development agencies and organizations such as chambers of commerce or small business centers, county economic development departments, state economic development agencies, or the U.S. Economic Development Administration. They are membership organizations that draw from all of these entities as well as others, including site location practitioners, real estate developers, utility companies, economic development consultants, and so forth.

The International Economic Development Council (IEDC) is the most significant economic development association in the United States and claims to be the world's largest economic development association (www.IEDConline.org). IEDC was formed in 2001 from the merger of the American Economic Development Council, which had been the largest and oldest economic development society (founded in 1926), and the Council for Urban Economic Development (founded in 1967). IEDC provides economic development advocacy, education, technical assistance, and networking. It has established a Certified Economic Developer program, which consists of meeting a minimum level of economic development work experience as well as taking (nondegree) coursework and passing an examination testing broad-based knowledge of economic development. Certified Economic Developers are also expected to adhere to a professional code of ethics. A recent initiative of IEDC, to be discussed later in the chapter, has been to identify the core competencies required of economic developers.

While individuals of any academic background can become Certified Economic Developers, the economic development field does have academic roots in the applied disciplines of geography, business administration, public finance, political economics, and urban and regional planning. Further, within the urban and regional planning field, there has long been an economic development specialization that grounds the practice in both theory and method. The American Planning Association, the professional association for all planners, has a division of economic development planning with its own officers that was established in 1978. The focus on economic development within the planning field is more explicitly directed toward the public interest than is found elsewhere in the practice.

The origins of the American economic development profession are typically associated with the rise of industrial recruiters in the late 19th century who literally bought factories for Southern cities. City business promoters and community boosters from chambers of commerce or similar business development agencies, as well as civic boosters, form another point of origin for the field.

Two decades ago, Levy (1990), writing from an urban and regional planning perspective, characterized the profession as a mixture of rational planning and salesmanship:

> The academicians who wish to increase the usefulness of [their] contribution to the practice of economic development at the local level or make useful suggestions regarding state and national policy direction must recognize the dominance of the sales side of the process in the practitioner's work. Efforts to tie local economic development into the broader context of community planning must be fitted into a setting in which sales is likely to remain the dominant mode. (p. 158)

Two years earlier, H. J. Rubin wrote an article characterizing the practice of economic development as "Shoot anything that flies, claim anything that falls" (1988). In this now classic article, Rubin observed that, in the practice of economic development, "[the] search for administrative certainty and task closure leads to the public sector's favoring business interests" (p. 236). He also observed that economic development practitioners perceive their work environment to be "complex and undefined" and to involve "a difficult effort in bridging the gap between the public and private sectors" (p. 237). Thus, to promote the appearance of certainty, they have adopted the philosophy of shooting anything that flies and claiming anything that falls.

A 2004 survey of economic development practitioners in local government, conducted by the International City/County Management Association (ICMA), found the same dynamics dominating the profession. Covering municipalities with populations of 10,000 or greater and counties with populations of 50,000 and more with council-administrator or council-elected executive forms of government, the survey found only 52% of local governments had written economic development plans (ICMA, 2004). In responding to questions about their economic development activities, these practitioners indicated the largest proportion of their effort was spent on business attraction/recruitment (44%), followed by business retention (41%), and small business development (19%). When asked about other programs that could foster economic development activities from within the locality, approximately half indicated that they supported community development corporations and job training. However, nearly three fifths indicated they did not have a community development loan fund, more than three quarters did not have a microenterprise program, and less than a third supported childcare programs.

Indeed, the predominant economic development activity in which local governments engaged continues to be marketing, with a heavy reliance on partnerships with private companies to carry this out. Even so, their efforts have been overwhelmingly ad hoc. Despite the fact that nearly 100% stated they wanted to attract new business, 70% indicated they did not have a written business-attraction plan. This serves to reinforce the finding of Rubin's (1988) earlier survey that practitioners were concerned their marketing and promotion efforts amounted to little more than boosterism.

IEDC offers training to strengthen the marketing capabilities of local government and economic development organizations. For example, in 2011, it offered training in "Economic Development Marketing and Attraction," which focused on topics such as site selection fundamentals, target audience identification, community marketing plans and branding, generating support for the marketing campaign, engaging social media, and evaluating the marketing plan (IEDC 2011 Annual Conference announcement).

Recurring themes in the economic development literature over the last two decades, particularly in response to globalization forces, have been that of the need to retain existing businesses as well as to foster homegrown, small businesses. Yet 77% of the ICMA survey respondents indicated they did not have a written business retention plan, while 83% did not have a written small business development plan. In contrast, more than 70% offered business incentives. The top five incentives were assistance with zoning and permits, improvements to infrastructure, tax increment financing, tax abatements, and one-stop permitting. This adds credence to another of Rubin's observations that economic developers believe the role of local government is to be "flexible enough with codes and regulations so as not to hamper business development" (p. 65).

More than 80% of local governments surveyed indicated that they measured the effectiveness of the business incentives they offered by the number of jobs created by new business (90%) and the amount of money invested in construction materials and labor (63%). However, nearly 90% indicated that they never required a percentage of new employees to be hired from within the community. Furthermore, when queried on whether they use performance measures to assess the effectiveness of their economic development efforts, such as program expenditures per estimated tax dollars generated, the majority (67%) responded negatively.

The emphasis on marketing and providing incentives to attract new business revealed by the ICMA survey is the most enduring characteristic of economic development practice.

The flexibility characterizing economic development can be an asset to practitioners who have limited resources with which to meet large but not always clear expectations. The flipside, however, is that the absence of standards makes it difficult to exclude any activities, even the most patently anticommunity activities, from being labeled as local economic development initiatives. Moreover, any government or local community group can (and sometimes does) merely change the name of its activity or the name on the door in order to label its activities as economic development.

From the nonprofit community perspective, economic development is more than "bricks and sticks" or marketing and recruitment. It is an effort to reweave the social and economic fabric of broken places and the people who live in them, often because they have no other choice. From a more recent set of interviews of economic developers, Rubin (2000) captures this feeling. One of his interviewees said:

> Our mission is to empower and educate and advocate. . . . It's not to produce anybody's anything or deliver anything. It's to empower and educate and advocate for the kinds of changes that will make the neighborhood a neat place to live. (p. 138)

Another interviewee remarked:

> We think of ourselves as catalysts . . . ignite activism and ignite a sense among people about what can be done when people work collectively and struggle for what is needed. (p. 139)

Yet another said:

> When there's an empty building we will serve as developer as a last resort. That's how we view ourselves. . . . We are losing money on the deal but it makes it all work. (p. 139)

Nonprofit community organizations take risks that for-profit developers would never assume. This risk entails organizing people of diverse ethnic and class backgrounds who sometimes fear and loathe one another. Although the nonprofits may or may not make money—mostly they don't—they are engaged in the hardest economic development work. That is, they are trying to make tough places livable.

The Role of the Economic Development Practitioner

The economic development profession can be viewed as comprising the interrelationships of five elements: locational factors, organizational role, task functions, nature of the clients served, and the individual practitioner orientation. The economic development (ED) practitioner role may be seen as a function of all these factors. Supplementing the five elements of the economic development profession that are discussed in greater detail below is the notion of competencies that these elements require of the ED practitioner. As previously mentioned, the International Economic Development Council has recently engaged in an effort to identify the competencies that the practitioner should have. IEDC distinguishes the needed competencies by whether the practitioner has an executive or administrative role versus a professional or staff role. As can be seen in Table 4.1, there are six competencies identified for ED staff and eight for ED executives. While there is considerable overlap in the competencies described, the ED executive needs higher levels of knowledge, as well as visioning and governing abilities.

Returning to the five elements, each *could* have the hallmarks of the "shoot anything that flies, claim anything that falls" point of view. In some instances, an individual economic development practitioner may achieve things the environment does not dictate and claim credit for the result. Further, the tasks the economic developer chooses or is assigned may themselves

Table 4.1 Economic Developer Competencies Identified by IEDC

Economic Development Professional/Staff Competencies

1. **Analysis and Decision-Making Skills**—Make elective decisions and solve problems in complex or ambiguous situations by gathering, diagnosing and judiciously analyzing the information about the situation and environment in order to identify and evaluate options and select the best course of action.

2. **Industry Understanding**—Aware of and interested in the economic development industry. Deeply learn service area(s). Develop professional capabilities.

3. **Leadership and Influence**—Inspire and influence by communicating a compelling vision of the future, conveying an executive presence (e.g., confidence, poise, connecting with others) and being sufficiently agile and self-assured to lead others electively.

4. **Relationships and Teaming**—Electively build relationships with individuals and teams across the organization and external stakeholders by being inclusive, considerate and responsive to the needs of others; by communicating electively, collaborating with others and sharing resources; and by being receptive to feedback.

5. **Responsibility and Achievement (Self Management, Ethical Integrity)**— Demonstrate initiative, commitment to excellence, and elective self-management skills, including integrity, ethical behavior, responsibility, dependability and follow through.

6. **Communications Skills**—Electively communicates through verbal and written media to stakeholders.

Economic Development Executive/Leader Competencies

1. **Analysis and Decision-Making Skills**—Make elective decisions and solve problems in complex or ambiguous situations by gathering, diagnosing and judiciously analyzing the information about the situation and environment in order to identify and evaluate options and select the best course of action.

2. **Economic Development Expertise**—Understand the principles and general trends within the economic development industry. Demonstrate experience in economic development programs. Speak the industry language to stakeholders.

3. **Governance Skills**—Build channels of information between all stakeholder groups. Provide feedback to the board. Look ahead and plan for the future business and leadership succession.

4. **Industry Vision**—Stay abreast of economic development industry knowledge. Identify opportunities for future growth. Think and act in an entrepreneurial manner.

5. **Leadership and Influence**—Inspire and influence by communicating a compelling vision of the future, conveying an executive presence and being sufficiently agile and self-assured to lead others electively.

6. **Management Skills**—Manage the work of others by providing direction, structure, and clear expectations; maintain an open flow of communication and a sense of urgency to drive results; hold others accountable; develop others by providing timely and relevant feedback and opportunities for development.

7. **Relationships and Teaming**—Electively build relationships with individuals and teams across the organization by being inclusive, considerate and responsive to the needs of others; by communicating electively, collaborating with others, and sharing resources; and by being receptive to feedback.

8. **Responsibility and Achievement (Self Management, Ethical Integrity)**—Demonstrate initiative, commitment to excellence and elective self-management skills, including: responsibility, dependability, planning and organization, detail-orientation, and the ability to follow through.

Source: The International Economic Development Council, Executive and Professional Economic Development Competencies, prepared by Corelli, Meyer and Associates, Washington, DC, 2012.

generate a productive or counterproductive environment. More than two decades ago, Luke and colleagues (1988) critically observed:

> The experience and working knowledge of the seasoned economic development manager are increasingly ineffective and, in many cases, even detrimental when applied to the new interconnected economic context. Competing with other cities for scarce industrial prospects creates adversarial, competitive relationships that can actually hinder future economic development. New collaborative strategies are required for several reasons. One is the expanding and crowded economic development arena . . . [p]olicy-making responsibility is dispersed and shared by a multiplicity of elected and appointed public officials. Another is a significantly reduced capacity for any one government agency or individual manager to effectively act unilaterally. A third is the slowness of policy formulation and implementation. . . . A fourth is the inevitable increase in vulnerability and openness to outside economic forces, with cities and states increasingly influenced by corporate investment decisions made in other cities on the globe. Economic development is now set in an intergovernmental and intersectoral web of pulling and pushing, and governments can seldom deal with economic problems independently. (Luke, Veattriss, Reed, and Reed, 1988, p. 227)

While the above critique is still too often relevant, there is also evidence of a sea change in the awareness and motivations of the profession. The discussion below is intended to help frame the context for this sea change.

The Community

Almost all communities or regions present different circumstances, irrespective of the causes of their economic ills. Many intervening factors can influence the situation. For example, one community may easily be mobilized because there is a clear pattern of leadership, while another has virtually no identifiable leaders. The goals in both circumstances may be identical and the tools or methods used by the practitioner may bear superficial similarity, but the precise mode of operation will vary based on the conditions. As a result, not only the objective circumstances but also the milieu for development are significant issues for the ED practitioner.

The total community or area circumstances must be taken into consideration when assessing economic development needs. The atmosphere in which the change is to be made is as important as the change itself. As a result, the ED practitioner must reach well beyond technical know-how to help the community see itself as a social and physical entity that in many instances goes well beyond the parochial boundaries of the municipality. This identification task is a necessary and important ingredient in the development process, and failure to come to grips with the real "locational" issues can doom even the most dedicated ED practitioner.

In addition to getting the economic geography right, the ED practitioner must also assist the community in getting the cause of economic problem(s) right. This is not an easy task. Many communities identify their problems as external, such as competing with lower-wage places of foreign nations or unfair international competition. This may or may not be the case. In most instances, however, dwelling on the external will not create any new options. Therefore, the ED practitioner's job is to identify the economic problems that can be solved within the context of that locality. This frequently means helping the community recognize that remedies selected elsewhere (high-tech, tourism, factory attraction, etc.) may not suit a particular locality. In essence, the situation determines both the means of and the limits on local economic development. The ED practitioner must be aware of this and use appropriate skills to assist the community to find the correct path to a sustainable economy.

The Organization

As previously discussed, local economic development activities are conducted by a variety of institutions at both the local and state levels. Primarily, the ED practitioner works in municipal or multijurisdictional local government organizations. Therefore, most of the comments in this section concern practice at the local level.

Each economic development organization is formed to fulfill some pre-conceived mission. That mission may be clear or fuzzy, but it forms the justification for the organization's existence and imposes a limitation on the authority of the ED practitioner. In many—perhaps most—circumstances, economic development organizations are coordinating bodies that take few direct actions themselves. In such instances, the ED practitioner is more of a resource person than an expert. Because other organizations are carrying out the action, the ED practitioner must possess the skill of encouraging without displacing and monitoring without ruling. It is a difficult role to play.

In other circumstances, the organization may view itself as a developer or development partner. In these circumstances, the ED practitioner must be creative and aggressive and seek opportunities to participate in new economic activities on a broad front, ranging from housing to industrial development to green development. The ED practitioner might even be required to design new financial instruments or help firms organize themselves to take advantage of government or other development programs.

Increasingly, the ED practitioner is part of a larger government or non-profit organization bureaucracy. As a government agent, the ED practitioner may have limitations imposed from a variety of sources, ranging from advisory boards to elected officials. The tensions created in this environment can be overwhelming, especially when different constituencies have widely varying concepts of the role and responsibilities of the ED practitioner.

Economic development organizations grow and specialize. As a result, the ED practitioner may operate within a large economic or planning bureaucracy. Organizations of this type expect the ED practitioner to have certain definable subareas of special skill such as housing, finance, entrepreneurship, and brownfield redevelopment.

Finally, economic development organizations operate in a wider framework of organizations and institutions at the local, state, and national levels and, more recently, at the international level. The interorganizational scope of local economic development is expanding. The need to create links with larger or more specialized organizations such as airport authorities or international development agencies, as well as the substantial lobbying required with state and federal legislatures, provides an exceptionally dynamic situation for the ED practitioner.

The Task Functions

The practitioner's task is complex, to say the least, but falls into the general categories of analysis, program development, and marketing. These activities are difficult to separate because they are intertwined in carrying out the activities of any practitioner. The marketing dimension involves activities associated with organizing people, selling ideas, and mobilizing resources for economic development. No amount of technically correct activity will help a community revitalize or direct its economy unless there is sufficient internal capacity. It is the process side of the ledger that helps build capacity in terms of leadership and organizational strength.

The analysis dimension refers to the set of strategies and approaches that the ED practitioner either fashions or identifies as suitable for the situation. Various types of analytical methods and processes will be elaborated upon in Chapter 6. They entail (1) identifying community problems, (2) providing technical and analytical assistance, (3) determining the resource mix required to meet the economic development needs of the situation, and the process skills of (4) developing networks among individuals and institutions and (5) stimulating interaction among diverse groups to achieve a common objective.

The specific tasks of ED practitioners are as follows:

1. *Building development organizations.* One of the most important functions of an ED practitioner is to develop a strong, viable, and continuing organization. Capacity building relates both to helping the organization gain expertise and to identifying and developing future leadership. In addition, the ED practitioner must assist the organization in strengthening its network with institutions at the local, national, and international levels.

2. *Inventory of area resources.* Keeping track of community or area resources goes well beyond physical assets inventories. An area's development resources extend to its culture, its leadership, and the quality of its community social life. The ED practitioner must not only know the resource base but also find new ways to use it to achieve community objectives. Of course, the ED practitioner must also find ways to build resources where there are deficiencies or to transform other resources to meet the need.

3. *Selecting strategies.* The community selects strategies, but the ED practitioner helps guide the community in the process. This is one of the most important process skills of a practitioner. The ED practitioner must be careful to "assist" rather than push or sell a particular strategy. Moreover, the ED practitioner must help the decision makers see the need for comprehensive approaches, incorporating several methods over single-component strategies, such as tourism.

4. *Marketing the area.* Marketing a community is not like marketing a product. Products remain constant in terms of their performance. Communities change. They both add and lose capacity depending on events. No matter what role the ED practitioner plays, marketing will be a component. The marketing of the place is also associated with the marketing of many other factors—for example, human resources, organizational capacity, and community incentive programs.

5. *Data development and analysis.* Economic development data are not always clear or clean. The ED practitioner constantly attempts to find good information on

the local situation, ranging from demographic to institutional analysis. Usually large-scale data sources are inadequate for the purpose. Therefore, the ED practitioner must refine data from the census and other sources, conduct surveys, or identify unobtrusive methods to measure any particular development dimension. Having data and determining what they mean are not easy tasks. As a result, the ED practitioner must frequently develop ways to display complex information for the layperson. This requires exceptionally good analytical and presentation skills.

All of the above tasks relate to the institutional and locational circumstances of the community. All five are required at different times.

The Clients

The economic development practitioner must work with a wide variety of clients. Clients are both individual and collective. In many respects, the total population of the community or area forms the client base. The ED practitioner usually has direct contact with a regular group and more limited contact with a wider constituent base. Generally, the ED practitioner will work with a single advisory body or group and maintain contact with others through organizations or other collective agencies.

Lay leaders are usually the clientele for local economic development. Such persons are generally volunteers working for the good of the community. As laypersons, they may have little or no preparation in the field. They may well represent community groups with considerable influence but without any special expertise. As a result, the ED practitioner must respect these individuals for the knowledge they bring from their constituents and use this information in program development. However, the professional must provide training and technical assistance to the group. This is a delicate role. The ED practitioner needs to balance the group's lay knowledge with professional expertise.

Local officials are frequently the employers of ED practitioners. Economic development departments or agencies are important components of local governments. ED practitioners may direct such departments and, in doing so, report directly to local elected officials. The ED practitioner's success in such circumstances depends on supporting these officials in meeting the needs of the community. This role may require anything from general economic development planning to community education to consultation with community groups.

Civic and economic development organizations are frequently the prime sponsors of economic development. These organizations, described earlier, are public–private institutions that take on the mantle of local development, generally with official sanction from the local or multijurisdictional authorities. Although these groups are also organized by volunteer laypersons, they frequently include individuals with considerable business expertise and resources.

The ED practitioner usually facilitates the activities of this type of agency. Because such groups tend to have substantial resources, the professional role requires coordinating economic development activities, including the hiring of additional specialized expertise. In addition, the ED practitioner acts as the principal contact person with other organizations and agencies.

In sum, the clientele for local economic development depends on the organizational form and task. The ED practitioner must be attuned to the circumstances of the community and work with laypersons as well as professionals. The ED practitioner role requires one to utilize the expertise of the clients as well as the profession to fashion economic development alternatives for the community.

The Professional Roles

The tasks of the economic development practitioner are also related to the three work roles of consultant, enabler, and community organizer. Sometimes, the circumstances prescribe the role of the ED professional; more often, the organization's mission defines it.

The *consultant* role does not refer to a professional occupation but to the mode of delivery. As consultant, the ED practitioner provides expertise and problem-solving skills in the situation. The consultant acts as the provider of accurate technical information, showing the options available to the decision-making group.

The *enabler* is essentially a facilitator. In this role, the ED practitioner is a catalytic leader who focuses on bringing people together and providing a structure for resolving community economic development issues. The enabler may also mobilize resources but seldom acts as the sole expert. Moreover, the enabler will attempt to create a continuing problem-solving capacity rather than addressing single economic or social issues (Luke et al., 1988).

The *community organizer* role has much more of an advocacy orientation. A community organizer is usually partisan or an advocate for a specific group or area and acts as the catalyst to propel it to political and economic action.

The organizer model requires a certain type of institutional structure, such as a community development corporation, to be effective in an economic development role.

Clearly, some of these roles are merged or even evolutionary. An ED practitioner might start out as a community organizer and subsequently adopt the role of enabler and consultant as the group increases its power and capacity. The essential factor is that both the "process" and the "content/methods" task be delivered to the community in some reasonably responsible manner. The framework here is merely an outline of the role models related to the task function of the ED practitioner, not a conclusive definition.

Economic Development Careers

There are many different career paths that economic development practitioners can take. Three of the most common are:

> *Manager.* The top level of manager involves managing economic development organizations as separate or component agencies and requires considerable managerial skill. The economic development manager must be an expert in process areas and have deep knowledge of the economic development fields as well as a good background in both business and economics. Within large economic development agencies, there can also be manager opportunities at the program level.
>
> *Analyst.* Nearly all economic development organizations and consultant firms require individuals with very strong analytical skills, particularly in the area of regional economic development, economics, or urban planning/business.
>
> *Neighborhood/community worker.* At the neighborhood and small community levels, overall development and process skills are required; community organization and development training is especially useful when working at this level.

Economic development practitioners are both process (community organization, leadership, and capacity building) and task (economic and data analysis) oriented. The tasks and roles of ED practitioners are related to the needs of the situation and the resources required. Individuals who want to become professional economic developers can build on degrees in urban and regional planning, public policy, economics, regional science, geography, or related disciplines, tailoring their coursework to focus on economic development. There are a few undergraduate economic development degrees in the country. Further, as previously discussed, there are opportunities for post-degree economic development training and certification through the International Economic Development Council.

Summary and Conclusion

The tasks and roles that economic development practitioners take have historically been contingent upon *where* they practice. ED practitioners working in smaller towns or counties typically define their jobs as marketing and industrial attraction. Industrial attraction also dominates the tasks for those who work in the economic development arms of utility companies and chambers of commerce. Those working in the planning departments or development agencies of large cities have a much wider range of responsibilities. In addition to marketing and recruitment, these can include small business development, industrial retention, commercial revitalization, implementation of tax increment financing districts, workforce and sector development, and brownfield redevelopment.

To date, economic development practitioners have been engaged primarily in marketing and recruitment, deal making, and program implementation. However, as the field matures, it is increasingly becoming self-reflective and self-critical, as the earlier discussion in this chapter suggests. This is a critical element of professionalization in general (Schön, 1987), as well as in establishing and meeting the goals of the economic development profession specifically. To date, the focus on strategic planning and implementation, wise use of resources, and development of standards and ethics has been based on traditional definitions and goals of economic development—that is, growth, wealth, and job creation. However, going forward, self-reflection and criticism will be especially necessary if economic development professionals are going to incorporate the criteria of equity and sustainability into their definition and practice of economic development to more effectively meet the challenges of a flatter and climate-challenged world.

References and Suggested Readings

Benveniste, Guy. 1983. *Bureaucracy.* San Francisco: Boyd and Fraser.
Blakely, Edward J. 1979. *Community Development Research: Concepts, Issues and Strategies.* New York: Human Services Press.
Christensen, James A., and Jerry W. Robinson. 1980. *Community Development in America.* Ames: Iowa State University Press.
International City/County Management Association (ICMA). 2004. *Economic Development Survey, 2004.* Accessed June 10, 2007 from http://www.icma.org.
Levy, John. 1990. What Economic Developers Actually Do: Location Quotients Versus Press Releases. *Journal of the American Planning Association* 56(2): 153–160.
Luke, Jeffrey S., Curtis Veattriss, Betty Jane Reed, and Christine Reed. 1988. *Managing Economic Development.* San Francisco: Jossey-Bass.
Rothman, John, Jack Erlich, and Joseph Teresa. 1975. *Promoting Innovation and Change in Organizations and Communities.* New York: John Wiley.
Rubin, Herbert J. 1988. Shoot Anything That Flies; Claim Anything That Falls: Conversations With Economic Development Practitioners. *Economic Development Quarterly* 2(3): 236–251.
———. 2000. *Renewing Hope: Within Neighborhoods of Despair.* Albany: State University of New York Press.
Schön, Donald. 1987. *Educating the Reflective Practitioner.* San Francisco: Jossey-Bass.
Vollmer, Howard M., and Donald L. Mills, eds. 1966. *Professionalization.* Englewood Cliffs, NJ: Prentice Hall.
Waterhouse, Mark D. 1997. Professionalizing the Economic Developer. *New Directions for Higher Education* 97: 84–95.
Weiner, Myron. 1982. *Human Services Management.* Homewood, IL: Dorsey.

5

The Local Economic
Development Planning Process

The planning of local economic development is a *process meant to deliver a product*. Most of us understand the possible products of economic growth—more and better jobs, increased wealth and income, increased opportunities for personal fulfillment, and so on. It is important to realize that the goal of community capacity building also involves a complex, multitasked process featuring many actors. Moreover, this process affects the entire environment of the community—physical, regulatory, and attitudinal—and determines the nature and quality of its economic products.

However, the planning process includes more than ascertaining when, where, and how new employment may be stimulated. In fact, the acquisition of more job opportunities may deliver little or no benefit to an area. For example, bringing high-tech jobs to a coal mining community may not assist currently unemployed coal miners, though it broadens the local economic base. Therefore, it is important to determine both the short-term and the long-term impacts of any proposed development alternative.

In recent decades, there have been some noteworthy planning misattempts. Real estate–oriented economic development in the 1980s aimed at increasing office workers in downtowns but neglected to match the new jobs to the existing population base. In the 1990s, every community in the nation turned its attention to small business start-ups, ranging from boutique enterprises like antique sales to Internet dotcoms. But, in too many instances, the fledgling enterprises required unavailable talent or created unexpected real estate demands, both on commercial properties and on housing, that effectively displaced the indigenous population.

Generally, new firms that are locally and regionally based or owned may have a greater impact on the stability and future of a community than branch plants. Similarly, recent research has shown that small, innovative businesses may be more labor intensive than larger plants. Nonetheless, the type of human resource assets and educational and training opportunities, along with the use of local infrastructure, should form the basis for any decision as to what kind of economic development strategy a community might pursue. In brief, local economic development planning takes hard work, careful analysis, well-defined goals, and long-term commitment of resources to achieve positive outcomes.

Preliminary Tasks of Local Economic Development Planning

Two tasks must precede the local economic development process. First, the organization or group of institutions responsible for implementing or coordinating the economic change must be identified and mobilized. Second, the geographic scope of the plan must be determined.

Identifying the Planners

Establishing an effective organizational structure for economic development is essential to the success of the effort. The most common organizational unit for a local economic development program is an economic development corporation (EDC) or similar specialized economic development organization charged with helping develop programs in a city, county, or region. Economic development agencies that are part of local government are also frequent nodes for development programs. In addition, chambers of commerce, business associations, workforce training agencies, or any other local group may become interested in promoting economic development. Strong organizational capacity is always based on communitywide participation, leadership, and legitimacy.

Participation. The primary task of the planning organization is to ensure the full participation of critical sectors of the community. Business must be involved along with government and civic-minded individuals. The importance of business involvement may seem obvious, but in too many cases local individuals in service clubs, labor organizations, or other community groups begin the economic development process without the active participation of business, labor, and government. As a result, while everyone may applaud the initiative, nothing comes of it.

Leadership. Economic development planning is the process of empowering a local leadership organization that has two key capacities: the vision to see economic potential and the ability to achieve widely shared desired results. Organizations must be willing and capable when it comes to taking on this leadership role, or they should not be selected to lead the economic development planning effort.

Legitimacy. A leadership organization should be perceived as legitimate—that is, it needs implicit approval from a wide range of community members to represent the community well-being. However, organizations often are not trusted because they represent only a single interest (e.g., an industry, a powerful family, the utilities) or because they are corrupt. Thus, legitimacy in the community is an earned quality and is easily eroded by secrecy, favoritism, and indecision.

Determining Geographic Scope

The second preliminary task of economic development planning is to target the effort's geographic scope. Areas or zones of concern can be as small as a city block that needs support or as large as a county, multicounty region, state, or even multistate region. Most important is that the economic area be a unit with internal consistency and cohesion. The area's economic configuration should be determined carefully because, irrespective of political boundaries—especially in areas with large counties—these seldom correspond to economic regions. In any case, the key to effective planning is to realize that no economy begins and ends with neighborhood or city boundaries.

The reality of economic development is that all small areas are ultimately nested in a larger regional enterprise that, of necessity, involves all communities sharing a common market, transportation system, and flow of goods and materials. The area to be focused upon is usually determined by the regional labor force (labor shed) or an equivalent interconnected zone that is physically and economically integrated. However, smaller and larger areas may also be the focus of effective economic development if desired. At its most efficient, the economic development process plans for an entire economic zone, maximizing the area's total resource base.

The Six Phases of Planning

After the preliminary tasks have been accomplished, the six widely recognized phases of the economic development process can begin. To a large extent, they follow the order shown in Table 5.1. Although there is no need to follow this order slavishly or to pass up a crucial opportunity because the final development strategy has not yet been set, ad hoc economic and employment development efforts may be both wasteful and unfortunate. Chapters 5 through 12 of this book describe the tasks associated with each phase of planning. A review of these tasks is included in subsequent chapters.

The basic planning approach for local economic development is self-education first, strategy development second, and projects third, according to the six phases.

In *Phase I,* planning organizations are involved in gathering information about the character of their economic base and the problems they have in generating more jobs and wealth. Without accurate, impartial data, development projects will surely be unable to maximize the use of community resources. In many cases, data gathering is complicated and requires surveys and sophisticated analysis, but in others it simply involves collecting data on industry, employment, the labor force, and institutional structures in the community.

In *Phase II,* planners select one of several broad strategies to solve the problems that were identified in Phase I. Chapter 7 describes the strategy selection process, and Chapters 8 through 11 document alternative strategies that can be used as the basis for meeting different development goals.

Phase III focuses on the projects that can be done within the selected strategy. Projects are concrete programs, facilities, investments, and marketing efforts that implement a strategy. Examples of projects are given throughout the book.

Once the projects are selected, the economic development planner begins *Phase IV*, building action plans to implement the projects. Action plans look at alternative ways of designing, financing, and doing a project. This subject is covered in Chapter 12.

Phase V continues planning for projects by specifying project details and establishing a monitoring and evaluation plan.

Finally, in *Phase VI* the project is implemented, facilitated by detailed financial plans, schedules, and other concrete arrangements. After an evaluation of community assets and support is completed, the project is launched.

Managing Planning Resources in the Community

Determining the Physical Environment

One way to approach Phase I of developmental planning is to research three aspects of the process that will need to be managed. These areas can also be considered as planning resources. Local governments are normally concerned with the physical environment—physical infrastructure—which is certainly important to business and industry. The private sector usually has both particular and general requirements for a physical environment. Particular needs often include special transportation services or waste-disposal services. In many cases, these forms of physical environment can be "custom made." In other words, local government can provide the special service or facility for a known and defined business or industry requirement, the fulfillment of which is likely to lead to new local jobs.

One of the most important factors influencing locational decisions for new private sector investment is the attractiveness or amenity of a particular area or city, more commonly referred to as *quality of life.* Many local governments

Table 5.1 Phases and Tasks of the Local Development Planning Process

Phase I	Data gathering and analysis
	Determining economic base
	Assessing current employment structure
	Examining opportunities for and constraints on economic development
	Examining institutional capacity
Phase II	Selecting a local development strategy
	Establishing goals and criteria
	Determining possible courses of action
	Developing a targeted strategy
Phase III	Selecting local development projects
	Identifying possible projects
	Assessing project viability
	– Community
	– Commercial
	– Location
	– Implementation
Phase IV	Building action plans
	Preassessing project outcomes
	Developing project inputs
	Establishing financial alternatives
	Identifying project structures
Phase V	Specifying project details
	Conducting detailed feasibility studies
	Preparing business plan
	Developing, monitoring, and evaluating program
Phase VI	Overall development plan preparation and implementation
	Preparing project plan implementation schedule
	Developing an overall development program
	Targeting and marketing community assets
	Marketing financial needs

and neighborhoods have been very much concerned about improving the quality of life in their municipalities, but how often have councils regarded a proposed performing arts center as increased potential for attracting private economic development? The same question applies to reduced vandalism or traffic congestion. Industry and business regard "livability" as an important locational factor, and local government is in the best position to improve the local quality of life.

Livability can mean different things to different people. Nearly every community possesses natural features, facilities, or simply an aesthetic quality that endears it to certain people. Local governments must identify their "quality of life" attributes, build on them, and effectively promote them to the business community. Indeed, many local governments have already begun this process.

Many urban and rural communities throughout the nation suffer serious economic problems and desperately need a revitalization of spirit and an effort to improve economic circumstances. A revitalized feeling can be created using various mechanisms. For example, small towns can undertake major improvement projects that create a sense of cohesion and beauty. These projects may be as small as improving street signs and trees or as major as the restoration of the whole civic center. The type of project undertaken should coincide with business improvements and should not merely be physical improvements for their own sake.

A good example of the use of physical resources as central to the planning process is the Le Droit neighborhood of Washington, D.C. This historic area bordering the campus of Howard University contains beautiful post–Civil War housing stock and a fenced-in reservoir at the center of the community. In 1999, the city of Washington, D.C., Fannie Mae, and Howard University, along with the community, entered into an innovative partnership to restore the housing, reduce crime, revitalize retailing, and rehabilitate the reservoir into a community park and recreational asset. There are thousands of similar examples of quality housing and underused infrastructure that can be repositioned to create a more livable environment, thus reattracting the vital middle class to neighborhoods. These assets can trigger the reinvestment by local businesses and entrepreneurs into the community as well as attract new investors.

Facing the Regulatory Environment as a Planning Resource

Financial incentives and policies are important inputs to the economic development process. Indeed, they are critical to creating an environment for economic development. Many local governments are now undertaking very thorough reviews of their procedures to ensure that "the cost of doing business" in their locales reflects their desire for economic growth. For example, some cities have recently established "one-stop" business-assistance centers. Such centers are still fairly novel in spite of much publicity regarding their effectiveness.

Regulation can be a boon or an impediment to the development process. Fast, responsive regulation is more important than reducing regulatory burdens. A blue-ribbon commission looking at the regulatory framework in the city of Los Angeles concluded that the conflicting interpretations of existing regulation by various bureaus and agencies combined with conflicting regulations were the culprits in discouraging business from the city. Many other cities have faced similar regulatory problems. A good example is the city of New York, which has consolidated arcane regulation, streamlined jurisdictional overlaps, and authorized the creation of business improvement districts that act as advocates for local businesses. This regulatory cleanup has reduced considerable friction between city agencies and local businesses.

Preparing the Attitudinal Environment

The decisions the private sector makes about investment expansion or relocation are not always based exclusively on hard data. In fact, final decisions—particularly between competing options—are most heavily swayed by "gut feelings" or "seat-of-the-pants" reactions. A business may choose not to locate in a certain area because residents are known to be hostile or antagonistic to business, for example. The company does not want to jeopardize its employees and may instead select the next best location on the basis of the latter's being more receptive and appreciative of the industry. Because all locations, worldwide, have increasingly equal market access, a community's presentability makes a very big difference to its future.

Often, local governments adopt a quasi-adversarial role toward developers rather than a facilitating one. Developers generally agree upon the difficulties in dealing with local neighborhood activists who are uninterested in the economic and social merits of any project. This criticism applies as well to many areas of local government administration, including the executive and technical levels. The unanimous criticism of developers is the primary problem of delay: delays in presenting applications to the city council and in receiving decisions. Another criticism applies to imposed conditions—that is, city officials who want to "win at all costs" and are reluctant to think beyond petty regulations. To counter this situation, all stakeholders need to adopt a positive attitude toward city planning matters (e.g., development applications, resubmissions, and rezonings) and deal expeditiously and reasonably with each one.

A number of small communities have combined information resources and other strategies to create a better attitudinal framework for local enterprises. Alvin Sokolow and Julia Spezia (1990) provide some instructive examples of

17 small rural communities—from Seaford, Delaware (population 5,500), to Maui County, Hawaii (population 85,000)—that have used attitudinal leadership resources as the keys to economic turnarounds. Although the projects in each of the communities differed (e.g., creating new industrial parks, attracting or retaining enterprises), the underlying theme in all cases "was the frequent boost in community identification and spirit. 'Attitudes have changed, and that feeling is contagious,' noted one mayor" (Sokolow and Spezia, 1990).

Good attitudes do not necessarily generate good projects, but "bad" attitudes—be they from individuals in political or business authority or from the community or other interest groups—can impede and may even kill a good idea. We all know of communities that are antidevelopment or organizations that challenge all forms of economic activity, irrespective of their merits.

As a matter of policy, cities can establish procedures for all development and other related planning applications and make these available as public information. A public chronology of all development decisions would be an effective way to disprove any unfounded or unfair claims of excessive delays by developers. At the same time, it would encourage a more efficient and time-effective approach by city staff. Some communities are assigning the exclusive responsibility for business/industrial development applications to a senior officer in the planning department. This includes the receipt, processing, and approval or rejection of applications as well as the monitoring of their progress to conclusion.

Selecting a Local Economic Development Role

Once the planners have been identified and the zone of concern specified, an initial planning step must be completed during Phase I. Any organization interested in local economic development needs to be clear about the role it wants to play in the process. The stance an organization takes will shape planning at all stages and determine the tools it can ultimately use to initiate economic development.

Organizations have constraints derived from their current or historic roles or set by their charters. It is always difficult for an organization to go beyond its mandate. Therefore, the role definition must precede any attempt to shape the local economic environment. There are basically four courses of action open to organizations: to act as the entrepreneur, the coordinator, the facilitator, the stimulator, or any combination of these roles.

Entrepreneur/Developer

In this role, the organization takes on the full responsibility of operating a business enterprise. Local government or community-based organizations may decide to operate commercial enterprises themselves. Land or buildings in local government control for conservation or for future development can be made available for economic purposes. Local governments may wish to retain commercial land and buildings in public ownership or turn over these resources to local community groups.

It seems apparent that local governments can make greater use of the commercial potential of land or buildings under their control. Beaches, road verges, reserves, and civic centers may be used for a variety of activities that provide jobs. Local governments could take an active approach to identifying and assessing the possible range of commercial opportunities and balancing these against other objectives. Development of a specialization or "theme" for particular localities may increase visitor traffic and, therefore, the potential for commercial operations.

Both rural and urban local governments have found new ways to promote small business and other creative enterprises by better use of existing facilities and opportunities. For example, an Internet kiosk has been established in South Central Los Angeles by the local transit authority as a service for commuters and a hub for new Internet and graphics entrepreneurs. Small towns have provided seed capital and land for the establishment of new enterprises like "aquaponics" in rural Floyd County, Kentucky (personal communication, Eddie Patton Clark Allison of Sandy RC&D Floyd County Fiscal Court, Kentucky). Clearly, some entrepreneurship and risk taking is required on the part of local elected officials and policymakers to promote new opportunities for local residents.

Community-based organizations are in a good position to run enterprises as employment generators where private enterprise is unable to do so, or to ensure provision of a service where private enterprise is unwilling to take the necessary risks. There may also be a case for local governments providing goods and services (and therefore employment) for their own operations, particularly where such goods and services would otherwise be imported from outside the area or region. Examples may include hotels, bakeries, and caravan parks in isolated areas, and concrete or crushing plants and nurseries in urban areas.

When a local government has as its objective the redevelopment of depressed industrial or commercial areas in order to increase local trade, employment, revenue, and so on, it can take an active role either individually or in partnership with community-based groups or private enterprise. Use of planning expertise, compulsory acquisition powers, and provision of incentives for relocation or upgrading of premises are some of the options available.

Coordinator

Local government or a community-based group can act as a coordination body to establish policy or propose strategies for an area's development.

Because services delivered both by governments and by community and business organizations have a local impact, local councils are increasingly attempting to provide some leadership in the planning and coordination of services within their areas. An extension of this role to economic development might involve community groups in collecting and evaluating economic information (e.g., employment levels, workforce, unemployment, establishments). It might also involve working with other government agencies, business, and community interests to evolve economic objectives, plans, and strategies. Such an approach ensures that all sectors focus their approaches and resources on similar goals and that limited resources are used in more effective ways. This approach can also ensure consistency with state economic programs and strategies so that the local economy receives maximum benefit from them.

Regional tourist development plans, or economic development plans that have been prepared in some areas, represent a possible approach where such plans are developed as joint statements between the three spheres of government and other sectors. Plans developed and imposed by government alone are unlikely to have the same level of commitment or resource input that joint plans will have.

Regional planning bodies with representation from each sector usually work most effectively with governments to produce these plans. A regional approach will normally be more effective because government attention will be focused on regional economies. It will also represent a more manageable level of cooperation between state and local governments. Regional bodies that adequately represent all sectors and that produce realistic analyses and approaches are likely to have high credibility with government and thus considerable political influence. Regional organizations formed by local governments are well placed to play an information and catalyst role for their members. Some communities have formed nonprofit organizations that assemble economic data for communities as well as provide a research capacity from which services can be shared.

Facilitator

Some community groups and/or local governments have decided they can best promote development by improving the attitudinal environment in the community or area. This might involve streamlining the development process and improving planning procedures and zoning regulations.

A city or community group may bring together a range of approaches from different functional areas into a policy statement on economic development. This need not involve the commitment of additional resources, but rather the provision of a statement of objectives. It would provide a focus for the local government's existing resources and energies and a base for additional programs as and when that course is determined.

Positive use of planning powers may also include establishing employment or development zones and standards that encourage a particular class, scale, or character of development. Although such approaches are often related to environmental conditions, they can also have economic objectives. These opportunity areas then have the potential to be marketed to prospective business clients through direct approaches and advertising in one form or another.

Finally, local council members, as elected community representatives, can advocate local concerns and bring economic problems and opportunities to the attention of higher levels of government. Their advocacy role will be strengthened to the extent that local government can demonstrate community and business sector support for this position and put forward realistic and achievable remedies.

Stimulator

Both community groups and city councils can stimulate business creation or expansion by taking specific action that induces firms to enter or remain in the community. Stimulation may range from developing brochures to actually building industrial estates or small manufacturing workshops.

In some cases, approaches have even included providing industrial buildings. In at least one state, small manufacturing workshops have been built and leased to operators at reduced rents for the first few years of operation. This is an option for local governments in areas where the provision of suitable premises is a problem.

In tourism, a local government may itself promote a particular "theme" or activity in a key venue when private sector action is not forthcoming. Outlets for crafts, craft demonstrations, or a periodic market are some of the possible uses for council-owned premises.

In numerous overseas examples, local governments have provided premises at reduced rents to community-based enterprises and cooperatives to help meet local employment objectives. The course(s) of action a local council decides to take will depend on the local situation. It would be inappropriate for a council not to use its resources in intelligent ways to benefit the total community. Although local development initiatives are not a panacea for local government or the solution to all local problems, they are significant complements to state as well as federal efforts to stimulate economic and employment development. The issue is seldom whether the council should or should not act, but what action to take and how to take it.

Typology of Planning Approaches

There are two conditions that affect any local planning approach: (1) the reality of current pressures exerted by international and domestic circumstances, and

(2) the fact that each place is affected differently—that is, some have growing industrial sectors while others are experiencing industrial decline.

What, then, are the effects of these conditions on community orientation toward economic development? The orientation or expectation of the community during Phase I shapes its view toward the economic development process. Moreover, localities need to be aware of their developmental orientation in order to improve or alter their strategy. For instance, there are two basic economic development perspectives: responsiveness to external needs and responsiveness to local community needs. For reasons mentioned earlier, responsiveness to external needs characterizes much of prevailing practice, and local responsiveness is identified with a new, emerging (or latent) practice.

This knowledge sets the stage for proposing a typology of four distinct planning orientations: two prevailing models (recruitment planning and impact planning) and two emerging models (contingency planning and strategic planning) for local economies that are growing or declining (Bergman, 1981). The first two models are in response to conditions as they emerge. Recruitment planning represents what is known as a *preactive* approach to external conditions. That is, the community initiates activities to build or maintain its economic base in response to competitive conditions. Impact planners wait until circumstances change. This is *reactive* planning in recognition of the loss of the existing industrial base. The subsequent two approaches are more thoughtful and responsive to the total dimensions of the regional and national economic conditions. Strategic planning is genuinely *proactive* and builds a long-term responsive community system to the conditions a locality faces, whereas the contingency approach is an *interactive* approach that recognizes the need to be flexible to conditions just as they emerge (see Table 5.2 for a summary of planning approaches).

Recruitment Planning (Preactive)

Recruitment planning is the traditional approach to economic development used by most localities to attract corporate expansion. Public involvement in this approach is quite limited. Private-sector vitality and initiative tend to displace expressions of local concern for explicit planning or policy making. Policies associated with this approach tend to operate on the assumption that all business is good for the community. Industrialization of the area is taken for granted as obvious policy. This is generally linked to a tacit understanding that industrialization will be beneficial to the entire community.

Typical planning for this approach includes a wide array of industrial inducements and efforts to enhance the image of the area's "business climate." Because it is the most familiar style of local economic development planning, variants of recruitment planning can be found in nearly every locality in the country.

Table 5.2   Planning Approaches

	Responsive Perspectives		Planning Perspectives	
	Preactive *(I)*	*Reactive* *(II)*	*Proactive* *(III)*	*Interactive* *(IV)*
Planning				
Model of practice planning model	Recruitment planning	Impact planning	Strategic planning	Contingency planning
Policy				
Industry	Industrialization	Deindustrialization	New indigenous firms	Building on existing firm base
Enterprise types	Corporate adjustment assistance	Government sponsored	High-tech/ new tech	Community-based
Development				
Intervention model	Industrial inducements	Government program expenditures	Public-initiated development	Community-initiated development

Source: Adapted from Bergman (1981). Used by permission.

Impact Planning (Reactive)

Impact planning is a more recent practice that tries to mitigate or reduce the worst effects of industrial losses in a local economy. It derives from a concern for the effects of plant shutdowns in some communities, particularly the impacts on the labor force, and is episodic in nature. For most of the nation, this activity constitutes the most recognizable public sector planning approach to economic development. The approach relies heavily on the continued availability of federal funds.

The main assumption underlying federal and local impact policies is that action is short term and taken only in time of crisis. The best example of this type of policy is the nearly $1 billion set aside to rebuild the business base of South Central Los Angeles subsequent to the Rodney King disturbances in April 1992.

This does not allow for flexibility in response and puts too much emphasis on securing external federal funds. Although federal policies are usually explicit, local policies are usually understood implicitly as background assumptions. Nonetheless, few planners would have difficulty in recognizing local industrial, labor, and enterprise policies if they were stated explicitly. In declining areas, firms close or gradually reduce operations in older, less profitable plants. This strategy, of course, is the mirror image of the industrial cycle for growing areas. Local communities can accept the risks associated with corporate modes of decision making and investment behavior, or they can develop their own strategies to deal with corporate decision making. By extension— although it is increasingly contested in most localities—the acceptance of risk involved with corporate market-driven decisions implies that corporations can move such plants and reinvest elsewhere without implied community obligations. Labor force impacts will be borne primarily by relocated workers and their families and indirectly by other workers in businesses whose employment depends on local wage purchasing power. Loss of wages, psychological and physiological distress, higher tax burdens, greater social program expenditures, and continued obligations to amortize industrial infrastructure are included in the costs that all workers in the community ultimately bear.

Development activities are clearly implied by the term *impact planning*. The typical model is a program brought on by sudden, unexpected plant closures and similar employment activity. Development policies and planning in this approach are formed in order to deal with the local impacts of necessary— but equally uncontrolled—acts of corporate mobility. The programs associated with such policies are generally targeted to the real long-term needs of the community.

Two consequences arise from planning solely for impact effects. First, because they rely on national and state programs in response to these needs, planners pay less attention to efforts to plan for the coherent development of their local economies. Directives that specify criteria for triggers, targets, and related aspects of program grant seeking displace thoughtful planning. Second, the planner's role in redeveloping a local economy is jeopardized when federal funds are withdrawn (as they often are), when localities can no longer afford the costs of standard impact program models, or when the economic development planners have no alternative style of planning to guide them.

Contingency Planning (Interactive)

Contingency planning is an emerging approach that grows out of the ineffectiveness of impact planning in declining areas and from awareness that planning must anticipate impacts rather than react to them. As plant shutdowns and adverse economic impacts increase, and as civic leaders come to recognize the scale of the problem, some have questioned the assumptions behind the reactive posture of the impact-planning model. Because impact planning responds to episodes of economic distress only *after* they happen, actions taken seldom fit into an overall plan for the area. Moreover, efforts to mitigate these impacts are primarily devised to reduce the effects of corporate relocation. Some local officials have now begun to question their past responsiveness to corporate needs.

Repeated episodes of plant closures, bank failures, and real estate debacles have altered the perspective of local officials toward economic development planning. Contingency planning anticipates the worst and best possible outcomes. It can help mobilize an area's resources and inherent capabilities to deflect or accommodate impacts brought on by external forces.

Contingency planning also assesses the strength of all economic sectors and anticipates prospects for plant shutdowns, plans potential economic redevelopment projects, and provides community organizations and leaders with the information necessary to initiate local actions. To carry out these tasks effectively, such planning needs the direction of a local economic development organization or an existing municipal planning and development department. The change of emphasis requires impact program planners to move beyond their grant-writing skills. They must now apply practical knowledge of how their local economy actually operates, analyze key elements of that economy, and design both economic development projects and policies that can be implemented effectively.

Under the contingency planning model, local policies toward industry, labor, and enterprises would respond to local need. Local development policy would attempt to stabilize industrial sectors with the long-term goal of protecting the locality's economic base. Local economic development planning would be responsible for estimating an area's "sustainable" level of industrial activity. Knowing the structure and linkages among the full complement of remaining industries and their likely tenure, as well as new industrial investment potential and the total need for local resources that can realistically be provided, planners would be expected to help local officials devise industrial stabilization policies geared to the realities of the situation.

Worker buyouts, employee stock option plans, producer cooperatives, worker–community enterprises, community development corporations, and other recent innovative efforts to stabilize job-loss economies are worthy of close examination. Many of these approaches require early public involvement in the planning, financing, and implementation phases. Local labor and enterprise policies should be established *before* the need arises. Here again, economic development requires the study of conditions and circumstances under which others have successfully stabilized local economies and prepared contingency plans for planners' active involvement in each of the phases.

The development activities associated with contingency planning include many of those discussed previously for recruitment and impact planning. But within the contingency planning style of economic development, these activities tend to be community initiated. It might be said that contingency planning, as a style, began to emerge only after community-initiated efforts demonstrated a clear need for them. Established first as a device for disadvantaged groups to exercise economic power in otherwise strong local economies, community economic development has gone beyond its early concerns to include worker- and community-initiated responses to plant shutdowns.

Strategic Planning (Proactive)

Strategic planning is the most appropriate approach for all communities. This is a future-oriented approach that builds a local economy on the basis of local needs. As used here, a dictionary definition of *strategic*—minus its military sense—provides all the essential elements: "Utilization of all of [a locality's] forces, through large-scale, long-range planning and development to ensure [success]."

To help ensure the successful development of a stable and prosperous economy, localities adopt a *long-range* view of economic development. This posture avoids the problems occasioned by rapid, almost haphazard growth so prevalent in growing areas. It also allows an area time to organize its capacity to plan for economic development and to accommodate desirable expansion of the economic base. Studying lessons learned the hard way in other places is well worth the time, even if local business leaders become a bit impatient with this deliberate approach. A long-term view fosters open discussion and full consideration of plans and policies that affect all segments of the community.

Strategic planning also necessarily entails a *large-scale* effort to deploy available resources. This does not necessarily mean heavy doses of local government expenditure or large state government subsidies—in fact, it could mean reducing current expenditures from all sources and lowering the risks of heavy long-term public and individual costs. The term *large-scale effort* implies that economic development becomes a long-term objective for all ongoing local community governance functions. The full set of regulations, tax policies, public works, and local government program expenditures is framed with long-term economic development objectives firmly in mind. A strategic view of planning would put economic development specialists at the focal point of budgets, tax policies, public procurement, expenditure patterns, and public finance. A local economic planning unit or development board would implement strategic management, targeting conflicting policies and areas with no direction. The strategic style of planning thus boils down to doing the everyday business of local government with one additional long-term objective firmly in mind: economic development.

Finally, the enterprise types to be developed are selected on the basis of the community needs and resources rather than on the availability of opportunities.

In this respect, nearly all actions subject to local decision making would favor no particular enterprise form. Thus, corporations, franchise businesses, small businesses, cooperatives, community–worker enterprises, and all other potential forms of economic enterprise would find themselves on an equal footing with respect to local economic development. Such a policy will doubtless require actions by localities to reduce favored treatment of some enterprises and to increase it for others.

The intervention model proposed here is dependent on publicly initiated development. Success comes from many public actions toward economic development, sophisticated strategic planning within appropriate departments and agencies, and integrated policy positions on the part of major actors. There is evidence that localities are considering the adoption of some of these features, but we know of no place implementing a fully developed version of strategic economic development.

Example of Proactive Strategic Planning

In 2002, the City of Paducah, Kentucky, established an innovative Artist Relocation Program to revitalize one of the community's oldest neighborhoods, Lowertown, which is adjacent to its downtown. The program has since attracted more than 80 artists from cities ranging from Los Angeles to New York to relocate to this northwest Kentucky town of 25,000. Its success can be attributed to the creative advertising campaign that targets arts publications and an incentives program that focuses on encouraging ownership and rehabilitation of existing structures. The available incentives include 100% financing for purchase and rehabilitation work, a 30-year fixed loan rate of 7%, free lots for new construction, and up to $2,500 for architectural or other professional services. Also key to the program's success are Lowertown's zoning regulations, which allow gallery owners to live and work in the same structure. Since the program's start, total private investment has been approximately $28.4 million, at a public sector expense of only $2.6 million. Thanks to a growing tourism industry focused on this new arts district, Paducah estimates potential sales are $20 million and growing (Barnett, 2007).

The program has also had a transformative physical impact on the Lowertown neighborhood. Figure 5.1 shows "before" and "after" pictures of some redevelopment projects funded by the Artist Relocation Program.

Features of Local Economic Development Planning

Local economic development planning is based on a number of key concepts that are still unfolding because the direction of the process is not yet fixed. Meanwhile, local economic development, as an area of practice, remains a

Figure 5.1 Before and After Images of Rehabilitated Properties in Paducah's Lowertown Neighborhood

Source: Photographs reprinted with permission from the City of Paducah.

collection of historical activities and reactions to current circumstances that guide its course. Although it is not a recognized area of government activity—like planning and zoning or even city administration—some local economic development practitioners work for local government in development departments. Others are associated with chambers of commerce or industrial development or attraction offices, and still others are employed by neighborhood- and community-based organizations.

Even though circumstances associated with local economic development are still quite diverse, the following salient features are truly developmental and, thus, important for all planners to consider.

Targeting Zones of Action

This central idea recognizes a geography of employment and economic distress. There is therefore a need to direct resources, concern, and energy to specific localities, irrespective of what macroeconomic or social policies are pursued. Local economic development programs are designed to intervene in the right place at the right time, affecting both people and place, irrespective of political boundaries.

Building Community-Level Institutions for Development

Locally relevant institutions and organizations can traverse political, economic, and social barriers in both the public and the private sectors in order to promote development. These institutions are inclusive, bringing together community actors who can effect change. Their mandate is to locate the capital necessary to combine with existing resources as the base for economic development.

Expanding Local Ownership

Creating new businesses or retaining existing ownership in a community is important because local firms form the base for development headquarters and use local resources, both human and physical, in their operations. In essence, they are usually good community citizens and contribute to the area's progress.

Merging the Resources of the Social Welfare System

Public social welfare is both the bane and boon of depressed communities. Although it provides an immediate shock absorber for the disadvantaged, it can also create a cycle of dependence. Corrective measures attempt to merge welfare and job skills formation into the same projects—for example, by using welfare payments as wage supports or involving recipients in various economic development programs. Social welfare also comes in the form of nonprofit organizations that provide a wide range of programs, including language and skills development, housing, and psychological care and drug treatment. When used in a positive manner, these resources can stimulate increased local economic activity. For example, simply using existing buildings to house these services may generate new foot traffic or create more security for an area.

Linking Employment and Economic Development Policies and Programs

One goal of local economic development is to diversify employment options within the local economy. Public resources can be used to improve the link between jobs available and people available to work. There will never be a perfect match, but there can be better matches.

Building Quality Jobs

Attracting firms is not always equivalent to improving circumstances in the community. It is important to determine which jobs "fit" the local populace while offering opportunities to increase skills to competitive levels, both currently and in the future. As an intervention in the market system, local economic development thus increases the potential for secure jobs, which in turn stabilizes the community, both economically and socially.

Public–Private Venturing

The hallmark of the U.S. experience in local economic development— whether in government or in the neighborhood—is the combining of the resources of the public sector and the private sector in just the correct balance to attain objectives neither could attain alone.

Conclusion

In sum, the circumstances and character of U.S. political institutions have forged a new and unusual blend of processes and institutions to create a concept called *local economic development*. Its key feature is the recognition of the capabilities and resources of local people. It depends on the self-help mentality of the community.

The national government has been a stimulator, a leveler, a financial resource, and a provider of technical assistance to localities. The national government, for good or for worse, has engaged in industrial and national development policy only by default, when other approaches have not worked. It has continued to modify market mechanisms rather than create new ones. It has used the existing local institutional base in the form of local governments—and more recently neighborhood-level institutions—by increasing their political standing.

For their part, national and local governments have steadfastly believed that the cure to any problem in spatial or human allocations of development will result from correcting imperfections in the existing market system. It is these imperfections, both large and small, to which localities must attend in order to build or rebuild their economic base and, thus, to ensure long-term economic viability.

Putting It All Together: Creating a Local Economic Development Strategy (Part I)

Case Study

Many communities in the Southeastern United States have lost significant jobs in the textile sector due to the movement of manufacturing operations to international labor markets with much lower wages. It is highly unlikely that these jobs will ever return. Consequently, there are high unemployment rates in many of these communities due to a lack of alternative employment opportunities for the persons laid off from the low-skilled textile jobs. Many of these historic mill towns have since engaged in ongoing efforts to reinvigorate their local economies.

One high-profile example is that of Kannapolis, North Carolina. In 2003, the economies of Kannapolis and its neighbor Concord were devastated when Pillowtex closed and, as a result, more than 3,000 jobs were lost. Now, thanks to the vision and generosity of David H. Murdock, owner of Castle & Cooke, Inc., and Dole Food Company, Inc., the community will soon become home to the approximately $1 billion North Carolina Research Campus (Textile Plant Closings and Layoffs, 2007).

Textiles is not the only U.S. manufacturing subsector to experience significant job losses, but there are others that, thus far, have not succumbed to the pressures destroying most of the U.S. textiles industry. These manufacturing sectors, particularly the "high-tech" sectors, are expected to be a continued source of job growth in the United States. The most promising sectors are those that rely on innovation and a higher-skilled workforce. Because the expected earnings for the U.S. workforce will likely never be able to compete with the low wages of international labor markets, this country will best be able to maintain a healthy economy if its current and future workforce has a skills-based competitive advantage.

The region of West Central Georgia is another example of a historic textile-dependent local economy. It is a 10-county region that is adjacent to the Alabama border; West Central Georgia reaches into the Atlanta metropolitan area (two of the counties are within the U.S. Census Bureau-defined metropolitan statistical area of Atlanta). The regional economy can be divided into three distinct subregions: Atlanta Area (Carroll and Coweta); Rural Area (Butts, Heard, Lamar, Meriwether, and Pike); and Textile Area (Spalding, Troup, and Upson). Troup is home to LaGrange, the largest city in the region, with 27,652 people in 2006 (U.S. Census Bureau, 2007).

The following are a few of the region's demographic factors of note:

- As illustrated in the map in Figure 5.2, the textile subregion (and the rural county of Meriwether) has had stagnant population growth compared with national growth rates.
- The region's population is diversifying, with a fast-growing Hispanic/Latino population and a proportionally larger Black/African American population than nationally.
- The region's population is older than average, as measured by the percentage of the population in the over-45, over-65, and over-85 age categories.
- A high percentage of the region's population is without a college education or even a high school diploma.
- Educational attainment is particularly low in the historic textile community of Thomaston in Upson County. (U.S. Census Bureau, 2007)

The region has had a number of job losses, many of which can be attributed to the textiles industry and its impact on other businesses in the regional
economy. Between 1997 and 2007, the region lost a total of 4,870 jobs due to
textile plant closings. The closing of Thomaston Mills alone resulted in 1,955
jobs lost in Upson County, 150 lost in Spalding County, and 145 lost in Pike
County. Westpoint Steven's closing resulted in 1,550 jobs lost in Troup County
(Textile Plant Closings and Layoffs, 2007).

There have been facility closings in other business sectors, but on a much
smaller scale than the textile losses. Recent nontextile plant closings have included
the 347-employee Cooper-Standard Automotive facility in Spalding County, the
308-employee Inflation Systems facility in Troup, and the 270-employee Nacom
Corporation facility in Spalding (Business Layoff/Closure Listing, 2007).

Textiles remain a component of the regional economy, with carpet manufacturer Milliken & Company one of the region's largest employers. Additional
large employers include Walmart, Southwire Company (manufacturer of wire
and cable products), Tanner Medical Center, and the University of West Georgia
(West Central Georgia Local Workforce Area Labor Profile, 2007).

Figure 5.2   Population Growth Rate, 1997–2006.

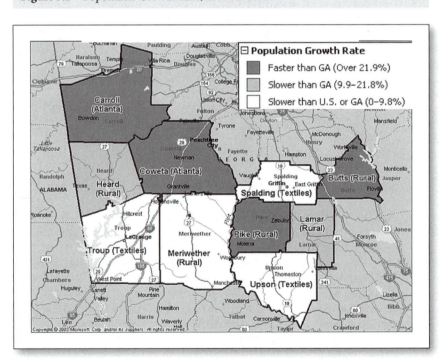

Source: U.S. Census Bureau, 2007.

The area's future has begun to look more hopeful, due in large part to the strengths of the Columbus, Georgia, economy, which is immediately south of the West Central region. Columbus is home to the U.S. military base Fort Benning (about 14,000 civilian employees once its planned expansion is complete; *Demographics*, 2007) and the national headquarters of insurance provider AFLAC (about 6,000 employees once its planned expansion is complete; *Demographics*, 2007). In 2009, a new 2,500-employee Kia auto manufacturing plant will open (*Valley Partnership Newsletter*, 2007).

Benefits of Columbus's growth are being felt in West Central Georgia from LaGrange to Thomaston. Numerous counties are working on spec buildings, hoping to entice Kia's suppliers and others to locate in the area. Pike County attributes its successful attraction of a Frito-Lay distribution center to the community's $700,000 infrastructure upgrade at its business park (West Central: Riding the Wave, 2007). In 2006, the Bank of Upson completed a $5 million expansion and the Upson Regional Medical Center completed its own $16 million expansion and renovation.

Putting It All Together: Creating a Local Economic Development Strategy

The economic future of West Central Georgia is hopeful, but the region continues to face the impact of job losses and an unemployed workforce skilled for textiles-based employment.

The West Central Georgia region case is intended to give you a chance to review the first four chapters of the book. You should read the case along with the theories and concepts of local economic development discussed in the four chapters. Based on your reading and understanding of the material, determine the following:

1. What are the national and international economic forces at work in Georgia's West Central region? How did they arise and what implication(s) do they have for the future of the community?

2. Who are the important actors in the economy of West Central Georgia?

3. What are West Central Georgia's assets and how do you propose to use them in building an economic development strategy for this region?

4. What is the role of government with respect to West Central Georgia? Consider all levels of government: local, state, and federal.

5. What planning approaches seem to be at work in West Central Georgia, if any? Explain why you think so.

6. Describe the economic planning approach you propose instead.

7. Within your economic development plan, what role should the local governments in West Central Georgia play?

References and Suggested Readings

Barnett, Tom. Director, Planning Department, City of Paducah. Interview with Dana King, December 10, 2007.

Beed, Thomas, and Robert Stimson, eds. 1985. *Survey Interviewing: Theory and Techniques.* Sydney, Australia: Allen and Unwin.

Bendavid-Val, Avrom. 1974. *Regional Economic Analysis for Practitioners.* New York: Praeger.

Bergman, Edward. 1981. *Citizen Guide to Economic Development in Job Loss Communities.* Chapel Hill, NC: Center for Urban and Regional Studies.

Business Layoff/Closure Listing. 2007. Georgia Department of Labor. Accessed November 17, 2007 from http://www.dol.state.ga.us/Access/Service/WarnIDListing

Butler, Lorna, and Robert Howell. 1980. *Coping With Growth: Community Needs Assessment Techniques.* Corvallis: Oregon State University, Western Rural Development Center.

Demographics. 2007. The Valley Partnership. Accessed November 17, 2007 from http://www.thevalleypartnership.com/demo.aspx#major_employers

Isard, Walter. 1975. *Introduction to Regional Science.* New York: Prentice Hall.

Jensen, Rodney Charles, T. D. Mandeville, and Neil D. Karunaratne. 1979. *Regional Economic Planning.* London: Croom Helm.

Kemp, Roger. 1992. *Strategic Planning in Local Government.* Chicago: American Planning Association Press.

Mahood, T., and A. Ghosh, eds. 1979. *Handbook for Community Economic Development.* Sponsored by the U.S. Department of Commerce, Economic Development Administration, Washington, DC. Los Angeles: Community Research Group of the East Los Angeles Community Union.

Sokolow, Alvin, and Julia Spezia. 1990. *Political Leaders as Entrepreneurs? Economic Development in Small Communities.* Economic Research Service: Rural Development Report no. 77. Washington, DC: U.S. Department of Agriculture.

Textile Plant Closings and Layoffs. 2007. National Council of Textile Organizations. Accessed November 17, 2007 from http://www.ncto.org/closings/NC.html

U.S. Census Bureau. 2007. *State and County Quickfacts.* Accessed November 18, 2007 from http://quickfacts.census.gov/qfd/states/13/13293.html

Valley Partnership Newsletter. 2007. Vol. 1, no. 3 (Fall). Accessed November 17, 2007 from http://www.columbusgachamber.com/ED/2007fall/#Kia

West Central Georgia Local Workforce Area Labor Profile. 2007. Atlanta: Georgia Department of Labor.

West Central: Riding the Wave. 2007. *Georgia Trend,* April. Accessed November 17, 2007 from http://explorer.dol.state.ga/mis/profiles/WIAs/wia08.pdf

6

Introduction to Analytical Methods for Local Economic Development Planning

Successful economic development planning is based on a solid analytical framework that accurately describes the local economic context, including the identification of groups that have special needs; the local resources available to address these needs; and the place of the community in the larger regional, state, national, and global context. The national economy is a composite of all the local economies within it, whether they are urban or rural, large or small, growing or declining. As we noted in Chapter 3, economic *development* occurs when a community's standard of living can be preserved and increased through a process of human physical development that is based on principles of equity and sustainability. The economic development planning process begins by analyzing the current economic conditions and capacities of the community.

Information and Analytical Requirements for Local Economic Development Planning

Economic development planning and implementation requires analyses across a wide range of categories that make up the local economy. These analyses can be descriptive, predictive, or evaluative. From descriptive analyses, the community can determine how its economy is faring relative to its position in the past or to its current position as measured against development goals that may have been set or measured against other referent economies (for example, the nation or a similar-sized country for which it competes for resources). Descriptive analyses are also often used for marketing purposes—that is, to provide information that can aid in attracting firms, major development projects, employers, employees, and residents.

Predictive analyses in economic development often take the form of impact or causal analysis. This type of analysis seeks to assess what the impacts of growth or development will be on the local economy but can be extended to a wider set of community concerns. For example, Edwards (2007) outlines a Development Impact Analysis that identifies anticipated economic, fiscal, environmental, social, and transportation-related impacts from specific development projects. Within this grouping, fiscal and socioeconomic impact analyses are most commonly used for economic development. Fiscal impact analysis estimates the impact of a particular development project on the costs and revenues of the local government units that will provide services to the development. Socioeconomic impact analysis assesses how development changes community demographics, demands for housing, retail and other services, levels of employment and income, as well as the aesthetic quality of the community (Edwards, 2007).

Much of what is labeled "impact analysis" specifically focuses on building and land development associated with new economic development activities. It is only over the last three decades or so that fiscal impact analysis has been practiced. A longer-term focus of causal economic development analysis (particularly as it intersects urban and regional analysis) has specifically been on forces affecting change in employment, since these in turn can create changes in population, migration, regional income, and a host of related phenomena (Isard et al., 1998).

Evaluative analysis seeks to determine how well specific goals of economic development planning efforts are being met, as well as to gauge shifts in economic development conditions. For example, have recent employment and business additions lessened or widened existing inequality in earnings? Have they significantly altered the cost of living? Did public investments in a specific industry cluster strategy lead to the creation of new firms and jobs, create more high-skilled jobs and higher average wages, or increase tax revenues? Of the three areas of economic development analyses, it is performed the least. In part, this is because rigorous evaluations require a control or comparison group to demonstrate that the economic development strategy or program implemented actually created results that would not have occurred on their own. It is difficult and expensive to create such comparison groups. Other reasons for lack of economic development evaluation have also been cited, including the fact that those paying for the evaluations are typically not the beneficiaries of the economic development program, and the suggestion that program administrators can be fearful of the consequences of a negative evaluation (Bartik and Bingham, 1993).

Each of the three areas of economic development analyses warrants substantial study on its own. Scholars in a wide range of academic disciplines engage in research that contributes to and advances these analytical areas, including (but not limited to) city and regional planning, demography, economics, geography, political science, and regional science. Serious students of local economic development planning will go on to take coursework specifically in methods of economic development analysis. Much of the remainder of this chapter will be devoted to providing an overview of descriptive analyses, which are the first step in preparing a strategic economic development plan as well as in gaining any true understanding of how the local economy works. These descriptive analyses cover a range of substantive areas that can reveal a community's strengths and weaknesses for advancing its local economic development, such as demographics, economics, land use, infrastructure, real estate, and finance. Following our examination of these analyses, the chapter discusses four key methods of local economic development analysis: economic base, shift-share, input–output, and cluster.

Understanding an Economy's Strengths and Weaknesses

Economic development intervention requires a detailed analytical understanding of the strengths and weaknesses of the local economy, as well as the forces that are constraining or driving it. Local matters must also be placed in the context of external economic forces from around the globe. New technology, changing availability of natural resources, and trade and monetary policy, for example, all strongly influence local economic needs and opportunities. The first step in understanding the strengths and weaknesses of the local economy involves creating a descriptive profile. To begin, the economic development analyst must determine the appropriate unit of analysis—that is, what are the geographic boundaries of the local economy? Is it a legally defined city or county, or a subarea such as a neighborhood planning unit? At times, the geographic focus of economic development planning does not coincide perfectly with the legal or administrative unit for which data are available. Further, as McLean and Voytek (1992) observe: "The range of impact of economic activity almost never coincides with the jurisdictional boundaries of political units. Spillovers occur in both directions: the policy decisions of one jurisdiction may affect economic activity in adjacent areas, even as economic activity flows easily across jurisdictional lines" (p. 10).

The economic analyst must also choose the time period of analysis, understanding that determining whether the local economy is better or worse off currently than at some earlier point in time, as well as determining exactly how it has changed over a period of time, is affected by two cyclical phenomena.

The first is the national business cycle. Demand for certain goods and services that make up the national economy can temporarily shift due to shocks such as energy price increases, natural disasters, or supply bottlenecks. Since the national economy is made up of all subnational (i.e., local) economies, many smaller economic units such as cities will be affected by a slowdown or surge in the national economy. This is not to say, however, that all subnational economies are simply smaller but complete versions of the national economy. Indeed, the smaller the economy, the more limited or specialized it is compared with the national economy. The degree to which the subnational economy will experience the effects of the business cycle depends on the proportion of industry sectors it has that are affected by the cycle. Due to increasing globalization, we now see evidence of local economies and national economies being impacted by slowdowns and surges in the international economy.

This also holds true for the second cyclical phenomenon, which is long term and structural and is often called *long wave*. In this phenomenon, significant and permanent shifts in economic activity occur. These can be sectoral—such as the shift from manufacturing to services industries that has occurred since the 1970s—or, within manufacturing, the shift over the last century from steam to coal to electricity to microelectronics-based production processes. Structural shifts toward nanotechnology-based manufacturing activity are now occurring so, if efforts to advance sustainability are successful, we can expect major structural shifts away from carbon-based manufacturing processes and products and perhaps a true industrial revolution.

Structural shifts can also be perceived as geographical. For example, a regional or local economy in which economic activity was largely associated with one particular sector may decline if the new sector originates in another region. The region of origin may in turn experience exceptional growth. Further, increasing internationalization has led to shifts of economic activity in both manufacturing and services out of local economies across the United States and into rising economies such as China, Korea, and India.

In the next section, we discuss the major categories of analysis that will help economic developers understand how their local economies are situated within the larger economic, industrial, and international systems.

The Economic Profile

We begin by presenting in Table 6.1 the major categories of descriptive statistics that should be included in a local area's economic profile, providing examples of the specific data that can be incorporated under each category. These statistics are the minimum amount of information that should be gathered for the economic profile. How much more information should be included will depend in part on the specific needs of the community, as well as on the availability of information for the size of community under consideration. In general, the smaller the community or the less its geographic boundaries coincide with administrative or political boundaries, the more difficult it becomes to obtain detailed economic information from secondary sources.

Table 6.1   Components of the Economic Profile

1. Demographics

Population by age group
Population by ethnicity
Households
Net migration last five years
Workforce education attainment
  • Less than high school
  • High school
  • Some college
  • College
  • Graduate

2. Quality of Life

Climate (average temperature, snow/rainfall, sunny days)
Housing supply and prices
Workforce housing supply
Education
  • Spending per student
  • Student–teacher ratios
  • Achievement test results
  • High school graduation rate
  • Percentage going on to college
  • Higher education (vocational and university)
Health care (hospitals, outpatient clinics, physicians, dentists)
Crime rate
Culture
  • Museums, performing arts, sports teams, and events
  • Green space and recreational outlets

3. Income and Wages
Median earnings and income level Distribution by quintile

(Continued)

Table 6.1 (Continued)

Working poor

Proportion of jobs with health and retirement benefits

4. Labor Force Characteristics

A. Civilian labor force

Unemployment rate

Participation rate

- Male
- Female
- Ethnicity
- Total

Working outside county of residence

Median commute time

B. Industry

Goods-producing

- Natural Resources and Mining
- Construction
- Manufacturing

Service-providing

- Trade, Transportation, and Utilities
- Information
- Financial Activities
- Professional and Business Services
- Education and health Services
- Leisure and Hospitality
- Other Services
- Public Administration

C. Occupation

Management Occupations

Business and Financial Operations Occupations

Computer and Mathematical Occupations

Architecture and Engineering Occupations

Life, Physical, and Social Science Occupations

Community and Social Services Occupations

Legal Occupations

Education, Training, and Library Occupations

Arts, Design, Entertainment, Sports, and Media Occupations

Health Care Practitioner and Technical Occupations

Health Care Support Occupations

Protective Service Occupations

Food Preparation and Serving Related Occupations

Building and Grounds Cleaning and Maintenance Occupations

Personal Care and Service Occupations

Sales and Related Occupations

Office and Administrative Support Occupations

Farming, Fishing, and Forestry Occupations

Construction and Extraction Occupations

Installation, Maintenance, and Repair Occupations

Production Occupations

Transportation and Material Moving Occupations

Military Specific Occupations

5. Business Establishments by Industry Sector and Employment Size

By industry and function (headquarters, back office, branch plant, R&D)

New to the area

Expansions/new facilities

Downsizing/closing/layoff

6. International Linkages

Foreign-owned companies

U.S. companies with foreign branches

Foreign bank branches

U.S. banks with international departments

Foreign consulates

Import/export bookers

International education programs

7. Research Base

Corporate, nonprofit, university, government

8. Higher Education Resources

9. Transportation

Commercial airport

• Hub status, carriers, daily nonstops, largest cities served

Railroads

Motor carriers/trucks

(Continued)

Table 6.1 (Continued)

Ports
Foreign Trade Zone designation
Overnight express services
Mass transit
10. Utilities
Water and sewage, electric power, natural gas, telecommunications
11. Taxes
Corporate
Personal income
Sales/use
Machinery and equipment
Property
12. Land/Building Availability
Business parks (industrial, office, research, mixed use)
Commercially zoned land and buildings
Vacancy rates and average rents (warehouse, industrial, office class A–C)
Approval length and type of local permits
13. Environmental Regulations
Attainment status for federal air pollution regulations
Average permit approval time (air, water, hazardous waste)
Landfills
Recycling regulations and programs

Sources: Derived from authors' research and practice, International Council of Economic Development (IEDC); U.S. Bureau of Labor Statistics (BLS); McLean and Voytek (1992); and Edwards (2007).

Demographics

A community's demographic characteristics tell whether it is large or small, growing or declining (when gathered for two or more periods of time), and whether its population is homogenous or diverse. The age profile (usually analyzed in 5-year segments, or three broad segments of less than working age, working age—16 to 64 years, or retirement age—65 years and older) indicates whether the community has a good distribution of all age groups or one that is weighted more toward a young labor force or a retirement community. The implications for economic development goals and strategies will differ depending on the age profile. The education attainment levels of the workforce can provide an indication of how advanced the economic development strategy can be.

Knowing the age profile of the local population also helps an economic developer understand what is likely to happen if elderly people retire. For instance, in several large cities, analysts have noted that skilled machinists or tool and die makers were all largely the same age, having been trained just after World War II. Because the industry in these communities remained stable, today there are no trained apprentices ready to replace these very skilled workers as they retire. Such trades are often pivotal to the success of other firms, and communities need to be attentive to finding replacement workers for critical occupations that require years of training.

It is also important to be able to answer questions such as how much mobility is in the workforce. For example, are young people working locally or leaving to work elsewhere? After high school, are they going to nearby cities to work or to attend college? Or, as is the case with many rural areas, do they never return to their local area because there are few job opportunities for them there?

Local community economic development often utilizes annual or semiannual *population estimates* that include the number of people in an area between census periods. Births are recorded and added to the population. Births, deaths, and migration factors (e.g., new houses, change of address, utility services, school enrollment, licenses) are added or subtracted from census data to give an estimate of current population in an area. Small areas are summed and balanced with larger county and state estimates.

Because few localities have any basis on which to estimate future migration patterns, either into or out of their area, trend data are used instead. In many cases, 5- and 10-year migration trends, such as those estimated from housing and school data, are extrapolated for the next 20 to 50 years. Consequently, the short-term trends typically distort future patterns and result in projections that are misleading. Economic developers need to be cautious using these projections, validating information with knowledgeable city planners and officials who have independent information by which to evaluate population trends.

Demographics also include knowing more about the changing ethnic mix in an area. A strong influx of specific ethnic groups can bring new opportunities and challenges to the economic development professional. For example, in spite of initial location around the nation, Hmong refugees (from Cambodia and Laos) displaced by the Vietnam War have tended to concentrate in a relatively few places, such as in California's central valley and in New York, and Russian immigrants have found their way in largest numbers to Brooklyn,

New York, and West Los Angeles, California. In the San Gabriel Valley, east of Los Angeles, large numbers of migrants from Hong Kong and Korea have created a vibrant international community.

Finally, retirement complexes have been particularly attractive to rural communities. A retiree coming into a rural community after selling a house in an urban area not only brings considerable money to buy a new house but also brings social security and pension income. Often, this income greatly exceeds what would be brought into the community by good factory jobs. In short, the demographics of a community shape the local workforce and economy.

Quality of Life

Quality-of-life indicators are an important consideration in economic development because they influence the ability to retain and attract firms and employees. In general, firms in more advanced industry sectors and workers in more advanced occupations have higher quality-of-life expectations. Opportunities for quality housing, education, health care, and cultural opportunities are important factors in a firm's or worker's location decisions. Increasingly, the supply of workforce housing is being recognized as a factor in quality of life. Housing price increases outpaced those of earnings in most urban areas for several decades and led to a shortage of decent and affordable housing for many workers. This was particularly acute in five vital occupations that receive low to moderate wages: janitors, elementary school teachers, police officers, licensed practical nurses, and retail salespersons (Bell, 2002). As a result, police officers and nurses have been unable to live within their employing communities, which would allow them to respond most rapidly to emergencies; local schools have trouble staffing and maintaining adequate student–teacher ratios, and the level of service in retail businesses is compromised. All of these reflect negatively on the local economy and its prospects for advancing.

While the Great Recession that began in 2007 caused a decline in housing prices ranging from 30% to 50% or more throughout most of the nation, this did not eliminate the shortage of workforce housing for either renters or buyers. In most communities, financing has become more difficult to obtain for those who want to buy, and the rate of foreclosures has created greater pressures on the rental market due to displaced homeowners.

Income and Wages

The income and wage subcategory is key to understanding what the standard of living is in the local economy. And, as previously discussed in Chapter 3, improving standard of living is one of three objectives of local economic development planning. Earnings and income levels are examined separately because not all households in the economy have earnings, or earnings are not the sole source of income. The distribution of income and wages by quintile is a key indicator of the level of inequality in the local economy, the reduction of which is also one of the three objectives of local economic development planning. The working poor indicator is computed by determining the number of workers in the local economy with year-round, full-time employment whose annual wages do not bring them above the poverty line. This represents a failure in economic development that should receive priority attention. Lastly, "good" jobs are often defined as those that provide health and retirement benefits along with adequate earnings. The cost of health and retirement benefits is typically 25% or more above the worker's wages. If employees must pay for these out of their earnings, then their overall standard of living is reduced. Further, in the case of low-wage workers for whom it is a struggle simply to provide housing and basic goods, the inability to self-fund health insurance can lead to financial disaster when they experience serious health incidents.

Labor Force Characteristics

A key activity in local economic development planning is job creation. Earnings from employment remain the primary source of income for individuals to support themselves and their families, and earnings define the standard of living for the vast majority of individuals. As we shall discuss subsequently, the income generated from earnings is a key factor in determining the economic base of a local economy. Thus, characteristics of the labor force of a local economy are vital for determining its future, and strengthening them is an important economic development goal.

The labor force characteristics section of Table 6.1 is the most detailed because of the importance of this aspect of the local economy. We start with a basic understanding of the civilian labor force. While some local economies have a sizeable portion of their labor force employed by the government and the military, the reality is that local economic development planning efforts can do little, if anything, to shape these sectors, and thus they focus on the civilian labor force.

A low unemployment rate suggests a tight labor market that cannot accommodate new firms unless there is growth in the local labor market. Conversely, a high unemployment rate suggests there is hardship in the local economy and active economic development efforts are needed. It is important to determine whether the unemployment is associated with specific industry sectors and occupations. It is also important to determine whether the unemployment is associated with a national downturn in the business cycle or is specific to the local economic composition to which specific planning efforts can be directed.

A low labor force participation rate for a specific gender or ethnic group may suggest a lack of opportunity, systematic discrimination, and the presence of discouraged workers. The latter are those who have given up on finding employment and, since they are no longer looking for work, they are no longer counted as being a part of the labor force.

Statistics on the proportion of the labor force that works outside the county of residence can be indicative of a lack of local job opportunities. The extent to which this is a valid issue will depend, in part, on the size of the county. For example, California, with a land mass of nearly 156,000 square miles, has only 58 counties. These counties can encompass many localities and local labor markets. On the other hand, Georgia, with a land mass of almost 58,000 square miles, has 156 counties. The small size of Georgia's counties suggests that many local labor markets will cross county lines. A more revealing indicator is "median commute time." Excessive commute times suggest a jobs–housing imbalance (whereby there are either not enough jobs in the worker's home community or there is a mismatch between local jobs and local residents' occupations) that should be a focus of economic development planning. The excessive commute times associated with jobs–housing imbalances not only lessen the quality of life of workers but also contribute to road congestion, air pollution, and deterioration in the community's quality of life.

The next subcategory under labor force characteristics is industry. All economic activity is classified into an industry sector. Industry composition varies across local economies, and these create different dynamics. Officially, an industry is defined as a group of establishments primarily engaged in producing or handling the same product or group of products or in rendering the same services. The industry listing in Table 6.1 is the official North American Industrial Classification System (NAICS) aggregated into the 11 sectors that the Bureau of Labor Statistics of the U.S. Department of Labor considers the relevant major groupings. NAICS falls under the responsibility of the federal Office of Management and Budget. NAICS and the U.S. Economic Classification Policy Committee recommend changes to the system (U.S. Bureau of the Census, online). NAICS uses a six-digit hierarchical coding system to classify all economic activity into 20 industry sectors, of which 5 sectors are mainly goods-producing sectors and 15 are entirely services-producing sectors (U.S. Bureau of Labor Statistics [BLS] 2012a). NAICS is revised every 5 years (in year 2 and 7 of each decade) in order to reflect ongoing changes in the industrial system. For example, the 2012 NAICS reduces the number of industry codes to 1,065 from the 1,175 used in 2007. It adds Alternative Energy Industries to the Utilities sector and reduces the number of 6-digit manufacturing industries by 108. All employment is classified into an industry sector, and likewise, all employment is classified into an occupation sector, the next subcategory in Table 6.1. There is also an official Standard Occupational Classification System (SOC) produced by the Bureau of Labor Statistics. Listed in Table 6.1 are the 23 major occupation groups. These 23 groups are an aggregation of 97 minor groups and 461 broad occupations. Further, for each of the 461 broad occupations, the SOC includes detailed occupation(s) requiring similar job duties, skills, education, or experience (BLS, 2012b). Occupation data within each industry group are also published. The SOC was revised in 2010 and is planned for another revision in 2018 and then every 10 years thereafter.

The official industry and occupation classification systems' revisions to reflect the emergence of new types of jobs and business activity can complicate trend analyses when economic activity is moved between categories from one system's revision to the next, or when the classification system reflects the addition of entirely new forms of economic activity or removal of obsolete activity. Official "crosswalks" are available that guide the analyst in comparing and combining data from previous and the latest classification systems. The NAICS was last revised in 2012, when changes were made to 7 of its 20 sectors. NAICS is actually a replacement for the previously used Standard Industrial Classification (SIC) system that was used from the 1930s to 1997. The renaming and revamping of the system occurred to allow standardized collection and analysis of economic activity for Canada, Mexico, and the United States as part of growing recognition of the increasing globalization and integration of these three economies. The SOC was last revised in 2010. The U.S. Department of Labor conducts ongoing studies to determine what new and emerging occupations will be taken into account in the next occupational classification system revision that is being considered for 2018. These occupations involve significantly different work than that which is found in current occupations. There were 24 new occupations included in the 2010 SOC revisions, including: Information Security Analysts, Web Developers, Community Health Workers, and Wind Turbine Service Technicians.

In a major development undertaken to help track the evolving green economy, since it cannot be done through NAICS or SOC, the Bureau of Labor Statistics began developing a new Green Jobs Classification in 2010. In 2011, it begin developing data on green jobs from establishment surveys of firms in 333 6-digit NAICS and will publish data annually for the nation, the states, and the District of Columbia that includes the number of jobs by industry and occupation engaged in producing green goods and services.

BLS defines green jobs as either:

A. Jobs in businesses that produce goods or provide services that benefit the environment or conserve natural resources

B. Jobs in which workers' duties involve making their establishment's production processes more environmentally friendly or use fewer natural resources. (BLS, 2012c)

Business Establishments

The fifth subcategory focuses on the characteristics of the business establishments found in the local economy. How many there are within a specific industry sector indicates whether the sector is competitively organized. The function of the business establishment provides clues as to its role in the overall economy. Those with research and development functions may be the sources of new innovation and companies. Those with headquarters functions may be longer lasting in the local economy than those with back-office and branch-plant functions.

International Linkages

Due to ongoing economic globalization, economic development planners should be familiar with and may want to encourage international linkages and support for export-oriented businesses within their local economies. Section 6 of Table 6.1 provides some key categories for consideration, but the analyst may want to go further, such as determining the extent to which locally produced goods and services are sold in international markets.

Research Base and Higher Education Resources

Sections 7 and 8 identify research activity that can become a source of innovation and new business creation. Beyond training the labor force, for which higher education was listed in the "Quality of Life" section, higher education institutions can also be a source of support for local economic development by contributing activities such as manufacturing extension partnerships, small business development centers, and business incubators.

Transportation, Utilities, Taxes, Land/Building Availability, and Environmental Regulations

The remaining five sections of the economic profile highlight traditional requirements and costs of doing business in a local economy. The transportation data indicate how connected the local economy is to other economic centers and how efficiently products and people can travel to and from the local economy. How influential the local cost of utility provision and the availability of specific utilities is to any business location decision is dependent on the production requirements of the business. For example, is it a business that uses large quantities of water in its production process, or does it rely on sophisticated telecommunication infrastructure to deliver an information-intensive service or product?

The subsection on taxes illustrates there is a range of taxes to which businesses and their employees can be subject. Taxation levels have traditionally been viewed as an issue of competitiveness in local economic development, though research results on how important they really are to business location decisions are mixed. The flipside to the issue is that too-low levels of taxation may indicate the locality is not investing sufficiently in physical and social infrastructure, and this can undermine long-term economic development.

The availability of land and buildings to house new and expanding business is a critical factor in local economic development. Communities that are built out (all land has been developed) or that have excess land but will not zone for commercial and industrial uses create disincentives for expanding existing businesses to stay or new businesses to locate in the community. In the business world, "time is money" such that lengthy building permit processes can raise the cost of doing business and serve as a barrier to economic development.

This issue is also pertinent in considering data for the last subsection on environmental regulations, which lists the kinds of environmental permits that businesses may have to secure, depending on their production processes. Difficulties in meeting the attainment status for federal air pollution regulations can become a major barrier to further economic development.

Landfills can be a significant issue in local economic development because some industries generate more waste byproducts than others, and those with hazardous waste byproducts are subject to rigorous (and costly) waste disposal regulations. Though there are some states and localities that consider operating landfills as an economic development activity, and they actually import waste from other localities to receive the revenue from disposal, the prevailing view is that landfills are costly to maintain safely, generate negative externalities for development surrounding them, and are to be minimized. One way in which disposal of industry waste can be minimized is through recycling regulations and programs. The most forward-thinking localities are promoting recycling as a way to minimize environmental pollution impacts as well as to promote economic development via the business and jobs that are created to reuse and recycle, as well as to create new products from waste (e.g., see Leigh and Patterson, 2006).

Building on Comparisons

Data for economic development analysis build on *comparisons* that look at a community in relation to someplace else that is a valid referent. Typically, planners compare the strengths and weaknesses of their zone of action (local, county, or multicounty) with a much larger area (a state, multistate region, or nation), depending on the size of the units. California and Texas, for example, are good references for communities within their states, but a community in Rhode Island or Vermont would better be compared with the New England region or the nation as a whole. As a result of comparison, planners may find that the local area has a higher proportion of electronics companies, or that its hospital and medical firms, while seemingly highly represented, in fact are actually below the number expected in ratio to areas like the state or region. In addition, local areas may discover that their unemployment rate is consistently above or below the same rate of the state or region, or that it changes differently over time. For example, some areas have rates that swing higher and lower than national cycles of unemployment, whereas other areas lag the national cycle, with unemployment peaking later and recovering more slowly.

Comparisons of a local area to its larger reference area must do more than simply count the employees or firms in each, because larger places would obviously have more firms or employees. The analytical task is to standardize the data with analytical tools that can account for the different sizes and scales of the various areas being compared. For example, economic developers use standard measures to compare areas in terms of average or per capita incomes (instead of total income), the unemployment rate (percentage of labor force not employed), the rate of small business formation (firms created as a ratio of all firms), or the number of doctors per thousand persons. In each of these cases, the economic factor of interest is standardized relative to the size of the place.

Data comparing local areas also need to be dynamic and show how change has occurred from one time period to another. This trend analysis describes how the local economy arrived at its present condition and projects what it may look like in the future, with and without intervention. Typically, economic development analysts look at change over periods from 5 to 10 years—long enough to show some dynamics, but short enough to capture local developments that are manageable by planning policy. The time period used is often dictated by the frequency of data publication of the relevant secondary sources of data such as the U.S. Census Bureau's Economic Censuses or American Community Survey. The selection of time schedules also seeks to take into account the effects of the business cycle. Data from several points of time show, for example, employment growth in certain industries, increases in unemployment rates, greater rates of female participation in the labor force, and the impact of inflation on real earning power.

Local economic planners need to combine professional statistical and quantitative analysis with an appreciation of the uniqueness of the local community. They should prepare for an analysis by first understanding gaps in a local area's analytical sophistication, need for data, or ability to use it. However, the analysis process frequently needs rethinking as *patterns* emerge—analysts learn more about the local economy and the community understands more about itself. Smaller communities often cannot support full-time economic development planning staff and thus seek the assistance of specialists who can assemble and help the community to understand relevant information as well as to develop an appropriate economic development planning process. Private economic development consulting firms, state and regional planning agencies, and university outreach centers may all be sources of economic development specialist assistance.

Gathering Available Descriptive Data

Data for local communities come from individual, government, and private sources, and each source has its strengths and weaknesses. The availability of this information is rapidly expanding, especially through Internet sources. Table 6.2 lists potential sources for the 13 categories of data suggested for the economic profile described earlier.

Table 6.2   Data Sources for Economic Profile

1. Demographic Characteristics
U.S. Bureau of the Census
Decennial Survey
American Community Survey
Local/Regional Planning Agency
2. Quality of Life
National Climatic Data Center
U.S. Bureau of the Census
National or Local Association of Realtors
State Department of Education or Public Instruction
Local School District
University System Office of the President
Federal Bureau of Investigation (FBI) Uniform
Crime Report for Locality
Local Business Directories
Local Medical Association

(Continued)

Table 6.2 (Continued)

Chamber of Commerce
Visitors Bureau
3. Income and Wages
U.S. Bureau of the Census
U.S. Bureau of Labor Statistics, National and Regional Offices
State Employment Security or Labor Departments
4. Labor Force Characteristics
BLS Local Area Unemployment Statistics
State Employment Security or Labor Departments
U.S. Bureau of the Census
County Business Patterns
Economic Census Geographic Area Series
Longitudinal Employer-Household Dynamics
Annual Survey of Manufacturers
5. Business Establishments by Industry Sector and Employment Size
Statistics of U.S. Businesses (U.S. Bureau of the Census)
Local Business Journals
Local and State Industrial/Economic Development Agencies
Local Surveys
6. International Linkages
USA Trade Online (U.S. Census Bureau)
Industry Trade Associations
Federal Reserve Board
7. Research Base
U.S. Patent and Trademark Office
Trade Associations
University Research Offices
8. Higher Education Resources
State University System Office of the President
Local Offices of University and Community College Presidents
Private College/University Offices of the President

9. Transportation
State Department of Transportation
U.S. Department of Transportation
Local Department of Transportation or Public Works
10. Utilities
State Utility Commission
Local Knowledge
11. Taxation
State Department of Finance or Revenue or Taxation
Local Office of Property Assessor
12. Land/Building Availability
National and Local Associations of Realtors
Commercial Real Estate Vendors
U.S. Census Bureau Residential Building Permits
13. Environmental Regulations
U.S. Environmental Protection Agency Envirofacts
State Environmental Agency
Local Government Environmental Departments

Local Agencies and Individuals

Already available in many communities is a vast array of existing data held by local planning or service agencies. There are also persons who have experienced the place in every conceivable way and from every conceivable angle—often over lengthy periods of time. People who live, work, and play in the community can be involved in contributing their knowledge and ideas to the local economic development planning process through community fact-finding techniques such as:

- personal interviews
- public hearings
- neighborhood meetings
- church, fraternal, and trade organizations
- press, radio, and television outlets
- existing reports, case studies, and feasibility studies

Beyond this, special efforts should be made to invite community leaders, as well as other interested and knowledgeable citizens, to participate in *advisory committees* and other formalized groups associated with the planning process. These people often reflect the collective thinking and awareness of many other citizens who have valuable perspectives or expertise but cannot actively participate.

Industrial Classifications

As referenced earlier, we use the North American Industrial Classification System (NAICS) to help us understand the multiplicity of parts in the economy. This system is the replacement for the Standard Industrial Classification (SIC) system that served for more than 60 years as the structure for the collection, aggregation, presentation, and analysis of the U.S. economy. An industry consists of a group of establishments primarily engaged in producing or handling the same product or group of products or in rendering the same services. NAICS uses a production-oriented conceptual framework, grouping establishments into industries based on the activity in which they are primarily engaged. Establishments using similar raw material inputs, similar capital equipment, and similar labor are classified in the same industry. In the switch from SICS to NAICS, a new Information sector was created that combined communications, publishing, motion picture and sound recording, and online services in recognition of the information-based economy. Manufacturing was restructured to account for new high-tech industries. A new subsector was created for computers and electronics, which includes reproduction of software. Eating and drinking places were transferred from the retail sector to a new Accommodation and Food Services sector. The distinction between the Retail and Wholesale sectors was changed to reflect the way each store conducted its business.

A key criticism of the old SIC system was that it did not reflect the growth in the economy of the service sector. The NAICS revision added nine new service sectors and 250 new service industries. NAICS has now been revised twice since its 2002 introduction in an effort to keep up with the nation's changing economy. Though the Census Bureau provides "crosswalks" to facilitate time series analysis when classification systems are revised, it is important to understand that the revisions from Standard Industrial Classification (SIC) to NAICS were so major as to hamper time series analyses for specific sectors.

Occupational Data

Revisions to the occupational classification system, like the industrial classification system, require the use of crosswalks to do time series analyses. However, unlike NAICS, the Standard Occupation Classification System (SOCS) is intended only for analyzing U.S. data.

SOCS data can be found in a number of public information sources. The U.S. Occupational Employment Statistics (OES) Program provides occupational employment and wage estimates by industry and across industries. State- and area-level data are provided by state Employment Security Agencies.

The Census Bureau publishes data on detailed occupations from the decennial censuses. Only aggregated data are published in paper form. Standard and customized tabulations of SOC data can be obtained through the Census Bureau's Web-based American Fact Finder site.

Biennially, the Bureau of Labor Statistics' Office of Employment Projections (OEP) publishes the *Occupational Outlook Handbook, Career Guide to Industries,* and *Occupational Projections and Training Data.* In addition, OEP publishes the *Occupational Outlook Quarterly* (www.bls.gov/soc/socguide.htm).

Census of the Population

Perhaps the most well-known source of economic data has been the U.S. Census, which collects data every 10 years. The census obtains from every household a small amount of data, such as age, race/ethnicity, gender, family, and a few housing items. Historically, about 1 in 20 households filled out a longer form that supplemented the personal data with an extensive bank of questions about many topics of interest to economic developers. The longer form reported on types of industry and occupation, income, education level, disabilities, and many other factors. The sample data were extrapolated to the entire population, but in areas with small populations, answers were aggregated to protect the confidentiality of respondents. Information from the long form guides the administration of federal programs and the distribution of federal dollars.

A new survey, the American Community Survey (ACS), has been implemented to replace the decennial long form. Because long-form data collection occurs only once every 10 years, they soon become out of date. Planners and other data users are reluctant to rely on them for decisions that are expensive and affect the quality of life of thousands of people. The ACS is intended to provide the data communities need every year instead of once in 10 years. The American Community Survey includes around 3 million households and makes estimates of demographic, housing, social, and economic characteristics for every county in the United States. Smaller areas will also be covered in the ACS, but it will take several years to accumulate sufficient data.

Census data have many advantages. First, the census has had a fairly standard set of questions and categories as well as a consistent methodology over many decades, which allows good long-term perspectives, often valid for 50 or more years. Although the analyst must be attentive to changes in industry and occupational classifications, census data are still the best source for long-term trend analysis. Second, census data reflect a hierarchy of geography, with smaller areas accumulated into larger areas. The nation, states, regions, counties, cities, towns, places, census tracts, and census blocks are some of the most important categories. In addition, data are provided for metropolitan areas, divisions, and other intermediary urban geographical sectors. Third, the widespread electronic availability of census data is permitting additional formats and estimated patterns. Thus, the census allows the widest geographical perspective.

However, the use of census data has certain limitations. First, census reports are based on where people live, not where they work. Although the census does ask about commuting, these data are not directly comparable to data on place of employment, especially if a large number of people work outside the area under study. Second, the census is collected only once every 10 years, and is thus often out of date. Furthermore, it usually takes 2 years from the time the census is taken until data are available on items of interest to economic developers. Third, economic data from the census are from a sample, and confidentiality limits the availability of important data in small geographical areas. Finally, and most important, census data are less complete in poor neighborhoods, among ethnically diverse communities, and where the population is in flux. Many challenges have been made to the census counts in central cities, in small rural communities, and in places where there are many undocumented immigrants. Homeless people, for example, are substantially undercounted. In spite of the fact that census data are the best we have, it is important to recognize potential gaps in coverage.

The census also makes periodic specialized censuses of importance to economic developers. Every 5 years, the census surveys manufacturing businesses, agriculture, and governments. These specialized reports provide detailed information within their topic. Even though this special census shows where manufacturing businesses are located, it does not include data on individual employees in each firm.

Employer Reports

Employers provide accurate, inclusive, and recurring reports as they get licenses and pay fees and taxes as part of their overall activities. These reports turn into data, which are collected by government agencies. Economic development planners are especially interested in two reports that all employers must make: quarterly payments for unemployment insurance to their state and social security deductions to the federal government. Thus, in the payment of these taxes, employers provide current and accurate data that can track the economy by specific industry SIC code in local areas.

As part of their unemployment insurance tax payments, all firms must report employment, payroll, and location, and their NAICS code is regularly checked. These detailed data are the backbone of the *Employment and Earnings Reports* produced by each state's employment security agency. These firm-level sources are reported not by where employees live but by where they work. Such data are excellent for coverage and are often available promptly to allow analysis of quarterly trends. In addition, many states are able to generate special reports based on particular geographical information (such as zip code) or showing detailed industrial categories (such as the fourth-digit level of the NAICS).

County Business Patterns data are collected from employer surveys as well as being obtained through administrative records on employers from the Social Security Administration, the Internal Revenue Service, and the U.S. Department of Labor. Like Employment and Earnings Reports, they are based on where people work, not where they live. As the name implies, County Business Patterns data provide data for the county level. More recently, however, these annually collected data have started to be published at the zip code level.

Government data series also rely on other specialized sources. For example, most states publish a report based on *sales tax collections*, which gives the dollars spent on taxable sales in counties or even cities by specific types of establishment. Depending on tax laws, taxable sales data may not include large parts of the retail sector (e.g., food or services that are not taxed, and most sales to businesses), but much retail analysis can rely on these data.

State income tax records are often analyzed both for business taxes and for individual income tax payments to provide information on earnings. *Agricultural data* are derived from crops planted, sales, and other information collected through marketing boards and reporting as part of inspections. Traffic monitoring leads to highway data on commuting and trucking. The purpose here is not to identify all the sources of data for economic development but to encourage planners to look for the data they need by identifying who might collect it for another purpose and then finding it.

Private Data

There has been a significant increase in private data sets that economic development analysts find useful. In some cases, these data sets are from public sources but are repackaged by private firms in a manner that makes them more useful for analysis. An example is the Business & Company Resource Center produced by the Gale Group. This is a subscription database that can usually be accessed at larger public and academic libraries. In other cases, a private data provider may be collecting data from businesses that it then processes and sells to customers. For example, Dun & Bradstreet provides privately generated data that are compiled and updated as part of its ongoing need to supply business credit information, such as the number of employees, sales, and the location of the firm. It provides data on privately held as well as small companies, unlike many other databases.

Private data have several advantages. First, confidentiality is less an issue with privately gathered data than with state or federal information. Several companies sell detailed data files on selected firms. Second, detailed geographical locations are available—even street addresses if needed. Third, special reports can be generated from the extensive data bank collected for sale to analysts and marketing firms who can pay the fee.

The limitations to private data sources are that the coverage is neither uniform nor exhaustive. For example, the only way a firm is listed in Dun & Bradstreet is if it requires a rating for credit. How serious a problem this is has been debated in the literature. Another limitation is that updates do not occur simultaneously. Dun & Bradstreet tries to make sure that every firm is updated every 3 years, but otherwise a firm's data are updated only when a new credit report is needed. And while publicly held firms that must report to the U.S. Securities and Exchange Commission can legally be liable for misrepresentation, there is no penalty for those that report to D&B.

There are other types of private data that can be useful for local economic development analysis, such as data on commercial or industrial real estate markets or trade association data that can help the analyst discern what kinds of challenges a locality's key businesses may be encountering or what potential exists for fostering greater clustering of a key industry.

Examining Analytical Techniques

There are at least five areas of analysis that the local economic development planner needs to understand:

1. What parts of the local economy are most valued by local residents and political leaders? How do the citizens see themselves compared with other communities?

2. What parts of the economy form the local economic base, accounting for the most substantial number of jobs and growth in wealth?

3. What parts of the local economy are growing most rapidly, forming jobs and generating opportunity? What can local leaders do about other parts that are declining?

4. How do changes multiply through the local economy? How does growth or decline in one part of the economy alter the other parts to which it sells or from which it buys?

5. What are the parts of the local economy that are most important because they are embedded in a strong and growing interdependent cluster of firms and related industries?

The answers to Questions 2 through 5 provide substantial insight into the economic system associated with every community. A version of this economic system is depicted in Figure 6.1. Healthy economies, as shown in the figure, export jobs, retain substantial income, and build internal linkages. Determining the size and performance of these economic relationships, as well as the community's ability to alter its relationship to other areas in the region, is the focus of the analytical techniques discussed in this chapter (Landis, 1985; Rochin, 1986).

The answers to Question 1 must come from primary data collection such as surveys, interviews, and focus groups. From our descriptive analyses using secondary data, we can gain insight into Questions 2 and 3. Further insight into Question 3, as well as into Questions 4 and 5, can be gained through additional analytical techniques. The remainder of this chapter will focus on the most commonly employed techniques.

Figure 6.1   Model of Local Economy

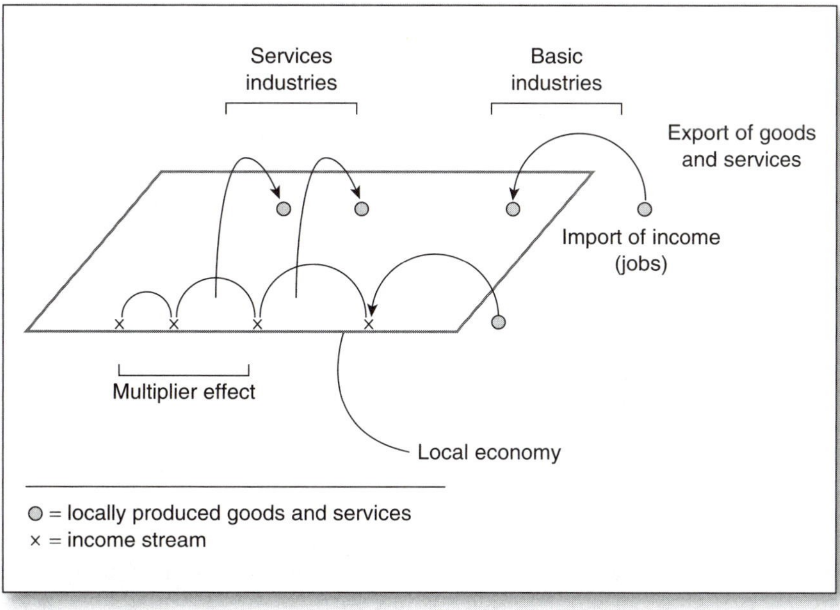

Source: Adapted from Agajanian (1987).

Economic Base Analysis as a Foundation for Economic Development Planning

Solid economic development planning hinges on an understanding of the factors that affect the level and growth of the local economy. These factors include how local firms meet the needs of people in their community and how these firms are shaped by external forces, such as markets for the export of local goods, imports, tourism, and even major changes in international trade (e.g., the rise or fall of the dollar relative to foreign currency). Every firm is part of an industry sector, and a local economy's industrial structure is the most fundamental factor that affects its growth.[1]

As McLean and Voytek (1992) have observed:

> The industries that are most crucial to local economic growth are those that produce goods and services sold outside the local economy, generating an inflow of income. These industries are known as an area's "economic base" or "export base." They generate the income that sustains the "local-serving" or "non-basic" sector of the economy—firms such as restaurants, grocery stores, automobile repair shops, laundries, and so on.

> In addition to exporting, local economies import goods and services that are demanded by local consumers and businesses but produced elsewhere. The extent and nature of a local economy's imports are also of interest for the analysis, since there may be opportunities to substitute locally produced goods and services for those being purchased from outside the area. (p. 60)

A simple economic base model can be depicted as:

Basic employment + Nonbasic employment = Total employment.

The principle of traditional economic base theory is that businesses that generate wealth should be targeted for attraction and nurtured with a higher priority than other firms. As Malizia and Feser (1999) have observed, the most common economic development strategy—industrial recruitment—is justified by economic base theory since the attraction of outside firms, which today can be manufacturing or service firms that export, will lead to increased demand for local firms. The interconnections between local serving and exporting firms of an economy and just how much export-based growth stimulates local-serving growth is most robustly analyzed via input–output analysis, a technique that is included in economic development methods courses and that we briefly discuss in this chapter. It is from input–output analysis that the most accurate estimates of multipliers are created. The concept of the multiplier is a much-focused-upon indicator in local economic development that is used to estimate how much change (for example, income, taxes, or jobs) will occur in the total local economy from an exogenous change in activity in the basic industries.

While economic base analysis has traditionally focused on industries as its unit of analysis, there has been something of a turn in local economic development analysis to focus on occupations as a driver of the economic base. This is particularly the case for occupations that are perceived to generate new forms of economic activity or fuel entrepreneurship. The Creative Class concept is one example of an occupation-centered economic base analysis.

In the next section, we discuss a simple-to-perform technique for analyzing the economic base that can be used to examine industrial or occupational structure. For simplicity of presentation, we use industry to describe the technique.

Location Quotients for Base Analysis

The location quotient is a technique used to identify the concentration of an industry sector in a local economy relative to a larger reference economy. Stated simply, an industry's share of the local economy is compared with the same share that industry has in the reference economy. The location quotient—sometimes called the concentration factor—is a static measure, picturing the economy at only one point in time. It does not say anything about whether an industry is growing or declining in importance relative to the local economy.

The location quotient is shown as a ratio between the percentage of employment in an industry locally to the percentage of employment in the same industry found in the state or nation being used as a reference. If the ratio of the local to the reference economy is greater than one, it means that the industry has a greater representation in the local area compared with the reference economy. If the ratio is less than one, however, the industry has a smaller representation. A location quotient (LQ) of 1.0 means that the local area and the reference economy have the same percentage of that industry in their respective economies. In economic base analysis, an LQ of 1 is interpreted as the local economy just meeting its needs for the products of that industry. An LQ less than 1 means the economy does not meet its needs internally. It is therefore considered local serving, and the locality may need to import the industry's products or services to fully meet its needs. On the other hand, an industry with a location quotient greater than 1 produces more than is needed locally, and the portion of the employment that leads to the LQ being greater than 1 is assigned to the locality's economic base that supports the economy as a whole. McLean and Voytek (1992) suggest that the analyst focus on industries with LQs greater than 1.25 or less than 0.75. Those with LQs of 1.25 or more are most clearly the export base industries whose further growth will stimulate the overall economy. Those with LQs less than 0.75 could also warrant focusing on because they offer opportunities for import substitution development strategies.

The standardized formula for depicting the location quotient is as follows:

$$LQ = \left(\frac{e_i}{e} \right) \div \left(\frac{E_i}{E} \right)$$

where

e_i = local employment in industry i

e = total local employment

E_i = national employment in industry i

E = total national employment

In essence, the LQ is an index of specialization. For example, if a rural locality has 10% of its local employment in the dairy industry and the state (the reference economy) has only 5% of its employment in dairy, the location quotient is the ratio of the first to the second, or 2.0 (i.e., divide the local percentage (10) by the reference percentage (5), to get the answer of a LQ of 2.0). But if an urban area only has 1% of its employment in dairy, the location quotient will be 0.2 (i.e., divide 1 by 5 to get 0.2). In the first case, the LQ of 2.0 indicates that the dairy industry constituted twice its expected share of the local economy, whereas in the second, the LQ of 0.2 indicates that the local share was only 20% of what would be expected if the local area was like the reference economy.

Analysts typically calculate location quotients for detailed industry classifications at the two-digit or greater levels. The danger in using one-digit industry data, such as for agriculture, is that either all or none of a sector's employment could be erroneously assigned to the economic base.

In Table 6.3, location quotients are presented for three metropolitan areas in the United States: Atlanta, Indianapolis, and Seattle. We will look for industry sectors with location quotients greater than 1.5 to get a sense of what are the greatest industry specializations in these three metro areas. Beginning with Atlanta, we can see that its greatest specialization is in air transportation (NAICS 481), with a very large LQ of 4.94. This correlates with the fact that the region's Hartfield-Jackson Airport is a major hub for both passenger and cargo transport. However, Atlanta also ranks high in what can more generally be called the information economy. It has location quotients of 2.37 in NAICS 517—Telecommunications. Additionally, it has a large LQ for NAICS 515—Broadcasting, except Internet. While Atlanta is the well-known home of CNN, if that were its only firm in this NAICS sector, we would not be able to calculate an LQ due to data disclosure rules. However, there are also a number of other broadcast firms in the metro area.

Three different areas of specialization are revealed in the Indianapolis metropolitan area. First, its economy is more specialized in what is often called

Table 6.3 Total Employment and Location Quotients for Two-Digit and Select Three-Digit NAICS Sectors, 2010 Quarterly Census of Employment and Earnings

Industry by Two-Digit and Select Three-Digit NAICS	U.S. Total	Atlanta-Sandy Springs-Marietta, GA MSA 1,816,730		Indianapolis-Carmel, IN MSA 708,417		Seattle-Tacoma-Bellevue, WA MSA 1,363,645	
		Jobs	LQ	Jobs	LQ	Jobs	LQ
Total, all industries	106,201,232						
NAICS 11 Agriculture, forestry, fishing and hunting	1,146,962	1,778	0.09	1,786	0.23	4,570	0.31
NAICS 114 Fishing, hunting and trapping	8,205	17	0.12	ND	ND	1,122	10.65
NAICS 21 Mining, quarrying, and oil and gas extraction	651,631	1,020	0.09	697	0.16	702	0.08
NAICS 22 Utilities	551,287	10,524	1.12	3,995	1.09	1,962	0.28
NAICS 221 Utilities	551,287	10,524	1.12	3,995	1.09	1,962	0.28
NAICS 23 Construction	5,489,499	87,263	0.93	36,654	1.00	77,687	1.10
NAICS 236 Construction of buildings	1,226,917	18,086	0.86	8,621	1.05	18,068	1.15
NAICS 238 Specialty trade contractors	3,451,459	56,299	0.95	23,461	1.02	50,312	1.14
NAICS 31-33 Manufacturing	11,487,496	140,959	0.72	82,271	1.07	165,556	1.12
NAICS 312 Beverage and tobacco product manufacturing	183,414	1,706	0.54	1,931	1.58	1,931	0.82

(Continued)

Table 6.3 (Continued)

Industry by Two-Digit and Select Three-Digit NAICS	U.S. Total	Atlanta-Sandy Springs-Marietta, GA MSA		Indianapolis-Carmel, IN MSA		Seattle-Tacoma-Bellevue, WA MSA	
NAICS 313 Textile mills	119,385	2,045	1.00	ND	ND	51	0.03
NAICS 314 Textile product mills	119,145	4,267	2.09	541	0.68	1,305	0.85
NAICS 322 Paper manufacturing	392,853	6,773	1.01	2,242	0.86	2,365	0.47
NAICS 323 Printing and related support activities	485,523	9,582	1.15	5,604	1.73	5,604	0.90
NAICS 325 Chemical manufacturing	785,283	9,297	0.69	14,730	2.81	14,730	1.46
NAICS 326 Plastics and rubber products manufacturing	623,259	11,826	1.11	2,600	0.63	4,015	0.50
NAICS 327 Nonmetallic mineral product manufacturing	368,097	7,036	1.12	2,738	1.12	4,756	1.01
NAICS 332 Fabricated metal product manufacturing	1,276,933	10,048	0.46	10,257	1.20	9,633	0.59
NAICS 333 Machinery manufacturing	991,039	7,249	0.43	6,763	1.02	6,763	0.53
NAICS 336 Transportation equipment manufacturing	1,327,169	13,451	0.59	13,187	1.49	83,253	4.89
NAICS 339 Miscellaneous manufacturing	566,479	6,696	0.69	6,499	1.72	6,956	0.96
NAICS 42 Wholesale trade	5,466,463	127,674	1.37	39,183	1.07	75,991	1.08

Industry by Two-Digit and Select Three-Digit NAICS	U.S. Total	Atlanta-Sandy Springs-Marietta, GA MSA		Indianapolis-Carmel, IN MSA		Seattle-Tacoma-Bellevue, WA MSA	
NAICS 423 Merchant wholesalers, durable goods	2,718,043	70,174	1.51	25,401	1.40	38,827	1.11
NAICS 424 Merchant wholesalers, nondurable goods	1,935,875	37,010	1.12	10,899	0.84	24,690	0.99
NAICS 425 Electronic markets and agents and brokers	812,545	20,490	1.47	2,884	0.53	12,475	1.20
NAICS 44-45 Retail trade	14,481,324	242,687	0.98	88,245	0.91	165,664	0.89
NAICS 441 Motor vehicle and parts dealers	1,630,802	28,995	1.04	10,637	0.98	18,060	0.86
NAICS 442 Furniture and home furnishings stores	436,314	8,111	1.09	2,886	0.99	5,795	1.03
NAICS 443 Electronics and appliance stores	502,036	8,996	1.05	3,339	1.00	5,381	0.83
NAICS 448 Clothing and clothing accessories stores	1,379,749	25,902	1.10	7,700	0.84	15,312	0.86
NAICS 451 Sporting goods, hobby, book and music stores	604,441	10,761	1.04	3,301	0.82	9,200	1.19
NAICS 452 General merchandise stores	2,988,606	51,232	1.00	20,376	1.02	32,650	0.85
NAICS 453 Miscellaneous store retailers	772,389	12,774	0.97	5,756	1.12	10,712	1.08
NAICS 454 Nonstore retailers	414,244	4,640	0.65	3,513	1.27	10,010	1.88
NAICS 48-49 Transportation and warehousing	3,943,659	105,891	1.57	43,987	1.67	53,143	1.05

(Continued)

Table 6.3 (Continued)

Industry by Two-Digit and Select Three-Digit NAICS	U.S. Total	Atlanta-Sandy Springs-Marietta, GA MSA		Indianapolis-Carmel, IN MSA		Seattle-Tacoma-Bellevue, WA MSA	
NAICS 481 Air transportation	448,145	37,895	4.94	3,874	1.30	9,495	1.65
NAICS 483 Water transportation	62,401	152	0.14	ND	ND	2,913	3.64
NAICS 484 Truck transportation	1,249,934	24,782	1.16	15,231	1.83	15,230	0.95
NAICS 487 Scenic and sightseeing transportation	26,399	ND	ND	42	0.24	454	1.34
NAICS 488 Support activities for transportation	540,988	10,190	1.10	3,176	0.88	12,838	1.85
NAICS 491 Postal service	4,424	69	0.91	ND	ND	117	2.06
NAICS 492 Couriers and messengers	519,434	14,369	1.62	9,643	2.78	9,643	1.45
NAICS 493 Warehousing and storage	629,934	15,234	1.41	11,206	2.67	11,206	1.39
NAICS 51 Information	2,703,886	75,531	1.63	14,506	0.80	87,250	2.51
NAICS 511 Publishing industries, except internet	754,903	18,782	1.45	5,155	1.02	53,831	5.55
NAICS 515 Broadcasting, except internet	293,533	9,954	1.98	1,485	0.76	2,300	0.61
NAICS 517 Telecommunications	902,691	36,546	2.37	5,693	0.95	19,478	1.68
NAICS 518 Data processing, hosting and related services	242,412	4,600	1.11	909	0.56	3,273	1.05

Industry by Two-Digit and Select Three-Digit NAICS	U.S. Total	Atlanta-Sandy Springs-Marietta, GA MSA		Indianapolis-Carmel, IN MSA		Seattle-Tacoma-Bellevue, WA MSA	
NAICS 519 Other information services	141,462	1,990	0.82	222	0.24	5,253	2.89
NAICS 52 Finance and insurance	5,486,241	94,491	1.01	40,220	1.10	57,052	0.81
NAICS 524 Insurance carriers and related activities	2,041,869	39,386	1.13	22,072	1.62	24,476	0.93
NAICS 53 Real estate and rental and leasing	1,915,571	38,456	1.17	13,934	1.09	29,743	1.21
NAICS 531 Real estate	1,382,794	26,948	1.14	9,460	1.03	23,380	1.32
NAICS 532 Rental and leasing services	507,470	10,626	1.22	4,203	1.24	5,385	0.83
NAICS 533 Lessors of nonfinancial intangible assets	25,307	880	2.03	161	0.95	170	0.52
NAICS 54 Professional and technical services	7,457,913	154,316	1.21	42,480	0.85	109,547	1.14
NAICS 541 Professional and technical services	7,457,913	154,316	1.21	42,480	0.85	109,547	1.14
NAICS 55 Management of companies and enterprises	1,854,778	38,746	1.22	10,687	0.86	24,620	1.03
NAICS 551 Management of companies and enterprises	1,854,778	38,746	1.22	10,687	0.86	24,620	1.03
NAICS 56 Administrative and waste services	7,399,320	160,668	1.27	60,157	1.22	83,301	0.88
NAICS 561 Administrative and support services	7,043,417	157,658	1.31	57,007	1.21	78,550	0.87

(Continued)

Table 6.3 (Continued)

Industry by Two-Digit and Select Three-Digit NAICS	U.S. Total	Atlanta-Sandy Springs-Marietta, GA MSA		Indianapolis-Carmel, IN MSA		Seattle-Tacoma-Bellevue, WA MSA	
NAICS 562 Waste management and remediation services	355,903	4,066	0.67	2,491	1.05	4,751	1.04
NAICS 61 Educational services	2,460,150	42,699	1.01	13,177	0.80	22,485	0.71
NAICS 611 Educational services	2,460,150	42,699	1.01	13,177	0.80	22,485	0.71
NAICS 62 Health care and social assistance	16,196,009	213,258	0.77	104,322	0.97	175,405	0.84
NAICS 622 Hospitals	4,639,079	70,736	0.89	36,372	1.18	37,211	0.62
NAICS 624 Social assistance	2,467,934	35,336	0.84	11,747	0.71	35,707	1.13
NAICS 71 Arts, entertainment, and recreation	1,903,739	25,747	0.79	11,463	0.90	28,676	1.17
NAICS 711 Performing arts and spectator sports	394,835	5,744	0.85	4,479	1.70	6,750	1.33
NAICS 712 Museums, historical sites, zoos, and parks	127,527	1,057	0.48	991	1.16	1,881	1.15
NAICS 713 Amusements, gambling, and recreation	1,381,377	18,661	0.79	6,985	0.76	20,046	1.13
NAICS 72 Accommodation and food services	11,103,075	192,467	1.01	70,953	0.96	124,814	0.88
NAICS 722 Food services and drinking places	9,355,821	170,944	1.07	65,026	1.04	109,735	0.91

Industry by Two-Digit and Select Three-Digit NAICS	U.S. Total	Atlanta-Sandy Springs-Marietta, GA MSA		Indianapolis-Carmel, IN MSA		Seattle-Tacoma-Bellevue, WA MSA	
NAICS 81 Other services, except public administration	4,349,563	55,065	0.74	26,221	0.90	75,485	1.35
NAICS 812 Personal and laundry services	1,266,794	21,626	1.00	8,201	0.97	18,231	1.12
NAICS 813 Membership associations and organizations	1,313,677	12,876	0.57	9,701	1.11	12,491	0.74
NAICS 814 Private households	633,973	2,400	0.22	1,033	0.24	18,352	2.25
NAICS 99 Unclassified	152,667	4,954	1.90	14	0.01	ND	ND
NAICS 999 Unclassified	152,667	4,954	1.90	14	0.01	ND	ND

Source: Bureau of Labor Statistics (BLS), 2010, *Quarterly Census of Employment and Earnings*, http://www.bls.gov/cew/data.htm.

(ND) Not Disclosable

Note: In order to provide the best possible disclosable data, for each NAICS the published data is the better available of either the metropolitan area figure, as reported by BLS, or the sum of the counties in the metropolitan area, as reported at the county-level by BLS. Some NAICS may still be underestimates due to not disclosure. The metropolitan area definitions are based on the metropolitan and micropolitan statistical areas, and metropolitan divisions, defined by the Office of Management and Budget, December 2009.

Location Quotient: Ratio of analysis-industry employment in the analysis area to base-industry employment in the analysis area divided by the ratio of analysis-industry employment in the base area to base-industry employment in the base area.

traditional industry, with large LQs for chemical manufacturing (NAICS 325) and transportation equipment manufacturing (NAICS 336), along with printing (NAICS). Indianapolis is also specialized in three sectors that suggest it is a significant distribution hub: NAICS 484—Truck transportation; NAICS 492—Couriers and messengers; and NAICS 493—Warehousing and storage. Finally, a location quotient analysis for Indianapolis reveals it specializes in arts and entertainment (NAICS 711—Performing arts and spectator sports).

Analysis of Seattle reveals it is narrowly specialized in three industry areas relative to the nation that are representative of three key phases of industrialization. First, it has a very high LQ of almost 11 for NAICS 114—Fishing, hunting, and trapping. Next, its LQ for NAICS 336—Transportation equipment manufacturing is more than three times that of Indianapolis, largely driven by the fact that Boeing has a major facility in the area. Third, the Seattle metropolitan area has high LQs for NAICS 511—Publishing industries, except Internet, and NAICS 519—Other information services. The first includes software—and, of course, the Seattle metro region is the home of Microsoft. Finally, Seattle has a high LQ for one of the lowest-paying industry sectors, NAICS 814—Private households.

It is important to understand that the location quotient analysis is an index of specialization relative to a reference economy. It does not necessarily indicate that an industry sector with a large LQ has a large number of employees in the local economy. For example, in the case of Seattle, while the LQ for the Private household industry sector was 2.91, this sector's number of employees represents only 1.3% of all employment (19,106 employees of 1,407,193 total). What this high LQ may suggest is that household help is more affordable in the Seattle metro area, or a greater proportion of higher-income households can afford to hire private domestic workers. Further, the LQ of 12.56 for the Fishing, hunting, and trapping sector represents less than one thousandth of total employment for the metro area. It is high because of Seattle's location on the Pacific coast, where a lot more of this activity naturally takes place.

Beyond indicating how specialized a local economy is relative to the larger economy of which it is a part, the location quotient is essential to determining the economic base of a local economy.

Data Requirements for Location Quotients

The basic data needed for calculating location quotients can come from any reliable statistical series for which the same categories of data are available for the local area and for the reference economy. The usual data series are employment by industry from the Employment and Earnings series or from County Business Patterns. Many analysts compare their local area to national data, while others choose to compare their local area to their state or multistate region. To some extent, the decision about which reference area to use depends on the size of the state and its applicability as a good reference. For example, because they are large, California, New York, and Texas are good references for calculating location quotients for the cities and counties in those states, whereas Vermont is not large enough to be a reference economy for its townships and counties. Vermont analysts may want to develop a New England (multistate) reference to facilitate their analysis.

While the location quotient is most often used with employment data, the same type of ratios can be calculated if the analyst has data on the industry sales, payroll, or any other related data series from which the industry share of the whole economy can be calculated. Indeed, only using employment as a base can send the wrong signal. For example, as efficiency and capital investment work through an industry, often employment falls. In some industries, falling employment may be one of the first signs not of weakness but of strength. Thus, in industries such as construction or farming in which efficiencies in employment are dramatic, a case can be made that analysts should use sales or other economic measures instead of employment.

The Growing Parts of a Local Economy: Understanding Where Jobs Will be in the Future

Just as it is important to know the current base of a local economy, the analyst must also assess (a) where the economy is going and (b) where the jobs will be. The process of making assessments of the projected future of local economies is very difficult—and extremely risky for the analyst, who could well be wrong. Local economic development agencies often contract with consultants for these analyses since the consultants have more experience and skills. However, to be a competent consumer of the projections of the consultants, every economic developer needs to understand the core issues.

In this section, we will help planners understand two components of the complex nature of assessing a changing local economy. First, we will describe the concepts and tools to go beyond the location quotient. This involves a *dynamic analysis* that shows what is growing and what is declining at more than one point in time. Then we will summarize *economic projections* and some of the principles of taking a trajectory of change into the future.

Rationale for a Dynamic Analysis

Analysts will want to know what is changing in the economy for several reasons. First, they will be able to invest public resources wisely and to allocate public infrastructure for appropriate industrial needs. In addition, knowing which industries are likely to grow most rapidly will allow economic developers to understand which jobs and skills are likely to increase, requiring allocation of job training efforts. The latter objective is central to the strategies of the national Workforce Investment Act (WIA) administered by the U.S. Department of Labor (see http://www.doleta.gov/usworkforce/wia/). Under WIA, state and local areas are mandated to project future job needs.

The data needed for a dynamic analysis of the changes in the local economy are the same as for a static analysis, but they need to be collected at two or more points in time. When choosing the two points in time, ideally the analyst will consider where they fall in the business cycle. For example, the analyst should avoid creating a distorted picture by comparing economic conditions of an economy at its peak or highest output level to the trough or lowest level of the business cycle. Some industries (appliance manufacturing is an historic example) will suffer temporary economic declines in a trough from which they subsequently fully recover. The changes the analyst would record from observing the data at the trough would inaccurately suggest a structural change had occurred in the economy.

A major tool for the analysis of the dynamic changes in a local economy is a set of tools that has been called *shift-share analysis.* Although few analysts actually use the entire shift-share approach, parts of it are essential to helping us understand answers to the key question: How is our area changing, and is it becoming more competitive?

Analysis Tool: Shift-Share Analysis

Shift-share analysis is a powerful technique for analyzing changes in the structure of the local economy in reference to the state or nation. Unlike the location quotient, shift-share deals with the changing economy, not just the way it is at one period of time. As with location quotients, the community under study can be as small as an incorporated town or as large as a metropolitan region. At the same time, the reference economy can be as small as a county or as large as the nation. As the reader might anticipate, this type of analytical technique is not useful at the neighborhood level.

The purpose of shift-share analysis is to disaggregate the growth of a local economy's industry structure. Again, shift-share can be calculated with employment or other economic data, but employment is usually used. According to the shift-share approach, economic growth or decline in a local area is a combination of three interrelated but distinct components:[1]

1. Economic growth in a local community benefits from or suffers from the changes in the overall national, state, or regional economy. Regardless of what industry it is, the overall growth or decline has an impact on the locality, and part of the change in employment (or sales, etc.) of a local industry has to do with what is happening in the broader economy. During economic expansion or recession, all industries are affected to some degree, and the overall direction of the economy is a context for all local firms and industries. The key here is the

---

[1]Shift-Share analysis is broken down into three components, though these components are not always given the same labels. In this revised fifth edition of the book, the labels for the three components of shift-share analysis have been changed to reflect those more commonly used; see Bendavid-Val (1991) or Shields (2003).

notion that the "rising or falling tide raises or lowers all boats." This is called the *national growth effect*. It is calculated as:

Growth: (employment in 2010 – employment in 2000)/employment in 2000.

2. The second factor is the relative change of an industry to the total of all industries. In shift-share language, this is called the *proportional shift* or *industry mix effect,* which measures the relative advantage or disadvantage that an industry has relative to the overall economic growth. If communications and health care, for example, are growing faster than the overall economy, they are proportionally more likely to contribute to the growth of the local area. On the other hand, if an industry is declining, such as forestry or agriculture employment, the local area will be shaped by these changes regardless of whether the economy is in expansion or recession. Thus, the second factor shaping the fate of a local community is how well the mix of industries in its area is doing relative to the overall mix of industries in the larger economy. The proportional shift allows one to identify industries that are contributing to growth and decline.

Industry Mix Effect = local industry employment ×
(national industry growth rate − national average growth rate).

3. The *differential shift* is what most economic development analysts focus on when they use shift-share. The differential shift, also called the *local share effect*, provides an indication of the competitive advantage of the local economy. It is the difference in the rate of growth or decline in a local industry relative to the rate of growth or decline in that same industry in the larger reference economy. Thus, in industries where the industry mix effect is flat (i.e., the industry as a whole is growing or declining at the same rate as the overall economy), local growth or decline shows that the local industry is doing better or worse than would be expected if the local area were just like the region. However, if the industry in the state or nation is rapidly growing, the differential shift is positive only if the local area is growing faster than the industry in the larger economy. Similarly, if an industry such as agriculture is losing employment overall in the economy, but the local area is losing employment at a lower rate, then it is advantaged. In short, local areas can be advantaged if they are declining less rapidly in declining industries, but they must be growing faster than expected in growing industries to have a positive differential shift. When the differential shift of a particular industry is positive, then it is assumed to be more competitive than the reference economy in this industry.

Local Share Effect = local industry employment in base year ×
(local industry growth rate − national industry growth rate)

The change in employment for each industry (and for the local economy overall) is equal to the sum of the national growth effect, industry mix effect, and local share effect. Shift-share analysis provides helpful insights into the local economy, but, as Shields (2003) notes, it has limitations: It minimizes business cycle impacts; while it shows where a comparative advantage may be, it cannot identify the cause; and its results are sensitive to the time period as well as level of industry aggregation chosen for calculating employment change.

A shift-share analysis for Cincinnati is presented in Table 6.4. Data are shown for both 2003 and 2010. Note that the first calculation (column G) is

Table 6.4 Calculation of Shift Share, Cincinnati, Ohio, Metropolitan Area

		Cincinnati MSA			United States			Shift-Share		
		A 2000 Employment	B 2006 Employment	C Percentage Change[a]	D 2000 Employment	E 2006 Employment	F Percentage Change[a]	G Shift (Overall Growth)	H Proportional Shift[b]	I Differential Shift[c]
11	Agriculture, Forestry, Fishing and Hunting	319	423	32.6%	1,201,637	1,167,004	-2.9%	3.3%	-6.2%	35.5%
21	Mining	488	496	1.6%	511,418	617,048	20.7%	3.3%	17.4%	-19.0%
22	Utilities	6,068	2,951	-51.4%	847,075	803,859	-5.1%	3.3%	-8.4%	-46.3%
23	Construction	47,905	48,792	1.9%	6,848,386	7,793,430	13.8%	3.3%	10.5%	-11.9%
31–33	Manufacturing	145,757	120,576	-17.3%	17,363,496	14,153,115	-18.5%	3.3%	-21.8%	1.2%
42	Wholesale Trade	51,773	55,630	7.4%	5,741,228	5,885,436	2.5%	3.3%	-0.8%	4.9%
44–45	Retail Trade	114,649	108,981	-4.9%	15,344,490	15,435,110	0.6%	3.3%	-2.7%	-5.5%
48–49	Transportation and Warehousing	45,342	40,139	-11.5%	5,386,807	5,302,583	-1.6%	3.3%	-4.9%	-9.9%
51	Information	20,314	16,247	-20.0%	3,757,053	3,185,907	-15.2%	3.3%	-18.5%	-4.8%

		Cincinnati MSA			United States			Shift-Share		
		A 2000 Employment	B 2006 Employment	C Percentage Change[a]	D 2000 Employment	E 2006 Employment	F Percentage Change[a]	G Shift (Overall Growth)	H Proportional Shift[b]	I Differential Shift[c]
52	Finance and Insurance	44,623	49,369	10.6%	5,578,028	6,037,467	8.2%	3.3%	4.9%	2.4%
53	Real Estate, Rental and Leasing	15,086	13,465	−10.7%	2,074,629	2,203,542	6.2%	3.3%	2.9%	−17.0%
54	Professional, Scientific, and Technical Services	50,303	52,427	4.2%	6,919,298	7,502,331	8.4%	3.3%	5.1%	−4.2%
55	Management of Companies and Enterprises	29,653	32,430	9.4%	1,783,807	1,785,257	0.1%	3.3%	−3.2%	9.3%
56	Administrative, Support, and Waste Management and Remediation Services	61,058	67,195	10.1%	8,125,498	8,376,060	3.1%	3.3%	−0.2%	7.0%
61	Educational Services	43,467	46,914	7.9%	10,554,237	11,734,366	11.2%	3.3%	7.9%	−3.3%
62	Health Care and Social Assistance	108,102	125,095	15.7%	14,233,766	16,480,734	15.8%	3.3%	12.5%	−0.1%

(Continued)

Table 6.4 (Continued)

	Cincinnati MSA			United States			Shift-Share		
	A 2000 Employment	B 2006 Employment	C Percentage Change[a]	D 2000 Employment	E 2006 Employment	F Percentage Change[a]	G Shift (Overall Growth)	H Proportional Shift[b]	I Differential Shift[c]
71 Arts, Entertainment, and Recreation	19,649	19,638	−0.1%	2,071,818	2,286,930	10.4%	3.3%	7.1%	−10.4%
72 Accommodation and Food Services	75,761	86,515	14.2%	10,055,329	11,189,512	11.3%	3.3%	8.0%	2.9%
81 Other Services	33,027	30,587	−7.4%	4,200,336	4,420,427	5.2%	3.3%	1.9%	−12.6%
92 Public Administration	30,975	34,214	10.5%	6,961,574	7,228,408	.8%	3.3%	0.5%	6.6%
99 Unclassified	n/a	617	n/a	n/a	245,310	n/a	3.3%	n/a	n/a
Total	**944,319**	**952,701**	**0.9%**	**129,559,910**	**133,833,836**	**3.3%**	**3.3%**	**0.0%**	**−2.4%**

Source: Bureau of Labor Statistics (BLS), 2003 and 2010, *Quarterly Census of Employment and Earnings,* http://www.bls.gov/cew/data.htm.

a. Rate of growth or decline for each industry is 2006 employment divided by 2000 employment, minus 1 (B/A − 1, or (B − A)/A).

b. Proportional shift is calculated by subtracting the total (all industry) rate of growth for the county from the industry-by-industry growth or decline (F − G). This shows which industries exceeded or lagged what would be expected if everything grew at the same rate as the nation.

c. Differential shift is calculated by subtracting the rate of growth of each industry at the national level from the rate of growth of the same industry at the local level (F − C).

the rate of change of each industry, not the share of the total as in location quotients. Two calculations of the rate of growth are required for each industry—one for the metro area county (column H) and one for the nation (column I). Some will be found to be positive and some negative. More industries will show positive growth if employment is growing, and most may be negative if employment is declining. It is expected that there will be differences in growth between the local area and the nation, because no local area's economic structure is identical to the nation's. Further, it is precisely the local economy's performance relative to the larger reference economy that shift-share analysis is designed to detect.

Shift-share can be useful to identify the industries in which a local area has a competitive advantage and that are growing faster than would be expected if they were performing just like the national economy. Shift-share analysis can also reveal a local economy's weaknesses. In the case of Cincinnati, we see that the metropolitan area did not grow between 2003 and 2010, while the nation grew slightly (−3.9% versus .02%). The proportional shift shows which national industries' employment exceeded or lagged what would have occurred if they had experienced the same rate as the national overall average. The differential shift reflects the difference between the growth rate of a particular industry in Cincinnati and its national growth rate. In interpreting the analysis in Table 6.4, it is important to note the actual employment numbers that are generating the shifts. Many of Cincinnati's industries grew less or declined more sharply than their national counterparts. The larger the industry, the greater the concern this should generate. At the same time, those industries with larger employment levels in 2003 that also grew at a higher rate than the national industry warrant attention as they suggest a competitive advantage for Cincinnati. There was really one significant industry in this category, "Management of Companies and Enterprises" (15.3%). While there is a very large differential shift of 57.5% for "Agriculture, forestry, fishing and hunting," employment in this area was too small to make this noteworthy (622 out of 946,500 in 2010).

Principles of Economic Projections

In an effort to plan for future changes in the local economy, economic development analysts make projections into the future based on changes that can be determined from present conditions. These can require sophisticated econometric and other analytical strategies for which local economic development planners often rely on outside consultants. However, the key to many economic projections is that they build on trajectories from the recent past. To start, economic developers can examine what would happen if the trends observed in the economy over the past decade were to continue into the future. Since the future is never exactly like the past, the recent past is best used as a starting point for analyzing the types of forces likely to change the direction things will take in the future. For example, in an area coming through a downturn in military spending and base closure, it would not be expected that the problems of military cutbacks will be as difficult for this community in the future as they were just after the base was closed. Similarly, communities that benefited from the dotcom boom and bust of the early 2000s knew that these changes were unlikely to repeat themselves in the next decade. On the other hand, communities seeing a steady growth in their tourism or medical industry may well expect that these trends will continue to dominate the future. Looking at previous trends and then examining the extent to which they will not continue into the future is a good reality check for all economic development analysis.

Economic development analysts also can make use of national or larger area projections to plan for changes in the economy. For example, the U.S. Bureau of Labor Statistics publishes 5-year projections of which occupations and which industries will grow or decline. The analyst can use this to examine the local economy and determine where there may be a need for new training programs and economic adjustment assistance.

Another aspect of economic projections is to consider how a change in the present or near future can be expected to have longer-term effects. This will be addressed in the next section.

How Do Changes Multiply Through the Economy?

The Concept of Cumulative Change

The dynamic quality of the local economy is not demonstrated by a lot of independent industries acting in isolation from each other. Instead, it is a highly interconnected network of economic exchanges, of which consumption or export is only the last step. When one buys a computer, for example, the company that produces it purchases parts from many other companies. The supply companies may not be in the same state or even nation as the company making the computer, but when the computer maker increases sales, so do the supply companies.

For instance, computer makers often buy memory chips from companies specializing in memory, and these companies in turn buy the many things they need to make the chips from yet other companies—silicon, metal contacts, chemicals, plastics, fabricating machinery, energy, packaging, and so forth.

Hard disk drive suppliers also supply computer manufacturers, and an increase in purchases of hard disks will also lead to an increase in purchases from a different set of suppliers. Thus, with an increase in computer purchases, all these suppliers and the suppliers of the suppliers will see an increase in their business as well. And, of course, a decline in computer purchases will lead to a decline in the sales of the suppliers.

Referring back to page 160, the fourth question local economic developers needs to ask, then, is how any particular changes in this interconnected economy will affect the entire economic base. For this, they use the concept of a *multiplier* to summarize the cumulative change or sum of all economic activity that results when any one part of the economy either grows or declines. The sum of the economic activity will be made up of direct and indirect effects. For example, the local multiplier for a computer industry that has obtained an order for an additional $1,000 of computers is as follows: a direct effect of $1,000, plus an indirect effect from the sales made by local serving firms due to the additional $1,000 coming into the local economy. These sales may be made to the computer industry for supplies to create the additional product, or they could come from employees of the firm making increased local purchases with additional income, or some combination thereof. If the sales made by local serving firms are $600, then the total increase in sales is $1,600, for a multiplier of 1.6. Multipliers can be computed for employment changes or income changes as well. In general, local multipliers are highest in areas where a large proportion of inputs are made locally and in industries in which there are many economic transactions along the way. For example, if the computer manufacturer is located in an area where no parts are made and all parts are purchased from another region, then the additional $1,000 in sales will have little additional impact locally. On the other hand, if the computer manufacturer is in Silicon Valley, the local multiplier will be high. As another example, labor-intensive businesses such as dry cleaners have few outside purchases when their business increases—they may need a bit more cleaning fluid (which is reused by the newest machines) and energy, but most of their cost is labor. Their multiplier will be small regardless of where their suppliers are located.

Economic developers need to understand how changes will multiply through the local economy, and the multiplier can help them to prepare for the total impacts if an existing industry grows, a new industry locates, or an industry leaves the local economy. The multiplier can also be used to consider whether public incentives provided to an industry are justified based on the total growth that may be expected from the added employment or sales that the industry is expected to create in the local economy.

Analysis Tool: Input–Output Analysis

The 1973 Nobel Laureate in Economics was awarded to Wassily Leontief for developing input–output analysis. His first major treatise on the topic in *The Structure of American Economy 1919–1939* was published in 1941. Leontief viewed the economy as a large system that had industries trading with each other. Given widespread computer and programming availability, a number of software programs are able to calculate local input–output analyses. IMPLAN is one of the best-known programs, and it runs on a personal computer. Although it is complicated and this text does not pretend to explain it, the program is in widespread use by economic development consultants and large economic development agencies.

The *framework* for an input–output analysis lists the industries in a region along both the horizontal and vertical axes of a table. The industries on the vertical plane are suppliers, and the industries on the horizontal plane are buyers. To develop a national input–output table, many firms were interviewed to determine what was needed to produce a dollar's worth of product. Because a typical firm buys from a limited number of industries, these were all identified. A firm also buys labor, which was estimated. Similarly, firms sell to a relatively limited number of buyers, which are other industries, and these were identified. Producers also sell to people who are consumers—what is called final demand. The national tables also estimate on average what people will buy when they receive additional income. Adding imports and exports, the tables were balanced to represent the total dollar transactions for the entire economy. Then the inputs and outputs were standardized as ratios between zero and one, which can be summarized to provide multipliers.

Input–output analysis starts with a national model and can be adapted to fit local areas. A number of alternative strategies can fit the national data to a local area, but they all work in roughly the same way. Taking the national coefficients, for example, IMPLAN adjusts production levels to fit states and counties based on what is known about the total output by industry in each state and county. IMPLAN balances local economic activity with other areas to total state and national totals, tracing the flow of goods as production increases or decreases. This provides a local area an idea of purchases and sales characteristic of its particular industrial mix.

Input–output analysis generates three types of multipliers that are of great interest to economic development professionals. The first type of multiplier includes just the first-order transactions of what an industry must buy to increase production by $1.00. For example, a pen manufacturer will need to buy certain amounts of plastic, metal, ink, and other materials to make a pen and will also buy some energy, buildings, and machinery. The firm will also hire a certain amount of labor, lawyers, and other business services. The first-order multiplier traces these direct expenditures by the pen manufacturer, and it is the smallest of the types of multiplier.

The second type of multiplier looks at the input–output consequences of these direct purchases. The firms that sell to the pen manufacturer will themselves have to buy more things unique to their industry in order to manufacture the goods or services they sell to the pen manufacturer. Thus, metal producers will need to buy ore, machinery, energy, and other things. The ink producer will have to buy the graphite, oil, and other chemicals that go into ink. The cascade of purchases goes on in that the ore producers, ink chemical makers, machinery manufacturers, and so on will also have to buy steel, energy, and other items. In fact, this cycle is nearly infinite, though the indirect purchases quickly become trivial. From a local perspective, this second-order multiplier is reduced to the extent that purchases are made by firms outside the region, and to the extent that outside firms do not buy things made locally.

There is also a third-level multiplier that takes into account another layer of impact. That is, at each step, the dollar increase in sales of pens goes to some part of a dollar in wages to employees, who earn wages with which to buy products and services. When they are purchased, they increase sales as well—of housing, cars, clothing, food, electronics gadgets, and so forth. (An average market basket of consumer items purchased by workers in each industry has been developed.) And each of these products or services a worker buys has its own cascade of production inputs.

The construction of the input–output tables did not entail tracking of the dollars spent by all these people who had indirect impacts on the economy due to the increase in sales of pens. Once the input–output table determines how much is spent in each transaction, mathematical models allow efficient calculations of all the millions of transactions until the impact becomes so small as to be uninteresting. The result produces estimates based on the average expenditure for each industry and individual.

Using Input–Output Analysis in Local Economic Development

While input–output analysis has many uses in economic development, it can be misinterpreted and lead to unreasonable claims such as overpredicting the final impact of a subsidy to a specific industry. In interpreting results, the analyst should consider the following:

- Input–output analyses and the multipliers derived from them are based on national models and not on local information. If a local area has unique industries, this may not be picked up by the national averages used in input–output analysis. For example, a local area specializing in making custom-designed furniture for wealthy clients will not have the same coefficients as the overall furniture industry, which largely mass produces items. This difference is not reflected in local tables.

- Multipliers at the local level are usually quite low. For example, many advocates for local industry claim that if a business comes to the local area, it will have a multiplier of three times or more. Therefore, they argue, offering local incentives to attract the firm will result in three times as much local economic activity as is now generated. In fact, rarely are multipliers for a local area above 2.0, and usually these are in the 1.5 to 1.75 range.

- Multipliers in rural areas are lower than in large metropolitan areas. In rural areas, few of the inputs that are needed by most other producers are available in the same county or region, so they must be imported from outside, "leaking" dollars out of the local economy. This large amount of leakage means that the multiplier will be very low. In some agricultural areas with seed, fertilizer, and processing facilities in the county, the multiplier for agriculture can be high, but the suppliers usually serve many other rural counties where the multipliers will thus be low. In large metropolitan areas such as Los Angeles, in contrast, a diversity of suppliers will be able to meet most local needs and the multipliers will be closer to 2.0 in many industries.

- Input–output analysis is available only on a subset of industries, depending on the source and the size of the local area being examined. The smaller set of industries does not necessarily have the level of detail that a full three- or four-digit analysis would provide, leaving much of the interesting detail unable to be studied.

- Input–output analysis and multipliers are simply starting points for an economic development analysis, and they need to be supported by interviews and extensive additional analysis.

Overall, the complex portrait provided by an input–output analysis of the local economy can enhance the economic development professional's understanding of the consequences of different development scenarios.

Identifying Industrial Clusters: The Most Important Parts of the Local Economy

Local Networks of Buying and Selling

The final analytical strategy for economic development we discuss in this chapter addresses the question of what are the most important parts of the local economy in terms of growth and strength. The typical local economy has a number of highly concentrated industries, several of which may be growing. In addition, many of these may be linked together into a strong local network of buying and selling. Local economic developers have recognized that not all businesses are the same in terms of their contribution to the growth of the local economy and their potential to create jobs and improve local wellbeing.

Economic developers have adopted the concept of industrial clusters to help them explain and nurture growing economies. A *cluster* is more than just the largest firms in a local area—it is the network of interrelated firms that buy and sell from the same suppliers, share markets, and are supported by a common specialized infrastructure.

The prototypical cluster is the electronics industry in Silicon Valley. There, a network of electronics firms has a global advantage because its members have a critical mass of firms in related fields, they are in proximity to firms and labs developing new technologies so they can learn about and adopt those advances before they become available elsewhere, they benefit from social infrastructure (e.g., universities, research centers, venture capital, and industry associations located nearby), and they have direct access to advantageous marketing channels (Bradshaw, 2000).

Other areas also have strong industrial clusters, but not all clusters are high technology. For example, California's Napa and Sonoma valleys are centers for the wine cluster; agricultural technology is located in the central valley; the apparel cluster is in Los Angeles around the fashion mart; and Sacramento is host to an expanding information technology cluster. Autos are clustered in Detroit; finance is in New York; plastics and rubber are in Akron. Many cities and regions have well-identified and highly visible clusters, but the promise of cluster analysis is to help identify clusters in places where they are not so visible and to help any place become aware of potential sets of industries that can be nurtured as a cluster. The proximity of multiple industries (or what economists call *agglomeration*) means that they gain benefit from their common location in addition to whatever each firm might be able to do by itself (Bradshaw, King, and Wahlstrom, 1999).

Analysis Tool: Cluster Analysis

Economic developers need to (a) understand the clusters in their region and (b) adapt programs to support the diverse needs of the firms in the cluster. To do these two things, clusters need to be identified. For purposes of analysis, industrial clusters can be defined as firms in related industries that:

- are geographically *concentrated* in a particular region,
- gain a *competitive advantage* because of their proximity to each other in the region,
- share specialized *supplier and buyer (marketing) advantages* because of their location, and
- are supported by *advantageous infrastructure* in the region, such as physical resources (e.g., a port or access to minerals), educational and research advantages (e.g., universities), financial institutions (e.g., venture capital), or labor advantages (e.g., training programs).

These four criteria are common to most definitions of clusters, though there is no agreed-upon methodology or formula for defining a cluster. Indeed, there are some economic developers who favor identification of local clusters by consensus of business and community leaders, not through a statistical analysis. On the other hand, some cluster identification techniques involve complex data analysis and statistical techniques that obfuscate the relationships that seem central to the concept.

The objective of a cluster analysis is to identify a set of interrelated industries composed of firms that have competitive advantages because they are co-located in a geographic area. The set of firms that has a competitive advantage may include firms in just a single two- or three-digit industry, or in several industries with similar NAICS codes, or in a wide assortment of industries that cut across many different parts of the NAICS code. Cluster analysis is also used in local economic development to identify emerging clusters of firms that may not yet have enough size to show up strongly in a quantitative analysis using standardized data. For example, if locally available data show that firms form a competitive cluster, but these firms are buried in NAICS codes that do not fully describe their output, the case still can be made for thinking of them as a cluster. To illustrate, locally based arts and crafts production is often classified with individual firms in jewelry, art, tableware, furniture, and so forth, and would consequently be buried in a standard cluster analysis. On the other hand, artisan crafts may go hand in hand with a tourism industry and be a major economic force in a community. In the end, cluster analysis techniques are limited by the data available, and the analyst must think creatively about the network of firms in the local area if the results are to be useful.

Four steps can guide a first-cut cluster analysis:

Step 1. Highly concentrated and competitive industries are the building blocks of a cluster. To construct a preliminary cluster analysis, data from the location quotient and the local differential from shift-share should be calculated for all industries in the local area at the two- and three-digit levels, if possible. As shown above, industries with a *location quotient greater than one* are concentrated in the local area and probably export their production to the wider area. Also, we showed above that industries with a *local differential greater than zero* had a competitive advantage of growing more rapidly. These two descriptions of industries, which show strength in the local economy, can be combined to form a four-quadrant table (see Figure 6.2), which collectively illustrates the findings of a location quotient and shift-share analysis.

Step 2. From candidate industries found in the upper-right quadrant of the fourfold table, clusters can initially be located. It is important at this point to note that concentrated and competitive industries are not necessarily also clusters and that all parts of a cluster are not necessarily in the upper quadrant. The

Figure 6.2   Four-Quadrant Table

	Not Competitive *(declining local shift)*	*Competitive* *(growing local shift)*	
	Transforming Industries	Growing Base Industries	*High-Local Concentration (location quotient over 1.0)*
	Declining Industries	Emerging Industries	*Low-Local Concentration (location quotient under 1.0)*

best strategy is to construct the four-quadrant table for both two- and three-digit industries. The key to cluster analysis is to start with industries that are both concentrated and competitive in the local area and then to refine this categorization—for example:

A. Local industries that are concentrated but known not to export should be eliminated. The typical concentrated industry that should be eliminated for this reason is construction, which may be concentrated and growing only in response to local population or economic growth. In growing areas, construction may generate a lot of jobs, but it sells nothing for use outside the local area.

B. Industries like transportation and utilities that are supportive of all industries are usually not parts of a cluster but constitute specialized infrastructure that benefits a wide array of firms.

C. Single firms that dominate an industry are often insulated from other businesses and do not constitute a cluster of firms in related industry. This is most common in rural areas.

After removing obviously inappropriate industries from the top-right category, the analyst should look for related industries that can be combined. Usually by the end of Step 2, a number of candidate clusters will have been identified. These need to be refined further and the top candidates selected. The issue in cluster analysis is not that a set of firms either is a cluster or is not a cluster. Clearly, there are different degrees to which a set of firms gains competitive advantage because of its common location. The economic developer is interested in strengthening these competitive advantages.

Step 3. After the analyst has narrowed the list of concentrated and competitive industries, the next step is to determine whether the candidate clusters do the following: (1) share advantages of having local supplier and marketing chains and (2) have an advantage of specialized infrastructure in the local area. The presence of local supplier linkages can be determined from the input–output table. First, the analyst will determine which suppliers are strongest for a given industry—both locally and in relation to whether local suppliers are more important than external suppliers. These data can be obtained from input–output tables. Identification of suppliers and markets can be understood as an hourglass-shaped set of linkages, with the core of the cluster (identified by Step 2) at the narrow middle point. The linkage of suppliers needs to be supplemented by an understanding of marketing channels for the products. Marketing drives the concentration of some industries. For example, Scott (1988) showed that the Fashion Mart in Los Angeles was such a major outlet for designer dresses that designers needed to be nearby, as well as sewing shops for top-line fashion. In addition, fabric suppliers, accessory suppliers, and other companies found it to their advantage to be near the top design shops. This specialization continued to stimulate even mass-production fashion firms, which needed to be near the designers. Thus, the market gave the local area its advantage. Specialized marketing firms and outlets in other industries play similar marketing roles.

Step 4. Finally, to complete the cluster analysis, one must examine the nature and presence of specialized local infrastructure that can assist in the development of the main cluster industries and their suppliers. The nature and strength of these relationships is unlikely to be determined by quantitative measures; rather, they will be ascertained by examining the type of industry and its business patterns. Around the country, different local infrastructure advantages help shape clusters. Military markets drove the advantages that defense and aerospace companies had in Los Angeles and that shipbuilding companies had around Virginia. Proximity to minerals shapes the location of iron-producing regions, as national parks influence tourism. Transportation routes also are important for some industries, including ports and airports, favoring cities on either the Pacific or Atlantic coast. As well, telecommunications lines (e.g., fiber optic cable and access to main hubs of the Internet) give certain areas advantages over places without this infrastructure. It is possible, but less common, for a cluster to develop without an identifiable specialized infrastructure.

Clusters are important because they form the core of regional economies, and they define the jobs that will be created as the economy grows and changes. Clusters in an area include firms that account for a disproportionate part of their industry in the state, and thus these are a core part of the existing economic base in a region. Furthermore, firms in a cluster have more rapid growth than other firms in their industry because they are competitive, and they are inherently networked, which helps identify related firms that are likely to grow along with the core.

Cluster Case Study: Cincinnati, Ohio, Metropolitan Area

In 2004, the Cincinnati USA Partnership, the economic development arm of the Cincinnati USA Regional Chamber, worked with the University of

Cincinnati's Economics Center for Education and Research (2004) to develop an industry cluster identification report. The May 2004 *Identification of Industry Clusters for Guiding Economic Development Efforts in Cincinnati USA* report used available data, new analysis, and the findings of six prior studies to determine the clusters on which the Partnership should focus its future economic development work.

The following summarizes the primary analytical techniques the Economics Center used to identify clusters in the Cincinnati region.

Part 1. The analysis began with a calculation of regional location quotients (LQ) for each two-digit level NAICS business sector code. These data were used to determine in which sectors the Cincinnati region has an apparent specialization, as measured by those with an LQ over 1.0.

The analysis found that the region no longer had its historic economic dependence on manufacturing, with management of companies and enterprises, transportation and warehousing, and wholesale trade each having a higher LQ than manufacturing. A brief county-by-county analysis of jobs distribution was also conducted to garner a better sense of subregional economic patterns.

Part 2. The next step was an analysis of occupational location quotients in 22 classification groups. The occupational analysis is beneficial because it is the best means of assessing the skills base of the current workforce, which impacts the types of jobs that can be attracted or grown, at least in the short term.

The initial occupational analysis found that the Cincinnati region had proportionately more jobs in production and transportation and material-moving occupations.

Further analysis was done of 34 more specific occupational groupings in which the region was found to have a high occupational LQ. This analysis also divided occupations by average wages to focus on jobs with higher earnings potential.

This additional occupational analysis found the region had a high number of jobs in management, marketing, promotions, advertising, and sales professions. Less specialized but also found to be noteworthy were occupations in the fields of finance, insurance, computer programming and science, architecture, engineering, and health care.

Part 3. The next phase of the analysis was to measure job growth rates by sector compared with national trends (from 1990 to 2000). The U.S. Bureau of Labor Statistics' national projected job growth rates (from 2002 to 2012) were also analyzed to determine what areas of the national economy appeared to be healthier than others. The primary finding was that service-based sectors were generally healthier than production-based sectors.

In a similar historic and projected growth analysis of occupations, the report found that the Cincinnati region had enjoyed strong growth in service, executive, professional, and technical occupations. Nationally, future growth was expected to be strongest in management, business, financial, professional, and service jobs. The report highlighted the fact that a number of these required at least a 4-year degree for employment.

Part 4. The next phase of the analysis looked at more qualitative factors in its consideration of how sectors related to each other in terms of supply-chain or competitive relationships. The research used the U.S. Department of Commerce Bureau of Economic Analysis's 1997 report, *Input-Output Transactions Between NAICS Sectors*, and its own factor analysis to identify 29 national clusters.

Those 29 clusters were analyzed using six measures that the Economics Center determined were a good basis for evaluating the health of a national cluster within the Cincinnati region (based on 2001 data):

- average wage higher than $35,000
- represents at least 1% of total jobs in the region
- exporter (primary customer base extends beyond the region)
- location quotient analysis (comparatively high percentage of total)
- healthy sector nationally, measured by job growth rate
- shift-share analysis (local growth outpaces national growth)

Based on that analysis, the report identified the following clusters for the Cincinnati region:

- Advanced Design Services
- Advanced Manufacturing (metalworking, industrial machinery, and primary nonferrous metals)
- Aerospace
- Biotechnology
- Business Management
- Chemicals and Plastics
- Digital Equipment and Telecommunications
- Financial Services
- Motor Vehicle Manufacturing
- Software and Data Processing

The identified targets were analyzed within the context of occupational groupings to determine whether the existing labor force could support them. The measure of analysis used was the number of "critical occupations," or those that were most difficult to fill because they either required a high skill level or represented a large proportion of the industry's total jobs. The Advanced Design Services cluster definition was refined somewhat based on these findings, but otherwise this analysis did not impact the identified clusters.

Part 5. To validate and further refine the cluster definitions, the list of identified clusters was compared with the findings of six previous studies conducted between 1999 and 2003. The scope of these ranged from Cincinnati's home county of Hamilton to the states of Ohio and Kentucky. The Economics Center's analysis determined that all but one of the clusters it identified (Advanced Design Services) were included in at least two of the previous studies.

The Hamilton County analysis—the April 2004 Hamilton County Regional Planning Commission report, *Hamilton County's Comparative and Competitive Advantages* (Hamilton County Regional Planning Commission Community Compass, 2004)—used the four-quadrant concept to illustrate the findings of its location quotient and shift-share analysis (see Figure 6.3).

Figure 6.3 Hamilton County Four-Quadrant Table

Not Competitive (declining local shift)	*Competitive (growing local shift)*	
Transforming Industries— "Emerging" • Arts, Entertainment, and Recreation • Information Technology	**Growing Base Industries—"Stars"** • Advanced Business and Financial Services • Advanced Manufacturing • Chemicals • Food Processing and Technology	*High-Local Concentration (location quotient over 1.0)*
Declining Industries— "Declining" • Transportation, Logistics, and Distribution • Advanced Materials	**Emerging Industries— "Transforming"** • Biomedical/ Biochemical • Information, Communications, and e-media	*Low-Local Concentration (location quotient under 1.0)*

Source: Hamilton County Regional Planning Commission.

Cincinnati USA Partnership Cluster Work 8 Years Later

Cluster identification is only the first stage in the process of pursuing a target-based approach to economic development. Since the Economics Center report's release in 2004, the Partnership has been working on using its findings to foster economic growth in the region. Primarily, progress has been made in the areas of Aerospace, Motor Vehicle Manufacturing, and Chemicals and Plastics.

During its economic development work, the Partnership has found that the region's clusters are more specialized and defined than the 2004 cluster definitions would suggest. For example, in Aerospace, Cincinnati's primary opportunities are in the power and propulsion-equipment side of the industry. In the area of Chemicals, Cincinnati's existing strength in food product flavoring is a promising subsector from which to leverage further growth.

Based on this experience, the Partnership has continued to examine the region's economy to determine more specific cluster definitions and monitor potential new clusters. It has now identified four emerging industry clusters that include Advanced Energy, Consumer Products and Creative Services, Information Technology, and Life Sciences. In the last cluster, the Cincinnati USA Partnership has identified more than 220 businesses engaged in research, testing, and production of pharmaceutical, medical, and agricultural products.

Cincinnati's experience is evidence of the reality that local regional cluster identification remains a moving target as local knowledge expands or new local or national economic realities take hold. While some consistency must be maintained for local target development activities to be effective, local economic development professionals must also be aware of the constant change that is inherent in a regional economic climate.

Using Clusters in Local Economic Analysis

The term *clusters* has become a common buzzword in economic development analysis and, as such, tends to be overused. Taking this fact into account, the economic developer can use the concept of clusters in several ways:

- *Specialized infrastructure strategies.* In this first strategy, the policy issue is to build the infrastructure that supports the core firms, their suppliers, and marketing. Many economic development programs focus on infrastructure, which looks at transportation, ports, telecommunications, industrial parks, redevelopment, natural resource extraction and availability, and other "hard" resources needed by industry. In addition, finance, legal specialization, regulatory environments, and other "soft" infrastructure may be needed. The most often noted and perhaps the largest contributors to many leading clusters are education and research facilities, such as university labs, technology transfer programs, and higher education degree programs. Specialized research, such as the University of California, Davis's research on wine, is often credited with being the core around which leading clusters build. Likewise, research programs at the University of California, Berkeley and at Stanford are often credited with supporting the electronics and biotechnology clusters in California, though others suggest the university role is overstated.

- *Missing link strategies.* The second way policymakers can expand the strength of a cluster or rescue a threatened one is to identify gaps in supply and marketing linkages. If a cluster is not achieving its potential national or global advantage because a key supplier or buyer is missing, steps may be taken to fill the gap. Because it is not the public's role to establish a firm to fill the open slot, economic development programs often target certain industries using cluster analysis to identify challenges and solutions. In the new economy, economic developers see their role as one of generating the information so that businesses fitting into the supplier or buyer linkages of a cluster are made aware of the advantage of locating in the local area.

- *Human resource strategies.* A third way to expand clusters is to increase the skill and training available to workers. By having a competent workforce, clusters have what they often consider the core resource for being more competitive. Communities can take advantage, for example, of Workforce Investment Act and school–higher education programs, as well as lifelong learning and retraining programs. In addition, human resource skills can be focused on likely growth industries that make every firm more successful. Occupations associated with these growth industries are good targets for training programs.

- *Marketing strategies.* Clusters are most successful when they are well known. If a cluster does not have market identification, it is most unlikely that it will grow and expand. The public role is to find ways to help identify and promote clusters. Public policies, from government procurement policy to public equivalents of marketing boards, can strongly influence the market for products. Public assistance in marketing ranges from proclamations of leadership (e.g., "artichoke capital of the world") to establishing convention centers, visitor centers, museums, and other facilities that assist marketing. Location of industry associations is also strongly associated with effective industrial marketing.

These four significant policy arenas cut across all types of clusters and provide strategies to address policy opportunities and needs that must be met.

Social Network Analysis

We have focused in this chapter on four key quantitative methods used by economic development analysts to understand and plan for their local economies, and the first three methods—location quotient, shift-share, and input-output analysis—can all be useful to help identify the fourth, cluster analysis. As we described earlier, cluster analysis identifies a set of interrelated industries composed of firms that have competitive advantages because they are co-located in a geographic area. The identification of the cluster is made through quantitative analysis.

Economic developers seeking to promote policies to strengthen clusters can benefit from a better understanding of the interorganizational network of their local economy's industry cluster. Social network analysis (SNA) is a relatively new tool that uses specialized software to identify the network of a cluster.

(For a recent review of international practices, see Guiliani and Pietrobelli, 2011.) It can be used as a descriptive or policy tool. The types of interactions between members of the cluster network are derived from qualitative data such as surveys of cluster members that ask about who they buy and sell to, have on corporate boards, have technology or research collaborations with, and other possible interactions. When combined with geographic information systems analysis, links between network members and nodes (areas of spatial concentration of network members) can be identified and help to inform efforts to strengthen the collaborations and connections of the network. This, in turn, can increase positive economic development outcomes.

The two figures below are highly simplistic representations of two different cluster development networks. In Figure 6.4a, the firms in the network are all connected to each other, which suggests high levels of mutually beneficial interactions occur that can lead to strong economic outcomes. In Figure 6.4b, there is a dense core of well-connected firms along with less-connected peripheral firms. The less-connected firms may not experience as great a benefit from the network. For example, firm G may be a supplier to firm D and would benefit from being able to also sell to firm C. However, neither firm G or C is aware of the other, and thus firm C buys the input that could be provided by firm G from a firm outside of the network and the local economy. A policy to strengthen the interactions between firms in the network represented in Figure 6.4b could lead greater sales for firm G and less leakage of income from the local economy, as G is no longer buying the needed input from the outside.

Conclusion

As we noted at the outset of this chapter, successful economic development is based on a solid analytical framework that accurately describes the local economic context, including the identification of groups that have special needs, the local resources available to address these needs, and the place of the community in the larger regional, state, national, and global context. However, analytical techniques alone can neither fully identify development problems nor help to select the means of solving them. Every local problem presents unique dimensions requiring insight and innovative strategies. The standard techniques presented here can prove useful to planners in suggesting both the point of intervention and ideal steps to be taken. Standard measuring systems help us assess the degree to which the community needs to improve with respect to its goals. After implementing new strategies, we ideally will perform economic development evaluations to determine the effectiveness of the strategies.

Figures 6.4a and 6.4b Cluster Development Networks

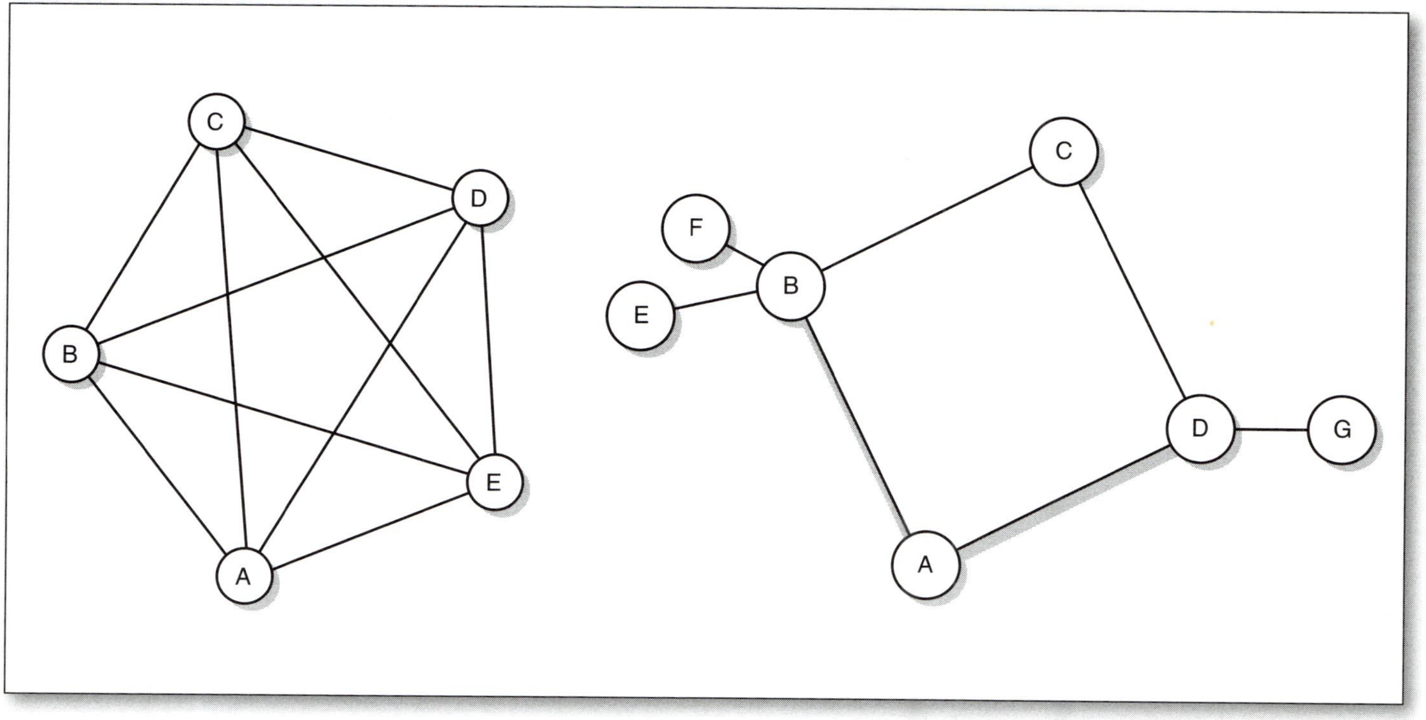

Putting It all Together: Creating a Local Economic Development Strategy (Part II)

Case Study, Part II

Now that you have more knowledge about strategies used by development analysts, you may be able to refine your suggestions for West Central Georgia's economic development plans (see the case study at the end of Chapter 5). First, study Tables 6.5 and 6.6 to get updated job data for different sectors in West Central Georgia compared with the nation, and then answer the following questions:

1. What are the existing sectors in West Central Georgia that are highly concentrated? To what extent are these sectors an outgrowth of the special history and character of the place?

2. Which of these sectors, if any, would West Central Georgia want to protect in an economic development plan? Explain.

3. What sectors in West Central Georgia might be the basis for a cluster? Construct a four-quadrant table.

4. Which West Central Georgia industries are competitive (positive differential shift)? To what extent are those sectors impacted by local and regional economic trends?

5. Which industries are neither concentrated nor competitive?

6. What would you need to know to complete a cluster analysis for West Central Georgia? How would you use the information, assuming that you could identify a set of clusters?

Note

1. Some firms may be engaged in activities that fall into more than one industry sector, particularly if they are large businesses. In such cases, the industry sector in which the largest portion of the firm's business is conducted is the one the firm falls into for economic survey purposes (BLS, 2012a).

References and Suggested Readings

Agajanian, S. 1987. *California Planner.* Sacramento: California Chapter, American Planning Association.

Bartik, Timothy J., and Richard D. Bingham. 1993. Can Economic Development Programs be Evaluated? In *Dilemmas of Urban Economic Development, Urban Affairs Annual Reviews 47,* edited by Richard D. Bingham and Robert Mier, pp. 247–277. Thousand Oaks, CA: Sage.

Table 6.5 Jobs by Employment Sector in West Central Georgia and the United States in 1998 and 2006

		West Central Georgia			United States			
		1998	2006	Change	% Change	1998	2006	Change	% Change
		A	B	C	D	E	F	G	H
11	Agriculture, Forestry, Fishing, and Hunting	226	155	−71	−31.4	1,206,059	1,167,004	−39,055	−3.2
21	Mining	*	*	*	*	568,640	617,048	48,408	8.5
22	Utilities	*	218	*	*	852,038	803,859	−48,179	−5.7
23	Construction	5,551	8,153	2,602	46.9	6,216,946	7,793,430	1,576,484	25.4
31–33	Manufacturing	32,966	29,535	−3,431	−10.4	17,668,078	14,153,115	−3,514,963	−19.9
42	Wholesale Trade	2,190	4,489	2,299	105.0	5,527,955	5,885,436	357,481	6.5
44–45	Retail Trade	16,856	19,643	2,787	16.5	14,694,552	15,435,110	740,558	5.0
48–49	Transportation and Warehousing	2,044	1,769	−275	−13.5	5,148,374	5,302,583	154,209	3.0

(Continued)

Table 6.5 (Continued)

		West Central Georgia				United States			
		1998	2006	Change	% Change	1998	2006	Change	% Change
		A	B	C	D	E	F	G	H
51	Information	2,166	2,970	804	37.1	3,359,021	3,185,907	−173,114	−5.2
52	Finance and Insurance	2,986	4,108	1,122	37.6	5,412,813	6,037,467	624,654	11.5
53	Real Estate, Rental and Leasing	1,092	1,263	171	15.7	1,982,356	2,203,542	221,186	11.2
54	Professional, Scientific, and Technical Services	1,616	2,226	610	37.7	6,218,214	7,502,331	1,284,117	20.7
55	Management of Companies and Enterprises	975	864	−111	−11.4	1,730,435	1,785,257	54,822	3.2

		West Central Georgia				United States			
		1998	2006	Change	% Change	1998	2006	Change	% Change
		A	B	C	D	E	F	G	H
56	Administrative, Support, and Waste Management and Remediation Services	5,946	8,460	2,514	42.3	7,337,847	8,376,060	1,038,213	14.1
61	Educational Services	6,178	12,162	5,984	96.9	9,964,361	11,734,366	1,770,005	17.8
62	Health Care and Social Assistance	9,222	14,215	4,993	54.1	13,793,525	16,480,734	2,687,209	19.5
71	Arts, Entertainment, and Recreation	956	1,161	205	21.4	1,932,221	2,286,930	354,709	18.4
72	Accommodation and Food Services	8,481	12,420	3,939	46.4	9,605,117	11,189,512	1,584,395	16.5
81	Other Services	3,015	2,786	−229	−7.6	4,046,965	4,420,427	373,462	9.2

(Continued)

Table 6.5 (Continued)

		West Central Georgia				United States			
		1998	2006	Change	% Change	1998	2006	Change	% Change
		A	B	C	D	E	F	G	H
92	Public Administration	3,089	6,913	3,824	123.8	6,669,838	7,228,408	558,570	8.4
99	Unclassified	*	98	*	*	*	245,310	245,310	*
Total		**105,555**	**133,608**	**28,053**	**26.6**	**123,935,355**	**133,833,836**	**9,898,481**	**8.0**

Source: Bureau of Labor Statistics (BLS). Data organized based on the NAICS system of classifying job data by business sector. (The 1998 data are from the BLS series, which reports 1998 SIC data reclassified into the new NAICS classification codes.)

*Data not disclosed by BLS in accordance with employer privacy protection policy.

A: Total jobs in 1998 in West Central Georgia (reported by BLS)

B: Total jobs in 2006 in West Central Georgia (reported by BLS)

C: Change in jobs from 1998 to 2006 in West Central Georgia (B – A)

D: Percentage change in jobs from 1998 to 2006 in West Central Georgia (C/A)

E: Total jobs in 1998 in United States (reported by BLS)

F: Total jobs in 2006 in United States (reported by BLS)

G: Change in jobs from 1998 to 2006 in United States (F – E)

H: Percentage change in jobs from 1998 to 2006 in West Central Georgia (G/E)

Table 6.6 Proportional and Differential Share in West Central Georgia in 2006

		Location Quotient Analysis				Shift-Share Analysis		
		% of Total Region	% Total U.S.	LQ	% Share	% Proportional Shift	% Differential Shift	Total
		I	J	K	L	M	N	O
11	Agriculture, Forestry, Fishing, and Hunting	0.1	0.9	0.13	8.0	−11.2	−28.2	−31.4
21	Mining	*	0.5	*	8.0	0.5	*	*
22	Utilities	0.2	0.6	0.27	8.0	−13.6	*	*
23	Construction	6.1	5.8	1.05	8.0	17.4	21.5	46.9
31–33	Manufacturing	22.1	10.6	2.09	8.0	−27.9	9.5	−10.4
42	Wholesale Trade	3.4	4.4	0.76	8.0	−1.5	98.5	105.0
44–45	Retail Trade	14.7	11.5	1.27	8.0	−2.9	11.5	16.5
48–49	Transportation and Warehousing	1.3	4.0	0.33	8.0	−5.0	−16.4	−13.5
51	Information	2.2	2.4	0.93	8.0	−13.1	42.3	37.1

(Continued)

Table 6.6 (Continued)

		Location Quotient Analysis				Shift-Share Analysis		
		% of Total Region	% Total U.S.	LQ	% Share	% Proportional Shift	% Differential Shift	Total
		I	J	K	L	M	N	O
52	Finance and Insurance	3.1	4.5	0.68	8.0	3.6	26.0	37.6
53	Real Estate, Rental and Leasing	0.9	1.6	0.57	8.0	3.2	4.5	15.7
54	Professional, Scientific, and Technical Services	1.7	5.6	0.30	8.0	12.7	17.1	37.7
55	Management of Companies and Enterprises	0.6	1.3	0.48	8.0	−4.8	−14.6	−11.4
56	Administrative, Support, and Waste Management and Remediation Services	6.3	6.3	1.01	8.0	6.2	28.1	42.3
61	Educational Services	9.1	8.8	1.04	8.0	9.8	79.1	96.9
62	Health Care and Social Assistance	10.6	12.3	0.86	8.0	11.5	34.7	54.1
71	Arts, Entertainment, and Recreation	0.9	1.7	0.51	8.0	10.4	3.1	21.4
72	Accommodation and Food Services	9.3	8.4	1.11	8.0	8.5	29.9	46.4

		Location Quotient Analysis				Shift-Share Analysis		
		% of Total Region	% Total U.S.	LQ	% Share	% Proportional Shift	% Differential Shift	Total
		I	J	K	L	M	N	O
81	Other Services	2.1	3.3	0.63	8.0	1.2	−16.8	−7.6
92	Public Administration	5.2	5.4	0.96	8.0	0.4	115.4	123.8
99	Unclassified	0.1	0.2	*	8.0	*	*	*
Total		100.0	100.0	1.00	8.0	0.0	18.6	26.6

Source: Bureau of Labor Statistics (BLS). Data organized based on the NAICS system of classifying job data by business sector. (The 1998 data are from the BLS series, which reports 1998 SIC data reclassified into the new NAICS classification codes.)

*Data not disclosed by BLS in accordance with employer privacy protection policy.

I: Percentage jobs in sector represents of total jobs in West Central Georgia (respective row of B/total of B)

J: Percentage jobs in sector represents of total jobs in United States (respective row of F/total of F)

K: Location quotient (I/J)

L: Share, percentage growth of total jobs in United States (total of H from Table 6.5)

M: Industry shift, percentage growth of sector in United States, minus percentage growth of total jobs in United States (H − L)

N: Local shift, percentage growth of sector in West Central Georgia, minus percentage growth of sector in United States (D − H)

O: Total of shift-share, to confirm sum equals percentage growth of sector in West Central Georgia (L + M + N)

Beed, Thomas, and Robert Stimson, eds. 1985. *Survey Interviewing: Theory and Techniques.* Sydney, Australia: Allen and Unwin.

Bell, Carolyn A. 2002. Workforce Housing: The New Economic Imperative? *Housing Facts & Findings* 4(2). Accessed July 22, from http://www.fanniemaefoundation.org/programs/hff/v4i2-workforce.html

Bendavid-Val, Avrom. 1980. *Local Economic Development Planning: From Goals to Projects.* Planning Advisory Service Report no. 353. Chicago: American Planning Association. Available from the publisher, 1313 E. 60th Street, Chicago, IL.

——. 1991. *Regional Economic Analysis for Practitioners.* 4th ed. New York: Praeger.

Blakely, Edward J. 1979. *Community Development Research.* New York: Human Sciences Press.

Bureau of Labor Statistics (BLS). 2003 and 2010. *Quarterly Census of Employment and Earnings.* Accessed April 2, 2010 from http://www.bls.gov/cew/data.htm

——. 2012a. *North American Industrial Classification System.* Accessed January 12, 2012 from http://www.bls.gov/bls/naics.htm

——. 2012b. *Standard Occupational Classification.* Accessed January 12, 2012 from http://www.bls.gov/soc/home.htm

——. 2012c, *Measuring Green Jobs.* Accessed January 13, 2012 from http://www.bls.gov/green/

Bosscher, Robert, and Kenneth Voytek. 1990. *Local Strategic Planning: A Primer for Local Area Analysis.* Washington, DC: U.S. Department of Commerce.

Bradshaw, Ted K. 2000. How Will the Central Valley Grow? *California Agriculture* 54(1): 41–47.

Bradshaw, Ted K., Jim King, and Stephen Wahlstrom. 1999. Catching on to Clusters. *Planning.* June: 18–22.

Braeschler, Curtis, John A. Kuehn, and John Croll. 1977. *The Community Economic Base: How to Compute, Evaluate and Use.* Guide DM3005. Columbia: University of Missouri Extension.

Butler, Gerry John, and Thomas Dwight Mandeville. 1981. *Regional Economics: An Australian Introduction.* Brisbane, Australia: University of Queensland Press.

Deller, Steven, James C. McConnon Jr., and Kenneth E. Stone. 1991. The Measurement of a Community's Retail Market. *Journal of the Community Development Society* 22(2): 68–83.

Economics Center for Education and Research, College of Business, University of Cincinnati, in collaboration with the Center for Business and Economic Research, University of Kentucky. 2004. *Identification of Industry Clusters for Guiding Economic Development Efforts in Cincinnati USA.* Prepared for the Cincinnati USA Partnership. May 19. Accessed November 23, 2004 from http://www.cincinnatichamber.com/pdf/eco/Final_Cluster_Report.pdf

Edwards, Mary. 2007. *Community Guide to Development Impact Analysis.* Accessed July 21, 2007 from www.lic.wisc.edu/shapingdane/facilitation/all_resources/ impacts/analysis_intro.ht7/2m

Gibson, Lay James, and Marshall A. Warden. 1981. Estimating the Economic Base Multiplier: A Test of Alternative Procedures. *Economic Geography* 57: 146–159.

Goldstein, Benjamin, and Ross Davis, eds. 1977. *Neighborhoods in the Urban Economy: Dynamics of Decline and Revitalization.* Lexington, MA: Lexington.

Giuliani, Elisa and Carlo Pietrobelli. 2011. *Social Network Analysis Methodologies for the Evaluation of Cluster Development Programs* Inter American Development Bank. http://www.iadb.org

Hamilton County Regional Planning Commission Community Compass. 2004. *Hamilton County's Comparative and Competitive Advantages, Community Compass Special Research Report No. 3–6, Business and Industry Clusters, 2003.* April. Accessed November 23, 2007 from http://www.communitycompass.org/ products/clusters/default.asp

Harmston, Floyd K. 1983. *The Community as an Economic System.* Ames: Iowa State University Press.

Huestedde, Ron, Ron Shaffer, and Glen Pulver. 1984. *Community Economic Analysis: A How-To Manual.* Ames, IA: North Central Regional Center for Rural Development.

Isard, Walter. 1975. *Introduction to Regional Science.* New York: Prentice Hall.

Isard, Walter, Iwan J. Azis, Matthew P. Drennan, Ronald E. Miller, Sidney Saltzman, and Erik Thorbecke. 1998. *Methods of Interregional and Regional Analysis.* Brookfield, VT: Ashgate.

Isserman, Andrew. 1977a. A Bracketing Approach for Estimating Regional Economic Impact Multipliers and a Procedure for Assessing Their Accuracy. *Environment and Planning A* 9: 1003–1011.

———. 1977b. The Location Quotient Approach to Estimating Regional Economic Impacts. *Journal of the American Institute of Planners* 57: 33–41.

Jensen, Rodney Charles, T. Mandeville, and Neil Karunarten. 1979. *Regional Economic Planning.* London: Croom Helm.

Jensen, Rodney Charles and G. R. West. 1983. The Nature of Australian Regional Input–Output Multipliers. *Prometheus* 1(1): 202–221.

———. 1984. *A Graduated Approach to the Construction of Input–Output Tables.* Paper presented at the Input–Output Workshop of the Ninth Conference of the Regional Science Association, Australia and New Zealand Section, University of Melbourne, December 3–5.

King, James. 2000. *Directions of the New Economy.* Sacramento, CA: Community Colleges, Economic Development Program.

Kruckeberg, Donald A., and Arthur L. Silvers. 1974. *Urban Planning Analysis: Methods and Models.* New York: John Wiley.

Landis, John. 1985. Electronic Spreadsheets in Planning. *Journal of the American Planning Association* (Planner's Notebook section) 51(2): n.p.

Leigh, Nancey Green, and Lynn M. Patterson 2006. Deconstructing to Redevelop: A Sustainable Alternative to Mechanical Demolition. *Journal of the American Planning Association* 72(2): 217–226.

Leontief, Wassily. 1941. *The Structure of American Economy 1919–1939.* New York: Oxford University Press.

Lewis, E., and R. E. Howells. 1981. *Coping With Growth: Community Needs Assessment Techniques.* Corvallis: Oregon State University, Western Rural Development Center.

Mahood, S. T., and A. K. Ghosh, eds. 1979. *Handbook for Community Economic Development.* Sponsored by the U.S. Department of Commerce, Economic Development Administration, Washington, DC. Los Angeles: Community Research Group of the East Los Angeles Community Union.

Malizia, Emil, and John Feser. 1999. *Understanding Local Economic Development.* New Brunswick, NJ: Rutgers University, Center for Urban Planning Research.

McLean, Mary L., and Kenneth P. Voytek. 1992. *Understanding Your Economy.* Chicago: Planners Press.

Murray, James. 1978. Population–Employment Ratios as Supplement to Location Quotients and Threshold Estimates. *Community Economics* 21: n.p.

Rochin, Refugio. 1986. *A Teaching Manual for Community Economic Development.* Davis: University of California, Department of Agricultural Economics.

Scott, Allen J. 1988. *Metropolis.* Berkeley: University of California Press.

Shaffer, Ron. 1989. *Community Economics.* Ames: Iowa State University Press.

Shields, Martin. 2003. *Using Employment Data to Better Understand Your Local Economy,* "Tool 4: Shift-Share Analysis Helps Identify Local Growth Engines." University Park: Penn State College of Agricultural Sciences, The Pennsylvania State University.

Stimson, Robert, and Edward J. Blakely. 1992. *Brisbane's Gateway Strategy for Economic Development: The Potential Impact of Intermodal International Transportation Initiatives.* Working Paper no. 548. Berkeley: Regional Development and Institute of Urban, University of California.

Voytek, Kenneth, and Harold Wolman. 1990. *Local Strategic Planning: A Manual for Local Economic Analysis.* Washington, DC: U.S. Department of Commerce, Economic Development Administration.

U.S. Bureau of the Census. "North American Industry Classification System Introduction." Accessed January 13, 2012 from http://www.census.gov/eos/www/naics/

Wadsworth, Y. n.d. *Do It Yourself Social Research.* Victorian Council of Social Service. Mimeo. Melbourne, Australia: Melbourne Family Care Organization.

Young, Frank, and Ruth Young. 1973. *Comparative Studies of Community Growth.* Monograph no. 2, Rural Sociological Society. Morgantown: West Virginia University Press.

7

Local Economic
Development Strategy

S trategic planning is now an accepted approach to determining direction
for firms, institutions, and regional economies. Selecting a strategy and
announcing it publicly has occupied much of the attention of planning agencies in many of the nation's cities. Globalization has given increased emphasis
to the notions of strategic planning for cities and regions. An entirely new
vocabulary has arisen to support the notions of strategic city/regional choices
in a competitive global economy. Saskia Sassen (2006) has been a leading pro-
ponent of the notion that the strategic global region is the new fulcrum for
international commerce. City states are employing a range of strategic tem-
plates to reposition their economies. Beyond the oft-cited Creative Class strategy (Florida, 2002), U.S. city-regions are positioning themselves as key centers
of finance (Charlotte, NC, is ascending), international logistics (Atlanta, GA),
information technology (Seattle and San Jose), pharmaceuticals (San Diego
and Raleigh, NC), biotechnology (Boston and San Francisco), and energy production (Houston), among others. Regional innovation strategies are increasingly the focus of economic development planning. Innovation strategist
AnnaLee Saxenian (2006) suggests that innovation springs from intelligent
strategies that spread innovation through networks of organizations and institutions across a well-defined regional space.

Economic development practitioners increasingly understand the value of
strategic approaches to rekindle distressed communities, both rural and urban.
Strategic economic development has a well-documented lineage. The long
economic boom of the 1990s coincided with one of the largest immigrant
population waves since the end of the 19th century. As the United States has
gained population and the economy expanded, some places have benefited
while others have been left behind. But the influx of people and new money
created new techniques using computer-based information systems to spread

the opportunities to revitalize inner-city urban areas and made some declining rural areas attractive for spawning new technology-based firms with a backdrop of recreation, retirement, and leisure. Most of the communities that have been successful point to some form of strategic choice—for example, Branson, Missouri's choice to build a new economy based on country music; or Indianapolis, Indiana's strategy of becoming the collegiate sport capital of the United States; or Pittsburgh, Pennsylvania's strategic choice to develop a new base in manufacturing and engineering technologies when its steel industry went into steep decline.

Interestingly, at the end of the 19th century, a similar phenomenon occurred. The Great Chicago Exhibition of 1893 focused on building the technology for the coming 20th century, such as the telephone, electricity, and new forms of power. This exhibition placed planning for a modern America at its core. In the first decade of the new century, planning for the nation's infrastructure must again be a national priority. The Bush administration tried to tackle both social and physical planning in the areas of social security and health care for the elderly. Earlier, the Clinton administration of the 1990s embarked on a large-scale search for national consensus on economic revitalization of the inner cities of the nation. However, state and local governments have been far more ambitious and astute than the national government in forging the future. States and localities have led the way in trying to reduce the settlement sprawl and develop smarter growth approaches for dealing with the consequences of post–World War II settlement patterns based on the highway and the automobile.

This local consensus recognizes several interrelated features. First, compact cities represent both a storehouse of infrastructure that can be revitalized at less expense than that involved in continuing sprawling development on the periphery of metropolitan areas. Second, transportation alternatives that reduce travel times must be found. This includes more mass transit and more condensed development closer to work and shopping locations. Urban sprawl has more than physical form consequences; it has social and economic impacts as well. Over the past three decades, urban areas have increased by more than 50% of their former geographic size, but their populations have increased by less than 5%. This expanding urban geography has been accompanied by increasing race and class separation.

No urban area has been exempt from increasing suburbanization. Old core cities like Chicago, St. Louis, and Detroit have seen dramatic declines in their populations. Urban core areas have not only lost population, they have also lost the vital middle class in the suburbanization process. Not only have the suburbs reduced the city population size, they have severely restricted central-city tax bases. Traditional industries have closed in the city, and central-city retail districts have became ghost towns in most midsized and even some large cities. As a result of this collapse, cities became holders of "stranded assets"—that is, underused capacity in infrastructure, schools, and industrial sectors and the population left behind. Physical assets were allowed to deteriorate, and no investments were made in the education and social services needed to fully develop the center cities' human capital.

Just how vulnerable a city can become in this unfortunate set of trends was made very clear when Hurricane Katrina hit New Orleans. Exposed to the world was an urban tragedy decades in the making, due to class and race separation and inadequate attention to critical urban infrastructure and natural resources. Hurricane Katrina demonstrated how severe the toll could be for suburban encroachment on the environment.

Nationwide, millions of acres of open space and critical watershed area have been lost, covered by new housing developments, strip development, and low-rise commercial centers. Environmentalists, city mayors, and other advocates are now united in decrying the consequences of urban sprawl. The Urban Land Institute has "recognized that conventional planning and development approaches are not effectively addressing growing traffic congestion and greater loss of open space" (Urban Land Institute, 1999, p. 1).

Not only is the physical environment in peril, but so is the nation's social fabric. As the suburbs grow, so does economic and racial disparity (Ewing and Rusk, 1995; Orfield, 1996). In an examination of four metropolitan areas— Atlanta, Cleveland, Philadelphia, and Portland, Oregon—Lee and Leigh (2007) found that, despite exhibiting different growth patterns and policies, the four metro regions all experienced increased intra-metropolitan spatial differentiation as well as inner-ring suburban decline between 1970 and 2000. Thus, inner-ring suburban decline—which is a spillover of problems from inner cities as well as the result of new immigrant populations increasingly occupying their aging housing stock—will require specifically targeted revitalization policies. Furthermore, as this negative trend was evident in metropolitan areas experiencing both high and low growth, we cannot expect it to be ameliorated by stronger overall metropolitan growth. Instead, it will require "smart growth" and antisprawl policies.

In contrast to the inner-ring suburbs, the downtown and inner-city subareas exhibited a gradual recovery from their decades-long patterns of distress. However, this recovery pattern has not been as strong in the two slow-growing metropolitan regions (Cleveland and Philadelphia). Their inner cities were still the most distressed subareas of the metropolitan area, while the outer-ring suburbs continued to thrive, drawing most of the new population and housing development.

Local development allies, together with older, inner-ring suburbs, have joined in supporting smart growth measures designed to increase urban densities, improve urban livability in all aspects (e.g., schools, mass transit), and boost inner-city retailing. The measures have ranged from proposals for urban growth boundaries (in Oregon and, in modified versions, in Maryland, Florida, New Jersey, and Vermont) to state-and local-supported inner-ring developments (in Georgia and Washington). However, Lee and Leigh (2007) found that, in spite of its urban growth boundary, the level of distress in the Portland inner-ring suburbs has actually increased over time. Thus, regional growth controls alone are inadequate for addressing inner-suburban decline. Instead, strategic neighborhood-level economic development planning is required.

Inner-city areas have recently become the net beneficiaries of an influx of development activity, such as higher-density apartment buildings in the urban cores of San Diego and Dallas, as well as increased investment in downtown malls and sports and entertainment complexes. Old downtowns (e.g., Santa Monica, Pasadena, San Jose, Boston, Baltimore, Chattanooga, and even Washington, D.C.) have undergone remarkable transformations. For example, Harlem is now the office location for former President Bill Clinton. It is one of the best retail addresses in the United States and the latest target for middle-class gentrification. Continued inner-city revitalization, however, is heavily dependent on continuing national prosperity, low crime rates, and some migration both from rural areas and new waves of urban pioneers from overseas to America's inner cities.

This chapter discusses how economic development planning is linked to an overall strategy for a community (urban or rural) to engage its human, physical, and economic resources.

Strategies, in this context, are planned actions for specific development goals of a community derived from the available opportunities—economic as well as social. While concern over sprawl and the toll on the environment and the economy initiated the Smart Growth movement in the 1990s, growing concerns in the first decade of the third millennium over climate change and inequality are now shaping sustainable approaches to local economic development planning and reframing some of the basic approaches discussed below.

Projects emerge from specific courses of action undertaken within a given strategy. The distinction between strategies and projects is necessary because, in too many instances, a single project or group of projects with no particular focus is described as a local economic strategy. In most instances, these ad hoc efforts are reactions to current circumstances. The most common rationale for the majority of these uncoordinated efforts is that "something had to be done."

Strategies, however, constitute an overarching set of principles that form concepts to guide general to specific actions (i.e., from goals to strategies to projects). Strategies are valuable in forcing clarity of thought and generating consensus during the local economic development process. It is, therefore, important to examine alternative strategies along with a set of specific projects or proposals as the basic building blocks of an economic development plan.

This is the approach that has been adopted here. Roger Kemp's *Strategic Planning in Local Government* (1992) provides a wide selection of informative strategic planning cases that students and practitioners may find beneficial to examine before embarking upon developmental projects.

The Goals of Local Economic Development

A key goal for any economic development strategy is to *provide quality jobs for the current population.* The thrust of workforce planning is to create employment for and with the resident population of the community. This is preferable to relying on approaches that attract new employers, who may require a different set of skills than those possessed by or that can be developed with the resident labor pool. Labor pools in many communities have changed dramatically over the past decade. Even though more immigrants with physical skills are arriving on our shores, many of them lack a good education and fundamental English-language skills. As a result of the fast pace of job creation, the labor pool does not always match the location or quality of the jobs created. Increasingly, small and large communities have the most individuals without the skills or capacities to enter good jobs in the new economy. It is important, then, to rethink job generation by starting with the supply side of the question—that is, who is in our population base? What skills do they bring and what kind of jobs might best fit them? This will require careful population data analysis along with intense focus groups and community surveys to determine where to apply economic development strategies.

Achieve local economic stability. Economic development will be successful only if the community has a specific approach to meet all the needs of business (i.e., land, finance, labor, infrastructure, and technical assistance, in addition to labor). Many cities don't even know the locations of available industrial sites or how a firm can identify requisite financing. If a community wants to obtain and retain jobs, it must have all its economic resources and socioeconomic data available in an organized form. In the new economy, communities also have to be able to match human resource capacities with telecommunication as resources. In other words, land and location mean far less than they once did. As a result, community economic development strategists have to design alternative mixes of resources to entice new technology firms or to retain existing firms as they expand or seek expanded international markets.

Build a diverse economic and employment base. No community with a single employer or set of employers is safe from fluctuating employment. Regardless of whether the community is high or low tech, it must have a broad base to provide continuing employment opportunities for residents. As firms become global, it is important for every community to develop regional strategies to create a web of economic and social infrastructure that will act as hubs for global firms. The dispersal of the Boeing headquarters from Seattle after 81 years to a three-city headquarter hub is one of the signals for any city that firms will move to human resources and capital and are not locked into any place because of tax rates or even raw materials.

Promote local sustainability. The three primary goals described above can all be employed in an approach that either does or does not also have the goal of promoting sustainable economic development. To incorporate sustainability into the process, the economic development strategy must explicitly consider the impacts of industries on the environment. It may specifically seek out innovative industries that are creating environmentally benign or remediating products and services. It may seek employers that adopt green practices and choose green buildings for their industrial, office, or commercial activities.

Prerequisites for Successful Strategy Formulation

The essential starting points for designing appropriate development strategies are the socioeconomic base analysis and development capacity analysis described in Chapter 6. At the conclusion of these analyses, a community can identify its opportunities and challenges and the resources available to meet them. A community should also, at this point, state explicitly its economic development goals. These goals should specify those sectors and groups that economic development is to serve.

When determining target sectors, industries, and social groups, one should keep several important points in mind. The best job-creation strategy is one that stresses increasing "basic" employment. Basic employment entails business activities that provide services primarily outside the local area via the sale of goods and services but whose revenue is directed to the local area in the form of wages, payments to local suppliers, and capital expenditures. Examples of business activities that could represent basic employment include resource-based manufacturing, transportation, and wholesale industrial sectors. When an office industry represents a headquarters for services, the result also is an increase in basic employment. "Nonbasic" employment, however, is associated with services and business activity that primarily serves the local area; revenue sources, therefore, are from the community. As a result, an analysis of the economic base should consider the following:

- determining which sectors play a dominant role in the local economy in terms of jobs, sales, taxes paid, and linkages to other local industries—for example, agriculture, forestry, some types of manufacturing, commerce, services, and government

- identifying important linkages between the local economy and the external economy to gauge the extent to which local sectors and infrastructure (e.g., international airports, world telecommunications links, and quality schools) respond to changes in the regional, national, and international economy
- assessing the local potential for economic growth, stability, and decline and identifying contingencies for economic development (e.g., major tourism or other resources) that can be used as a buffer for changes in other components of the local and regional economy and complement each trend
- exploring contingencies important to the local population or political leadership that could have major impacts on jobs, sales, incomes, public revenues and expenditures, economic productivity, job quality, and local quality of life

With target economic sectors and social groups as firm points of reference, the process of identifying and assessing alternative development strategies will be a clear but difficult task. The identified economic development opportunities probably will not provide all of the employment for the disadvantaged groups of the community. Thus, more than one economic development strategy will be required to meet local needs.

Selecting Strategic Options

It is well known that localities with severe economic problems face a morass of complex, interrelated issues. Such local situations result from a mixture of people needing jobs, firms closing or leaving, and factors that attract or produce more jobs. No single facet of the economic/employment problem is easily resolved. Too frequently, however, a single dimension or aspect of the problem is highlighted without full comprehension of its interaction with other components. To provide a better perspective of the situation faced by local governments and community groups, the strategic model created here portrays options as the components of an overall local development strategy. Each of the options listed presents an alternative approach to meeting one or more aspects of a community's needs.

City and neighborhood leaders must decide how each of these components should be combined in order to create a unique strategy that will secure the types of jobs and requisite job balance for the community, given the resources available and local development objectives.

There are four strategic approaches. These are strategies that emphasize (1) locality or physical development strategy, (2) business development, (3) human resources development, and (4) community-based development. In most instances, a strategic plan will incorporate different elements of these approaches, depending on local needs and circumstances.

Each of these major components is part of the mixture of approaches the community develops to create a local economic development strategy. That is, strategies—like problems—are unique in their development and in their application.

The Locality Development Strategy Option (the Built Environment Dimension)

As major developers of parks, roads, drainage, parking lots, and in some cases water and electricity supplies, local governments influence the establishment and operating costs of businesses. By developing a program to upgrade a locality designated for industrial and/or commercial uses, local government may have a positive influence on local business development. Quality and affordable housing, as well as safe neighborhoods and good schools, are central to achieving a quality living environment. Places like Redman, Washington, just outside Seattle, and Rochester, Minnesota, home of the Mayo Clinic, are consistently rated among the best places in the United States to live and work because these communities have low crime rates and little racial segregation. Large cities can attain similar reputations. Places like Seattle, Washington; Portland, Oregon; and even San Jose and San Diego, California, have low crime rates and high employment levels. There are a number of natural and community assets a community can decide to upgrade (for example, parks and theaters) to attract executives, entrepreneurs, and creative professionals, who seek places with high and visible quality of life attributes to raise their families.

The tools for accomplishing locality development goals are numerous and include the following:

- *Planning and development controls.* Positive use of these controls improves the image of councils with business and has a positive influence on the investment climate.
- *Economic and enterprise zones.* These are designed to revitalize aging and underused inner-city and rural retail areas.
- *Transportation and major infrastructure.* These developments increase the use of major civic assets (e.g., riverfronts, city core areas, parks, and the like).
- *Landscaping and streetscaping.* Economic upturn in town commercial centers can be achieved by making improvements to the street (e.g., planting shade trees) and to local business premises (e.g., improving window displays and the physical standards of commercial buildings).
- *Household services and housing.* A well-housed and well-serviced labor force is an inducement to businesses; in addition, activities in this sector also have the potential to generate employment.

The full array of locality development tools available is discussed in Chapter 8.

The Business Development Strategy Option (the Demand Side)

In most places, there are not enough jobs within existing firms to meet local population needs. Therefore, new ways have to be found to encourage new businesses, to attract existing businesses to relocate in the area, and to sustain and expand existing local firms. This should result in a net increase in total jobs. Several mechanisms can be employed, including the following:

- *small business and innovation assistance centers* to provide accessible management training, counseling, consulting, and research services for small firms or inventors as a means of improving their economic performance and possibly helping them to expand their workforce
- *technology and business parks* to provide the specific infrastructure requirements of sought-after industries
- *venture financing companies* to provide venture capital to selected firms unable to obtain financing from other traditional lending institutions
- *one-stop business information centers* to expedite the information needs of existing and potential new businesses
- *micro-enterprise programs* that provide seed capital in a group lending approach that builds both collective social capital in the group and increases emphasis on local ownership and capital formation

The methods used to improve local business development are discussed in greater detail in Chapter 9.

The Human Resource Development Option (the Supply Side)

This strategic option forges close connections between the employment needs of certain segments of the local population and the job-formation process. The goal is to alter the human resource system in ways that increase opportunities for good jobs for the unemployed and underemployed in the community. The new emphasis on creative human capacity emphasizes people as the wealth-generating resource in the 21st century. Furthermore, due to the abolition of permanent welfare recipients in the reforms to welfare legislation, there is a greater need to create jobs than ever before. Finally, a new emphasis on women in the workforce and seniors as expanded intellectual and human capital increases the need for communities to identify the resources required to develop human resource banks as a central goal for economic development. The methods include the following:

- *customized training,* providing the employer with specific training based on the firm's requirements
- *creative venue development,* through the organization of space and programs that provide for inventors and others to expand their talents and invent new products and services in space provided for by local government

- *targeted placement*, ensuring that employers who receive government assistance are obliged to hire qualified local personnel as the first source of employees
- *welfare to work*, which is required under Temporary Assistance to Needy Families (TANF). Under this legislation, welfare recipients are required to seek employment in the private sector with some local assistance. Local employment institutions have been designed to serve this end
- *school-to-work programs*, aimed at improving the prospects of young people, particularly from disadvantaged communities, to find employment while at school and/or to link the educational process directly to employers' needs
- *local employment programs*, developing employment offices in the community that run training and personal skills development programs to help especially disadvantaged social groups gain employment or acquire increased skills

These approaches are coupled with several related tools that can be used to develop local human resources, as discussed in Chapter 10.

Economic Development Plans Within the Context of Comprehensive Plans

Comprehensive land-use plan development is a widely utilized local planning practice primarily intended to reserve underdeveloped land for a future "highest and best use." Increasingly, communities are recognizing the value of pursuing an economic development strategy in conjunction with a comprehensive planning process. Land-use planning decisions can be of higher value when they are determined based on the agreed-upon priorities of the community's economic development goals.

As a final option for pursuing an economic development strategy, the comprehensive approach can be of most value if it embodies not only the interests of the traditional land-use plan but also those of the locality, business, human resource, and community-based strategy options. The most promising economic development programs are those that recognize that success depends not on any one initiative, but on a multipronged approach that addresses all the factors that impact a community's economic health.

The Community-Based Employment Development Strategy Option (the Neighborhood Dimension)

This option is designed to promote economic development at the neighborhood/small community level and create employment opportunities for persons who are long-term unemployed, new entrants to the labor force, or groups seeking to play unconventional roles in the economic system. In this approach, activities are intended to function as intermediaries between the social welfare system and the local economy. They are aimed at providing alternative employment opportunities for individuals who require new skills or skill upgrading. In addition, these alternative socioeconomic structures may serve those who wish to contribute to society through enterprise firms that promote economic democracy. Community-based organizations can represent the intersection between the social sectors by acting as the institutions that provide the opportunity to bring individuals and groups in the lowest and immigrant ranks or with blemished social histories, such as brushes with the law, back into society. Finally, community-based organizations are the major provider of low-cost and affordable housing for the nation's workforce. Basic activities include the following:

- *community-based development organizations,* nonprofit organizations that own and/or operate entrepreneurial activities and also provide a wide range of community services (the purpose of providing both business and services in the same organization is to facilitate, without stress, the movement of usually difficult-to-employ individuals through the progressive stages of employment)
- *cooperatives,* worker-owned and -managed businesses in which the group shares the responsibility and liability for generating wealth and/or employment using jointly held resources
- *community capital institutions,* a new set of community-based capital institutions that are emerging across the nation. Some of these are engaged in microcredit, trying to develop small loans and collective borrowing strategies in low-income neighborhoods, while others are fully fledged banking institutions ranging from credit unions to community development finance institutions that finance community-based housing and similar enterprises
- *affordable housing corporations,* which provide housing for workers, low- and moderate-income groups, and special-needs populations, at the same time creating new employment and business opportunities
- *land trust and similar community ownership instruments,* which create vehicles for local control and ownership of economic activity in the community

Clearly, these alternative approaches to local economic development can and will be mixed to meet the requirements of a given situation. Different strategy options will suit different socioeconomic circumstances. Each of the following three basic types of socioeconomies—growing, unstable, and those that are restructuring, including distressed mature economies and declining or chronically depressed economies—requires a different strategy or approach.

Common Traps in Strategy Formulation

When selecting economic development strategies, community leaders will face several traps. These pitfalls are usually derived from civic leaders' anxiety to move quickly and get results. In their haste, however, they frequently overlook important fundamentals, such as the following:

1. *Leading with grants without a strategic program and clear goals.* Local development practitioners often accept foundation and government programs as their strategies with no assessment as to whether they fit their locale or population. Public officials and community organizations usually attempt to make local needs fit national government programs rather than basing approaches on local need. All too often, such attempts overlook employment or economic problems and divert attention from the real assets of the community and/or its economic development limitations. Moreover, when the government or foundation program goes away, often the local economic strategy also disappears. The new approach is for government and foundations to provide financing and not funding. This means any organization needs to find ways to develop long-term stability by generating income for services or diversifying its funding base from a wide variety of public and private sources.

2. *Letting the tool(s) determine the strategy.* Civic leaders often confuse a particular development tool with a comprehensive strategy plan. Instruments such as industrial parks, enterprise zones, small business assistance, one-stop business information offices, tax relief, or even more sophisticated public–private financial schemes are ingredients of an economic strategy, not the plan itself.

3. *Starting at the wrong end of the problem.* Although employment creation is the usual goal of most communities, human resources are seldom the focus of local economic planning. Usually, local planning groups attempt to attract any firm in the anticipation that the local workforce will obtain most of the jobs. This desired economic result seldom occurs because too little attention has been paid to the actual skill levels, training requirements, or abilities of the local population. Because human resources are more important than natural resources or even location, initial planning must focus on current as well as projected labor force skills. An unskilled or even technically but unsuitably trained workforce can rarely meet the labor market conditions of new firms.

4. *Following the fad.* High technology, small business, tourism, and convention centers dominate current municipal economic strategies. Communities adopt these trendy approaches on scant economic evidence and without any particular ability to provide the necessary infrastructure for these firms. A substantial body of recent research indicates that there is little support for most communities' aspirations for a high-technology, tourism, or convention scenario. In fact, unless a community has unique attributes, with the necessary reinforcing institutions (such as a university's relationship to high technology), prospects for such development are dismal no matter how many artificial stimulants or inducements are provided.

5. *Overlooking development capacity.* Too often, local governments or neighborhood groups have adopted development strategies and proceeded without assessing the overall development capacities described earlier. Groups should undertake serious examination of the capacity to develop and manage any project to avoid this pitfall. In many instances, planning efforts have failed. Development strategies and projects must be designed to fit not only the area's or region's resources but

also its competencies. Indeed, the success of a local development strategy depends on a long-term commitment by a sustained coalition of local public officials and corporate and labor leaders to carry out the program or activities.

Assembling the Elements of a Strategy

A strategy is a collection of actions and activities that help achieve a predetermined goal. The methods used to assemble the strategy, as depicted in Figure 7.1, are critical in building one that is long term in nature. The following factors form the base for assembling such a strategy.

Target Characteristics

Target characteristics include such items as the strategy's scope. Is it multijurisdictional, single city, or neighborhood? The strategy may also focus on a specific sector for revitalization and emphasize certain types of enterprises, such as small businesses or large export firms. In addition, the strategy can address the direction of economic growth by selecting new firms versus existing enterprises, or it may single out some elements of both. Finally, a strategy must address the critical environmental constraints that may impede its successful implementation.

Methods of Development

A good strategy uses appropriate methods to accomplish intended objectives. These methods might include direct assistance to firms, such as financial incentives, land assembly, and other tools. Alternatively, the strategy may emphasize improving the procedures or processes available within the local environment for firms to establish or expand into new markets. The means to accomplish these objectives range from improving the existing permit procedures to business education and marketing assistance.

Forms of Local Organization

In many instances, the form of the economic development organization is selected before a strategy is designed. As a result, the institutional form is not compatible with the strategy. For example, local governments are not very good vehicles for taking ownership of declining enterprises or for starting new businesses.

The organizational form needs to be well thought out before economic development strategies are selected. Voluntary organizations, nonprofit community development corporations, local development corporations, business associations, and neighborhood organizations all have strengths and many limitations when it comes to local economic development.

Figure 7.1   Elements of Strategies for Local Economic Development

Target Characteristics
- Source of enterprise—local, regional, state, national, international
- Product sector—resource development, manufacturing, services, government
- Scale of enterprise—small, medium, large
- Type of enterprise—new firm, expansion, branch
- Critical constraints—environmental pollution, wage levels

Methods of Development
- Direct assistance to firms
  - Land assembly, purchase, writedown
  - Labor mobilization and training
  - Capital—fixed and working; loans, grants, equity
- Development process assistance
  - Permitting
  - Technical information and assistance
  - Marketing assistance

Forms of Local Organization
- Local government agency—economic development department, county or city
- Local development corporation—profit or nonprofit
- Voluntary informational organization

Time Frame
- Short term—three to six months
- Medium to long term—three to five years

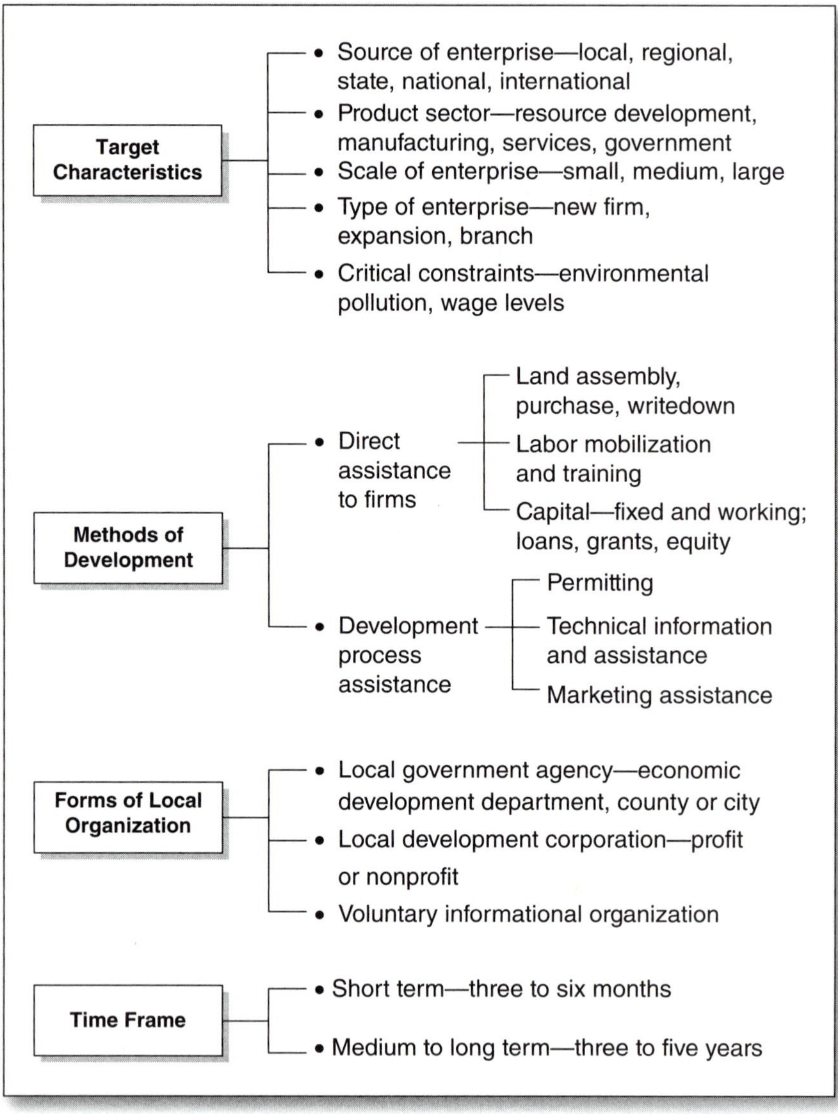

Source: Teitz and Blakely (1985). Used with permission.

Time Frame

A local economic development strategy must include both short-term, visible objectives and long-term, process objectives. It is important that the local decision makers consider clearly how to incorporate both shorter-term as well as longer-term goals in any economic development strategy.

Projects From Strategies

Having formed a development strategy, the next step is to build an action plan for each of its viable projects. Action plans are documents describing the components of a proposed project that match the economic development strategy. The principal purpose of the project action plan is to provide sufficient information to test the project's viability—that is, to determine whether the necessary economic, technical, management, and other support systems will indeed be adequate to support the proposed project. Taken as a whole, all the projects with detailed action plans constitute the community's overall development program.

The components of an action plan are shown in Figure 7.2. They include a statement of project inputs, a management structure and institutional plan, and a statement of project outputs. Each of these components is discussed below.

Figure 7.2   Components of an Action Plan

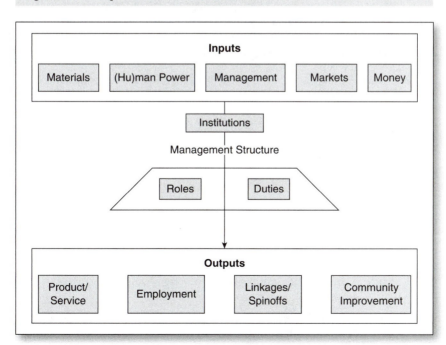

Describing Project Outcomes

Planning cannot commence without an examination of project outputs, because one cannot specify exactly either project inputs or a project management and institutional plan without knowing what the project is to produce.

The first task in building an action plan should be that of *specifying the goods and/or services* that the proposed project will produce and/or sell. All of the other factors in the action plan will relate to this definition. Other project outputs that should also be described at this time include employment impacts, linkages and spinoffs, and community improvements.

Employment Impacts

Job creation generally is important, but it is more important to create the right jobs for those in need in the community. As mentioned earlier, it is far easier to create jobs for the existing human resources than it is to move people to new jobs or to attempt to retrain them for other forms of employment. It is therefore important to ascertain the types of jobs created in relationship to the existing employment requirements of the community. Although this will necessarily be a rough estimate, it will provide a framework for ensuring a better fit of jobs to people.

A statement of employment impacts should include answers to at least the following questions:

- How many new jobs will be directly associated with the proposed project?
- In which occupational category and wage range will the new jobs fall?
- Will the new jobs provide better-paying jobs, better working conditions, or better career advancement possibilities compared with existing employment opportunities?
- How many of the new jobs are likely to be filled by local residents? How many by newcomers?
- How many of the new jobs for local residents are likely to be filled by unemployed people, women, or minorities? Would job training be required to accomplish this? If so, what kind?
- Will the new project result in the elimination of jobs, directly or indirectly, in other local businesses?

Linkages and Spinoffs

The extent to which new projects fit into the existing business and industrial base is an important consideration. If new businesses drive out existing firms, little is gained from the development planning process. On the other hand, some projects expand or improve the existing business base or even create new industry bases.

The attraction, expansion, or startup of businesses or services that have linkages with existing economic activities in the region will have a more beneficial socioeconomic impact than industries with no local linkages. Socioeconomic linkages can include the following:

- use of local raw materials
- use of locally produced goods or services as inputs
- employment of local personnel (particularly if they have been locally trained)
- sale of the goods/services produced to the local market
- attraction of new investment to the area
- attraction of ancillary employers to the area

Projects that strengthen socioeconomic linkages are usually also projects with a competitive advantage.

Community Improvement

Development planning is not merely (or solely) a business development activity. Culture, recreation, community appearance, and related factors are integral to development planning. As a result, each project should be measured for its contributions in these areas in addition to the areas of direct employment and economic development. For example, projects that build the self-esteem and identity of youth can significantly alter a community's social and economic climate. These aspects of a project, which enhance the total livability of an area, should be documented under the heading *community improvement*. To reiterate, the specification of outputs for proposed projects forms the definition and guide for the entire development process. One cannot determine other project requirements without discussing with knowledgeable people the full potential for success and failure. Similarly, platitudes about job creation or improving the overall economy are meaningless. The real focus for economic development comes from trying to work through specific activities that improve actual situations using known or attainable resources.

Specifying Strategic Resources: The Five Ms

Economic growth and development can be seen as analogous to a living plant's growth and development: The key elements of heat, light, water, and other nutrients must be present in proper amounts for a plant to grow. If one key element is missing, growth will not occur, even if other elements are present in abundance. Similarly, five key elements, loosely termed the *five Ms*, must be present for economic development to occur. These elements are (1) materials, (2) (hu)man power, (3) markets, (4) management, and (5) money. Each must be considered by communities in developing an economic development plan. This section defines these elements (see Table 7.1) and discusses their importance to economic development programs.

Table 7.1   The Five Key Resources for Economic Development

Materials
Land
Buildings
Location
Infrastructure/natural resources
(Hu)man power/labor
Skilled personnel
Available workforce
Education and training capacity
Markets
Markets analysis
Competition
Penetration
Marketing strategy
Management
Organizational structure
Managers/operators
Research and development (R&D)
Marketing and sales
Legal
Money
Equity/ownership capital
Debt/borrowed funds
Capitalizing institutions
Subsidy and substitutes for direct capital

1. *Materials* may be thought of as all existing physical resources, including both natural resources and human-made facilities or infrastructures, such as roads, ports, electric power distribution systems, and buildings. Natural resources, of course, encompass all useful, naturally existing materials and conditions in such forms as soil, terrain, minerals, climate, water sources, plant and animal life, and geographic locations. A community should understand that, although these resources may be limited in quantity and availability, they might be combined in any number of ways to produce a wide variety of products and services. Because absence of materials can restrict the types of goods that may be

produced in an area, however, the existence of these resources should be investigated before attention is given to potential products and their production in the effort to provide jobs.

2. *[Hu]man power* represents the labor used to create a product or service for sale. For example, labor includes the person operating a machine, repairing a machine, supervising the process, or delivering the final goods produced. Specific skills may be needed for different stages of a process, and those skills may be acquired through experience or training. These skills amount to an investment that has a clear "payoff" in the form of improved productivity. A trained and experienced person will be more disciplined, make fewer mistakes, and be more innovative. The skilled person is therefore an asset and can be thought of as human capital within the economic development process.

   o The amount of human capital available for work in an area depends on the size of the working population and people's willingness and ability to work. Willingness to work depends on the sociocultural background of the individuals, the type of work available, and the prevailing wage rates. Ability to work depends on the age of the population and the level of education and training. Existing human power in an area is a significant resource.

3. *Markets* are the places where there is demand for certain products or services. Demand size depends on the number of people or organizations desiring the product; the qualities of the product; the price at which it is offered; and the ability to inform possible consumers of the product's quality, price, and availability. The market area for a product is not fixed. A change in population characteristics, the local or international economy, or general social values and attitudes may create potential customers. Similarly, new methods of communicating price and product characteristics create the potential for new demands. New markets may be created through better product pricing, superior transportation, better production techniques, and/or penetration of more local or overseas markets. The point is that markets are normally very flexible and can be expanded through imagination and hard work. Identifying potential consumers, knowing what kind of product they want and at what price, and being able to inform them of the product's availability are examples of using a market area to maximum effect.

4. *Management* is a special type of human capital. A good manager is the person able to combine materials, money, and personnel to produce and market a product or service successfully. Without the catalyst of effective management, economic development cannot occur. The most effective managers also tend to be visionaries, risk takers, and innovators, as well as motivators and coordinators.

   o Economic development is a multifaceted process, and for it to be successful, there must be effective coordination between government and industry as well as between various agencies and levels of government. Most important, the local community must provide support and involvement. Successful links among these diverse groups require top management talent in both the public and the private sectors of the economy. Local government or other initiators of economic development programs designed to stimulate employment may have to be especially creative in finding ways to contribute to the availability and use of effective management talent.

5. *Money* is the financing directly involved in establishing and operating a proposed project. Money is required to initiate an economic development project in order to provide necessary facilities, to hire and train staff, to pay for materials if a product is to be manufactured, to transport the product, and to market the product or service.

   o When there is a need to provide missing elements or components for a successful project, money must be found to purchase, hire, organize, or in some other way make these elements available. For example, funds may have to be found to acquire the use of buildings, hire accountants or management consultants, train workers in specific skills, or extend sewer lines and roads. Funds for the necessary project components may come from private or public sources, and the components themselves may be provided by public or private agencies. In the next section, we will describe a variety of alternative approaches to finance.

Plan Financing and Implementation

Money, the last of the five Ms, causes the greatest problem for most local governments or development organizations because it is too often thought of as "funding" rather than "financing." In the public sector, funding refers to obtaining all of the fiscal resources to develop and manage a project or program. In essence, government agencies usually think of a continuing commitment of tax dollars to support a public activity, regardless of any income generated from it. However, *financing* refers to identifying sources of capital (often private) to provide the initial financial resources. It is further anticipated, based on careful analysis, that the project will generate sufficient income to pay for itself. For a detailed discussion of project finance, see Giles and Blakely (2001).

No matter how it is constructed, an economic development strategy is only as successful as its implementation allows. Critical to the process is assembling the personnel and resources necessary to develop, oversee, and update (as needed) the approaches identified in the strategy.

The right personnel include both the leadership and staff-level support necessary for the new initiatives to achieve positive results. The most successful initiatives are often those that are able to develop a leadership structure that provides program "ownership" to key stakeholders in the public and private sectors. From strategy conception to full-scale implementation, buy-in from the community's primary political, institutional, and business entities is vital. For example, those entities may include city and county governments, universities, community and technical colleges, chambers of commerce, business associations, nonprofit foundations, or other community organizations.

Sufficient financing is key to successful implementation, as it ensures that the most-qualified staff, most-needed resources, and other key programmatic elements are secured. To achieve both financing and much-needed support from the public and private sectors, many economic development programs are structured as 501(c)(3) entities. By using this designation, the programs are able to garner donations, annual allocations, and grant monies from public, private, and nonprofit sources.

To help finance a 501(c)(3) or alternatively structured economic development entity, a community would be remiss to overlook the numerous grant opportunities available from local, regional, and national nonprofit foundations, their state government, and the federal government. The most widely recognized grants for financing general program activities are Community Development Block Grants (CDBGs), which are the U.S. Department of Housing and Urban Development–funded grants allocated by the states to eligible applicant communities. There are numerous additional grant opportunities to help finance economic development from the general to the very specific initiative. For example, in September 2007, AT&T announced a $1.5 million competitive grant program to help local educational programs fund wireless Internet service and infrastructure (AT&T Foundation Competitive Grant Program, 2008).

For locality- or community-based strategies, there are also specific tax-related and other measures that can be used to help fund economic development. Some widely used examples are:

Business Improvement Districts (BID): An organized effort to use public and private monies to maintain and restore a commercial neighborhood

Empowerment Zones (EZ): Businesses in these designated areas of need are eligible for special incentives to open or expand operations

Tax Increment Financing (TIF): A typically district-based designation that allows projected future tax gains to be used to finance today's infrastructure improvements

Project financing requires the flexible use of existing assets combined with solid project planning. For example, city-owned land may form the basic fiscal resource for financing a local agency's building project. Similarly, local governments have become adept at selling development rights for the construction of needed office space above parking structures or other community facilities. Some cities have used civic assets (e.g., museums, city halls) as their contribution to commercial and retail developments in which the city government is a major investor. Many cities have used a lease agreement for the major portion of a commercial structure, thus encouraging a private developer to build a new multistory administrative building and civic library. In other words, project financing requires imagination more than actual money. A well-documented economic demand for a service or the use of city government space, development rights, or other factors can assist the community in achieving its objectives without using local taxes. Project identification follows the assembly of the appropriate local fiscal resources to meet the community's goals. Good project ideas are the key to development.

In a typical situation, identifying economic development projects will require compromises and tradeoffs. There may be projects that improve people's well-being, increase productivity and economic viability, or enhance the quality of life and work—but there may be no markets available for such products. An economist would say that wants and needs are greater than effective demand (that is, the ability to pay). In the typical situation, there would have to be tradeoffs between meeting local development needs and making money. Thus, the most general guideline for identifying projects is to look for those that enhance local economic development and generate acceptable profits, simultaneously, at reasonable levels of risk. An obvious but important implication of this guideline is that local communities should avoid at all costs projects with high risk and/or no profit. If an acceptable cash flow cannot be anticipated from a potential project, the project should be discarded. With the criteria of economic development potential, profitability, and risk in mind, these guidelines form the minimum mean test for a community's participation.

The general implementation guidelines discussed in this section can make the difference between a strategy that results in sustainable economic vitality and a strategic document that sits on a shelf. By carefully fostering the relationships and securing the financing necessary to make implementation a public–private partnership, local economic development practitioners can significantly improve their chance of measurable success.

Conclusion

A set of conceptual parameters for local economic development planning has been laid out here, forming its basis: strategy development and program design. The planning system or orientation taken by any community will shape the goals of the process and the resources used.

The collective experience of many hundreds of local areas working to develop their economies will shape new strategic models. Unavoidably, perspectives favoring corporate and local needs will exist side by side in the same locality. Similarly, nearly every area comprises some growing industrial sectors and others that are declining. Thus, these areas will exhibit simultaneously two or three requirements for economic development. Communities cannot remain complacent or indifferent to questions of economic development, as they have in the past. The careful economic development planner will sort through the economic development models outlined. Strategies emerge from the circumstances. None will conform to ideal types depicted here. In the following chapters, these strategies are explored in greater detail and combined with case studies that illustrate how they are integrated into a community environment.

References and Suggested Readings

AT&T Foundation Competitive Grant Program. 2008. *AT&T Corporate Social Responsibility*. Accessed January 5, 2008 from http://www.att.com/gen/corporate-citizenship?pid=10582

Barnes, N., et al. 1976. *Strategies for an Effective Public–Private Relationship in City Industrial Development*. Prepared for the Society of Industrial Realtors. Washington, DC: Economic Development Administration (NTIS).

Bendavid-Val, Avrom. 1980. *Local Economic Development Planning: From Goals to Projects*. Report no. 353. Chicago: Planning and Advisory Service.

Blakely, Edward J. 2000. Economic Development. In *The Practice of Local Government Planning*, edited by Charles Hoch, Linda Dalton, and Frank So, 3rd ed. Washington, DC: International City/County Management Association (The Green Book).

Bluestone, Barry, and Bennett Harrison. 1980. *Capital and Communities: The Causes and Consequences of Private Disinvestment*. Washington, DC: Progressive Alliance.

Carlisle, Rick. 1978. New Strategies for Local Economic Development. *Carolina Planning* 2(4): 14–18.

Castells, Manuel. 2002. *The Information Society and the Welfare State*. London: Oxford University Press.

Ewing, Reid, and David Rusk. 1995. *Cities Without Suburbs*. Washington, DC: Woodrow Wilson Center.

Florida, Richard. 2002. *Rise of the Creative Class: And How It Is Transforming Work, Leisure, Community, and Everyday Life*. New York: Basic Books.

Gardner, Linda M. 1983. *Community Economic Development Strategies: Creating Successful Businesses: Vol. 1. Building the Base*. Berkeley, CA: National Economic Development and Law Center.

Giles, Susan, and Edward J. Blakely. 2001. *Elements of Local Economic Development Finance*. Thousand Oaks, CA: Sage.

Kelly, Rita Mae. 1976. *Community Participation in Directing Economic Development*. Cambridge, MA: Center for Continuing Economic Development.

Kemp, Roger A. 1992. *Strategic Planning in Local Government*. Chicago: American Planning Association Press.

Lee, Sugie, and Nancey Green Leigh. 2007. Intra-Metropolitan Spatial Differentiation and Decline of Inner-Ring Suburbs. *Journal of Planning Education and Research* 27(2): 146–154.

Mahood, S., and A. Ghosh, eds. 1979. *Handbook for Community Economic Development*. Sponsored by the U.S. Department of Commerce, Economic Development Administration, Washington, DC. Los Angeles: Community Research Group of the East Los Angeles Community Union.

Malizia, Emil. 1981a. *Contingency Planning: A New Approach to Local Economic Development Planning*. Unpublished paper.

——. 1981b. *A Guide to Planning Economic Development in Small Communities and Rural Areas.* Charlotte, NC: Division of Community Assistance, North Carolina Department of Natural Resources and Community Development.

——. 1981c. *Planning Economic Development in Smaller Communities.* Paper prepared for the National Planning Conference, Rural and Small Town Planning Division Session, Boston, April 28.

Nathanson, J. 1980. *Early Warning Information Systems for Business Relocation.* Washington, DC: U.S. Department of Commerce, Urban Consortium.

National Council for Urban Economic Development (NCUED). 1977. *Strengthening the Economic Development Capacities of Urban Governments.* Washington, DC: Author.

Orfield, Gary. 1996. *Metropolitics.* Washington, DC: Brookings Institution.

Putnam, Robert. 2004. *Better Together: Restoring the American Community.* New York: Simon & Schuster.

Sassen, Saskia. 2006. *Cities in a World Economy,* 3rd ed. Thousand Oaks, CA: Pine Forge.

Saxenian, AnnaLee. 2006. *The New Argonauts: Regional Advantage in a Global Economy.* Cambridge, MA: Harvard University Press.

Schmenner, Roger. 1980. How Corporations Select Communities for New Manufacturing Plants. In *Firm Size Market Structure and Social Performance,* edited by J. Siegfried. Washington, DC: Government Printing Office.

Teitz, Michael B., and Edward J. Blakely. 1985. Unpublished course materials. University of California, Berkeley.

Tremoulet, Andree, and Ellen Walker. 1980. *Predicting Corporate Failure and Plant Closings: Resources for Local Employment Planners.* Unpublished working paper. Chapel Hill: University of North Carolina, Department of City and Regional Planning.

Urban Land Institute. 1999. *Smart Growth: Myth and Fact.* Washington, DC: Author.

8

Locality Development

L ocality development has traditionally focused on the ownership, regulation, and management of land and the buildings placed upon it. These are the sites on which economic activity occurs. Locality development highlights how transportation planning and urban design are essential contributors to quality local economic development and overall quality of life. Good transportation systems are required for the efficient movement of goods and people within the local economy. Increasingly, the transportation focus is being expanded to incorporate the notion of accessibility. Thus, the key issue is not the physical distance between economic and community activities but rather the ease and time required to access them. Urban design also addresses these issues by creating the vehicular and pedestrian networks of the locality as well as providing attractive ways to combine a mixture of land uses (residential, business, community) that enhances functionality and property values. Urban design helps to create the locality's image through the application of design standards, as well as to establish the fundamental framework on which evolving economic and community activity occurs.

Locality development needs to focus on minimizing environmental impacts of land development and building construction to respond to growing concerns about climate change and desires to create greater sustainability. That is, we should expect a "greening" of locality development that is only beginning to be seen in current practice.

Land is one of the most important resources in local economic development, so it must be managed carefully. Without control of land, local development is essentially impossible. Thus, land management and land deals should form an important component of any economic development program. A local or community development plan will be thwarted if suitable sites and buildings for selected projects cannot be furnished. Moreover, this management must aim to improve existing land-use practices and the appearance of the community, paying special heed to design standards associated with urban space. The newest concept in locality development is called "smart growth" or "new urbanism."

Both terms refer to strategies that are antisprawl and call for the reuse of existing urban space at higher densities and with more mixed uses to increase neighborhood walkability and community social contacts.

Livability is another extremely important component of smart growth and new urbanism as the catalyst for economic development. Because both residents and nonresidents tend to spend their time and money in the most pleasant of the available environments, tree-lined streets, covered walkways, and clean, well-managed retail areas can help build local business. An attractive entrance to and exit from a city tell the visitor a great deal about the pride and community spirit of its residents. Indeed, for tourism, there are few factors more important than community appearance. Visitors do "judge the book by its cover."

In fact, judging cities by their appearance and their social/economic climate has become a major assessment tool of economic development professionals. For example, the Rand McNally quality-of-life survey is viewed by some economic development practitioners as a legitimate locational preference index for corporate real estate managers. In addition, *Fortune, Money, Financial World,* and other leading business periodicals present annual assessments of civic performance on the basis of the local capacity to do business with the private sector, along with the physical and social appeal of the community to its indigenous population and visitors. One result of these polls is the transformation of the desirability of communities like Chattanooga, Charleston, Pittsburgh, Seattle, Sioux Falls, Baltimore, and Oakland, California, over the past two decades. In particular, communities with the right physical attributes, such as Old Town Pasadena, California, LoDo in Denver, and 18th & Vine in Kansas City, Missouri, have created living environments that are nationally attractive. The cityscape and the total natural environment are essential attributes of the quality of life economic developers seek to highlight. Good environmental management, which includes developing open space and preserving valuable habitat in the community and the surrounding region, is an important corollary to good economic development.

Local officials find it increasingly important to do "image management" in the face of global competition for corporate location. As a result, they must carefully develop their land, building assets, and "presentation features." The motivation behind developing land management and control systems should not be to prevent the worst things from happening, but rather to get the right things to happen. This requires land-use planning that goes beyond coloring maps and issuing regulations. It calls for the development of a visual theme that (1) creates a sense of identity, (2) improves the amenity base or livability of the community, (3) preserves and protects sensitive land areas and recognizes environmental equity in the community (e.g., adequate parks and open space within the urban areas and across the region), and (4) improves the attractiveness of the civic center with smart growth and related strategies to mix residential and commercial spaces in an effort to improve local business and quality of life. Table 8.1 reviews

Table 8.1   Location Development Tools and Criteria

Tool	Objective		
	Image Building	*Amenity Improvement*	*Business Improvement*
Urban Design	X	X	X
Landbanking		X	X
Infrastructure provision		X	X
Speculative buildings			X
Incentive zoning		X	X
Regulation improvement	X		X
Tourism planning	X	X	X
Townscaping	X	X	X
Shopsteading	X		X
Housing and neighborhood improvement	X	X	
Community services	X	X	X

the most commonly used locality development tools to achieve these ends. Each of these tools is described in the next section.

The Link Between Economic Development and Urban Design

While not typically considered in economic development texts, urban design is a fundamental component of locality development. Urban design focuses on subdivision of land, open space (parks, greenways . . .), sidewalks, streets, and spaces between buildings. It is essential to recognize that land subdivision patterns are the most permanent aspect of a city and its neighborhoods. That is, buildings and land uses are temporary when compared to the durability of the subdivision of land into streets, blocks, and lots. Many types of buildings are converted to different uses—factories and offices to residential, industrial to commercial (stores, hotels, restaurants), old schools to lofts, to name a few examples. But the blocks and streets on which these uses are located stay the same, and it is on these blocks and streets that private and public businesses and the employees they hire are located.

Growth management and urban design strategies for strong and weak economies are more effective when the locality is structured as small blocks and streets instead of superblocks, cul de sacs, and the gated enclaves of housing, offices, or industry that have characterized much of postwar suburban development. Good urban design enables strong and self-renewing local economies, while poor urban design significantly inhibits revitalization efforts. To be effective, both urban design and economic development must reflect the idea that the use of a building or parcel of land is always temporary. Change is inevitable, and the pace of change has accelerated in our global economy. U.S. cities have also experienced significant change from business cycles and recessions, with the most recent recession creating some of the most profound change. Throughout the United States, cities and towns have higher levels of business closures and abandoned housing and subdivision projects as a result of the financial crisis, all requiring new strategies and users to restore the neighborhoods in which they are located.

Effective local economic development is enabled by urban design principles of incremental development, organization of territory, layering of infrastructure, definition of boundaries, and creation of public space, which are described briefly below.[1]

The first principle of incremental development maintains that design should reflect the uncertainty of the future. More fundamentally, urban development is understood as an ongoing process that has no determinant end form and requires a strategic framework that allows the city and its neighborhoods to continually reinvent and reconstruct themselves while providing an organizing structure for growth. Instead of attempting to control a master planned outcome, urban design should remain flexible, adaptable, and indeterminate such that a wide range of future development scenarios, foreseen or unforeseen, can be accommodated.

While incremental development establishes a critical strategy for urban design, the second principle—organization of territory—directly informs the staging of incremental development. How a site is organized internally influences how and where development occurs. Thus, territory should be organized in a way that specific uses and programs are allowed to change without altering the underlying ordering strategy. The traditional lot, street, and block arrangements

---

[1]This section consists of excerpts from "The Economic Development-Urban Design Link in Brownfield Redevelopment: Learning from Atlantic Station," by Kevin Bacon, Richard Dagenhart, Nancey Green Leigh, and John Skach. *The IEDC Economic Development Journal* 7(2): 30–39.

found in cities across the world are organizations of territory that have proven to accommodate change over centuries. Large single-use parcels, whether large industrial brownfield sites or suburban superblocks, do not have the capacity to easily change. Instead of letting market analysis, which by definition is always short term, determine how territory is organized, the territory should be thought of as a part of a city and organized into patterns of lot, street, and block structures that are empirically proven to work. In great cities, land and economic use adapts to urban form and structure, not vice versa, enabling the continuing changes and processes of economic development.

How a territory is internally organized brings into discussion the third principle: layering of infrastructure. The traditional street grid has provided efficient organization of territory, accessibility, and mobility. However, widespread acceptance and use of a hierarchal street system—arterials, collectors, and distributors—has shifted the focus more toward mobility, almost to the point where any other design element has disappeared. Historically, streets have not only provided for vehicular movement, but they have shaped public space, encouraged economic development, incorporated the needs of transit and pedestrians, and connected to other urban infrastructure systems like water management and power distribution (Jacobs, 1993; Mossop, 2006).

The permanent nature of infrastructure necessitates that it reclaim its traditional ability to function as a critical organizing element, serving as the skeleton for a given site or larger territory. This is particularly important since one of the main forms of economic development incentives is to fund infrastructure improvements. Infrastructure outlasts land uses and should be designed as such.

Definition of boundaries, the fourth principle, underlies both the principles of organization and infrastructure and focuses on how [development] sites are physically connected or bound to their surrounding context. One aspect of binding a site to its context is physical connections—extending streets to connect in as many places as possible with the surroundings. But it is also about economic connections—the economic processes on one site are bound to others.

The last principle, creation of public space, deals with physical design and the redevelopment process itself. As design, the principle of creating public space serves as an extension of the boundary, infrastructure, and organization conditions by designating locations for key public parks and programs. However, as process, creation of public space implicates public involvement in making spatial choices beyond the standard practice of reviewing and approving completed plans for redevelopment. True creation of public space validates surrounding communities, attracts users, and catalyzes development (Frenchman, 2004). Of course, it also strengthens economic development processes. In other words, public space "fertilizes" the economy.

If a locality follows the urban design principles described here, its use of many of the tools discussed subsequently will be more successful.

Landbanking and Community Land Trusts

Landbanking is the practice of acquiring and improving contiguous parcels of land. Local development organizations can use landbanking to put together good development sites for business or industry. Landbanking does not necessarily mean vacant site acquisition. In fact, local governments accomplish some of the most creative landbanking. A number of cities have rented or leased land or buildings acquired through tax sales or eminent domain to assist in starting up new businesses or developing new markets. For example, some cities have leased land acquired through street widening or located under freeways to new environmental enterprises. In other instances, cities have reused vacant warehouses as community ice skating or roller skating rinks prior to razing the facility for another use. In each of these cases, the community has used an underutilized asset to establish a new enterprise that can be relocated when the land or buildings are converted. Nothing is more unsightly than vacant and derelict buildings.

Landbanking is a powerful locational incentive, done primarily in older communities where little land is available for development or where there is significant vacant land that the community seeks to strategically position for an economic development strategy. It is also used in newer communities to reserve good sites for future development. Landbank sites often include land that is city-owned surplus, donated, acquired through condemnation, purchased from private sources, considered a forest or watershed, former stockyards, or former military installations. To develop a landbank, a locality should set up a real estate division to search continuously for underutilized or underdeveloped properties, catalogue these properties by size and location, and computerize the information for rapid updating and quick reference.

At the neighborhood or community level, a *community land trust* offers a unique means to maintain control over physical assets. Community land trusts are local groups that establish themselves as nonprofit land trusts. The trust board and leadership are generally composed of local neighborhood activists, businesspersons, and relevant professionals (e.g., planners, architects, and finance and real estate brokers). The initiating group can call on technical assistance from the Institute for Community Economics in Springfield, Massachusetts.

The most common community trust usually acquires vacant homes through a loan, gift, or city reconveyance in blighted neighborhoods or in areas undergoing significant disinvestments. The trust identifies low- or moderate-income families and assists them in rehabilitating the property. The families' "sweat equity" may be used as a down payment for the house. The trust sells the home but maintains a land lease on the ground that requires owner occupancy and limits the resale price on the property. In some instances, state housing financing agencies offer the mortgage loans, and in others, banks or bank intermediaries fulfill their Community Reinvestment Act quota through such loans.

Community land trusts have expanded to include the purchase of farmland from hard-pressed farmers, releasing the land to the farmer under the condition that he or she maintains the land in agriculture.

Landbanks or community trusts require substantial capital. Potential sources of funds for land acquisition and preparation include national, state, or local capital programs, Community Reinvestment Act funds, program-related investments of foundations and intermediary institutions, such as the Local Initiative Support Corporation of the Ford Foundation, and industrial development bonds. If money for land acquisition cannot be found, however, an alternative approach is to gain control of suitable parcels of land by purchasing an option on them and later selling the option and land to a suitable developer.

Brownfield Redevelopment: A Priority of Locality Development

As noted in Chapter 2, the problems of brownfields—or previously developed properties with known or perceived contamination—have been a major focus of federal economic development efforts over the last decade and a half. The U.S. EPA responded to communities' concerns raised about how environmental cleanup legislation (CERCLA) created a strong disincentive for redeveloping contaminated properties, thereby affecting prospects for economic revitalization in general and economic development efforts in low-income communities especially. Further, brownfields are often major visual blights for a community and detract from the attractiveness of the locality.

While predominantly associated with older cities and towns, brownfields can also be located in rural areas or anywhere economic activity has left behind hazardous waste. Further, brownfield creation is not just an artifact of the past: new brownfields are still being created, primarily due to illegal activities. For example, a new source comes from "methfields," or brownfields created by clandestine drug labs. These have rapidly multiplied throughout urban and rural areas. The dumping of their waste—estimated at five pounds for every one pound of methamphetamine produced—is contaminating drain fields, soils, and surface waters. It is likely that this new source of brownfields will be disproportionately located in disadvantaged neighborhoods and areas.

The U.S. EPA's proactive stance to overcoming the problems of brownfields was significantly enhanced with the 2002 enactment of the Small Business Liability Relief and Brownfields Revitalization Act. This act furthered the establishment of a brownfields marketplace by authorizing funding for site assessment and cleanup, clarifying legal liability, and allowing states to sign off on completed brownfield remediations in their Voluntary Clean-Up Programs.

U.S. EPA legislation and programs have also been a critical catalyst for the creation of a sophisticated brownfield industry that includes specializations in environmental consulting, finance and investment, law, insurance, real estate, engineering and remediation, and research and development of new remediation technologies. Localities seeking to redevelop their brownfields can and should draw on this expertise.

Throughout the country, cities have begun to proactively address the problem of vacant land. This is distinct from greenfields that have never been developed and instead is land that has been developed and is no longer in productive use. Brownfields are a key contributor to the problem because many owners of contaminated sites find the remediation costs that must be incurred to sell the property cannot be recouped. The strategy of landbanking introduced above is being tested as a means of resolving this problem. The City of Cleveland established an Industrial/Commercial Land Bank in 2005 to attempt to create market-ready properties for firms seeking to locate or expand in Cleveland. The lessons they have learned so far are that it is much easier and less costly to acquire land that does not have buildings that must be demolished. Further, it is far more cost effective to process larger properties than smaller ones (Furio and Hoelzel, 2007).

Brownfields and other kinds of vacant land act as a drag on overall prospects for neighborhood and community revitalization. Research by Leigh and Coffin (2005) has found that the presence of brownfield properties stigmatizes and devalues surrounding nonbrownfield properties, acting as a barrier to neighborhood revitalization. By lowering the property values of surrounding properties, brownfields reduce overall neighborhood property taxes with which to pay for schools, infrastructure, and other essential economic development services. In turn, these neighborhoods are left further behind from those in which brownfields are being revitalized, which tend to be the larger and best-located properties, or the "low-hanging fruit." The rationale for the public sector focus has been to maximize return on public investment, while the private sector logically and appropriately is seeking to maximize profits. But this rationale does not take into account the potential for widening inequality between neighborhoods within a community.

An important component of locality development is to develop a picture of the extent of the community's brownfield problem through inventories and mapping and to develop a proactive strategy to revitalize brownfields. This strategy should balance the desire and need for maximizing returns on public investment, which considers only immediate costs, with the need to prioritize revitalization of the community's poorest neighborhoods to reduce spatial and human inequalities.

Physical Infrastructure Development on Industrial and Commercial Land

Industrial and commercial land and buildings are often more attractive to potential businesses and industries if they have already been improved. The advantages to a company buying or leasing improved land are twofold: The time between acquisition and operation can be greatly reduced, and the expense and bother of site improvement are avoided. Thus, many towns and industrial development corporations have the requisite building inventory and physical infrastructure already in place to attract new companies and retain existing, expanding companies. Some have been successful, others have not. When considering this tool, be sure it is used only in relation to businesses truly suited to an area.

Adaptive reuse is another alternative for community infrastructure revitalization. A number of cities have developed policies to reclaim old, underused industrial property for other uses. Factory space has been transformed into housing, live-work space, offices, art studios, restaurants, and shopping malls. The city usually uses its resources to reconfigure the streets, build parking structures, and reinforce the building to meet the basic requirements of the new users. Federal and state rehabilitation tax credits allow the developers to receive tax breaks for a period of 5 or more years for the conversion investments.

There is a variety of additional ways in which a community can improve land and buildings to create incentives. Most common is the provision of water and sewerage lines, street lighting, access roads, and sidewalks. Lowell, Massachusetts, converted 11 major textile mills into office and demonstration space for a national urban park with the city providing offsite improvements and parking. North Adams, Massachusetts, converted an old abandoned factory into a museum of contemporary art that draws more than 100,000 visitors a year. Older industrial and port cities, such as Charlestown, South Carolina, have provided landscaping for privately financed historic preservation efforts of industrial, commercial, and housing estates. The Tennessee Valley Authority provided technical assistance to small rural communities for the transformation of old city motels into residential space called "hometels" (Homets, 1992).

Speculative Buildings

Speculative buildings are "shell" buildings. Their interiors are left largely unfinished until a tenant is found. They are a marketing tool for attracting firms to an area and for retaining existing companies that are expanding. They provide work space—a key factor in a firm's decision making on site location. By providing the space, a city or neighborhood can significantly reduce a firm's startup or expansion time.

Speculative buildings are best used by localities that suffer from a shortage of industrial space but have an adequate labor force, a transportation system, and a sufficient supply of public services, including utilities, police, and fire services.

One inventive and low-risk approach to speculative building is for a locality to build fully serviced storage units with water and power. These units, if properly designed, can be turned into small factoryette spaces, repair shops, and business incubators. A number of communities in the Northwest have either assisted in such space development or converted their own underutilized corporate yards to this type of incubator space. Perhaps the best example of this type of investment in the United States is the very successful biotechnology incubator space provided in Emeryville, California, adjacent to the University of California, Berkeley, and Silicon Alley in New York City's Greenwich Village.

Zoning Regulations

Zoning policy can promote economic and commercial development by setting aside a sufficient amount of land for industrial and commercial use and by allowing flexible zones and rules in the local zoning code. A number of techniques have been developed that overcome deficiencies of single-use, strict limit designations of height and density—thus making land use more flexible. Such zoning tools include incentive zoning, overlay zoning, and special districts. Because the local government controls these regulations, only local planning and zoning officials can use these tools.

Incentive zoning is often used to overcome strict site regulations of height and/or bulk. It provides a developer with flexibility and encourages certain land uses and project features. These incentives may be applied in a variety of ways, but they are generally used to obtain public benefits in exchange for design concessions to a developer. The most prevalent type of incentive zoning is bonus zoning, in which additional densities or increased floor areas, beyond those specified in the zoning codes, are awarded in exchange for public benefits (access to mass transit facilities, open space, etc.).

Overlay (or floating) zoning is a regulatory tool used when local government's general zoning and development standards do not address a subarea's unique issues and conditions (Fitzgerald and Leigh, 2002). The overlay zone is a special zoning district that is placed over the existing zoning base, thereby superseding, modifying, or supplementing its requirements. The overlay can add special provisions for land uses, design standards, or preservation of unique features, as in the case of historic preservation zoning overlays. For economic development purposes, the overlay zone can be used to create specialized commercial or industrial districts. In addition, overlay zones can be used as a device to market development rights by selling to developers the right to increase plot ratios in a specific area while maintaining the same overall citywide density limits.

Another excellent example of the use of overlay zoning is the historic corridor district developed in Gastonia, North Carolina. Gastonia's overlay zone is a supplemental zoning area bordering its historic residential district. The overlay zone protects the underlying historic district residential character and design, and the overlay provides a development corridor in the area that allows professional offices, banks, specialty shops, and small restaurants in keeping with the overall historic theme. As a result, commercial development and residential character have both been enhanced.

In essence, overlay zoning merely allows the shifting of densities and zoning applications around the city within prescribed limits. It also allows the market to work more effectively and efficiently. Developers can place facilities where demand exists rather than where planners think they ought to be. Finally, in growing areas, this tool is a tremendous fundraising device, allowing the local government to acquire capital for other civic improvements without going back to the taxpayers. At times, this practice alone generates sufficient income to finance the community's economic development office and/or program.

Business Improvement Districts

There is little doubt that Business Improvement Districts (BIDs) have restored New York City's retail areas. Basically, an improvement district is like a special-purpose zoning or taxing area, but it is organized by the businesses and gains legal form through a majority of the businesses voting for its existence. They are also agreeing to assess or tax themselves to raise the funds needed to pursue improvements to the district. These funds can be augmented by securing public grants and can be used for a variety of locality-improving purposes such as cleanup, enhanced pedestrian and transportation projects, policing, marketing programs, building façade improvements, and so on. The most well-known BIDs—New York City's Grand Central Station (see Figure 8.1) and Times Square BIDs—have been responsible for the restoration of these important areas by providing added police services, local hourly cleanups, and joint merchant services.

Figure 8.1 Grand Central Station, New York, Community Business
District Team

Businesses and sometimes apartment or condominium owners agree to form an organization to provide basic community services (e.g., street sweeping, supplementary police services, area-wide advertising) that promote the location and bring it new retailing and residential occupants. A local board of business and community leaders, including local schools, is established and, with city permission and usually encouragement, the district is established and allowed to tax local businesses a small amount for services.

BIDs have been set up in many major cities, with impressive results. Crime and vandalism have declined markedly, and patronage of local merchants has far outweighed the small monthly assessments of the districts. In many of these districts, the district leadership has formed a compact with the local schools and community service organizations to promote after-school programs that support both in-school and out-of-school sports and recreation, as well as engage local volunteers for school programs. The BIDs also host speakers programs and other activities, such as holiday celebrations, that pull the community together.

Not all communities or businesses favor BIDs. Many merchants view this as no more than a new tax with few benefits. Moreover, the BID is another level of government, creating a new excuse for local government not to provide the tax-mandated services. Furthermore, it is argued that the BIDs create a new establishment in some communities that makes its own rules with little real accountability to the entire community. In spite of these arguments, BIDs are increasingly popular in both large and medium-sized cities because of the results they bring in terms of improved physical appearance and a feeling of security to residents and patrons in the area.

Regulatory Improvement Through Simplification

An excellent method of evaluating a community's regulatory system is to place a local public official in the developer's role and have him or her walk through a typical permit or code enforcement routine. This will provide the local official with insight, from a developer's point of view, into any flaws and problems associated with the development approval process, such as conflicting regulations, time-consuming delays, or a negative or adversarial view of development. If this procedure indicates procedural and regulatory shortcomings, the community should alter its regulations and simplify the approval process. The Loma Prieta earthquake in San Francisco in 1989, the Oakland, California, firestorm in 1991, Hurricane Andrew, New York's terrorism attacks on lower Manhattan in 2001, as well as the Hurricane Katrina experience in New Orleans in 2005 forced local government officials to undertake intense and expensive reviews of their existing zoning procedures. The aftermath of each of these events provided local officials with a better understanding of how their planning and building systems were ill equipped to respond to the development process.

Recently, many communities have established local interdepartmental panels, one-stop permit offices, or committees to review development impacts and overcome the aggravation and uncertainty involved in the process.

Townscaping

Many small towns believe tourism is the antidote to the collapse of their town centers. Although tourist dollars are important, local trade is important as well. Tourism is both cyclical and fickle. Commercial centers must ultimately survive on local traffic. Communities must therefore do everything they can to make shopping in their civic center attractive and worthwhile for local residents as well as for outsiders. One of the best ways to make the downtown area attractive is to embark on programs that give it character or restore some character to it.

Townscaping—a physical, attitudinal, and management process—is one means of achieving these objectives. The physical component basically entails the development of a visual theme for the central town area by local merchants, city planners, and citizen groups. The theme may be based on the area's history or be a more contemporary expression of the community's identity. A typical manifestation of this idea is the Main Street program, in which the town theme is incorporated into plans for building or rebuilding the existing landscape and built environment. For example, small communities in the Midwest have developed modest but well-designed approaches to townscaping that make them exceptionally visually appealing. Many small communities have experienced increased local business traffic and tourism as a result of improving their visual image while preserving their rural or small-town character.

The attitudinal component of townscaping relates to the actions local businesses take with regard to their town center. Some communities have resurrected or formed new local chambers of commerce to provide business with a forum in which to discuss common problems such as improving the skill level of shop assistants and increasing the type and range of advertising on television or radio as a group advertising effort.

One of the most clever townscaping programs in the nation is the restoration of downtown Pasadena, California (see Figure 8.2). For all of its native beauty, sunshine, and national attention via the Rose Parade, Pasadena was an economic disaster in the1970s. However, with the assistance of a group of planners and architects, the core of Colorado Boulevard was restored on its Art Deco base. Along with well-appointed alley shops, tree-lined streets, and exceptionally well-hidden but accessible parking, Pasadena is now one of Southern California's major tourist destinations.

Figure 8.2   Shopping Area, Pasadena, California: Interior Buildingscape

The management aspects of townscaping include such measures as hiring consultants or even civic center managers to help analyze methods for increasing sales, improving product offerings, maintaining cleanliness and attractiveness, and advocating civic improvements that will improve retail opportunities.

Shopsteading

Shopsteading is a relatively new approach to community or inner-city neighborhood revitalization. It is a tool that can be used to address the problem of vacant commercial property. It involves the sale of abandoned shop facilities to businesspeople willing to renovate them and then operate their business there. The success of shopsteading hinges on two main factors, the first of which is the availability of vacant properties in areas that have considerable potential for economic revitalization. This means that there must be an identifiable market for goods and services in the shopstead area.

The second necessary component is the availability of individuals able to satisfy shopsteading requirements. Before settling on the property, shopsteaders are usually required to provide evidence of equity capital and to submit detailed specifications for rehabilitating the property. They also must have estimated all capital requirements for reconstruction and obtained commitments for the necessary financing. Shortly after settlement, the shopsteaders must begin improving the property. Within a few months, the building must comply with the local building code, and within a year, the shopsteaders must have completed the renovations. If not, the property reverts to the city. Within a year, the shopsteaders must also begin operating the business and continue in operation for at least 2 years before it may be sold.

Shopsteading is designed to promote both business retention and business-attraction activities. For businesspeople, the most important benefit is low-cost—sometimes even rent-free—property; the shopsteaders have the immediate advantage of purchasing property at a cost considerably below the market value. Owning the building where his or her business is located gives the small businessperson an incentive to improve it. Shopsteading probably provides one of the best opportunities for people who wish to open retail and specialty shops, service-oriented firms, and other small businesses.

For the city or town, shopsteading has the potential for improving land-use patterns in marginal commercial areas and providing incentives for other private investors to renovate the remaining buildings on the block. Before deciding to initiate this program, however, local governments and community groups must study the opportunity costs of shopsteading (i.e., how the available resources might be used for another project).

Housing and Neighborhood Improvement

Housing is one of the most obvious community resources, yet it is rarely considered by most cities when it comes to economic development. There are two aspects of the housing–economic development nexus. One is the need to provide diverse housing types to provide homes for all groups in the community. The other is the need to provide households with services ranging from child care to community facilities, such as swimming pools. The traditional approach taken to these opportunity areas has been merely to wait for the state or someone else to act. City councils, however, are becoming increasingly aware of how the availability of housing and household services influences the local economic development climate. As a result, some cities are becoming aggressive housing developers through the use of their land. For example, BRIDGE Housing Corporation in San Francisco is the largest nonprofit housing producer in the nation. BRIDGE produces more than 1,000 units of housing annually for both sale and rental. BRIDGE developments are almost entirely based on local land contributions to support the project.

There are more than 1,000 nonprofit housing development corporations in the country that pursue similar strategies. Chicago devised a very ambitious plan to revitalize its entire public housing stock, replacing it with a mixture of moderate- and low-income housing and including both rental and homeowner units in the same development. Another example is Oakland, California. Its downtown and its entire city have been revitalized by Mayor Jerry Brown's aggressive housing program that has restored or developed more than 10,000 mixed-income housing units at the heart of the city (see Figure 8.3).

Housing development need not be a prohibitively expensive process if a community is prudent about land acquisition. By purchasing or trading land, community groups or city governments can put themselves in the position of inviting in quality developers to build diverse housing. However, land cost is a critical determinant of whether good affordable housing can be provided. New Orleans is undertaking a very aggressive strategy to reduce blighted housing that predated the hurricanes. The City of New Orleans, with a combination of foundation and city resources, is purchasing and condemning properties that have been abandoned or have taxes in arrears in distressed neighborhoods to create new affordable and market-rate housing.

Figure 8.3   Neighborhood Housing, Oakland, California

Household Services

Household services represent another area in which there are new opportunities for enterprising local governments. Some local councils have built new recreation and sport facilities under lease agreements with private operators rather than providing and maintaining these facilities themselves. In addition, community-based organizations can provide household and community services on a contract basis for neighborhood development and job generation.

Community Services

Local government provides a wide range of services, from household to commercial (see Figure 8.4). Communities are also becoming involved in providing services, such as running trailer parks, operating summer youth

Figure 8.4   Street Closure for Farmers' Market, Berkeley, California

projects, writing local histories, and maintaining museums and art galleries. In other instances, councils are beginning to operate motion picture theaters and similar labor-intensive services. These services are frequently a drain on city resources. However, there are ways for communities to reduce these costs, and in some instances turn them into money-making propositions.

Local government and community-based organizations have used a number of techniques to make community services pay for themselves. Local governments have sublet their visitor centers to entrepreneurs who run them as combination gift shops and information centers. In addition, as communities embark on tourism as an economic activity, they discover that tourist services must pay for themselves directly. Visitor bureaus and similar activities are expensive. There are ways to finance these services, however. For example, some visitor centers publish tourism newsletters with advertising for local merchants. This helps defray some of the cost of the center.

The approaches communities use to provide services while reducing costs and creating jobs is limited only by the imagination. The traditional fiscal municipal management philosophy of "we won't do it unless we've got the money" is no longer acceptable. For example, communities in Florida and Maine aim at attracting tourists willing to pay more to "sustain" the natural environment. Local officials have the responsibility of finding a way to do it rather than a reason for not doing it. Recognizing this, a local government should develop alternative mixes of public and private resources, combined with incentives, to achieve its objectives. Similarly, community groups cannot take "no" for an answer. They must also develop a strong blend of existing and new resources to meet their goals. The examples in Box 8.1 and the following teaching cases represent means by which a community can use its civic assets.

Box 8.1 Example 8.1: Building on the Past

The Le Droit neighborhood is an excellent example of a community that had good assets but suffered from bad perceptions as well as the non-supportive actions of its large university neighbor.

The 135-year-old Le Droit neighborhood is in the northeast section of Washington, D.C., on the major arterial traffic route that connects the capital with Maryland. It is an area with a rich history, remarkable physical attributes, and what could have been—and ultimately has become—the significant asset of Howard University. The largest historically Black university in the country, with 11,000 students and almost 6,000 staff, Howard University includes a major teaching hospital complex, easy access to the central city, and nearby attractions such as the Smithsonian Air and Space Museum and the National Gallery of Art.

Le Droit is strategically located with more than 60,000 vehicle trips per day passing through the area. Another important asset is the McMillan Reservoir, designed by Frederick Law Olmsted, Jr. The reservoir represented a significant opportunity for a community park of several hundred acres. In addition, the community possesses some of the most magnificent post–Civil War historic architecture in the nation.

Like many areas, after the riots of the 1960s, both White and Black middle-class residents abandoned this area. In the 1970s, drug dealers moved in and the area gained a reputation for crime, drug dealing, and

(Continued)

(Continued)

prostitution. As a result, Howard University took the defensive strategy of closing off its campus. It also began a campaign of land banking for expansion purposes. In so doing, dozens of home and vacant lots were purchased, boarded up, and left to deteriorate (French, 2004). The Le Droit community, consequently, did not feel that Howard University was a good neighbor.

Le Droit's fortunes began to change in the mid-1990s when a new president came to Howard University. French (2004) writes, "On a tour of the neighborhood, [H. Patrick Swygert] was appalled by the degree of deterioration that had taken place since his days as a student in the 1960s" (p. 110). The first step the university took to turn around the Le Droit neighborhood was to move a number of university entities into vacant buildings on the main commercial street, Georgia Avenue, near the campus. These included the technology center, the bookstore, the Howard Community Association, and a new visitor center (French, 2004).

This step turned out to be the first phase of what has become a four-phase strategy of redevelopment in which the university has engaged. Along the way, it has developed significant partnerships to realize its goals, including those with the District government, community groups, and Fannie Mae, which developed low-interest home and business loans. In Phase 2, homeownership opportunities were created from converting 29 boarded-up properties and 17 vacant lots. By the end of Phase 3, a total of 45 homes had been constructed or rehabilitated, and these are owned by Howard University employees, public school teachers, and members of the community, as well as municipal firefighters and police. Significant infrastructure improvements have been made in Phase 3, including "street resurfacing, installation of new street lighting, bricking of sidewalks, tree planting and traffic calming measures undertaken by the City with $5 million in federal grants awarded to the University" (Swygert, 2008, p. 2). Phase 4 of The Le Droit Park Initiative is an ambitious mixed-use project of nearly half a million square feet that was scheduled to start in 2008. This project was projected to include 300 market-rate rental residential units with parking, and 70,000 square feet for retail uses, including a 35,000-square-foot grocery store.

Howard University's Le Droit Revitalization Initiative has won national recognition for its successful redevelopment, along with 11 national awards (French, 2004).

Sources: French, Desiree. 2000. Hassan Minor, Community Builders Profile. *Urban Land,* July 2004; *Le Droit Neighborhood, Washington, D.C.* (2000); Swygert, H. Patrick letter to Howard University Community, May 21, 2008. Accessed December 19, 2008 from http://whygentrify.wordpress.eom/page/2/.

Box 8.1	Example 8.2: Target Areas Approach Locality Development in New Orleans

In efforts to rebuild New Orleans after Hurricane Katrina, the adoption of a targeted locality development approach has been essential due to the extensive damage the city suffered and subsequent difficulty in generating sufficient resources for redevelopment. An extensive planning effort, in which coauthor Edward J. Blakely played a key role as the Director of the Office of Recovery Management, led to the area prioritization depicted in the map in Figure 8.6.

Rebuild

New Orleans East Plaza—District Center

New Orleans East, developed in 1960, makes up 67% of the city's land and pre-Katrina had 96,000 people. The New Orleans East Plaza, at 1-10 and Read Road, was established in 1974 and served as a major shopping center for this suburban area. Over 70% of the residences in this area were deemed substantially damaged by Katrina, yet today homes are being rebuilt and families are returning. One vision is to redevelop the 80-acre Plaza as a town center that includes residential, retail, and commercial aspects. Nearby Joe Brown Park and the Louisiana Nature Center form a wonderful regional 187-acre wildlife and recreation center.

Lower Ninth

The Lower Ninth Ward was populated after the Civil War by scores of struggling freedmen who had settled in the area. The Lower Ninth Ward's rural feel and reputation for neighborliness formed its character, as did its history of civil rights activism, which created one of the first integrated elementary schools in the South. It is home to musicians such as Fats Domino and Kermit Ruffins. In the Holy Cross area, fine examples of traditional New Orleans architecture and two historic landmarks, the Doullut Steamboat Houses, survived the storm. Unfortunately, 90% of the Lower Ninth was significantly damaged. The vision is to support the development of economic and community redevelopment opportunities, including clustering of properties closer to the river. Global Green has broken ground on the first energy efficient housing complex in the city.

(Continued)

(Continued)

Figure 8.5 City of New Orleans Recovery Target Areas

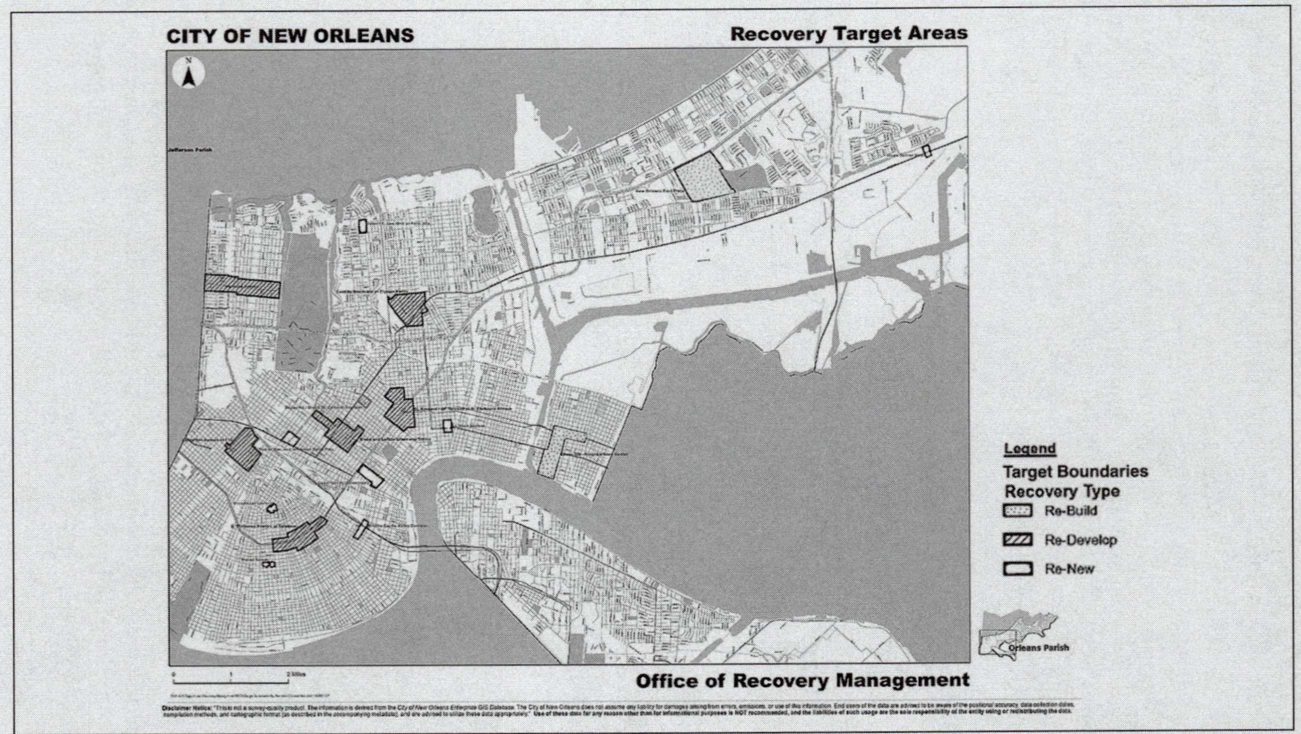

Source: Created for Edward J. Blakely by New Orleans Department of Information Services, September 2007. City of New Orleans, Office of Recovery Management.

Redevelop

Gentilly Boulevard @ Elysian Fields

Always an important transportation route, this intersection now links businesses, several neighborhoods of middle-income family dwellings, and four higher education institutions. Nearby Gentilly Terrace is a national historic district, which has the largest collection of California bungalow-style houses in the South. Dillard University, the University of New Orleans, Southern University at New Orleans, and the Southern Baptist Theological Seminary are in proximity to this important intersection, bringing students and faculty to this area on a regular basis. Plans for this area include the redevelopment of the shopping center at this intersection into a mixed-use facility and new landscaping to make it a more pedestrian-friendly location.

South Claiborne @ Toledano

South Claiborne is a busy six-lane thoroughfare with a large green neutral ground. At Toledano, halfway between uptown and downtown, two neighborhoods meet: Central City and Broadmoor. This has for many years been a point for businesses serving these mixed-income neighborhoods with high residential density. The community wishes to redevelop abandoned housing and eradicate blight in the area. The shopping center here is also targeted for redevelopment, with a vision of upgraded facilities that bring smart growth and economic sustainability.

Figure 8.6   Streetcars Moving Once Again in New Orleans

Source: Photo by Edward J. Blakely, April 2007.

Renew

Alcee Fortier Boulevard

New Orleans is home to 12,000 Vietnamese Americans, many of whom live in Village de l'Est, a small portion of the 32,000-acre tract of land in New Orleans East that was first developed in 1961. The first Vietnamese came in 1975 after the fall of Saigon, South Vietnam's capital, and quickly adapted to the fishing and industries of the area.

(Continued)

(Continued)

The center of this community is The Mary Queen of Vietnam Church, which played a pivotal role in the rapid post–Katrina recovery of this area. The area is rich with Vietnamese restaurants, as well as nearby pictur-esque traditional gardens and weekly vegetable markets. Alcee Fortier Boulevard, the main commercial center of the area, will receive street beautification to support continued redevelopment.

Broadmoor

Located in Uptown New Orleans, Broadmoor is a well-established, multi-racial/multi-ethnic community. The residential architecture in the area is expansive, ranging from Spanish-style, double shotgun, Greek revival, Louisiana Victorian, Louisiana Classical, and a handful of Arts and Crafts. Broadmoor is also the home of the Rosa Keller Branch Library, one of the most recognizable landmarks in the neighborhood. Due to its architectural significance, the New Orleans Historic Districts/Landmarks Commission designated the home a historic landmark in 1986.

While suffering from significant damage after the hurricanes, the work of the Broadmoor Improvement Association, founded in 1969, has helped to stabilize the neighborhood. Many homes have been elevated and families and businesses are returning. The community's vision includes the expansion of the Rosa Keller library and the development of a museum dedicated to the history of New Orleans' famous pumping system.

What Is New and Creative About This Plan and What Leadership Does It Show?

This plan emerged from the complex processes described. It not only built on the work of the community, but justified it in concrete terms. The Target Areas Plan has become the catalyst for civic action. The Target Areas are the new community drivers and the rallying points for the "Citywide" recovery. They have provided a sense of hope for all segments of the community after over two years of squabbling, dissent, anger, and animosity. The plan has led the healing process.

A Plan to Live By and Go By

The New Orleans Plan is more than just a document. It has restored the community's faith in itself and led to new investment across the city. The initial plan investment is $1.1 billion. This is not enough money to do the total city restoration, but it will make a great start.

The plan is already bearing fruit, with new businesses and housing opening in the target areas. In late August 2007, the Veterans Administration and the Louisiana State University announced their contributions to the plan, with each pledging over $1 billion in new medical and bioscience facilities to anchor the downtown (Canal Street) portion of the plan.

New Orleans is not just rebuilding a city. It is recapturing a spirit that is unique in America, and one of the best reflections of American diversity. As such, rebuilding New Orleans helps to restore America's soul. This is the plan.

Teaching Case 8.1

Community Building Through Ownership

Chesterfield has had an impressive recent record of innovation in urban revitalization. It was one of the first cities to respond to the need for rehabilitated housing and to recognize the opportunity of abandoned, vacant city-owned houses by developing the urban homesteading program. City residents willing to rehabilitate and live in the buildings could buy them for just one dollar. Chesterfield has become a city that planners, urban government officials, and private developers use as an example of a city willing and able to develop innovative programs to meet the needs of all its residents.

Part of the reason for Chesterfield's success has been the city's ability to build on the strength of its neighborhoods. That process has involved a willingness to listen to neighborhood concerns, and to adapt city policies and programs to meet those concerns. Keeping the neighborhood shopping areas alive and healthy has been an important part of that effort.

One of the problems with many city programs is that they attack only one facet of a problem. Cities focus on putting in street improvements or a mall and then hope for the storeowners to do their part. They expect homeowners and apartment owners to improve their properties. The city of Chesterfield recognized that public improvements would not, by themselves, have any long-term effect unless there was a total approach to the needs of the shopping areas and homeowners.

The city's staff worked closely with a locally developed City Economic Development Task Force to identify the commercial and housing needs of an area and then organize programs of activities to meet those needs. The program included four major components: public improvements, housing and storefront improvements, management, and financing.

The city's task force recommended a program in which commercial buildings, multiple-unit dwellings, and a few single-family units used as

(Continued)

(Continued)

"crackpads" were seized for payment of delinquent taxes or fines. These buildings are being recycled for community use. In the program, as designed by the task force, the city pays for mutually agreed upon public improvements such as public housing, police protection, parking, land-scaping, benches, and other street furniture in a designated neighbor-hood. The citizens of the selected area must work for a nonprofit community-based Community Land Trust (CLT). The CLT purchases dis-tressed properties from the city at cost. CLT properties are then placed in one of three programs: the Lease Purchase Program, the Homeward Bound Program, or the Multifamily Program. Under the CLT Lease Purchase Program, qualified low-income working families who cannot raise the down payment but can make lease payments of $200 to $300 per month can lease a home or apartment with an option to purchase. Families must put at least $2,000 in sweat equity into the home via repairs before they can move into the unit. The low-income prospective owner must present a plan to rehabilitate the property at his or her expense. During the lease period, the family must keep up the property or face lease termination.

The Homeward Bound Program is aimed at young people who have moved away from their neighborhoods. It is similar to the Lease Purchase Program but aimed at higher-income families who still cannot afford a down payment. These families take on mortgage payments of $1,000 to $1,400 per month. Families purchase the property with a low down pay-ment and a second mortgage. They can refinance the project in as little as three years, and take on the full first mortgage themselves. CLT maintains a ground lease on these properties that specifies owner occupancy and sets a formula for a sales price. If the property is sold for a price higher than the agreed-upon formula, the land lease is terminated and the back land rent is due and payable in full.

Finally, the Multifamily Program provides for the rehabilitation of mul-tifamily units by CLT for rental. CLT has a separate housing management company to service the nearly 400 units of apartment units it currently operates.

A fourth critical area of the Chesterfield program is management assis-tance. The city has the staff and expertise to do all of the things needed to manage property. The city's program provides that expertise to building owners too small to afford it on their own. The city offers a neighborhood development manager in each district who will carry out an analysis of retail demand in the neighborhood so merchants can offer the goods and services their customers want. It also helps merchants plan and carry out promotional events such as street fairs, tours, and market days, and assists with advertising campaigns.

The city is contemplating moving beyond this program to revitalize neighborhood areas. The new approach would be to establish a local community development bank to help finance community- or neighborhood-based projects. The development bank would be formed as a community development bank trust with a local board composed of both neighborhood and business representatives. The city economic development staff, which proposed the idea, are suggesting that the city council place a portion of the city employee pension fund assets in this bank, and the income stream from downtown redevelopment projects as well as the $1 million private sector commitment, into the bank, The proposal has generated heated debate in the city council and the community. The *Chesterfield Tribune* has editorialized that such a use of city pension and investment funds in this manner would be "totally irresponsible." What are the pros and cons of this type of investment approach? Should the city risk its pension funds and city redevelopment income on such projects?

Teaching Case 8.2

Revitalizing the Center

The key to a city downtown revitalization strategy is a dynamic public–private partnership. During the late 1960s, Centerville began to decline economically. As in many other moderate-sized, industrial American cities, Centerville's retail sector moved to the suburbs and its industrial base shrank. The 1990 census showed a continuing decline in the city population from 690,000 in 1960 to 499,000 three decades later. Meanwhile, the metropolitan area's population increased from 792,000 to 1,570,000. In the late 1960s and early 1970s, Centerville realized that a dramatic move had to be made to revive the city. That move was a strategy to invest significant public funds to encourage private investment in the city's decaying downtown. Those funds upgraded public facilities and improved sites, opening up new development opportunities for private investors. Spurred by public support, a series of projects has led to a fairly significant comeback for Centerville's downtown. Centerville's success is a useful model for other cities of moderate size in the midst of revitalizing their downtowns.

As a medium-sized city, Centerville had a close-knit and generally progressive business community. The business leaders knew and trusted each other. Those relationships helped to convince them to take some risks to revitalize their downtown. The camaraderie was so strong that, once the process began, no one wanted to be left out. That feeling was essential. The

(Continued)

(Continued)

city leaders felt that the redevelopment would never have happened if any one participant had failed to join—that is, if the public–private partnership were less than complete.

In Centerville, 90% of all deals involving public commitments include the city's economic development corporation, Civic Central Area, Inc., a private, nonprofit business organization. The economic development corporation is headed by an executive director, and employs 32 people who work to attract new development, retain business, assist small businesses, and package financing. This active municipal component, along with Centerville's mayor, initiated and promoted the downtown revitalization strategy. The public commitment to development has been consistent and predictable, thus making the development environment more hospitable. Centerville's strategy was to initiate development through bold steps that would ripple through the downtown.

The city's early redevelopment efforts were convincing evidence of the need for this direction. One of the first projects conceived in the late 1960s and constructed in the early 1970s was a six-block pedestrian mall on Fourth Avenue, downtown. When the mall was on the drawing board, the retail sector had not completely deteriorated but the suburban shopping trend was clear. By the time the mall was completed, a second suburban shopping center had opened and the true impact on downtown was felt. The mall, unfortunately, was an example of too little, too late. That experience, however, taught Centerville a lesson: Only a large investment would affect the downtown's economy.

Centerville's size is also a plus. Although the city has suffered economic decline, as have many Midwestern industrial cities, Centerville does not have the larger pockets of poverty characteristic of larger cities. The extent of poverty, housing problems, and economic decline is not so extreme, and solutions are easier to find.

Yet the citizens' attitude toward the downtown in a moderate-sized city like Centerville is harder to break than in a larger city. In Centerville, the public saw no possibility of reviving the downtown. In large cities, the central business district frequently has kept its traditional office function, making retail core revitalization easier, but in medium-sized cities such as this one, the public often perceives the downtown as dead for all purposes. Therefore, Centerville launched a major public relations campaign to overcome this negative attitude.

To formulate a new strategy, the city and Civic Central Area, Inc., formed a committee to study the downtown's problems. At that time, the city had a strong governmental complex at its western edge, a large medical complex on the east side, and the Belvedere Hotel on the north. Fourth Avenue, the heart of the CBD (central business district), was clearly suffering.

The committee recommended the construction of the Pigeon Dome, a new center-city sports complex, combined with retailing to be located in the heart of the downtown, in order to fill the hole in the donut. The city provided the seed money to plan the Pigeon Dome. The plan envisioned an integrated project of an office, retail, restaurant, and hotel attached to the 25,000-seat indoor sports arena. Municipal support for the project was reinforced with a pledge from the business community to assist in developing necessary feasibility studies and assistance in land assembly. With that commitment, the committee was entertaining a deal with the team owner Al David. Al wanted the community to finance the entire project and pay no rent for the first 10 years. In addition, Al asked for the Pigeons basketball team to control the revenues for the entire stadium parking for the life of their 20-year lease.

The total project cost, $142.5 million, would be financed by the city and state, federal grants, and private sources. Federal funds would be used to acquire land and construct a department store, leased to its operator. City funds constructed the garage from the land monies and built the public open space, including the Pigeon skyboxes. They organized financial and public support from downtown business owners, the city leadership, and the state made a strong partnership—and, the codeveloper believed, an essential one—to make the project work.

However, very significant community opposition has developed. Neighborhood activists have attacked the project as a giveaway to wealthy sports owners. Schools and community groups claim that $150 million could go a long way toward restoring all of the programs cut out of the school budget, lowering class size, and providing housing for the homeless.

Proponents for the Pigeons argue that the dome is an investment and cannot be compared with funding the schools or homeless projects. Furthermore, bringing the Pigeons to downtown will prove that a major project in a city of this size would give high visibility all over the Midwest. The project is demanding public attention and dominates the media. The value of the Pigeons playing downtown will bring millions in unpaid advertising to the city. This visibility is a major component in an overall strategy for cities of moderate size, particularly in overcoming negative attitudes and replacing them with civic pride in the downtown.

The mayor of Centerville argues that physical redevelopment must precede business and jobs. An important way to attract new firms is to show potential companies an exciting city with a major sports franchise at its heart. The private and public sectors, working together, can make this happen.

African American leaders have been especially critical of the downtown Pigeon Dome proposal. They point out that, other than a few star players, few Blacks will benefit from the arena. They have come to the city with a plan

(Continued)

(Continued)

that would require that African Americans be given opportunities for equity participation in all future downtown projects. The proposal before the city council would require that 20% of the equity in the Pigeon Dome be set aside for local Black investors. Half of this 20%—or 10%—would be from city funds invested in the projects and passed on to a coalition of African American leaders to be held in a trust fund for minority education. The remaining percentage would be allocated by the developer to Black residents who would either provide services, cash, or secured notes to gain their share of the project. Finally, the coalition is requiring Al David to donate 5% of the team's ownership stakes to a minority development corporation.

Assume you are on the mayor's chief economic development advisory board and develop a winning strategy for the mayor that does not contribute to racial injustice.

Teaching Case 8.3

The Portside Plan

One of the newest trends for raising capital in cities involves minority equity participation programs intended to increase the participation of minorities and women in new development. Such plans are designed to help pay for affordable housing, economic development, and other needs in city neighborhoods. Communities all across the nation from San Francisco to Boston, from Seattle to Jersey City, are attempting to find ways to bring minorities and women and neighborhoods into the development process. The concept is to design a system that provides for a combination of taxes and incentives to make developers involve minorities and women in city development projects.

The Portside Minority Equity Participation Program is an innovative "bottom-up" strategy that uses downtown development to fuel growth in the city's neighborhoods. The Portside Minority Equity Participation Program is essential to the city's health in that it can help create self-reliant, locally based entrepreneurship in low-income, minority neighborhoods. Such programs stress self-employment, small businesses, and worker or community ownership, emphasizing adequate wages and benefits, decent working conditions, stability, job control, and opportunities for upward mobility. A city is thus rebuilt neighborhood by neighborhood, as small, locally controlled enterprises create jobs for nearby residents.

Portside is giving a whole new meaning to bottom-up development programs by earmarking downtown development through its Minority

Equity Participation Program. The program has three components. First, a new Minority/Community Equity Participation (MCEP) Commission is being appointed. The new commission will have responsibility for establishing guidelines for minimum minority/female participation in all projects with city investments of more than $100,000. The commission is to establish a point system as part of the bidding process so that developers can bid for projects with varying amounts of minority participation, jobs, and other benefits in any project. The project with the greatest overall city benefit would be awarded the opportunity to develop the specified site. Second, the Minority Equity Trust fund is being established. This trust fund is designed as an alternative to direct equity or jobs participation. Developers can contribute to the trust fund in lieu of or in addition to meeting other community goals. Finally, the Minority/Community Equity Participation Commission was authorized to recommend a downtown development fee (tax) on all downtown developments on a per-square-foot basis. The fees collected would be designated for the trust fund.

Within this framework, the Minority/Community Equity Participation Advisory Board has proposed that a linked development requirement be instituted for downtown commercial development. This would require the developer to design a companion project in one of several low-income neighborhoods. Innovative programs proposed by the committee included a variety of loans for start-up enterprises headed by low-income people, minorities, and women as well as housing and job training projects. One loan program, for example, would provide these businesses with working capital at low interest rates and favorable repayment terms.

Another component of the MCEP Board's plan was first-source hiring agreements to ensure that the city's most needy residents would benefit from the jobs created by downtown development. Any employer who receives a publicly subsidized grant or loan or who is involved in a commercial project involving city financial participation would have to use the mayor's Office of Employment and Training as a "first source" of employment referrals for any new jobs created.

A third component of the MCEP Board's recommendations is a plan for Portside city government to make half its purchases from city small businesses and 25% from businesses owned by minorities and women.

The Minority Equity Participation Program was adopted without a single dissenting vote in the city council. However, now that the commission is in operation, the city attorney and business groups are raising questions about the legality and the advisability of the MCEP's proposals. The city attorney is arguing that the point system is a violation of the *Croson v. City of Richmond* decision of the U.S. Supreme Court, which prohibits any plan based solely on race. Moreover, the commission, City Attorney Jane

(Continued)

(Continued)

Gonzales argues, has not established a nexus between downtown development and the proposed development fee. This, she states, is a clear violation of the *Nollan v. California* decision, which requires a nexus between any tax or fee and the actual project impacts.

The chamber of commerce is livid because the use tax and exaction fees are perceived as antidevelopment. The chamber argues that the office market is too soft to withstand these taxes and that the result of their implementation would be a rapid acceleration of suburban office construction and job growth. "We have talked to developers and those who have done major rehabs, and they say that an additional $2 a square foot [the average exaction fee] can kill a deal," asserts the president of a local business organization.

Several factors have prevented implementation of most of the Portside MCEP proposals. These have included city council fear, developer and real estate opposition, and the unsettled legal questions. The mayor thinks that the city attorney's objection is correct but that her approach is incorrect. What the mayor and a majority of council members want is to find an acceptable formula for implementing the MCEP commission recommendations. Can you figure out a way to resolve the impasse for the mayor, the advisory board, and the city attorney?

Conclusion

Locality development is the most well-known technique for stimulating economic development. City officials are generally comfortable with most aspects of this concept. Everyone wants to live in an orderly, well-maintained community that is proud of itself. Every community needs to be able to successfully adapt to changes in its economy. This does not happen by chance. A city's urban design plays a critical role in its ability to adapt to negative and positive economic trends. In addition, farsighted leadership combined with the prudent use of incentives and disincentives can enable the community to meet its economic goals. No community can afford to "sit on its assets."

References and Suggested Readings

Bacon, Kevin, Richard Dagenhart, Nancey Green Leigh, and John Skach. 2008. The Economic Development-Urban Design Link in Brownfield Redevelopment: Learning from Atlantic Station. *The IEDC Economic Development Journal* 7(2): 30–39.

Blakely, Edward J. 1992. This City is Not for Burning. *Natural Hazards Journal* 16(6): 1–3.

Day, P., and D. Perkins. 1984. Carrot or the Stick? The Incentives in Development Control. *Urban Policy and Research* 2(3): 2–14.

Farley, Josh, and Norm Glickman. 1986. R&D as an Economic Development Strategy. *Journal of the American Planning Association* 77(1): 407–418.

Farr, Cheryl. 1984. *Shaping the Local Economy.* Washington, DC: International City/County Management Association.

Fitzgerald, Joan, and Nancey Green Leigh. 2002. *Cases and Strategies for City and Suburb.* Thousand Oaks, CA: Sage.

Freidman, Bernard, and Lynne Sagalyn. 1989. *Downtown Inc: How America Rebuilds Cities.* Cambridge: MIT Press.

French, Desiree. 2004. Hassan Minor, Community Builders Profile. *Urban Land* July: 110–111.

Frenchman. D. 2004. Event-places in North America: City Meaning and Making. *Places* 16(3): 36–49.

Furio, Brooke A., and Nate Z. Hoelzel. 2007. Lessons Learned. Cleveland's Industrial/Commercial Land Bank Pilot Program. November 28. Accessed February 25, 2008 from http://www.epa.state.oh.us/derr/Brownfield_Conference/presentation%20docs/Land%20Bank.pdf

Haar, Charles M., and Jerold S. Kayden. 1989. *Zoning and the American Dream.* Chicago: Planners Press.

Hester, Randy. 1985. 12 Steps to Community Development. *Landscape Architecture* 75: 78–85.

Homets, J. 1992. *Small Town and Rural Planning Newsletter* 11(1–2): 7.

Jacobs, Allan B. 1993. *Great Streets.* Cambridge, MA: MIT Press.

Le Droit Neighborhood, Washington, D.C. 2000. In *Howard University–Le Droit Park Revitalization Initiative.* Washington, DC: Concord Partners for the District of Columbia Government.

Leigh, Nancey Green, and Sarah L. Coffin. 2005. Modeling the Relationship Among Brownfields, Property Values, and Community Revitalization. *Housing Policy Debate* 16(2): 257–280.

Mossop, E. 2006. Landscapes of Infrastructure. In C. Waldheim (Ed.), *The Landscape Urbanism Reader* (pp. 163–177). New York: Princeton Architectural Press

Museum Brings Town Back to Life. 2000. *New York Times,* May 30, p. A1.

Neutze, Max. 1984. *Land Use Planning and Local Economic Development Plan,* March. Unpublished manuscript.

Oke, Graham. 1986. Targeting Economic Development. *Australian Urban Studies* February 4: 13.

Purcell, Amelia. 1982. Shopsteading: New Business in Old Neighborhoods. *Commentary* (Spring), n.p.

Reardon, C. 1993. The Unconquered Spirit. *Ford Foundation Newsletter* 24(2): 3–7.

Sagalyn, Lynne. 1990. Exploring the Improbable: Local Redevelopment in the Wake of Federal Cutbacks. *Journal of the American Planning Association* 56(4): 429–441. This is a revised version of a paper presented to the New South Wales Local Government Planners Association Conference, Macquarie University, 15 February, 1984.

Schwab, Jim. 1989. Riverfront Gamblers. *Planning* 55: 15–18.

Swygert, H. Patrick. 2008. Letter to Howard University Community, May 21. Accessed December 19, 2008 from http://whygentrify.wordpress.com/page/2

Walsh, Tommy. 1992. Dress Up for Company. *Economic Development Digest* 1(9): 1.

9

Business Development

B usiness development is an essential component of local economic development planning because the creation, attraction, and retention of business activities builds and maintains a healthy local economy. Active business development is required in both good and bad economic times. When our national economy was booming in the recent past, there were still soft areas in fast-growing economies like Silicon Valley, where neighboring East Palo Alto benefited very little from the robust economy. Other areas, such as much of rural Appalachia, saw some improvements in low-wage jobs but little real economic gain. Clearly, many inner-city residents, such as Harlem's long-standing low-income Black and Hispanic residents, benefited little from the robust New York economic resurgence that welcomed former President Clinton to the community and led to rising real estate prices, pushing longtime renter households out of the community.

No matter how poor a local economy appears to be, however, it still has economic potential internally and opportunities to reach larger external markets. For example, America's inner cities, which had been in continual decline due to postwar suburbanization, came to be seen as new markets ripe for picking at the end of the 1990s (Cuomo, 1999). This vast potential was first tapped by just a handful of pioneering retailers, but the trend grew exponentially, bolstered by the New Urbanism and Smart Growth movements, resulting in the "back to the downtown" movement of housing, headquarters, offices, hotels, and restaurants as well as retail activity. The movement came from local entrepreneurs and national/international developers, businesses, and franchise holders. Today, there is a growing emphasis on stabilizing inner-city economies through deepening the local economic base with industrial activity (Leigh and Hoelzel, 2012).

Retailers and other business can come into distressed communities only if new partnerships can be forged between community and business interests.

These new partnerships are developed by public planners in the name of community. As Frieden (1990) says,

> Planners have many compelling reasons for taking on the function of public sector developers. For professionals whose usual complaint is lack of influence, public sector development offers a rare opportunity to get major projects done. For professionals whose usual output consists of planning documents, it provides visible, measurable accomplishment on the ground. And for professionals usually required to have the time-sense of a geologist, it offers the satisfactions of making an impact within a few years.
>
> Getting the projects done poses challenges that many people find exciting. The public sector developer has to mediate between public and private interests in order to find solutions that meet both an economic and a political bottom line. Achieving success means delivering a project that is economically sound and that serves public purposes beyond financial returns. For a planner who wants to influence the character of a city on a large scale, and wants to do it reasonably early in his or her career, public sector development is a promising choice. (p. 427)

Business development is intended to redress the balance between community as a social construct and business as an instrument of wealth generation for planners. As Lockhart (1987) puts it:

> Community [is] more than a bedroom and service annex to alien commercial interests. Such a notion of community begins with the recognition of the crucial role that the building of shared commitments to the common well-being plays in the attainment of social health and individual satisfaction. (p. 57)

In this context, community and business development are merged as a vehicle to mobilize essential community resources for the generation of shared wealth, both in terms of individual and collective well-being and in terms of a stronger set of economic institutions that can compete both locally and globally. Andrew Cuomo (1999), former U.S. Department of Housing and Urban Development (HUD) secretary (1996–2000), articulates this concept: "Increased business investment can transform many inner cities from places left behind by the new economy into places leading the way to economic success—bringing shoppers, billions of dollars in consumer spending, and new jobs to urban America" (p. vii). Even though business opportunities are important to minority communities, this should not lead to the conclusion that small business is the only way to create such opportunities. For example, the 600,000 to 800,000 new U.S. companies created annually include many self-employed workers. The Department of Labor estimates that nearly 11% of Americans were self-employed in 2009. This includes those professionals who work on their own, such as consultants and actors, as well as people who work from home in asso-ciation with millions of small businesses. Rates of self-employment are highest among Whites (7.4%), men (8.3%), and older workers (18.1%). These 2009 data reflect a continuing trend (Hipple, 2010).

Regardless of whether we are promoting new businesses or retaining existing enterprises, there are at least 12 basic tools or techniques normally considered central to business development. They include one-stop centers, start-up and venture financing companies, small business development centers, women's enterprises, group marketing systems, promotion and tourism programs, research and development programs, incubation centers, micro-enterprises, tech-nology and business parks, enterprise zones, and entrepreneur development courses.

The choice of tools depends on the local business development strategy. Business development strategies can have one or more of four basic dimensions: to encourage new business start-ups, to attract new firms to the area, to sustain and expand existing businesses in the area, and to increase innovation and entrepreneurship within the community. Table 9.1 illustrates how the tools emphasize the different dimensions. Clearly, they can be mixed together to incorporate several dimensions, depending on the circumstances. In fact, few communities use one tool alone. Most communities use a combination of tools integrated into the total local or community economic development strategy.

Table 9.1   Matching Business Development Tools and Objectives

Tool	Objective			
	Business Start-Ups	*Business Attraction*	*Business Expansion/ Retention*	*Nurturing Innovation and Entrepreneurship*
One-stop center	X	X	X	
Start-up and venture financing company	X	X	X	
Small business assistance center	X		X	X
Group marketing system	X		X	X
Promotion and tourism programming	X	X	X	

Tool	Objective			
	Business Start-Ups	Business Attraction	Business Expansion/ Retention	Nurturing Innovation and Entrepreneurship
Research and development				X
Incubation center	X			X
Technology and business park	X	X	X	
Enterprise zone	X	X	X	
Entrepreneurship development activity	X			X
Women's enterprise	X			X
Micro-enterprise	X		X	X

Creating a Good Business Climate

A "climate" conducive to business development is often created with the participation of local governments and neighborhoods. There are published business climate studies in leading business and professional magazines worldwide. The significance of these studies of states, cities, and metropolitan regions remains clouded. After examining their methods and uses, Rodney Erickson (1987) concluded,

> There are clearly shortcomings of business climate studies. . . . Does that mean that we should forget about competitive position and business climate studies? . . . In my mind the answer is "no." Whether we like it or not, business climate studies are here to stay. . . . [G]ood business climate studies can help to focus attention on the particular nature of problem issues and lead to some worthwhile introspection. (p. 62)

Business climate studies receive media attention externally and internally. Citizens feel better about a well-ranked community, whether or not there is a real difference in the economic or social outcomes associated with the subjective measure used in such studies. Most business climate studies measure the comparative aspects of conducting business in one community over another.

However, issues in firm location or relocation have more to do with the comparative advantages a city offers for the particular enterprise, such as the nearby location of important suppliers, customers, or scientific information. The key to a good climate is determining what kinds of regulatory and policy tools will facilitate business development for the type of firms that use the locality's asset base, such as a harbor, university, or supplier. This is not an easy task, but it can be achieved. There is no strict, standard mixture with respect to the kinds of incentives and support programs offered. The main goal is to fit the program to the businesses desired and to be flexible.

Therefore, both local neighborhoods and cities need to look at existing regulations to see whether they "guide development" to the places and types of activities desired or merely prevent those activities considered undesirable. Finally, the issue of environmental outcomes must be considered. The fact that a community has space or facilities for some environmentally contaminating uses does not mean that these should be the best or only industries a community attempts to attract.

Entrepreneur Development and Economic Gardening[1]

An entrepreneurial community strategy seeks to grow local businesses and create jobs from within the local economy. It requires a critical mass of entrepreneurs, strong support networks, and a community that is ready for change and seeks innovations (Litchenstein, Lyons, and Kutzhanova, 2004).

An entrepreneur, as defined in the *Oxford English Dictionary*, is someone who undertakes a business or enterprise with chance of profit or loss. Put more simply, an entrepreneur is a risk taker. Not all risk takers are successful, however. To be successful, the entrepreneur needs to be proficient in all aspects of decision making. Successful decision making by entrepreneurs involves three skills:

1. *self-knowledge,* or the knowledge to specify the objective; imagination and analytical ability to focus on the factors that lead to decisive action

2. *research skills,* necessary for collection of data and foresight to estimate data

3. *decision-making and implementation skills,* which require computational skills for applying the data to the decision rule and communication skills for formulating implementation plans. In addition, the entrepreneur needs to have delegation and organizational skills to involve and utilize specialists as required.

The entrepreneur's goal is to "create or capitalize on new economic opportunities through innovation—by finding new solutions to existing problems, or by connecting existing solutions to unmet needs or new opportunities" (Lichtenstein and Lyons, 1996). We highlight here six methods that can be used to foster an entrepreneurship local economic development strategy; these are elaborated on to some extent in other sections of this chapter.[2]

1. *Develop diverse sources of capital:* local venture capital firms, organized networks of angel investors, and public or private seed capital funds.

2. *Create an enabling community culture:* This should be founded on the entrepreneurs' common vision for the community's future, their commitment to giving time and money back to the community, and their willingness to share ideas and information.

3. *Foster networking:* "[C]onsummate entrepreneurs are networkers who thrive in communities. Networks are essential because they link entrepreneurs to potential sources of capital, new employees, strategic alliances, and service providers such as lawyers, accountants, and consultants" (Edward Lowe Foundation, 2002).

4. *Provide supportive infrastructure:* Perhaps most significant is the presence of a local college or university because of its role in education, research and development, and fostering an open-minded, risk-taking local culture. However, more traditional infrastructure, such as transportation and high-speed Internet access, is also important.

5. *Make government entrepreneur friendly:* Local governments that streamline processes work in a spirit of entrepreneurship instead of bureaucracy, so it is easier for local entrepreneurs to do business.

6. *Foster entrepreneurship education:* This education should be targeted to primary and secondary schools as well as adult education. Linking entrepreneurship with education develops human capital and makes this method of economic development more sustainable (Dabson et al., 2003).

Cities can facilitate the identification of people with entrepreneurial talent and interests and develop them via the creation of social and professional networks, as well as through secondary and postsecondary education programs.

Social and professional networks connect business owners with service providers as well as grant access to resources, materials, labor, financing, and new markets. Mentoring, another critical aspect of fostering entrepreneurship, occurs on a voluntary basis. The cost for both networks and mentoring programs is typically small and supports logistical and organizational activities.

Youth business programs can be established in high schools, while entrepreneurial training programs can be established in the junior or community colleges. Some big-city newspapers such as the *Oakland Tribune* in California have sponsored business start-up fairs and training sessions to release local entrepreneurial talents in the resident population.

While it is difficult to compare the budget of an entrepreneurial strategy with those of traditional business recruitment incentive packages, it is clear that the costs of this strategy can be significantly lower than the latter category of economic development expenditures. For example, the incentive packages that seven states offered in 1996 for just a single manufacturing plant ranged from $2.35 million to $12.475 million (Spicer, 1996). In contrast, the 2005 total budget for a Littleton, Colorado, economic gardening strategy (described below) was $600,000, or one quarter of that of the lowest amount spent on a single manufacturing plant by any of the seven states in the mid-1990s.

Entrepreneurial Community Program: Growing an Economic Garden

In 1987, the City Council of Littleton, Colorado, decided it wanted to grow jobs by fostering entrepreneurship within the community rather than by recruiting companies to relocate to or expand in the area.[3] It developed an economic gardening program based on the idea that business success comes from (1) an ability to adapt to changes while retaining an identity, (2) a sense of self-organization that encourages action at the individual level versus top-heavy organizational structures, and (3) a local culture that favors risk taking, innovation, and diversity (Gibbons, 2005).

Littleton's economic gardening program has three core activities. First, it provides tactical and strategic information to existing or potential local businesses. This is called "competitive intelligence" (Society of Competitive Intelligence Professionals, n.d.)[4] and involves providing information to local Littleton businesses that is usually available only to large companies. The intelligence provided can include marketability studies, the tracking of new products, legal research, and answers to specific business questions.

Second, Littleton has ensured that necessary infrastructure improvements were made for supporting business. This includes not only physical improvements but also ways to enhance quality of life, such as providing enjoyable open space, sponsoring community events, and an creating an intellectual framework through offering courses and training to promote competitive business practices.

Third, the entrepreneurial strategy focused on creating connections between Littleton's business community and outside organizations, including trade associations, research and development firms, think tanks, and academic institutions such as the University of Colorado and Denver University.

Littleton's Department of Business and Industry Affairs, which created the economic gardening concept, annually assists 200 to 300 businesses with the competitive intelligence aspect of its program (Gibbons, 2005; Hamilton-Pennell, 2004). In the 14 years prior to Littleton's adoption of economic gardening in 1989, business recruitment strategies attracted a total of 4,000 jobs to the city. From 1989 to 2004, employment grew from 15,000 to 29,000, for a total increase of 14,000 jobs. During this period, *no* money was spent on attracting outside industries (Hamilton-Pennell, 2004). Thus, the number of employees grew by 93%; however, Littleton's population increased by only 30% from 1989 to 2004. Using business retention strategies, an annual average of 278 jobs was created. With economic gardening, employment grew by an annual average of 1,000 jobs. There are now more than 2,000 companies located in Littleton, the majority of which are small businesses.

One-Stop Business Assistance Centers

One-stop business centers are relatively common components of local government today. In many cases, the one-stop center has a small business mediation function located in the office of the mayor, the city manager, or economic development.

The traditional role for a one-stop center is an information center designed to serve as a key contact point between businesses of all kinds and local government. To be a one-stop advice service for businesses, the center must contain information on all planning and development matters of interest and concern to businesses—local economic indicators and labor market statistics, local development plans, land availability, building regulations and permits, all aspects of finance, and other useful business information. It must also be able to make this information available promptly. Clearly, the center's size will be a function of the size and complexity of the economic zone it serves. In large cities and towns, for example, a one-stop center for businesses might employ several people. In neighborhoods or community-level and rural places, in contrast, it might employ one person on a full-time or even a part-time basis.

A one-stop center is a valuable business development tool. It benefits businesses by eliminating frustrating referrals from one department to another and by saving time that would have been spent—perhaps without result—trying to procure information on local regulations on their own. In addition to assisting businesses, a one-stop center provides valuable services to local government. Statistics from the center can be used as the basis for reports that describe the number, nature, and geographical breakdown of all business requests. The center's data can also indicate short-term business trends or identify potential business development problems. Moreover, the establishment of an organized professional approach to information dissemination for enterprises strengthens business confidence, as well as local governments or neighborhoods.

Start-Up and Venture Financing Companies and Development Banks

Small firms constitute the vast majority of all business enterprises. The formation of new small businesses has effectively utilized both capital and human resources, resulting in employment growth. However, few financial institutions specialize in meeting the needs of small enterprises.

A small business is usually formed using venture capital from the entrepreneur and his or her relatives and friends. If the business is successful, growth is rapid, and the available funds are quickly consumed in buying equipment and/or stock. At this stage, growing small firms need venture capital, which will both improve their profitability and lower their risk of failure. The small business owner then usually approaches a bank for finance. However, the existing financial system is not equipped to provide adequate venture capital to stimulate the growth of innovative small-size enterprises. Reasons for this shortcoming include constraints on different classes of institutions, an inability of existing financial institutions to evaluate the asset value of highly technical or market-driven innovation, and a general insistence on physical assets as collateral for loans. Banks are primarily lenders to rather than investors in small business. Their emphasis on financial security requires some small firms with an inadequate security or equity base but sound profit expectations to seek either higher-cost sources of finance or to defer or cancel development plans if such alternative sources are unavailable. Venture capital is available primarily from private investors or stock issues. However, many projects and business start-ups in the retail or community service sectors cannot raise funds via the stock exchange, and there are seldom sufficient active local private investors.

The establishment of a mechanism that allows local people to invest in local businesses is therefore an important business development initiative. This can be done through the formation of a start-up and venture financing company—specifically, a community development finance institution (CDFI). CDFIs are a new class of institution with a variety of roots. Some CDFIs are traditional community development corporations that now, with federal government support, offer venture and equity capital. This business development tool can provide venture capital to selected eligible small firms unable to obtain finances from traditional lending institutions and thereby contribute to local economic and employment development. CDFIs, according to Avis Vidal (1995), are not a substitute for ensuring that conventional finance institutions provide equal access to credit and other services in poor inner-city neighborhoods and [rural] communities of color—places where that access is now clearly deficient. CDFIs appear to be playing a useful role both in pressing conventional institutions to do this and in demonstrating how to do it (p. 194).

The Northern California Loan Fund (NCLF) is an illustration of this form of investment organization. Headquartered in San Francisco, the NCLF provides small start-up loans to emerging enterprises in disadvantaged and rural communities. The NCLF obtains its loan funds from private investors who agree to invest in the fund and forgo the interest return on their funds and from foundations and private corporations interested in socially responsible investments.

Development banks are a larger and more established mechanism to provide capital for low-income and female- and minority-owned enterprises. A development bank is a regular lending institution that devotes its resources to fostering economic development (Parzen and Kieschnick, 1992). A development bank might take the form of a savings and loan, a bank, or a community credit union. There is now an association of 40 institutions forming the National Association of Community Development Loan Funds. Massachusetts, New York, and Wisconsin have statewide programs with very similar orientations, and the Ford Foundation's Local Initiative Support Corporation (LISC) provides loan funds or capital support for community development or community enterprise funds on a regional basis for some community development corporations. By providing venture capital, local development groups become shareholders in the companies in which they invest. A community shares with other stockholders in the success (or failure) of investments; it is therefore vitally concerned with their long-term development. Groups like the NCLF provide the opportunity for residents within a community to invest in small business and share in its success without the risk of investing in just a single enterprise.

To be successful, a CDFI or other community venture group must invest only in those small businesses, existing or new, that are commercially viable and have the greatest potential. LISCs or similar groups should not invest in businesses that are not commercially viable, even for social reasons. The community investment program must be run by a board of directors made up of commercially aware and experienced businesspeople with relevant business expertise.

In sum, community-based (CDFI) groups should prefer to invest in small businesses that

- have an innovation in product, process, or marketing
- have potential for rapid growth
- have potential for future sales outside the region
- can demonstrate sound management skills or, if those are absent, are willing to put them in place
- are willing, if selected, to establish, with the help of the community, an experienced board of directors to assist in planning the future growth of the business (the composition of this board should complement the skills of the small business owner in financial, marketing, and management)

By using these criteria, a good community venture group can embrace a wide range of innovations or technologies in traditional business areas or in the newer high-technology enterprises. A CDFI, in particular, should seek to support a business, not run it, by holding a share of up to 50%. Moreover, because an investment is worthwhile only if at some stage the investor can get his or her money back, a CDFI must have a method of exit via one of the following:

- selling its share back to the entrepreneur
- selling its share to another private investor
- selling its share through the stock market

Finance—particularly local finance that can stimulate new creative enterprises—is the core of small business development. Therefore, every city or neighborhood that wants to pursue this avenue of business development must be prepared at some level to put its money on the line. Timothy Bates (2000), one of the leading scholars on small business in general and minority small business in particular, warns that we must examine all the euphoria about small business as a good investment. In fact, he points out that few small, minority businesses are good investments for anyone, including government. Most successful enterprises of this type that pay back loans and investors are Asian small restaurants and similar services employing captive linguistically challenged populations who work in poor conditions and are paid low wages. Even so, many of these enterprises barely provide a living for their owners. Bates warns that "students of economic development should take note: Honest reporting of small business loan losses is rare in the world of local economic development institutions. . . . Absent of subsidies, the insistence of government sponsored CDFIs to actively fund high-risk, high-cost loans is a recipe for disaster" (p. 240). Bates is correct in his observations. The concept that small business is the cornerstone of neighborhood recovery in inner-city communities has been somewhat oversold. Bates and others admit that there is room for businesses, both large and small, in the inner city; however, to consider local ownership via small enterprises as the best or only solution is not warranted and is bad advice.

Small Business Development Centers

Despite the importance of small businesses as employers and sources of entrepreneurial drive, research evidence suggests that the failure (as distinct from discontinuance) rate among new and small firms is substantial. Poor management is the most frequently cited reason for this. An obvious and arguably cost-effective means of improving the economic performance of the small business sector is to establish small business development centers.

These centers provide management training, counseling/consulting, and research services to small firms, with training as the dominant activity. A small business development center should support the training function in various ways. The center that provides these activities could effectively achieve five interrelated objectives:

- encourage a higher rate of new business starts with the potential to succeed
- reduce the level of business failures
- improve the general financial performance and growth rate of the small-firm sector
- raise the potential of small firms to create new jobs and improve employment levels
- raise the general level of technological innovation and productivity

Although small business training/research/counseling activities may be provided through any of several alternative organizations, the best form is a specialist institution organized in close association with rather than within appropriate educational institutions (e.g., university business schools, advanced education, and technical colleges).

Another approach is to turn unemployed workers into business owners and operators through a business resource center. The purpose of these centers is to tap the entrepreneurial talents of laid-off workers and find niches in the local market in which they might start their own enterprises. Business resource centers are usually started by local service clubs, the chamber of commerce, local employment and training institutes, or even a separate nonprofit development and training company. This type of nonprofit organization is designed to use the skills of the underemployed as a basis for generating new employment using business resource centers. These centers provide the following:

- practical training in business start-ups
- low-cost, small premises
- centralized services, such as photocopying, telephone answering, and accounting
- a big brother or sister for the new business

Micro-Enterprise

In 2006, Mohammad Yunus won the Nobel Peace Prize for pioneering the concept of micro-enterprise supported by the Grameen Bank. The spread of the micro-enterprise and associated microlending concept is a rare example of the transference of an economic development tool that originated in the developing world to the developed world. In the United States, in particular, both rural areas and inner cities are adopting this tool.

The basic micro-enterprise concept is to loan funds to a group of borrowers who plan to go into very small labor-intensive businesses in the same community. Micro-enterprises are usually operated from the home or on the street. They include such enterprises as homemade jewelry or garments, handmade shoes, or specialty foods for restaurants.

Micro-enterprise programs usually make very small loans to a group of 5 to 10 borrowers, each borrowing under $1,000. The group is responsible for each member making his or her loan payments on time. There is usually some form of prebusiness training and group building before loans are made to potential entrepreneurs. These programs are now in place in many parts of the country, although it is too early to assess their efforts. The programs include the Micro Industry Credit Organization in Tucson, the Self-Employment Circle (a subsidiary of the South Shore Bank in Chicago), and the Lakota Fund on the Pine Ridge Reservation in Kyle, South Dakota. Micro-enterprise development is not a panacea for the poor, according to Lisa Servon (1999). However, she maintains that the locally initiated nature of micro-enterprise programs makes them particularly responsive to their constituencies. This local orientation has allowed them to stay flexible, boosting training capacity, broadening or narrowing the target population, increasing loan-size ceilings, and so forth.

Women's Enterprises

One of the most underutilized resources in the nation is the entrepreneurial talent of millions of women. In the mid-1980s, a pioneering organization was established in Minneapolis-St. Paul to assist women of low income and on welfare to start their own businesses. The mission of this organization, called WEDCO and now known as Women Venture, was to assist women developing small enterprises through an intensive self-help program.

Women Venture has more than 10 affiliate operations around the country. Each is based on a very similar model. Low- and moderate-income women are put through a seven-week intensive training program. The program focuses on assisting them to identify their talents and interests and on building the self-confidence to start a competitive enterprise. The program is rigorous, with few dropouts. Although not all women start their own business, many complete the training with enough confidence to seek work in challenging and rewarding fields.

Servon (1999) provides an insightful analysis of women's microenterprises in that they offer a means of changing attitudes more than incomes. At the conclusion of her book of case studies, she remarks, "Perhaps one of the most important things that micro-enterprise programs accomplish is that they help change people's attitudes by creating forward motion, giving them the hope they need to believe they can take charge of their own lives."

Promotion and Tourism Programs

The tourism industry has grown rapidly over recent years. Communities have favored and continue to promote tourism in the belief that it is a significant economic and employment development tool. However, surprisingly little is known about the economic and employment implications of the tourism industry. Empirical economic studies of the tourism industry remain few in number. Such studies have been hampered by a lack of consistent data, particularly at the regional level. Objective studies of tourism that measure the economic impacts indicate that tourism at a national and state level is not a major industry in terms of its contribution to the gross domestic product or employment.

However, these results obscure the vital fact that tourism is spatially selective. Tourism is not ubiquitously but regionally located. As yet, we have no comprehensive studies of the local regional significance of tourism. Nonetheless, three types of regions can be recognized with respect to the role of tourism:

Regions lacking tourism significance. These are predominantly rural inland regions with no particular or unique attraction for the public traveling for recreational purposes, and towns off the main business travel routes. They include most of the nation's small towns, particularly those in the Midwest and Southwest. However, even a community without observable tourism significance can alter its destiny by offering an unusual opportunity, such as "weekend on the farm," or capitalizing on a specific historical event such as the birthplace of a famous or infamous personality.

Regions of high tourist significance. These are areas with substantial scenic wonders and/or excellent climate. They have national and international appeal without increased promotion. They are generally in or near large metropolitan areas. Among those that come to mind immediately are such places as Yosemite, San Francisco, or Miami.

Centers of some tourist interest. These are places that have tourism as a component of some other major economic activity. Southern California's film and television industry provides this form of tourism/recreation opportunity.

Although tourism can be an asset, it does not provide the solution for most of the regional/urban areas currently in a state of low growth or decline and should not be promoted as an economic recovery solution. Indeed, research on regional economics indicates that local demand for goods and services is more important than visitor demand. Even in those instances in which the tourist industry has been a major source of growth or decline, there is some doubt that it has ever reached a level of economic importance equal to that of the local permanent population growth. If this is the case, it follows that local planning authorities might focus more on attracting permanent residents—retirees, business managers, and the like—than on seeking to boost tourism from distant places as a source of economic and employment development. Of course, the need for social and physical infrastructure development to keep pace with the rate of population growth must be borne in mind. In sum, for the majority of American communities, tourism is best seen as one component of an economic development strategy rather than as the entire strategy itself.

To be successful, a tourism program of any kind must be well planned and managed. It must have explicit objectives, such as business development, as well as the active support of all local parties with an interest in and effect upon tourism. It should be planned around specific themes, such as business conventions for the industries identified in the region's industrial development strategy. It should also be targeted toward specific populations, such as nonlocal businesspeople, and be promoted and marketed in the places of residence of these populations.

Research and Development

A dominant feature of today's economies is the knowledge-intensive high-technology enterprise. World market competition requires nations to develop value-added and research-intensive products to remain competitive. As a result, technological developments require an increased knowledge base for industry cultivation. The microcomputer industry, which both receives and supplies information, is a prime example of the use of intelligence as a product. But many other new information and telecommunication-related technologies exert profound influences on traditional production technologies. Indeed, it can be said that all tomorrow's industries will be knowledge intensive or they just will not exist at all.

An economy is emerging based on new environmental industries, biotechnology, and information technology. Since the first edition of this book in 1989, for example, the cellular telephone business has emerged and now dominates telecommunications marketing. Many other start-up industries need a place to begin. They require a community interested in mixing uses, such as housing and retail. Communities that provide the right atmosphere for start-up firms will attract them. If they nurture these firms by providing the right kind of atmosphere, they can become the headquarters for new companies or the centers of revitalization of older ones.

Local communities are well placed to identify their target technology sectors and activities. Moreover, those investments should be directed toward developing infrastructure to suit new firms. Improved links between universities and other research organizations, as well as industrial and business companies, should be encouraged and more joint funds established by companies and universities for common research and new product commercialization.

Inventors need a supporting environment during the crucial period between the conception of a new idea and its development to the point at which it can be taken to the venture capitalist. The lack of a supporting environment during that critical period can result in many fine ideas never taking off. Incubation centers (also known as "technology development centers") are intended to provide this supporting environment. They provide low-rent workplaces and are usually located adjacent to educational institutions, which provide small inventors with equipment, facilities, and advice on business management and work support from student assistance to put together business plans and approach venture capitalists. Control Data has pioneered in the establishment of incubator centers. Other centers can be found within some technology and business parks.

Technology and business parks, in this context, refer to parks that house commercial activities rather than research and development activities. They usually cover several acres and have the following general features:

- a campus-style physical environment
- a mixture of ownership and management, ranging from government to the private sector
- a frequent association with some form of university- or science-oriented establishment
- low-density development with high-quality buildings
- specific criteria for the eligibility of prospective occupants to ensure that all the activities within the park are compatible with each other

The technology and business park development is still a relatively recent strategy, so it is difficult to draw any significant conclusions about its likely success. However, ingredients for success apparently include the following:

- adherence to a carefully thought-out and very specific development objective, including type of desired activities
- availability of good management and entrepreneurial skills
- access to venture capital and the accompanying advice on how to use it
- involvement of the private sector in planning the development
- presence of meaningful community support

Other locational elements that appear to be influential include transport access, the availability of skilled labor, an attractive living environment, proximity to appropriate research facilities, and the presence of a suitable major manufacturing enterprise that acts as a catalyst. These findings are derived from a range of empirical studies on technology parks. It is important to note that these studies commonly suggest that the development times for technology and business parks are varied, generally 10 to 20 years.

Enterprise Zones

An enterprise zone is a defined area in which planning controls are kept to a minimum and attractive financial incentives are offered to prospective developers and occupants.

The concept of enterprise zones was introduced in the United Kingdom in the late 1970s based on the Hong Kong record of increased job attraction through reduced regulation. They were designed as a last, desperate measure to be tried only on a small scale in depressed areas where conventional economic and employment development policies and tools had failed to arrest decline. An underlying assumption is that the removal or streamlining of certain statutory and administrative controls will encourage entrepreneurs to create or expand businesses, providing the jobs and taxes that distressed areas so badly need.

To achieve this objective, policymakers need to emphasize labor-intensive industries that match the skill levels of potential workers. This can be achieved by offering strong wage subsidies in addition to tax relief packages and land.

Thirty-seven states have created enterprise zone legislation. Louisiana has 750 enterprise zones, and in Ohio, virtually all of Toledo and Cleveland have been declared enterprise zones under state legislation. Federal legislation provided for between 50 and 100 enterprise zones during the Clinton administration. Although enterprise zones have many advocates, the jury is still out on their real benefits. Recent studies indicate that enterprise zones do generate jobs only because of the concentrated attention of policymakers and not entirely because of the incentives provided by localities or states (Green, 1991; Rubin and Wilder, 1989). However, the few assessments of the latest wave of enterprise zones in Harlem and Detroit indicate renewed retail and commercial activity. In Harlem, Magic Johnson, Old Navy, and Starbucks are now part of the retail base. In Detroit, General Motors is headquartered in the city center, along with two new professional sports parks and a gambling casino—all of which were lured by packages of tax and enterprise zone incentives.

Nevertheless, policymakers need to avoid thinking that tax giveaways are the only or best tool to generate new economic activity. Policymakers also need to be careful about the temptation to view enterprise zones as potential for high-technology parks, ignoring any relation between the employment structures of high-technology firms and the skill levels of the local workforces. Other disadvantages of zones of any kind are that large developers and well-established corporations are likely to be the major beneficiaries. Such areas also place an unfair burden on existing commercial taxpayers outside the zones.

The Use of Financial Incentives for Business Development

Local governments seeking to foster business development have long resorted to their status as taxing bodies to provide financial assistance to firms and development projects. Local governments can provide financial incentives to firms based on their power to tax and the fact that the debt they take on is tax exempt. In the first case, local governments can create Tax Increment Finance, or TIF, districts in which the increment in tax revenues generated by a business location or district revitalization is used to pay for the specific projects that created this economic development rather than being used by the taxing jurisdiction for routine expenditures. In the second case, local governments can issue tax-exempt bonds to pay for economic development projects. For example, with the industrial development bond, they provide lower-cost loans to manufacturers who need to build new facilities or expand their facilities by raising capital in the marketplace. The motivation for the purchasers of the tax-exempt bonds is that the interest income they earn off of the bonds is exempt from both federal and state income taxes. The realized savings can be passed on to borrowers as below-market interest rates.

The widespread use of financial incentives has been criticized for creating a sense of entitlement among firms and questioned with regard to whether the accompanying development activity truly warranted a subsidy or incentive. Concern that the provision of incentives can erode the ability to pay for basic community functions such as public schools and infrastructure is increasing, especially in slow-growth or declining areas. Advocacy groups such as Good Jobs First track the use of financial incentives and recommend steps to ensure that the intended benefits are realized by the locality providing the benefits.

Local economic development practice will increasingly be called upon to account for its use of financial incentives. To do so, it can employ tools such as community benefit agreements that require firms receiving public subsidies to hire local workers and provide other investments in the community or clawback provisions that require firms to reimburse communities when they do not provide the jobs promised or do not remain in the community long enough for the public subsidies to be recouped by the private enterprise's contribution to the economy.

Conclusion

Business is the engine of economic development. All business originates from a sense of opportunity to serve or gain. Irrespective of the motivation to start a business or maintain it, this motivation can be hampered or retarded by the actions of communities or local governments. No business wants to be where it is not wanted. However, communities need to consider carefully the types of businesses they want to host. Linking economic and employment objectives to the types of firms in the locality is an essential task for the community. (See Table 9.2 for a sampling of business development project starters.)

Businesses, and particularly small new innovative businesses, may become the large firms of the future. It was not that long ago that Microsoft was a small firm, but now it is a giant subject to antitrust action. Microsoft is a significant component of Seattle's economy. Bill Gates could have gone elsewhere. On the other hand, around three out of every five small businesses started will fail. Further, even if a small firm has an excellent business plan, if it is poorly capitalized, its survival chances will be very low.

The means communities use to attract firms will depend on what resources are available. The most important factor in firm location is knowing the area's assets as well as having the correct attitudes and infrastructure to support the firm. Every community must develop special activities and tools to build the right type of infrastructure for the development and the employment it wants. Chasing tourists or high-tech firms should not top the agenda unless the community is particularly well situated for this form of economic development. The most important activity is building soft infrastructure, such as information and finance, to make the community attractive to enterprise. In essence, the community must become entrepreneurial in the use of its resources if it wants to attract and retain firms as a major component of its economic development strategy.

Table 9.2   Business Development Project Starters

Tool	Project Idea Starter
Attraction	*Organization development:* A local development commission with state finance backing loans funds to a nonlocal dying industry suited to the region to assist that industry to relocate and develop as a business development venture and possibly also as a tourist attraction (e.g., a local development commission's sponsoring surfboard-making industry). *Work space and support facilities for small business:* This aims to establish a privately or publicly owned project using a workhouse building or the like to provide work space and a support framework for small firms with common facilities (e.g., reception, telephones, Internet, copiers, cleaning, maintenance, conference rooms).
Small business and new venture start-ups	*Community business advice project:* This is an organization formed to provide professional advice and assistance to small businesses in the areas of management, marketing, accounting, financing, locating resources, and problem solving. One such organization is a nonprofit organization run by a committee that decides which clients to help and how much to charge them (e.g., no charge for low-income groups and marginal businesses and standard consultant fee to established firms). It employs a full-time business adviser who works directly with clients in their home or places of business.

Tool	Project Idea Starter
Business expansion/retention	*Export promotion scheme:* This is a scheme to assist small and medium-sized firms in exploring new export markets by representing them at trade fairs and missions. *Regional technology center:* This is a center to research and identify technologies appropriate to the region's socioeconomic base and to help people who are developing these techniques start up a business. It provides the necessary backup support facilities and management advice.
Local government	*Joint public–private ventures:* Joint venture agreements for construction of business venture facilities to revitalize the central business district, generate employment, and create revenue for the city government. These facilities could include a cinema complex or an administrative center with shops, parking garage, and sports facilities.

Box 9.1 | **Example 9.1: TARGETing Retail Gaps in a Low- to Moderate-Income City[5]**

The City of Azusa is one of eight San Gabriel Valley Foothill communities of Los Angeles County, California. It has 45,000 residents and 13,000 households, most of whom are Hispanic. Less than 20% percent of Azusa's residents over 24 years of age have earned college degrees (the state average is 30 percent; U.S. Census Quickfacts). Compared to the other seven Foothill communities, Azusa has the lowest home ownership rate and median housing sales price (City of Azusa, 2010). Azusa has had diffi-

Photo 9.1   Target Azusa

Source: Photo by Austin Gordon, Senior Economics Major, Azusa Pacific University; Ken Rhinehart; http://www.iwillride.org/?p=917

culty competing with surrounding communities due to declining neighborhoods, falling property values, and reinvestment activity, as well as increasing crime and rental property turnover. This was particularly the case for its retail

(Continued)

(Continued)

economy, in which sales per capita in Azusa lagged behind those of the Los Angeles region by more than $2,000.

A 2006 study found Azusa's leakage of retail sales amounted to nearly $20 million (Klingensmith and Strother, 2006). The study calculated the market serving index (MSI) for each retail category. The MSI is a form of location quotient in which the proportion of firms for Azusa in a specific retail category is compared to the proportion for the larger retail market of which it is a part, in this case, the Los Angeles metropolitan area. Several retail categories for Azusa had MSIs of zero; that is, there were no retailers within the city limits. Among these categories were nursery and garden centers; men's clothing stores; hobby, toy, and game stores; book, periodical, and music stores; office supplies, stationery, and gift stores; and department stores. Other categories in which sales were lower than estimated demand included women's clothing stores, jewelry stores, furnishing stores, and shoe stores. From identification of these retail gaps, Azusa concluded its retail economy could best be strengthened by attracting a large value retailer such as Target. While Target normally looks for a more urban and upscale market than that found in Azusa, the city approached Target and was able to convince it to open a store due to several factors.

First, countering the weak retail market indicators was the fact that Azusa has two universities, Azusa Pacific and Citrus College, with a combined student population of more than 20,000. This effectively increases Azusa's consumer base by 50 percent. Locating near the two college campuses would significantly add to retail sales, since Target carries product lines with particular appeal to the college market.

Second, the regional transit system called the Metro Gold Line planned to add two Azusa stops. The city proposed to locate Target at one of these stops developed as a transit-oriented development close to the colleges. Because the Gold Line would connect Azusa with neighboring cities, including Pasadena and Los Angeles, Target would help fill a gap in Azusa's retail needs as well as draw in new consumers from outside communities when the light rail extension is completed in 2013 (Klingensmith and Strother, 2006).

Third, the city assembled the land for the store using its redevelopment authority and sold it to Target at less than cost. It also paid for the streetscaping of the site.

Several issues about the project arose during the planning phase, including the desire to preserve trees near the site; concern about nighttime lighting and visual cohesiveness with the surrounding area; the need to prevent theft of shopping carts; air quality and noise impact of delivery trucks, along with the relationship of delivery entry points in relation to the planned Metro line; and traffic flows and parking needs (City of Azusa Draft Environmental Impact Report, 2008).

Target submitted plans and technical specifications for the building in April 2009. The plans addressed many of the issues raised. The property's exterior was built to blend in with the Spanish architecture of nearby City Hall and the greater community. The building itself is identified as a "unique" Target due to its alternative layout and appearance from the tra- ditional big box, single-level store models. Because the site's footprint is limited to a single city block, designers had to be creative in maximizing its utility. The store has two floors, with the shopping level located above a ground-level garage with more than 400 parking spaces (Gresham, 2010).

Target opened ahead of schedule in 2010. In addition to its usual prod- uct line, the site contains a pharmacy, a fresh grocery, an alcohol selection, a Pizza Hut, and a Starbucks. Councilman Uriel Macias declared the suc- cessful recruitment of Target a "crowning achievement" in Azusa's rebirth (Tedford, 2010). Pointing to the City's effort to use the store as a cornerstone for future economic development and additional foot traffic, he said: "Our downtown has completely changed from what it used to be. It used to be something you would drive by. Now it is a destination point" (Tedford, 2010).

Economic and Community Development Director Kurt Christiansen believes Target provides a "win-win" for the city: not only is it a convenient one-stop-shop for residents with limited transit options, it provides additional tax revenue as well as revenue from increased municipal electricity and water sales (Christiansen, 2012). Another benefit worth noting is that Target invests 5% of its income from the Azusa store in grants to local schools, the library, nonprofits, and supporting city sponsored events. The store has also provided much-needed jobs to the city; Target hired 225 employees, making it the city's ninth largest employer. All in all, the project has helped to address Azusa's retail leakage, provided jobs for the local economy, and assisted in the commercial revitalization of Azusa's downtown.

Box 9.1   Example 9.2: A Cow Bank in India

A cow bank sounds utterly silly, but it is a very serious venture. Building wealth requires resources and, in some cultures in India, a cow is a very important and expansive resource. Students at the business school at La Sierra College in Riverside, California, are helping Karandi, India, establish a cow bank. The idea is to establish a self-sufficient project that creates wealth on a continuing basis. The cow bank is designed to produce a cow

(Continued)

(Continued)

stock that will produce milk. Milk can then be sold in the village and to surrounding villages, creating income for the community.

The bank's initial capital is three cows. The bank will have the cows artificially inseminated, and their calves will increase the number of cows. The cows can be loaned out to families that can keep and/or sell the cow's milk and eventually own a cow of their own from their sales or savings, which they can buy from the bank. The goal is to eventually have a bank of 20 cows as the bank's stock. If the bank is successful, the village will increase its wealth, and villagers will have a new resource that can reproduce itself.

Banking can take many forms, as this case shows. New resources and self-sustaining wealth creation should be a role of any bank. This technique is not just for developing nations. For example, tool banks have been very useful in helping former homeless people get back on their feet by doing local repairs and so forth.

Source: Based on information from Don Benson, business staff reporter, Inland Empire newspaper *The Business Press,* November 15, 1999.

Box 9.1	**Example 9.3: Mobile Entrepreneurs: Portland Food Carts***

"Street food" is an urban industry that has thrived because of rather in spite of the Great Recession. Benefitting from lower overhead costs and greater flexibility than that of a restaurant, food carts have been an emerging sector in cities across the country. With hundreds of food carts and strong city policy support, Portland, Oregon is a leader in this mobile entrepreneurship movement that creates jobs, public revenues from business licenses and sales taxes, and demand for supplies often locally provided. Many food truck operators hope ultimately to open up brick-and-mortar businesses when they accumulate the necessary start-up capital.

In Portland, many of the food carts operate in "pods" of several carts clustered together in open spaces, especially along the edges of surface lots and vacant parcels. As of December 2010, Portland was home to 25 of these pods, one of which had 30 carts. Planners have welcomed this arrangement as a way to activate public space. Food carts generate pedestrian activity and encourage interaction among customers in common outdoor spaces. Like other forms of street vending, food carts provide a viable temporary use of land that that may ultimately have more permanent development when economic conditions are more favorable. Food carts can also contribute to urban safety by providing another set of eyes on the street, as illustrated by the New York City street vendor whose presence is credited with thwarting the attempted 2010 car-bombing of Times Square.

While many of Portland's carts operate in parking lots or on temporarily vacant land, some developers have begun incorporating space for permanent pods in private developments. The first and perhaps most well known, example is Roger Goldingay's Mississippi Marketplace. Goldingay's parcel of land had been slated for condo development prior to the recession. Goldingay built a market center instead and included a 10,000-square-foot lot specifically designed to accommodate 10 food carts, covered seating, electrical outlets, and recycling bins.

A study of Portland street food found that food carts benefitted local economic development because they fostered entrepreneurship and microenterprise, street vitality, and social interaction among consumers. Commissioned by the Portland Bureau of Planning and conducted by graduate urban planning students at Portland State University, the study found Portland's food carts provide an important opportunity for immigrants to become entrepreneurs, as roughly half of the street vendors surveyed were born outside the country. Citing the desires to be independent, to eventually open up a restaurant, to be a cook, and to have a flexible schedule, food cart operators were found to enjoy their trade and the relationship they have with customers.

Among the 78 vendors surveyed in the study, 63% agreed that street vending was a good way to earn a living to support themselves and their families. According to the study, start-up costs for a high-end food cart are less than half that of a small brick-and-mortar business with a single employee. While there are lower barriers to entry for food cart entrepreneurs starting a business, finding financial and other assistance to do so still proved to be a challenge for many vendors. Only 18% of vendors surveyed received any job training for their venture. About half of the food cart owners obtained start-up capital from family members and from their own savings. Eight percent utilized a home equity loan, and only 2% received financial assistance from an outside organization. Many never pursued bank financing. This suggests a role for community economic developers if there is a desire to grow the industry.

Another Portland State University study, "Food Carts as Retail Real Estate," assessed the impact of food carts on local economic development. In 2010, 461 licensed food carts paid an average monthly rent of between $300 and $550, accounting for combined yearly rents of between $2 and $3 million dollars. Food cart operators spend between 13 and 14% of their revenues on rent. Much of this rent revenue benefits private property owners, as food carts often occupy private land. The study made rather wide-ranging estimates for job creation—between

(Continued)

(Continued)

500 and 1,800 local jobs—and total sale revenues of between $14 and $23 million.

While some restaurant owners believe the nearby presence of food carts can help business by increasing area foot traffic, others are concerned they have a negative effect on their business. Citing fewer government regulations and lower permit fees and overhead costs, many brick-and-mortar restaurant owners view food carts as unfair competition, cannibalizing business from restaurants. The Oregon Restaurant Association states that carts should be categorized as restaurants and be subject to the same fees. Because food carts are technically mobile vehicles, permit holders do not pay personal property taxes on kitchen equipment like restaurants do. When business is bad in one area, cart owners may be able to relocate to a new area.

On the other hand, food cart business is subject to weather conditions, as 65% of food cart patrons walk to make their purchases from the carts. Further, the food cart customer base is also more vulnerable, as the carts do not have fixed, permanent locations. Finding a location for their business can be a key challenge for food cart operators.

While street food vendors have always operated in various cities across the country that allowed their activity, urban food carts are emerging as a significant new economic development in entrepreneurship. The food carts provide an eclectic range of choices in a retail food economy dominated by chains and brand names. Consequently, they can contribute to locality development and a community's sense of place.

---

*Research assistance by Patrick Terranova.

Box 9.1 | Example 9.4: Determination Helped Snatch This Town From the Jaws of Economic Death

Cuba, Mo.—The metallic brown Ford van came barreling down the gravel road, kicking clouds of dust toward the overcast sky, its horn beating out a rhythmic warning sound.

"Oh, my gracious," said Dennis Roedemeier, president of the Industrial Development Board of this little Missouri town, "something's gone wrong."

As the van came skidding to a halt, grim-faced Mayor Ray Mortimeyer leaned out of the window and said, "We've lost the grant."

"What went wrong?" Roedemeier asked. Even as he asked, he knew nothing had gone wrong, because the mayor could not contain himself any longer and broke into a broad grin, extending his beefy hand in heartfelt congratulations.

Minutes before, the state community development block grant office had notified the mayor that the city had been awarded $900,000 in state grants to enable the Bailey Corporation to open a facility in Cuba's new industrial park. Bailey is the fifth new company to locate in Cuba this year. In addition, two local companies have expanded their operations, and a shoe plant that had closed down has reopened. These moves have created 450 jobs. Cuba, unlike so many other small towns in rural America that have been victimized by cheap imports and regional recession, did not roll over and die. It has bounced back from the dark days of the autumn of 1984 when this town of 2,100 people lost 125 jobs and saw its unemployment rate soar to 13 percent.

It took dreaming and scheming, naive faith and dogged persistence for Cuba to turn its fortunes around.

Cuba lies alongside Interstate 44 in south central Missouri, about a third of the way between St. Louis and Springfield. The city advertises itself as "the gateway to the Ozarks"—a testament to the region's beauty, but also its poverty.

Two out of every three people in Cuba live below the state poverty level; until recently, things were getting worse as the area's principal industries— lead and iron mining and shoes—declined in the face of foreign imports. "We're surrounded by small towns that built their future on the one little factory," Mortimeyer said. "As that plant closed its doors, so did hope."

Cuba seemed destined for the same fate . . . But there were people in Cuba who refused to let their town die. Mortimeyer, who had operated a local home heating fuel business since 1969, was elected mayor in April 1984 on a platform promising an activist government that would run Cuba more efficiently.

One of the things the new mayor did was to convene the local Industrial Development Board, which had been in existence since September 1983, but never met. He asked Roedemeier, a local entrepreneur who had recently sold his business, to become the volunteer president of the board. Roedemeier initially demurred but finally relented after assurances that business executives would run the show and politicians would not interfere.

Roedemeier knew that Cuba had to act quickly. "We had been slowly bleeding to death and then we began to hemorrhage," he said. In September 1984, 55 more jobs were lost when Prismo Paint Company and Echo Shoes closed their doors. In November, the Mid-America Shoe Company announced that it would close by the end of the year, taking with it 70 jobs.

Roedemeier visited neighboring communities. He talked to their business leaders and elected officials to see what they had done right and

(Continued)

(Continued)

where they had gone wrong. He prowled the corridors of the state capital in Jefferson City, learning all he could about the myriad of state assistance programs for business development.

That dogged determination paid off. From January to November 1985, Cuba received $1.6 million in state grants to attract new industry, to help existing companies refurbish, and to provide necessary improvement in public services.

Such financial assistance coupled with a new spirit of entrepreneurial creativity rapidly began to show results. In February, the Mid-America Shoe Company, which had shut down, reopened as Whistles, Inc., planning to overcome mounting foreign competition with local commitment and innovation. The plant's former manager and salesman mortgaged their homes and bought out Mid-America's owners.

The city received a state development action grant of $119,000 and lent it to Whistles at a 7 percent rate to enable the company to purchase new equipment. A group of concerned local business executives bought the company's buildings and agreed to lease it back for a nominal sum.

Teaching Case 9.1

Community-Based Business

"The bankers aren't interested. They tried this in the 1960s, but they had a high rate of loss." The speaker was the head of the new government-guaranteed bank program. Reunion, a community business development bank, had approached local commercial banks seeking participation in a loan program to finance new inner-city ventures. The Reunion Development Bank was making overtures to use the commercial bank's Community Reinvestment funds for community purposes. The commercial banks they were approaching had tried inner-city loan funds in the 1980s and 1990s and were disappointed in the loan losses.

Commercial, small, and minority business loan funds of the 1980s and 1990s suffered from a number of major shortcomings. These funds often employed weak loan criteria and had little or no oversight, and bank managers showed little concern when the loss rates began to mount. In recent years, however, new community-oriented funds have emerged that have learned from past mistakes. Although the community development banks are a new instrument, they have shown considerably greater success in their repayment rates.

The Reunion Bank's Loan Committee has nine new projects identified across the city that illustrate the success of the community development bank concept. One of the best examples of community-oriented loan programs is the Business Development Corporation of Centerville (BDCC). The emphasis of the Centerville BDCC is on Hispanic entrepreneurship to provide jobs for the area's unemployed population. Although capitalized with nearly $1 million in city funds, BDCC's first years were disappointing, in part because the group followed the SBA model of administration. Community representatives, inexperienced in banking, made decisions. By BDCC's third year in business, the loan loss rate was reported to have reached nearly 60%.

In that year, the city restructured the loan committee to include banking professionals, and a former commercial bank official was brought in as executive director. Then the picture began to change. During a three-year period, BDC made 32 loans to small businesses, most of them in the range of $10,000 to $50,000, with three- to five-year repayment schemes. At present, only three of the loans are in default.

Four key ingredients make the new loan funds effective. They are the following:

1. *Professional criteria.* It is important to use strict criteria in financing decisions. These criteria include the applicant's experience in the field, his or her investment of capital, and a convincing business plan.

2. *Careful monitoring.* Try to keep a manageable volume of loans so that each one can be closely monitored and identified if management assistance is needed.

3. *Training and technical assistance.* This complements the basic entrepreneurship and should be offered to and in most instances required of loan recipients.

4. *Involving others.* Most of the new loan funds, unlike their predecessors, provide only part of the total loan needed to start a business. For example, the CDC will provide financing for only up to one third of the total package, requiring applicants to find other private sources. The involvement of other lenders provides additional analysis of business plans and enables the loan funds to leverage their participation.

The loan funds of the 1980s and 1990s had disappointing results, but the new loan funds have benefited from the mistakes of the past. They can

(Continued)

(Continued)

grow into a major antipoverty force if only they can hold true to entrepreneurial values: creativity, decentralization, and market discipline.

The Cadillac Foundation has become interested in minority lending.
The foundation directors, chaired by John Jonas, have directed the staff to
consider forming a loan guarantee plan for Community Development
Banks. Cadillac wants to support loans to the homeless on a model similar
to the women's enterprise programs. How would such a program be
designed by the community development bank, or is this just too risky?
Mr. Jonas is adamant about introducing a microloan for the homeless, but
how would you devise a program using all of the methods detailed above
to move the homeless from their current status to self-sufficiency?

Teaching Case 9.2

A Small Town Determines Its Own Destiny

Steelnet's dream evaporated almost overnight. The Midwest Iron Range
community, located on a two-lane county road in the northern Great Lakes
region, began for just one reason: a low-grade iron ore called taconite. The
Reservation Mining Company built the town in 1939 expressly for its workers, who earned good wages, financed their houses on easy terms through
an employee credit union, and often had money to burn.

For years, Reservation's taconite mine, a joint venture of the Inland
and Republic steel companies, was the most productive in the world. But
decline in the U.S. steel industry and competition from other taconite
sources finally closed the mine, decimating the town that at its peak was
home to 30,700 people. Lacking proximity to anything but its iron mines,
Steelnet had to scramble for economic survival. So did its residents, many
of whom left as unemployment soared to 85%. The rapid exodus cut the
population from more than 30,000 to today's 12,300. The average housing
price plummeted to less than $15,000 per single-family home.

Steelnet could have become a ghost town. When the mine reopened
a few years later, it recalled just 100 of its 1,500 former workers. What has
kept the town alive—and optimistic—is the tenacity of its citizens and the
mayor, Don Cole, a retired mine foreman. A smile and an easy laugh are
part of the salesman's repertoire, and Cole is a salesman for Steelnet. His
first priority was to train the town to market itself through a program
launched by the state's Department of Energy and Economic Development.
Named Star Cities, the program is designed to highlight and strengthen the
state's most aggressive local development programs.

The certification requirements to become a Star City would daunt many small cities, but Steelnet had one key asset: a pool of unemployed volunteers who combined their talents to make the town a Star City in a record four and a half months. The achievement won it visibility among state officials, which paid handsome dividends later.

The Steelnet city council also formed the Steelnet Area Development Association (SADA), inviting joint efforts with a nearby township that shares the same school district. Cole and the council never planned to settle for a passive role, even though a small board of citizens assumed control of economic development efforts. The same civic enthusiasm that had achieved a speedy Star Cities designation enlisted 435 individual and 29 business members to sustain SADA's projects and committees.

Mayor Cole joined the search for funding sources. He recalls an effort to solicit foundation officials who had never heard of Steelnet and had no idea where it was or why they should care. Cole was a good salesman. He was able to attract foundation grants that provided $55,000 for the city's revolving loan fund, targeted for small business loans to local people who could not qualify for bank credit. Steelnet's skilled but largely unemployed workforce would become its main source of entrepreneurial talent for these loans.

Because the city had relocated its offices to a retail/office complex in a converted school building, the old city hall became an ideal trial site for SADA's efforts. A community development block grant financed renovation of the building, while SADA loans allowed a pool table manufacturer and a small software games products firm to occupy it. SADA has relied heavily on board members' personal knowledge of loan applicants in taking risks. Yet SADA's 20 loans have shown a perfect repayment rate. The city did less well at first, however, in trying to attract new businesses from other areas. On the bright side, Reservation Mining's steady decline offered new opportunities for the reuse of abandoned buildings. A rubber tire plant, expanding to fill the Firestone disaster tire needs, located in a building formerly used by a pneumatic drill manufacturer. The city owned this facility, having purchased it for only $500,000. The new Kelos tire plant is being leased from the city for nearly $50,000 per year, and the tire plant is expected eventually to create 60 new jobs. Two other firms that will also locate in Steelnet to make use of the rubber for auto racing and high-speed windshields may add twice as many jobs by the end of the year.

Steelnet's strategies finally seem to have paid off. This little town didn't give up or die. There is a lesson here for many small towns dependent on natural resources or a single industry.

One of the union leaders is opposing the plan for the reuse of the mining facility by an outside firm. He argues that outsiders are nonunion and that these union-busting firms are the cause of Steelnet's problems. Joe

(Continued)

(Continued)

Bartowski, a former union steward, argues that "we should loan some of that money to ourselves and reopen the rubber plant ourselves. After all, we worked in it before," he says. "Who knows the market and the products better than we do?" Mayor Cole thinks Joe is a little crazy. "Working in a place ain't like running it." Who is right? Maybe they both are for different reasons. Or is there something in what Joe says that can be used by Steelnet before they let the new firm in?

Teaching Case 9.3

An Incubator as a Revitalization Tool

When the Kanter Corporation, a metal fabricating company, abandoned a 73,000-square-foot facility on three acres of land one mile north of Jonesboro, Kanter gave the land and buildings to the city for $1. Jonesboro originally wanted to use the facility for a new community college, but a feasibility study showed this would not be financially prudent. The Greater Region Economic Development Foundation then asked the city council to allow it to investigate the site's suitability for an incubator facility.

Canton was able to obtain a Small Cities Block Grant to perform a feasibility study. The study, which included a building and site evaluation, marketing strategy, and incubator plan and program, came back favorable to an incubator facility. The Greater Region Economic Development Foundation obtained a $70,000 matching grant from a private donor and a $70,000, 5% loan from the city, with repayment beginning in three years. In addition, the city charges the incubator no rent. The $70,000 from the city is money that the city would have needed to spend on security, maintenance, and so forth for the incubator building if it had remained empty.

The Women's Equity Development Corporation Center will run a business incubator for women-owned firms in Canton. Women who want to rent or lease space may do so only after they have completed a special training program organized by the Women's Equity Development Corporation (WEDCO). The incubator offers newly established businesses the opportunity to rent space at below-market rates and have access to free telephone receptionist services, secretarial services, business management assistance, custodial and maintenance service, and a business technical library. In addition, the businesses have an opportunity to network with each other. Most of the entrepreneurs at WEDCO Center are either first-time female business owners or are moving to the incubator from their garage, basement, or barn.

The WEDCO incubator currently houses eight businesses, including a manufacturer of wooden playground equipment, a company that sells bagged ice to convenience stores and bait shops, a firm that makes tools for air conditioner repair, and a computer services business. Lake College also plans to relocate its Business and Industrial Institute to the incubator. The institute will offer 50 different programs, including technical manual writing, computer training, management training, and blueprint reading. Each business in the incubator will be entitled to one free class. The Lake College programs are developing into an entrepreneurial training institute for businesspeople in the area.

The primary function of the incubator's Operating Committee is to screen applicants. More prospective tenants are rejected than are accepted. The major criterion for acceptance is the business's ability to create jobs for women, either now or in the future. The incubator is not promoting professional people or service sector businesses that offer limited job creation, emphasizing manufacturing and information processing businesses.

The incubator staff assists approved businesses to prepare a business plan and steers them in the direction of local lenders who have been extremely supportive in lending start-up capital to incubator businesses. Each company occupies 500 to 2,000 square feet at a rental rate of $3 per square foot per year. Leases can be for up to five years, but no business has signed on for more than two years, hoping to move to larger quarters by that time. The incubator is expected to create 120 jobs and currently has a 65% occupancy rate, ahead of the 15% predicted by the end of one year of operation.

The community goals of the incubator are to create jobs and ownership for women. Some of the incubator businesses may be able to move to the city industrial park in a few years to help revitalize this city-owned, underutilized facility. By the third year of the incubator's operation, it should be self-sufficient and able to begin repaying the city loan.

The mayor and Regional Development Foundation are now in the process of calculating the return on investment. They are unfamiliar with the appropriate methods to use. The building with improvements is valued at $1 million. Most of the rental spaces will rent at less than market rates, as discussed earlier. A consultant has been hired to assist making the calculations; however, the committee wants to provide the consultant with the parameters for the study before it commences. What are the variables that need to be considered, and how will the city know if it is in fact making both a social and economic profit?

Notes

1. Georgia Tech graduate students Ellen Anderson, Jason Chernock, and Melissa Mailloux contributed to this section.

2. The first five methods have been identified from the work of the Edward Lowe Foundation, a nonprofit organization devoted to developing entrepreneurship (Edward

Lowe Foundation, 2002). The sixth is drawn from recent work by the Corporation for Enterprise Development (Dabson, 2003).

3. The official title it gave to this effort was the New Economy Project.

4. Defined by the Society of Competitive Intelligence Professionals (now the Society of Strategic and Competitive Intelligence Professionals) as "a systematic and ethical program for gathering, analyzing and managing external information that can affect your company's plans, decisions and operations." Accessed December 8, 2005 from http://www.scip.org/ci/.

5. Georgia Tech graduate student Patrick Terranova contributed to this section.

References and Suggested Readings

Bates, Timothy. 2000. Financing the Development of Urban Minority Communities: Lessons of History. *Economic Development Quarterly* 14(3): 240.

Christiansen, Kurt. 2012. City of Azusa Economic and Community Development Director, personal interview with Nancey Green Leigh, April 2.

City of Azusa. 2010. *2008–2014 Housing Element.* Accessed April 2, 2012 from www .ci.azusa.ca.us/DocumentView.aspx?DID=5185

City of Azusa. 2011. Target Store Redevelopment Project: Draft EIR. Accessed November 19, 2011, from http://www.ci.azusa.ca.us/DocumentCenter/View/1118

Cuomo, Andrew. 1999. *New Markets: Untapped Retail Power in America's Inner Cities.* Washington, DC: U.S. Department of Housing and Urban Development.

Dabson, Brian et al. 2003. *Mapping Rural Entrepreneurship.* Washington, DC: Corporation for Enterprise Development.

Edward Lowe Foundation. 2002. *Building Entrepreneurial Communities.* Cassopolis, MI: Author.

Erickson, Rodney. 1987. Business Climate Studies: A Critical Evaluation. *Economic Development Quarterly* 1(1): 62–71.

Frieden, Bernard. 1990. City Center Transformed. *Journal of the American Planning Association* 56(4): 432–438.

Gibbons, Christian. 2005. *Economic Gardening.* City of Littleton Business/Industry Affairs. Accessed February 19, 2009 from http://www.littletongov.org

Green, Roy E. 1991. *Enterprise Zones: New Directions for Economic Development.* Newbury Park, CA: Sage.

Gresham, Rachel. 2010. Target Prepares City for Unique Opening. *Azusa Pacific University Student Press.* http://www.theclause.org/2010/09/target-prepares-city-for-unique-opening/

Hamilton-Pennell, Christine. 2004. CI for Small Businesses: The City of Littleton's Economic Gardening Program. *Society of Competitive Intelligence Professionals Newsletter* 6(7).

Hipple, Steven F. 2010. "Self-employment in the United States." *Monthly Labor Review.* Bureau of Labor Statistics. http://www.bls.gov/opub/mlr/2010/09/art2full.pdf

Klingensmith, Megan and Stuart Strother. 2011. *Azusa Retail Development Analysis: A Report to the City of Azusa.* School of Business and Management, Azusa Pacific University. Accessed November 19, 2011, from http://www.cbfa.org/lemaster_strothers_hutchison22006.pdf

Leigh, Nancey Green and Nathanael Z. Hoelzel. 2012. Smart Growth's Blindside: Sustainable Cities Need to Protect Productive Urban Industrial Land. *Journal of the American Planning Association* 78(1), 87–103.

Lewis, Sylvia. 1993. The Bank With a Heart. *Planning* 59(4): 23.

Lichtenstein, Gregg A., and Thomas S. Lyons. 1996. *Incubating New Enterprises: A Guide to Successful Practice.* Washington, DC: The Aspen Institute.

Lichtenstein, Gregg A., Thomas S. Lyons, and Nailya Kutzhanova. 2004. Building Entrepreneurial Communities: The Appropriate Role of Enterprise Development Activities. *Journal of Community Development* 35(1): 6–7.

Lockhart, A. 1987. Community-Based Economic Development and Conventional Economics in the Canadian North. In *Social Intervention Theory and Practice,* edited by E. Bennett. Lewiston, NY: Mellen.

National Association of Development Organizations. 2000. Entrepreneurship: The Appalachian Regional Commission Approach. *Economic Development Digest* (November): 7.

Parzen, Julia Ann, and Michael Kieschnick. 1992. *Credit Where It's Due: Development Banking for Communities.* Philadelphia: Temple University Press.

Rubin, Barry, and Margaret Wilder. 1989. Urban Enterprise Zones: Employment Impacts and Fiscal Incentives. *Journal of the American Planning Association* 55(4): 418–431.

Servon, Lisa. 1999. *Bootstrap Capital: Microenterprises and the American Poor.* Washington, DC: Brookings Institution.

Society of Competitive Intelligence Professionals. Accessed December 8, 2005 from http://www.scip.org

Spicer, David E. 1996. *A State-by-State Analysis of Estimated Incentive Packages and Taxes.* Boston: Harvard Business School. Accessed February 19, 2009 from http://www.hks.harvard.edu/case/ncbattle/briefing/incentiv/incpack.htm

Stokes, Barry. 1985. Determination Helped Snatch This Town From the Jaws of Economic Death. *National Journal,* December 21, n.p.

Target.com. 2011. Store Locator: Azusa, CA. Accessed November 19, 2011, from http://sites.target.com/site/en/spot/search_results.jsp?&mapType=enhanced&startAddres s=azusa%2C+ca&startingLat=34.133609771728516&startingLong=-117.905883 7890625&_requestid=278545

Target.com. 2011. Community Outreach: Grants. Accessed November 19, 2011, from http://sites.target.com/site/en/company/page.jsp ?contentId=WCMP04-031767

Tedford, Daniel. 2010. Cornerstone of Azusa's Downtown, Target Has "Soft Opening." *Pasadena Star-News.* http://www.pasadenastarnews.com/news/ci_16261031?IAD ID=Search-www.pasadenastarnews.com-www.pasadenastarnews.com#ixzz1 umrO9vEZ

U.S. Census QuickFacts: Azusa, California. n.d. Accessed November 19, 2011 from http://quickfacts.census.gov/qfd/states/06/0603386.html

Vidal, Avis. 1995. Reintegrating Disadvantaged Communities into the Fabric of Urban Life: The Role of Community Development. *Housing Policy Debate* 6(1): 194.

10

Human Resource Development

I n this chapter, we focus on two critical aspects of human resource development. We begin with the traditional economic development focus on workforce development, surveying the range of practice and efforts to make workforce development more effective in responding to the challenges of the knowledge-based 21st century. Then we turn our focus to education, the essential foundation to workforce and economic development that the practice of economic development has neglected.

Workforce Development

> Workforce development is not a problem—it is an opportunity—the chance to unleash the creative, productive, and innovative forces, found only in people, for the economic and social betterment of our cities, states, and nations. People-centered development has the unique advantage of promising increased equity, efficiency, and economic vitality. (Garmise, 2006, p. 146)

The author of the above quote is urging us to turn around the traditional problem-focused approach to workforce development. Consistent with the definition of economic development guiding this book, Shari Garmise (2006) argues that equity is extended by increasing access to skill and talent development. Further, this extension is essential for an economic development strategy to succeed in the global economy of the 21st century, in which people and place survival skills are being placed directly on creative and innovative abilities.

We will begin our discussion with a review of the problems that have preoccupied the practice of workforce development in recent decades. There is the concern that certain individuals and groups in society are not able to compete in the emerging growth sectors of biotechnology, electronics, information, computing, and health industries. Another concern is that jobs have literally been moving away from people to suburbs and other nations. In the first case, the new locations for jobs are physically far away from where people (inner-city residents and rural communities) are most in need of work. In other cases, jobs are transforming or disappearing faster than the population has been able to adapt. The clearest evidence of this is the rapid decline in the labor input to the manufacturing sector. However, many service jobs are also being deskilled or eliminated as a result of automation. At the same time, while the postrecession unemployment rate had yet to fall below 8% in mid 2012, employers across all sectors complained they could not find employees to hire with the right skills.

Realities of an Undertrained Workforce

American workers are undertrained for their current jobs and not prepared for future opportunities. While about $60 billion was spent on "human capital investment," the annual survey of U.S. employers by *Training* magazine found there was a significant decline in company education and training expenditures during the early 2000s (O'Toole and Lawler, 2006).

Large companies are more likely to offer workforce training than are small companies (fewer than 50 employees), but O'Toole and Lawler (2006) cite a University of Michigan survey finding that less than 20% of workers took advantage of employer-offered training. They concluded:

> Given the nation's growing competitive challenges and the need to create greater mobility (and good careers) for workers, the decrease in the amount spent on training—coupled with the number of employees who apparently are not participating in training programs—leads us to conclude that the already undereducated American workforce also is being under-trained. (p. 128)

Or, as Mark Elliott (cited in Kleinman, 2000) of Public/Private Ventures puts it, "It's hard to compete in the global economy with a lame workforce" (p. 2). This is even more the case when the undertrained workers are also some of the most expensive in the world, as can be seen in Table 10.1.

The nation is not preparing its human resources for competition today or tomorrow. Furthermore, even in good times, minority workers are not as well rewarded as White workers, as is illustrated in Figure 10.1, which shows hourly wages for workers with low and high education levels for similar work in the Boston metropolitan area. Race and wage rates in Boston reflect a pattern similar to that of the nation. Race matters, but so do skills. No matter what color the worker, education and training pay. The average families with two or more professionals with professional degrees had incomes of more than $147,000 annually versus a similar family of high school graduates, who had a combined family income of only $48,000 per year. Although even the low-income number is well out of the poverty range, the fact that it takes several

Table 10.1   All Employees: Indexes of Hourly Compensation in Manufacturing, Selected Countries, 2006

Country or Area	Index
Americas	
United States	100
Argentina	22
Brazil	20
Canada	98
Mexico	13
Asia and Oceania	
Australia	102
Israel	49
Japan	82
Korea, Republic of	57
New Zealand	54
Philippines	5
Singapore	46
Taiwan	27
Europe	
Austria	124
Belgium	123
Czech Republic	—
Denmark	129
Finland	119
France	114
Germany	139
Hungary	28
Ireland	105

Country or Area	Index
Italy	97
Netherlands	119
Norway	156
Poland	21
Portugal	32
Slovakia	22
Spain	74
Sweden	116
Switzerland	121
United Kingdom	114

Source: U.S. Department of Labor, Bureau of Labor Statistics, Economic News Release, January 2008, Table 7.

Note: Dash means data not available.

members of the household to get this income means that catching up with the professional "Joneses" is impossible to do without an education.

Even as jobs are being shed, people remain an important community resource and are crucial to a locality's economic recovery. Good labor that adds value to production is always the critical asset when it comes to firm location. The United States has tended to place more of its national resources in income-support programs than on job skills development and maintenance schemes. In contrast, other developed nations, such as Sweden, have recognized the need to make job skills development the key component of their labor market programs. This need is only now being recognized here.

Public Role in Workforce Development

Human resource development has long been a public–private partnership, one that dates back a hundred years or more and has involved the public schools.

Initially, informal employment training agreements were made between employers and schools that set certain expectations for the roles to be played by public and private interests to ensure that workers could perform in the work-place. Basically, schools had the responsibility to prepare people to enter the

Figure 10.1   Human Capital Endowment by Race, Boston

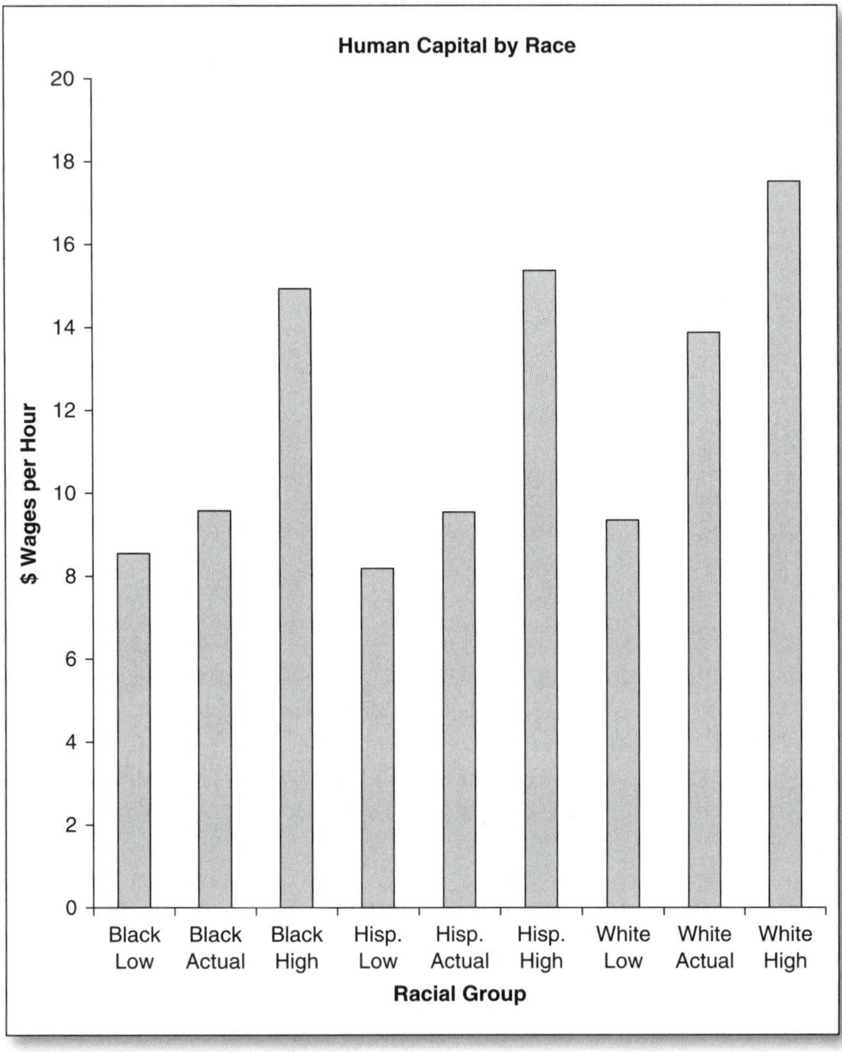

Source: Bluestone and Stevenson (2000).

Note: Low means low education. *High* means high education—some college or specialized training.

workforce, and the employer had the responsibility to train the worker for the specific tasks that needed to be done at work. Preparation for entering the workforce involved literacy skills, simple math, and a sense of civic responsibility. Some generic skills were also taught, such as measuring and the use of simple tools.

Once students got to the workplace, they were trained in specific skills needed by their employers. On-the-job training was often simple, with factory work being learned quickly. Moreover, people stayed in the same job for many years, gradually progressing through higher skill levels in the company based on performance. Apprentice training was the model for more complex training in crafts, which combined classroom instruction with structured on-the-job training under the supervision of master craftspersons.

Structural economic changes have altered that old compact, beginning with the shift to what has been labeled the New Economy. In general, this term refers to the substantial shifts in industry structure from the effects of the information and communications revolution. But the new economy continues to evolve as new industries develop, such as biotechnology and nanotechnology, which themselves have profound impacts for traditional as well as emerging industry. The overall result is that the kind and level of training required to enter the workforce for many jobs are greater and must be responsive to the needs of quickly evolving industry.

While it has been estimated that 90% of the fastest-growing jobs will require postsecondary education, an increasing number of people come to the workplace without even the basic skills expected (GAO, 2007). Recent adult immigrants, for example, lack language and work skills, and people who get displaced from certain jobs because of technology need to acquire a number of basic skills just to be able to undertake regular training programs. People older than school age thus find themselves needing special programs, which may be available only through partnerships with employers. Furthermore, the very high dropout rate from high school by low-income and minority youth, including many first-generation immigrants, also creates many barriers for participation in the new economy.

Government at all levels—federal, state, and local—has an important role in providing support for a workforce development system. The last major federal program development for this resulted from the passage of the Workforce Investment Act (WIA) in 1998. By 2012, the WIA was considered long overdue for reauthorization and criticized for not responding to changes in the economy. The National Skills Coalition observes that "The law's original emphasis on short-term training and rapid re-employment is increasingly inconsistent with growing demands for longer-term training aligned to high-growth and emerging industries" (National Skills Coalition, undated). The current structure of the WIA is described below.

Under WIA, responsibility for managing the programs devolved from the federal government to the states, and ultimately to local Workforce Investment Boards (WIBs), which make most of the decisions. In contrast to previous approaches, the WIA recognized that training needed to respond to:

- Economic swings that had more to do with the readjustment of the competitiveness of major industries than periodic cycles.
- Global competition that led to unexpected swings in markets with consequent employment impacts.
- Firms and employees that did not change would be left behind and suffer not only unprofitability but extinction.

- Employees were likely to change jobs and careers as many as 10 to 15 times in their working lives due to necessity and opportunity.
- Unskilled or static-skilled workers would be left out of the new economy.

The WIA asked for stronger coordination among multiple training and service providers in the context of one-stop career centers that would allow individuals more flexibility to choose from a larger number of training options linked to employer needs. Thus, a majority of the WIB membership is composed of business representatives. For the first time, the WIA program permitted the use of resources to train employed persons. Previously, funding was restricted to unemployed persons. The WIA also provided new employment-generation tools that states can use to transform their workforce development programs.

Economic developers have found that partnerships with institutions engaged in workforce development provide many benefits. From the training providers' perspective, changes in the economy and federal regulations have combined to force them into a three-way partnership with business on one hand and economic development organizations and training providers on the other. Consequently, government resources and private resources are being used more effectively as trainers seek to ensure the service they provide is directly related to what business really wants and that the people they train can find jobs in the most promising firms. Economic developers in turn realize that they need the training professionals to produce a top-quality workforce that is able to meet the needs of existing businesses or the businesses that might be attracted to the area.

The economic developer wanting to utilize a human resource approach to building jobs and creating a stronger economic base in the community must first identify the existing programs at the core of the workforce development system. These major training institutions increasingly are partners in economic development, a recent trend necessitated by the growing awareness that training programs can partner with job development programs and thereby make both systems more effective. Thus, the primary training providers are increasingly also the leading strategic economic development resources for local community leaders. Some examples follow.

- *Job training programs.* The federal job-training providers are typically nonprofit contractors who work with the federal programs to train people in specific skills or sets of skills. This also includes state-supported training programs, which often contribute funds to businesses that provide their own curriculum and instructors.
- *Nonprofit community development corporations.* Increasingly, nonprofit housing, social service, and other programs are providing job training to their clients, often including disadvantaged groups, immigrants, women, inner-city residents, and so forth.

- *High schools.* The high school, as a resource for community economic development, offers an untapped but growing potential for students and teachers. The schools have many opportunities to couple teaching with internships, business formation, and summer activities for both students and faculty.
- *Adult education programs.* The public school system in most communities also sponsors an adult school that offers courses in English as a second language, job skills, and recreational and cultural topics.
- *Nonaccredited postsecondary training programs.* Training institutions are often connected with industries and certificate programs that train students. These programs are typically run by business associations, unions, or equipment suppliers specifically for a set of firms. Nonaccredited programs are also provided by schools that charge students fees, promising them training for jobs related to cosmetics, truck driving, sales, or computer repair.
- *Accredited colleges and universities.* The range of accredited programs starts with 4-year colleges and universities, in which new programs are linking coursework with industry areas. In addition, and increasingly important in economic development, are community colleges that provide specialized training for industries on a fee basis. Community colleges also partner with other economic development programs to provide training and technical assistance to local firms.

In addition, federal and state programs link employment training with other programs. For example, in the area of health and welfare, programs include senior community service, job services, veterans' programs, Wagner-Peyser funds, trade adjustment assistance, vocational rehabilitation and supported employment, food stamps, employment and training, and refugee assistance. Many states have conservation corps and programs for troubled youth. In areas of housing and community development, many job training programs and employment services are targeted to residents. Finally, the Stewart B. McKinney homeless assistance program and inmate employment and vocational education for incarcerated youths and adults also provide training resources.

Coordinating these various training resources is a massive task that is increasingly assigned to WIBs and their one-stop service centers. The types of activities undertaken by these human resource coordinating programs depend on the local situation. Generally, their task involves doing more than just assuring that training is available, such as:

- managing workforce training schemes, such as group apprentice schemes, adult retraining, and new training initiatives
- offering business support services that increase employment
- developing shared facilities for training activities
- operating general literacy and community education projects
- developing on-the-job training and work experience activities for young adults
- attempting to reduce discrimination in employment for disadvantaged groups

These many training avenues can actually achieve significant economic development goals in a local community and result in good partnerships for all. Using a human resources strategy implies that community economic development goals are pursued in tandem with the training and educational assets of the workers, helping businesses to grow and to locate in the local community.

Goals of Human Resource Programs

Human resource programs are typically focused on one of four categories of workers who are developing skills needed by employers:

> First, programs focus on people *entering the workforce for the first time.* Typically, these are youth or high school students, but also immigrants, homemakers, welfare recipients, disabled people, and other groups. Programs for these people include considerable attention to basic work skills and work readiness, as well as help in the job search.

> First-time entrants to the workforce have traditionally been helped in schools, but the schools have not always done an adequate job of preparing people for work due to the emphasis given to preparing people for college. A national program called the School-to-Work program has helped schools better address the students not going to college. Other programs throughout the country help individuals gain practical work skills, prepare resumes, and learn job search skills.

> Second, some human resource programs focus on people who have been *displaced from the workforce* and are unemployed, seeking to return to work. The old model assumed that when individuals lost their jobs, unemployment would be temporary and they would be recalled when economic conditions improved. However, increasingly, the people losing their jobs are finding that the layoffs are permanent.

> Traditionally, workforce development personnel were reluctant to train displaced workers for two reasons. Trainers believed that workers were temporarily laid off and that, at a moment's notice, they would go back to work. It was also believed that such programs were unnecessary for laid-off workers because they presumably had adequate skills for the job.

> Third, workforce programs have focused on providing training for *incumbent workers* who need to upgrade their skills in order to remain competitive in their firm and for the firm to remain competitive with other firms. Business itself is the largest provider of workforce training, without assistance from government or economic development programs. Reportedly, business spends some $6 billion on training each year, though the majority of that goes to management and high-ranking professionals. Nonetheless, throughout companies, considerable training goes on to improve workforce skills. These efforts are strongly supported by training programs that are tailor made for

certain skills. Courses in commonly used software or in safety when working around high-voltage lines are examples. In addition, businesses that require licenses for certain jobs need to provide both initial training and recertification programs. Professional conferences typically train people in new techniques and legal requirements that affect their business.

Workforce programs can also be targeted to *potential employees* of firms that are being attracted, that are moving into an area, or that are expanding. These firms see worker training as a major cost of doing business in an area and often look to workforce development programs to help support training their new workers. Typically, worker training benefits account for a large proportion of the incentives given workers under business attraction schemes (see Chapter 8), as they are a large one-time cost associated with a relocation or expansion. In these cases, specialized training programs are funded by using either training professionals from the firm or faculty at specific training institutions, such as community colleges or private training firms.

Matching Human Resource Programs and Economic Development Objectives

The following paragraphs give more detail about the various types of human resources development and training programs in existence. The correlation between job placement efforts and economic development is also discussed.

Workforce Investment Boards

Generally, local employment and training boards, formerly known as Private Industry Councils (PICs) and now WIBs, are more than happy to cooperate with local employment strategies if they are aware of the economic development goals of the community. They have been created to repair the continuing gulf between employment and training efforts and economic development, particularly for the disadvantaged. In the past, preparation for employment has been a "revolving door" for many people. They attend courses that frequently lead to dead-end or unsatisfying occupations, only to be sent to additional training as a remedy for their unemployment. Recently, with the help of WIBs, community groups have attempted to pull together local business and community-based economic development programs into a single employment network.

For example, WIBs attempt to coordinate the frequently fragmented efforts of parties interested in employment within a region. Although they vary in composition, WIBs generally include representation from key local firms, local government, state government, unions, and educational institutions. The members of the board must commit themselves to creating more flexibility in both training systems and job entry arrangements.

WIBs must also pull together multiple government-sponsored training initiatives and integrate them with local economic development. One of their major responsibilities is to identify and encourage new ventures that have skill requirements readily met by local people. Another is to match local training activities with the needs of local employers.

Community employment programs (discussed in the previous chapter) offer an appropriate mechanism for coordinating economic development and employment. They offer a vehicle for communities that wish to combine the community-based concept with more traditional economic development activities.

First-Source or Targeted Hiring Agreements

"First-source agreement" refers to a contractual obligation entered into by firms that receive substantial government assistance, such as tax holidays and government loans. Under the contract, the assisted firm agrees to interview, as the first source, local people for the available positions. After reviewing them, the employer may select anyone for the vacancy. This agreement generally stipulates the referral source and the number of referrals required before the employer can place advertisements or interview persons from outside the specified geographic area. First-source agreements historically have been targeted to firms directly. More recently, a variant of these agreements is being incorporated into community benefit agreements (CBAs) targeted toward developers of large-scale projects. That is, in the legally enforceable contract between community groups and a developer that the CBA represents, targeted hiring is one of the specific benefits being spelled out. This is done to ensure that the promises of job creation that come from developers and from local government agencies promoting the development will benefit the community from which both parties seek cooperation and approval.

In their manual on CBAs, Gross, LeRoy, and Janis-Aparicio (2005) suggest that possible target populations might include:

- individuals whose jobs are displaced by the development
- residents of the neighborhood immediately surrounding the development
- residents of low-income neighborhoods anywhere in the metropolitan area
- individuals referred by local, community-based job training organizations
- low-income individuals generally
- "special needs" individuals, such as public assistance recipients or ex-offenders (pp. 45–46)

In some instances, firms will request local referral voluntarily as a civic obligation in high-unemployment areas. These voluntary efforts are also used to stimulate employers to look at local youth as a first source. Youth-oriented first-source agreements generally have a "job tryout" component.

Employment Maintenance

Employment maintenance or support programs use unemployment funds to develop jobs for hard-to-place people. In this scheme, a local government or nonprofit organization receives the welfare payment as a subsidy for employing a person at the full wage level. A large number of community development corporations have employed this approach with considerable success. This type of project was one of the keystone initiatives of the Clinton administration. Many urban and rural local governments have indicated an interest in this type of program as a means of restoring teachers' aides, playground supervisors, assistant librarians, and many other paraprofessional positions.

Skill Banks

This is a relatively simple concept, aided by the advent of the microcomputer. The idea is that the employment officer or a local volunteer group or other person(s) collects refined information on the skills and backgrounds of local unemployed persons. This skill inventory can be used for a number of purposes. First, it serves as a source of community data on the nature of the job-development needs of the unemployed. Frequently, communities know that there is high unemployment, but they do not know what kinds of skills the unemployed have or the kinds of jobs they need. The skill bank helps address this problem. Second, the dominant use of the skill bank is its inventory of skills that can be matched to available vacancies in the local area. Finally, skill banks collect unemployed people into cooperatives or community-based employment initiatives. A skill bank is an invaluable tool for assessing local abilities and building new jobs or services on the basis of these skills.

To initiate a skill bank, organizers should first do a survey to document the demand for various occupations or skills and the availability of skilled labor to fill those needs. As a second step, the existing training and education facilities in the region should be assessed by their accessibility, suitability, and ability to meet further labor market needs. Recommendations for upgrading, extending, or modifying education/training programs have been made on the basis of these studies.

Training Programs

Particularly in the last decade, an observable convergence of trends has heightened the need for more, and better, job training: the increasing speed of technology change, the increasing sophistication of foreign competitors, the export of manufacturing jobs, downsizing due to pressures to increase productivity, shortcomings in the quality of formal education (particularly at the high school level), and the aging of the workforce. All told, those trends amount to an almost perfect storm, creating an ever-increasing need for workers to update their skills regularly and, often, to develop entirely new ones. (O'Toole and Lawler, 2006, p. 127)

In this section, we review a range of training concepts developed, with more or less success, to tackle labor force problems in local economic development. Most contain provisions for special courses to meet the needs of local employers and include upgrade training, apprenticeship courses, retraining of dislocated workers or of women re-entering the workforce, as well as traditional course offerings. Local training councils, such as WIBs, help to integrate these efforts with local development strategies. For example, communities that embark on tourism strategies need to develop courses that provide initial education and upgrade the skills of those already in the hospitality industry. Wolman, Lichtman, and Barnes (1991), after examining education, training, and skills, conclude that training in a specific skill area does have a significant payoff for the underskilled. Specialized training approaches include the following.

Customized Training

The concept of customized training is relatively simple. It provides training either at the employer's site or at the local college through courses specifically designed to meet employer expectations. Human resources are thus used to attract business because of the reduced cost of staff development.

Although this type of program is usually reserved for new firms moving into an area, it may also be used by existing firms that are expanding. One of the most innovative customized training efforts in the nation is the Ohio High Unemployment Population Program (HUPP), which targets training and employment services to chronically unemployed minority males. In this program, the employer's premises are used as a home base or site to aid participants in on-the-job training and education for a credential or degree. The basic idea is for a person to develop job habits and a job resume while gaining a degree. Although it is too early to evaluate this approach, early returns indicate that it is working and attracting hard-to-reach, long-term-unemployed individuals.

Competency-Based Training

In competency-based training, human resource professionals work with a group of employers to articulate the competencies that are required for workers in a particular industry. For example, a group of banks simplified their training into three sets of tasks (i.e., cashier, financial analysis, customer service) and developed the specific skills that were necessary in each. A hierarchy of skills allowed people to be trained for simple tasks first and more complex functions later so that they could progress in their track and receive more challenging jobs. As they received training, each employee received a certificate that was recognized by other banks.

Overall, this strategy is similar to the training in many apprentice programs sponsored by unions, and it allows workers to move easily from one employer to another. From an economic development perspective, it can simplify training programs and reduce costs for all the firms involved. Although many tasks in the new economy do not fit well into competency-based programs, an increasing number of employers can benefit from the better training such programs provide.

Comprehensive Training to Meet Social Needs

The strong link between human resource development and meeting the social needs of people outside the workforce is readily apparent to anyone working with persistently unemployed persons. For example, a key barrier for many welfare families is the lack of child care. In other cases, substance dependency or physical disabilities may be a barrier to steady employment.

Community-based organizations serving groups with barriers to full participation in work often are in a position to provide multiple services and training. One example is a program in Oakland, California, that used various public and private funding to assist the hardest-to-place persons. This program was comprehensive in that it did full intake assessments and started with work readiness training, such as being on time, work attire, persistence, and so on. Participants were assisted in solving important social problems like finding housing and child care, getting proper clothes or tools, and being sober and safe. They were also helped to identify at least three jobs and careers paying at least $14 per hour for which they could be trained, based on prearranged contacts with potential employers who agreed to take the graduates. Students were then placed for trial periods at the workplaces, where they could observe each job. Many found that the job they thought they wanted was not good for them (e.g., a student thought she wanted to be a nurse but discovered a fear of blood). After choosing their job, students received intensive training supported by internships and on-the-job supervision as they progressed. Upon graduation, they remained in touch with the program to ensure that problems could be solved.

This program was so successful that students had a high level of security that they would remain employable, with only a few needing more training.

But this approach is expensive and intensive, something for which funding is not always adequate.

Youth Enterprise

There is growing interest in helping young people to become acquainted with business development. In part, this is an attempt to rekindle entrepreneurial spirit in the nation's youth. It also represents a new emphasis on helping people create jobs for themselves rather than waiting for jobs to be created for them.

Youth enterprises have been started through the Community Youth Employment programs as well as various service clubs, community-based organizations, and schools. These vary in size and focus, and a few have become major self-supporting enterprises.

The basic idea is to start businesses within the skill range of youth to give them some experience in how the business system works (see Figures 10.2 and 10.3). Community-based groups have considerable resources and training to foster such activities. They can offer vacant space or equipment to the youth enterprise as well as mobilize service clubs and others to provide the technical assistance for the projects. Youth enterprise has even developed to meet critical needs of communities.

The Bulldog Express is a student-run grocery store in the small rural town of Leeton, Missouri. It began in 2009 and has drawn national attention. The town had lost its only grocery store 10 years earlier and the closest grocery store was 15 miles away. The store is located in what was a closed bank building. Leeton school administrators and students worked together to form the store and received broad support from the community. Students staff, stock, and manage the store, receiving earnings and valuable business experience in the process. The store provides essential goods to the community, a gathering place for the small town, and is particularly appreciated by senior citizens for whom driving has become more difficult.

University–Industry Technology Transfer

One of the most interesting sets of human resource programs involves universities sharing their research with local businesses. Although some technology-transfer programs are limited to patents and products, many find that the most effective flow of technology is through students trained in specific programs to meet specific needs of industry. For example, university programs in biotechnology can meet the needs of industry, whereas less specialized biology programs may not.

University programs operate either by providing specific project support to firms wanting new technology or by making scientific results available to businesses with whom they are shared. Many states have created specialized technology programs in which business funds part or all of specific research projects. Examples are the Ohio Ben Franklin and the New York Centers for Applied Technology. All these programs leverage private funding of faculty research and train students—usually graduate students—who apply their knowledge in industry, often in nearby industrial parks.

University programs that maintain specific project-by-project collaboration with industry benefit all participants. For example, the University of California Toxic Substances Research and Training Program leverages faculty interests by linking with firm needs. In this instance, graduates of the university program not only receive good industry-university education but also the benefit of a new generation of products and processes to detect, control, and remediate toxic substance problems in the environment.

Although university relations with industry are most clearly seen in tech parks, such as Stanford Industrial Park (electronics industry) and Research Triangle Park (North Carolina), college and university programs in fact work with industry at many unseen levels because of the common flow of people and ideas from university to business.

Self-Employment Initiatives

These initiatives attempt to assist unemployed people of any age to create employment ventures themselves, using their own labor as the primary resource. They include small business start-up efforts in which the unemployed receive small loans and grants to initiate a new, independent, community-serving business. During the period when the business is being organized, unemployed persons receive an allowance equivalent to an unemployment benefit. This allows the enterprise to reach the stability point before wages have to be paid.

There also are programs available that support self-employment ventures organized by a group rather than by an individual. In these projects, such as the microloan programs discussed in Chapter 9, a specialist works with groups to examine opportunities and exploit them using unemployed persons as the basic resource.

Career Ladders

Career ladder programs are aimed at helping workers in low-skill and low-wage jobs move into higher-level and more secure employment. For example,

Fitzgerald notes career ladder programs have helped nurses' aides to become licensed practical nurses and clerical workers to become information technology workers. The career ladder programs identify the training and education needed for the worker to move up the ladder and provide support services and financial aid to help the worker prepare (Fitzgerald, 2005).

Disabled Persons Skills Development

Physically, emotionally, and educationally disabled persons have always had difficult placement problems. Intervention in this situation ranges from sheltered workshops to employing a special disability placement officer (DPO).

The DPO is responsible for seeking out employment opportunities for disabled persons that fit their capabilities. With modern equipment, there are more of these opportunities than most employers realize. The DPO's job, then, is to see how the work environment can be made to fit the person rather than the person fitting the job. The DPO also provides employers with information on assistance schemes for disabled persons and their employers. Local governments can assist DPOs and the disabled by being positive examples, such as including the disabled in the development planning process and by allowing council offices to be used by the DPO or others working on issues of the disabled.

Education as the Foundation of Human Resource Development

There are two major reasons that economic developers focus on human resource development. First, referring to our definition of local economic development, we seek to provide sufficient and rising standards of living for all persons in the economy, reducing inequality in the process. This requires giving individuals the opportunity to attain this standard of living through quality employment and good compensation packages. This, in turn, requires providing quality education opportunities. It has been estimated, for example, that every additional year of education increases a worker's earnings by 10% (Schweke, 2004).

Even if we were to fall back to the traditional definition of economic development that simply emphasizes job and wealth creation, the importance of a well-educated labor force should be clear. At a minimum, employers need workers with strong basic skills. The most desirable employment in today's knowledge-based economy, however, requires advanced education and skill levels.

Thus, it seems logical that when economic development has focused on the role of education, it has done so primarily at the university or postsecondary level. We discussed above the role that community colleges and vocational and technical training institutions play in providing employee training. There has been a long-term trend away from employers providing in-house training to workers; the role of voc-tech schools and community colleges has become more important as a result. Working closely with these institutions is a key component of a human resource–based economic development strategy.

Less appreciated is the idea that local economic developers should also be concerned with the quality of the local prekindergarten and kindergarten through high school education systems. With regard to prekindergarten or early childhood education programs, economists have found that investments in these programs bring significant public and private returns on investment (as much as 16%). Indeed, Grunewald and Rolnick (quoted in Schweke, 2004, p. 16) state, "We are unaware of any other economic development effort that has such a public return, and yet early childhood development is rarely viewed in economic development terms."

Additionally, there are a number of reasons economic developers should concern themselves with the quality of the local K–12 school systems. First, quality primary and secondary school systems generate higher proportions of students who qualify for advanced education and training that generates higher-quality employment and earnings opportunities. Second, quality primary and secondary school systems can help to attract the firms that make up the knowledge-intensive sector of the economy. These firms may seek to hire local workers as well as seek high-quality communities for their existing employees. The lack of quality primary and secondary education has been shown, for example, to be a barrier to growing the biotechnology sector because firms cannot attract needed research scientists (Leigh, Wilkins, and Riall, 2001).

Third, providing high-quality school systems, particularly in low-income areas, increases the likelihood that disadvantaged or at-risk youth will graduate. This, in turn, has been shown to reduce crime and incarceration rates as well as welfare dependency (Schweke, 2004). All of these factors increase the attractiveness of a local community as well as free up public resources that can be devoted to improving the local economy.

Implementing a Human Resource Development Strategy

Economic developers interested in applying a human resource development strategy in their community to expand jobs and improve community well-being need to discover how the increase in skills of current or potential workers can expand opportunities for groups of people or businesses currently not fully participating in the local community.

Knowing about training gaps and workforce problems of employers is key to identifying a possible development opportunity. The examples in Box 10.1 and the following teaching cases show how some businesses and communities responded to changes in the economic climate of their community. Table 10.2 offers several ideas to help get a human resource project started.

Table 10.2 Human Resource Development Tools and Techniques

| Tool | Goal | | | |
	Vocational Training and Education	Job Placement	Client-Oriented Job Creation	Job Maintenance
Customized training	X		X	X
First-source agreements		X		
Supported work program				X
Local employment officer	X	X	X	
Skill banks	X	X	X	
Training programs	X	X		
Youth enterprise	X		X	
Self-employment initiatives	X		X	
Disabled skills development	X	X	X	

Conclusion

Unemployed persons are generally viewed as incapable. This is far from the truth. The unemployed are a resource. They can help themselves as well as the community. The programs discussed in this chapter are usually auxiliary or adjunct to other efforts. That does not mean that they are unimportant or that they should be an afterthought. They can, especially in the short term, be a major component in the overall local/regional economic development strategy. Irrespective of whether a council is part of a regional scheme, there are opportunities in this area that can be taken to meet the particular training and employment needs of community members.

Box 10.1   Example 10.1: Calling Kansas City

Sprint, a world leader in telecommunication headquartered in Kansas City, Missouri, generated about $800 billion in revenues. Sprint made a logical decision to place one of its world call centers in a Kansas City suburb. Sprint was happy with its decision to locate in the suburbs until the turn-over rate and employee training expenses reached unacceptable levels. In the late 1990s, Sprint management turned to the inner city to reinvigorate its workforce and stabilize its business. Sprint entered into a partnership with several local community-based organizations to locate a satellite call center in inner-city Kansas City.

Sprint was able, with the help of the local Kansas City Development Corporation, to find a building in the heart of the inner city and establish a call center. The call center with the support of local community-based training organizations is developing good-paying jobs for inner-city residents, including former welfare recipients. The center trains 300 people per month and many of these find work with Sprint or other local call centers. But the call center and training are only part of the story. The Sprint call center is located on 18th and Vine in the heart of the Enterprise Zone at the community renewal program. As a result, it contributes to the renewal of the job base and the economic base of this reemerging community.

Source: Initiative for a Competitive Inner City (1999).

Box 10.1   Example 10.2: The Machine Action Project

The Machine Action Project (MAP), located in Springfield, Massachusetts, exemplifies how labor's involvement can lead to innovative local approaches to training and retraining and manufacturing retention. MAP is an affiliate organization of the Federation for Industrial Retention and Renewal (FIRR), a network of labor–community coalitions committed to maintaining and developing the U.S. manufacturing sector and the high-paying jobs it provides. The FIRR model of industrial retention focuses on three issues: future ownership, integration of minorities and women, and maintaining manufacturing competitiveness. FIRR recognizes that if the U.S. manufacturing sector is to become more competitive, new high-performance forms of workplace organization will have to be adopted, which will require a substantial investment in worker training.

(Continued)

(Continued)

MAP'S involvement in training emerged in response to restructuring of the local metalworking industry. Without MAP'S efforts at identifying and developing a response to a skills mismatch in metalworking firms, this essential part of the Springfield area economy would have been lost. The effectiveness and uniqueness of their approach has been recognized widely. In 1988, MAP was the recipient of a Ford Foundation-Kennedy School of Government award as one of the ten most innovative community projects in the country. In 1990, MAP received another innovation award from the Arthur D. Little Foundation.

The late 1970s and early 1980s were a time of intensive restructuring of the metalworking industry in the Springfield, Massachusetts, area. Large, highly automated firms were closing and small producers employing flexible production techniques were growing. Approximately 15,000 metalworking jobs were lost between 1980 and 1985, virtually all in large facilities.

In 1985, the local International Union of Electrical Workers (IUE) union members at the American Bosch plant in Springfield began to notice signs of disinvestment. Through business manager Bob Forrant, the union began warning state and local political representatives and the local economic development community that this plant employing 1,000 workers was likely to close. The response from all quarters was that of disbelief. The IUE was told their early-warning indicators were responding to a false alarm.

When American Bosch announced its closing in 1986, dismantling and movement of production offshore was already in process. Although union activists were able to negotiate a better severance package, they were unable to convince local economic development actors to support an eminent domain takeover of the facility, and were frustrated by their lack of influence. The union then worked with the local private industry and labor councils to seek state funding for designation as a State Industry Action Project. Funds were awarded in 1986 to organize MAP to conduct local labor market research and to develop worker training strategies. MAP'S research revealed a previously unidentified skills mismatch. While much attention had been paid to the loss of major metalworking employers, many small producers were thriving. In contrast to the large automated facilities, the smaller shops employed flexible production processes. Workers in small facilities needed higher skill levels, requiring them to set up and operate three or more machine tools, to read and assemble parts from blueprints, and to maintain their own tools. Few workers in large automated plants possessed these skills. A key difference between these and the central government programs is their focus on retention and expansion of manufacturing in order to maintain economic competitiveness and high-paying, blue-collar jobs.

Thus, workers displaced from the large firms did not have the skills needed by the small flexible producers. The lack of skilled labor to feed the small producers was also a result of a general perception in the area that metalworking was a dying industry and that blue-collar work was inferior to service occupations. As a result, new labor force entrants did not consider employment in metalworking.

In 1988, MAP was funded by the Massachusetts Department of Education to offer adult education programs in five vocational high schools in the region. The courses developed were targeted to upgrade the skills of those employed in area metalworking shops, although they also served the unemployed and high school students as well. MAP entered into a memorandum of agreement with Springfield Technical Community College, the local chapter of the National Tooling and Machining Association, and several federal, state, and local agencies on a common curriculum to be used by all local metalworking training institutions. MAP assumed a coordination and informational role in the agreement, conducting research on the region's training needs, developing recruiting strategies to target women and racial and linguistic minorities, securing funding, and following up on trainees.

The program served the needs of the small metalworking shops, the employees, and the schools. The firms paid minimal fees for state-of-the-art instruction they could not provide on their own. The coordination of courses, a common intake assessment, and a competency-based curriculum allowed trainees to take courses with different providers without losing program continuity. Furthermore, the articulation agreement between the schools allowed trainees to accumulate credits toward an associate's degree in metalworking technology. The state funds and tuition were used to update the schools' curricula with one recently approved by the National Machining Association and to buy equipment. Furthermore, MAP cosponsored a summer institute on new manufacturing technologies for 20 local secondary vocational education teachers to keep them updated in the latest manufacturing technologies.

MAP also received U.S. Department of Labor Women's Bureau funds to develop a program to increase the presence of women in the machine trades. MAP commissioned the Massachusetts Career Development Institute (MCDI), a nonprofit training provider targeting low-income youth and adults, to provide the training. MCDI already offered its trainees a number of support services, including child care, to eliminate barriers to program completion.

Source: Fitzgerald, Joan, and Allan McGregor. 1993. Labor-Community Initiatives in Worker Training. *Economic Development Quarterly: The Journal of American Economic Revitalization* 7(2): 176–179. Copyright © Sage Publications, Inc. Reprinted with permission.

Box 10.1	Example 10.3: The Inverclyde Training Trust

More than any other community on the River Clyde, Inverclyde (consisting largely of the towns of Greenock and Port Glasgow) depended most heavily on shipbuilding. Even after a protracted period of shipbuilding decline, shipbuilding still accounted for 17% (roughly 6,500 jobs) of all employment in Inverclyde in 1981. By the end of the 1980s, fewer than 1,000 shipbuilding jobs were left. This is a dramatic decline bearing in mind that the area's major shipbuilder, Scott Lithgow, alone accounted for 9,000 workers in the mid-1970s.

The impact has been highly localized as there was a very strong workplace–residence overlap due to the historical tradition of shipbuilding in the area, and its relative isolation from the larger Glasgow area. The unemployment situation in Inverclyde deteriorated dramatically over the period of this job loss. In the early 1980s, the unemployment rate was roughly 20% above the Scottish average, and by the late 1980s, it was 50% higher. This was despite a population decline from 105,000 to 98,000 between 1976 and 1985.

A number of responses were developed in an attempt to combat the decline in shipbuilding employment. A key innovative measure was the development of Inverclyde Training Trust (ITT) in 1986. Although control of ITT was local, the initial funding for its activities was provided by a regional economic development organization, the Scottish Development Agency. ITT organizers realized that the jobs lost in the shipbuilding industry would not be recovered, due to international overcapacity. Furthermore, they recognized that in a stagnant national and regional economy, possibilities for attracting mobile capital were limited and competition between areas for that capital was fierce. Thus, their emphasis was on providing displaced workers with new skills to equip them for alternative employment or self-employment.

To link training and local economic development, ITT focused on providing skills for the unemployed both to fill existing vacancies and to attract inward investors, and for the employed to enhance the productivity and performance of local companies. To accomplish its goals, the organization would have to convince local unemployed people and employers of the benefits of training and retraining, and obtain the resources to make local training programs more effective.

Two features of ITT enable it to perform a difficult and innovative role in the local economy. First, it was established as a training broker, and not as a provider of training. ITT sits in the middle of Inverclyde's training system, establishing the needs of the local unemployed and employers and trying to find means of meeting those needs. In a sense, it is a catalytic organization whose presence in the local system generates dynamic change or development in training. Second, it is a free-standing organization with only minor core funding and resource support. ITT essentially trades in training services. In this capacity, it makes use of existing UK national and local government programs as well as training programs funded by the Social Fund of the European Common Market.

A major part of ITT's training portfolio is supported by the Social Fund. Many trainees are eligible for a training allowance, and a survey of trainees revealed that 25% would not have been able to participate without this support. This distinguishes ITT's training from the "benefit plus" regime of the national program, ET.

ITT's 95% completion rate indicated that the thorough monitoring and feedback of participants is a critical component of the program. The post-training placement rates, however, reveal a less positive outcome. Whereas half of the former shipyard workers were either employed or in further education or training, the corresponding figure for trainees from other industrial backgrounds was only one third. The difficulties in shifting people from unemployment to self-employment are evident, although the figures are somewhat better than those achieved in some of the large-scale redundancies elsewhere in the UK.

The high rates of unemployment vividly illustrate how training itself is not a solution to the problem of redundancy or unemployment. It can facilitate the redeployment of reasonable numbers and help the local unemployed generally to find work, but it needs to be accompanied by corresponding measures to replace some proportion of the net job loss resulting from the redundancy. This conclusion is supported further by a survey of trainees that indicated that only 50% of former shipbuilders felt that their training helped them directly in getting a job. Nevertheless, 91% valued the ESF training sufficiently to recommend it to other unemployed people. This figure indicates that workers obtain value other than direct and immediate employability from their training. Indeed, although nearly 60% of former shipyard workers saw the acquisition of job-related skills as the key advantage of training, 33% stressed enhanced personal confidence. For many trainees, personal confidence and related factors significantly outweighed job-related skills as the key advantage. By improving morale and self-esteem, training keeps the local workforce in a position to take advantage of new jobs that may locate in the area. As Inverclyde is hoping to attract additional employment as a result of the establishment of the Inverclyde Enterprise Zone, maintaining motivation is critical.

Teaching Case 10.1

Employment Planning as Economic Development

How does an older Northeastern city with a declining industrial base, high unemployment, uncoordinated federal economic programs, and a reputation for poor service in job training and placement overcome its handicaps and use its federal resources to build a job training and referral system that draws industry back into town, creates jobs, and wins the respect of private industry?

In Eastport, which has come a fair way toward achieving these goals, the answer rests in a combination of the city's commitment to provide real job service to the private sector and its determination to save neighborhoods by seeing that there are jobs for the people who live in them. Indeed, the key to the economic turnaround of Eastport is jobs, especially new jobs in the heart of the city to replace those lost. The blueprint for achieving this is Eastport's Employment Development Plan, with a realistic approach to urban planning and a coordinated use of federal funds. The plan's principal goal is creating jobs and assuring people's access to them.

The essence of the Eastport Plan is the coordination of the efforts of all the federal urban economic stimulus programs into one local agency used to build a base for both short- and long-term improvements in the city's economy. Federal funding for public works, economic development, and training and employment had been coming into the city under separate programs. The plan provides a means to combine these programs at the local level. Its goal is to create 14,000 new permanent jobs over 5 years.

The city of Eastport had some successful experience in downtown revitalization to draw on in putting together the plan. The city had already faced all the problems of many older cities—a declining inner-city tax base, movement of the middle class to the suburbs, increased demands for social services by those remaining, and a growing unemployment problem. As one response to its problems, the city chose to make a direct investment in the downtown waterfront, transforming this decaying and obsolete commercial area into a housing, commercial, and tourist center that has attracted national interest. The success of the downtown revitalization effort demonstrated to residents that the city could be made livable again. The city proposed to revitalize several neighborhoods. Residents, who had seen the downtown successfully restored, had reason to hope that the new plan might work in their neighborhoods.

One of the first steps the city took was to reorganize the city's various employment and economic development activities into a single agency, the

Employment and Economic Policy Administration (EEPA), and to give it responsibility for providing new or expanding industries in the area with trained workers or federal job training program enrollees whom a firm could train.

Before the city could undertake job training and referral services for the private sector, it had a major handicap to overcome—its reputation for providing poor-quality employment services to those industries. Private employers felt that the city had provided inadequate job-orientation services to the potential workers it referred. Many trainees had dropped out of the program in which they were placed, or the employers were so dissatisfied with them that they did not go back to the program for more. There were few links between the city employment program and the community organizations that understood the special needs of the cultural and ethnic groups living in the inner city, from which many of the prospective workers were drawn. Private employers felt that the city did not give a high priority to the services it provided.

The EEPA set out to correct this situation. The city sponsored a survey of employers to find out what specific problems they had experienced in the past, and asked for their advice on how to improve the situation. One problem frequently identified was a lack of direct involvement on the part of the city officials in dealing with private-sector industry. To correct this, the city first transferred on-the-job training activities from the independent agency that had been acting for the city to the EEPA. The EEPA then formed a coalition with the National Association of Business (NAB) and the Urban League to provide the close contacts among the city, jobs, and people, which were lacking before.

Later, the on-the-job training program of the EEPA formally merged with the NAB. The two agencies are now housed together, with each agency maintaining its own role in the employment process. The NAB staff aggressively approached the business community to find jobs for the economically disadvantaged. Firms that agreed to participate could hire individuals directly or through an on-the-job training program. The payoff to the firms is the screening, job orientation, and employability counseling provided to each person by the city agency before the initial employment.

One illustrative program is a training program underway to provide long-range training opportunities in the marine and computer fields. The harbor is the site of a major new industrial park that will provide jobs for 3,500 skilled and unskilled workers. Using a variety of funding

(Continued)

(Continued)

sources, the city renovated and equipped one of the buildings in the park to serve as a job training center—the only vocational training facility directly linking the growing marine industry with a skills training program.

The center's staff identified specific highly skilled occupations that required no more than 10 months of training. They then verified the need for workers with these skills with the firms operating the Marine Industrial Park. Under the agreements entered into between a potential employer and the center, each employer must appoint a training supervisor to assist in the design of the training programs. Each of the participating firms must use the plandeveloped as the basis of the agreement with the job training center. The job trainees are trained either at the center or on the job site. All employers using the center's services must make a commitment to hire first the individuals trained through the center program. This has not been a problem, because the agreements provide for heavy employer involvement in the specification and design of the training courses in all skill trades with known labor shortages.

Eastport seems to be well on its way to a healthier job base than it has had in some time. But there is more to the plan than the link between jobs and economic development, although that is a key element. Through the strengthening of the city's economic base and by providing jobs to unemployed city residents, the city's leaders believe they will reduce the problems of crime, poor housing, inadequate health facilities, and inaccessible recreational facilities.

One of the most exciting features of the plan is the one providing unemployed workers with loans to start their own businesses. Under this program, the unemployed continue to receive their unemployment insurance payments for a full year with a supplemental payment while they start their new business. Participants must take up to 6 weeks of small business training before they open a business and become involved in the SCORE (Service Corps of Retired Executives) program for technical assistance to their new firm. The program has received a lot of criticism from local merchants, who claim that their firms were not subsidized at the outset and these new businesses represent unfair competition. On the other hand, the program guidelines are relatively strict on the new firm competition area by restricting new start-up firms to business types not represented in the local community. What do you think of the complaints of the local businesspersons and how might their issues be resolved, if at all?

Teaching Case 10.2

Moving the Poor off Welfare

Many cities are experiencing very different economic circumstances as a result of the national economic transformation. Although the Midwest has a high unemployment rate and large concentrations of poverty, both the Northeast and the Far West are booming economies with relatively few jobless people. All of the cities agree that they must initiate programs to move substantial numbers of chronically poor people off welfare and into relatively well-paying jobs.

The secret to achieving this, some experts suggest, is to involve the poor in counseling, education, and training programs far more intensive than any attempted in the past and to guarantee continued support services, such as medical insurance and child care, until they are secure in their jobs.

Margarita Majias was one of 30,000 welfare clients who officials say found employment under the state's program in the past 3 years in Holyport, a Northeastern city still suffering from the closing of industrial plants. As a single mother with one child, she had tried working, with a job in a shoe factory for about $4 an hour. Soon, she said in an interview, she found she could do better by going on welfare, which also provided food stamps and medical insurance through Medicaid.

After several years on welfare, she was persuaded by state counselors to enter training, which included instruction in how and where to apply for work. Eventually, she found a job as assistant property manager for an apartment complex. Her income went from $500 a month on welfare to $960, along with a free apartment in the complex and a promise of raises in the future, with benefits.

"It's good work, and gives me a sense of purpose because other people are depending on me. Sure it's hard, but I like it," she said. "And I don't have to worry about medical insurance for my daughter. It is provided with respectability for the first time in my life."

Few experts believe these efforts will be successful with every welfare case. But most agree that long-term welfare dependence can be reduced substantially by innovative efforts, which may eventually help to break cycles of poverty, broken families, crime, drug addiction, and teenage pregnancies.

The Holyport program is voluntary, unlike some other cities' programs. Eligible applicants can elect regular welfare payments or a stipend for the work performed in lieu of welfare. Most choose the check because it is a symbol of moving away from welfare. The program includes close

(Continued)

(Continued)

counseling, education, training if needed, and job placement with the promise that Medicaid, the medical insurance program for the poor, will continue for a year if the employer does not provide it. That is important because many women say they would rather stay on welfare and receive Medicaid than take a job paying marginally more that does not have medical insurance.

In addition, Holyport has added a new wrinkle to the current efforts. A proposed program called Work Assistance allows a select group of non-profit community development corporations (CDCs) to hire and train welfare recipients at subsidized wages. The Holyport Spanish Speaking CDC operates a gasoline station, a community supermarket, a rental car agency, and several health clinics, as well as a day care center. Under the plan, the city will subsidize the employment of welfare recipients in all firms operated by the Holyport Spanish Speaking CDC. The CDC must pay above the minimum wage and guarantee to place the participants in unsubsidized jobs within 6 months.

At the last meeting of the Holyport Employment Council, Ernesto Gutierrez asked that the subsidy be raised and the length of time increased because the quality of applicants was so low that more remediation was necessary. The Employment Council is upset by the request because it feels that the program is really too expensive and that Spanish Speaking CDC is using too much of its funding in English and literacy instruction. Based on an assessment of the local, primarily Hispanic welfare clientele, would you consider the Spanish Speaking CDC's actions reasonable? If so, why? You might look at some local data and interview welfare and community organizations to determine the job readiness of the local welfare population. What would it take to put most of your local limited English-speaking welfare population into unsubsidized employment?

Teaching Case 10.3

Young Need a Job—Make Your Own!

Tung Ng was offered a job as a Vietnamese youth director by the Viet Family Life Center but wasn't sure if the ideas he had for the job would be acceptable to the organizers of the Viet Family Life Committee. That was 2 years ago, and Tung now draws $2,000 a month for work that has become a mission.

(Continued)

Tung's idea for the largely Vietnamese and Cambodian lower-income Crestview Park neighborhood was a program that would teach youngsters aged 14 to 21 about business, personal money management, and entrepreneurial savvy. Tung brought a lot of business know-how with him from Vietnam. He had worked for the U.S. Air Force in the Base Store. His family ran restaurants and variety stores in Saigon. He felt that the American-born and -raised Vietnamese and Cambodian youth were using their entrepreneurial skills to form gangs instead of starting their own businesses.

Tung started his program, called Youth Action, with only 20 youngsters. Based at a local center, the program is open to any child in the community. Only about 30% of its members belong to the Viet Family Life Center. Tung admits Youth Action has many components similar to Junior Achievement. However, Youth Action is more professional because it is geared to help young people actually own and operate businesses in their communities. It also differs from standard job training programs because it doesn't teach them how to do a particular task in someone else's business. Youth Action shows youths how to develop "minibusinesses" of their own. They learn by attending a 10-week training program after school and on weekends. They also act as interns in jobs they can accommodate year round, after school, and on weekends.

At the conclusion of the training program, each youth has a business plan. These plans are screened by a panel of local Asian businesspeople. Those that meet the test of business worthiness are seed-funded with a grant of $2,000 and a small loan. The business must be in community-related areas and fit a community need. The youth cannot merely find a nice white-collar occupation outside the community as the answer to their problem.

"We live in a world where even many white-collar jobs in big and smaller companies are becoming scarce for experienced, educated adults," Tung points out. "Asian youngsters must be trained early to turn their talents and skills into jobs they create for themselves."

The basis for Youth Action, says Tung, is "working to re-create historic values of building something for yourself and fostering a self-dignity, independence, and pride essential to long-term achievement." Tung hopes to expand the program if it continues to be successful.

The Family Life Center provides facilities for Youth Action activities but takes no money from them. All the money Youth Action generates is used to support its projects and for the youngsters' salaries. Members must give 15% of their earnings back to Youth Action. These funds are

(Continued)

(Continued)

held in a trust account for each member's future education at the college or vocational level. A person who does not go to college forfeits his or her accumulation.

Since the program began, the teenagers have launched a prospering catering business, a computer training center, a word processing service, a photography business, a summer tutorial program for elementary school children, and an answering service. In addition to those ongoing services, Youth Action has sponsored several one-time projects such as yard sales, breakfasts, bake sales, and an ice cream store day (they made the ice cream at a local outlet and sold it). In the planning stages are a babysitting service, a Vietnamese and Cambodian book fair to encourage cultural restoration among inner-city youngsters, and a children's computer and electronic swap meet. To encourage sound money management, members must plan a personal budget and establish a savings account at the Korean-owned Community Savings & Loan Association. That bank was chosen, Tung noted, because he wants the youngsters to get in the habit of supporting local Asian business.

"The bank officers know them so well now that they've gone a long way toward establishing a sound relationship with a bank," said Tung. "I explained to them how important that will be when they're [old enough] to apply for credit and need good references."

I've found that most of these kids have lots of talent," Tung said. "They all have things they can do. If I say I need a sign made, or whatever, someone will say 'I can do it,' and they do it."

The adult board of Youth Action wants to consolidate all businesses under a single corporate or limited partnership status. The rationale for this move is that the business license and other procedures are too complicated and make business startup more difficult than business operations. Several board members counter that this is the essence of the experience. Tung objects to this change. The cost of opening these ventures is time consuming and creates a liability for the Family Life Board. Assume the board has come to you as an economic development expert and asked you to chart an alternative plan for the youth businesses that is less expensive and reaches more youth.

References and Suggested Readings

Ashenfelter, Orley. 1978. Estimating the Effect of Training Programs on Earnings. *Review of Economics and Statistics* 60(1): 47–57.

Becker, Gary. 1975. *Human Capital*, 2nd ed. New York: Columbia University Press.

Blakely, Edward, J. 1982. Economic Development and Job Creation: Some Ideas and Examples for the United States. In *Job Creation Through the Public Sector? A Strategy for Employment Growth.* Melbourne, Australia: Brotherhood of St. Laurence.

Blichfeldt, Jan Frode. 1975. The Relations Between School and the Place of Work. In *School and Community*, edited by G. Blichfeldt. Paris: CERI/OECD.

Bluestone, Barry, and Mary Huff Stevenson. 2000. *The Boston Renaissance.* New York: Russell Sage Foundation.

Choate, Pat. 1982. *Retooling the American Workforce: Towards a National Strategy.* Washington, DC: Northeast-Midwest Institute.

Field, Frank. 1977. *Education and the Urban Crisis.* London: Routledge & Kegan Paul.

Fitzgerald, Joan. 2005. *Moving Up in the New Economy.* Ithaca, NY: ILR Press.

Fitzgerald, Joan, and Allan McGregor. 1993. Labor–Community Initiatives in Worker Training. *Economic Development Quarterly* 7(2): 176–179.

Furst, Lyndon. 1979. Work: An Educational Alternative to Schooling. *Urban Review* 11(3): n.p.

GAO. 2007. *Higher Education: Tuition Continues to Rise, but Patterns Vary by Institution Type, Enrollment, and Educational Expenditures.* Report to the Chairman, Committee on Education and Labor, House of Representatives. GAO-08-245, www.gao.gov

Garmise, Shari. 2006. *People and the Competitive Advantage of Place: Building a Workforce for the 21st Century.* Armonk, NY: M.E. Sharpe.

Gleaser, E. 1980. *The Community College in the United States.* Paper presented at the OECD Conference, Higher Education and the Community, Paris, France, February.

Goldstein, Harold. 1977. *Training and Education by Industry.* Washington, DC: National Institute for Work and Learning.

Goodman, Robert. 1973. *After the Planners.* New York: Simon & Schuster.

Gross, Julian, Greg LeRoy, and Madeline Janis-Aparicio. 2005. *Community Benefit Agreements: Making Development Projects Accountable.* Washington, DC: Good Jobs First.

Hamilton, M. 1980. On Creating Work Experience Programs: Design and Implementation. In *Youthwork National Policy Study.* Occasional Paper no. 3. Ithaca, NY: Cornell University.

Have Factory, Will Travel. 2000. *The Economist* 355(8172): 61–62.

Holloway, W. 1980. Youth Participation: A Strategy to Increase the Role of School Youth in Creating Job Opportunities. In *Youthwork National Policy Study.* Occasional Paper no. 3. Ithaca, NY: Cornell University.

Information Technology Association. 2000. *Technology Updates.* Arlington, VA: Author.

Initiative for a Competitive Inner City. 1999. *Calling Kansas City: Sprint as New Economy Job Developer.* Boston: Author.

Jones, P. 1978. *Community Education in Practice: A Review.* Oxford, UK: Social Evaluation Unit.

Kleinman, Neil Scott. 2000. *The Skills Crisis.* New York: Center for an Urban Future.

Leigh, Nancey Green, Joy Wilkins, and Bill Riall. 2001. *The Economic Development Potential of Georgia's Biotechnology Industry.* Atlanta: Georgia Department of Industry, Trade, and Tourism and Georgia Tech Economic Development Research Program.

National Skills Coalition. n.d. Workforce Investment Act, Title 1. Accessed May 6, 2012 from http://www.nationalskillscoalition.org/resources/reports/tpib/nsc_tpib_wia_titlei.pdf

O'Toole, James, and Edward E. Lawler, III. 2006. *The New American Workplace.* New York: Palgrave Macmillan.

Schaaf, Michael. 1977. *Cooperatives at the Crossroads: The Potential for a Major New Economic and Social Role.* Washington, DC: Exploratory Project for Economic Alternatives.

Schweke, William. 2004. *Smart Money: Education and Economic Development.* Washington, DC: Economic Policy Institute.

Sher, Jonathan. 1979. *Rural Education in Urbanized Nations: Issues and Innovation.* Boulder, CO: Westview.

Swack, Michael, and Donald Mason. 1987. Community Economic Development as a Strategy for Social Intervention. In *Social Intervention Strategies*, edited by E. Bennett. Lewiston, NY: Mellen.

Willis, Robert J., and Sherwin Rosen. 1970. Education and Self-Selection. *Journal of Political Economy* 87(2): 350–366.

Wolman, Harold, Cary Lichtman, and Suzie Barnes. 1991. The Impact of Credentials, Skill Levels, Worker Training and the Motivation on Employment Outcomes: Sorting Out the Implications for Economic Development Policy. *Economic Development Quarterly* 5(2): 140–151.

11

Community Economic Development

The difference between community development and economic development is often a source of confusion, especially for new students of local economic development planning. The confusion can be cleared up by noting that *community* development focuses on a broad range of development issues that include housing, business and job development, health and safety, and child development, as well as education and other critical public services. Business and job development can readily be identified as components of the economic side of community development. However, it is important to understand the spatial scale at which the economic aspects of community development are addressed. As Ferguson and Dickens (1999) note, "No one argues that community development can effectively counteract the business cycle or fend off major transformation in the macroeconomy. Neither can it compete with income-transfer programs as short-run responses to poverty" (p. 2).

Community economic development focuses on the neighborhood scale of socioeconomic transformation in a distressed locality. Community economic development seeks to improve conditions within a geographic area that is populated by the disadvantaged and unable to control its socioeconomic direction or resources, both human and physical. The development efforts focusing on improving internal conditions within the neighborhood may very well need to focus on strengthening linkages external to the neighborhood. Strengthening those linkages often entails the economic side of community development by linking neighborhood residents to opportunities for work outside of their neighborhood, as well as by attracting new investment and businesses (and therefore jobs) to the neighborhood.

Fundamentally, *community economic* development has a narrower focus within the broader community development sector that is aimed at improving conditions and overall quality of life in poor and working-class neighborhoods.

William H. Simon (2001) defines community economic development as engaging in "(1) efforts to develop housing, jobs or business opportunities for low-income people, (2) in which a leading role is played by nonprofit, nongovernmental organizations, (3) that are accountable to residentially defined communities" (p. 4).

He also notes that the community economic development movement has spawned significant legal and institutional innovations. These include the use of peripheral legal forms such as charitable corporations and cooperatives (Simon, 2001). Further, one of the most significant innovations was the passage of the Community Reinvestment Act, which requires banks to demonstrate lending and business development in disadvantaged communities.

The community economic development movement has grown more sophisticated in recent years. For example, the Center for Community Economic Development (CCED) is part of a national network of organizations creating local-level Families for Economic Security (FES) projects. According to CCED (2008), the FES project is a

> broad-based coalition comprised of legislators, advocates, direct service providers and foundations who support policies that build economic security for families, elders, and the communities in which they live. We define economic security as having enough money to cover the basics like rent, food, child care, health care, transportation, and taxes, *and* enough money to develop savings and assets. Savings and assets are what allow people to weather the inevitable economic ups and downs of life, and to build a more stable future. CFES [Californians for Family Economic Security] advocates that policymakers use more realistic measures of what it takes to make ends meet as they develop policies and allocate limited resources.

Efforts such as that of CCED have proliferated over the past several years due to the failure of the general economy to serve the needs of particularly disadvantaged communities. These development initiatives aim to generate *socially useful, labor-intensive* projects that meet their expenses or make a profit while improving the employability of the participants. They also seek to create greater local control and ownership in a community. Parzen and Kieschnick (1992) observe:

> Ownership is integral to the notion of economic development. It has become commonplace to describe economic development by citing the old parable that you can feed someone for a day by giving them fish, or you can feed someone for life by teaching them to fish. This may be true. But the twentieth century postscript to the story is that what really matters is who owns the pond with the fish. There is surely a difference between two communities, one with all of its tangible assets owned by distant investors and one with a significant degree of local ownership. The absence of local ownership implies either a lack of local capital or a lack of confidence in local investing on the part of local owners of capital—neither is consistent with a policy of economic development. (p. 5)

The basic objective of these initiatives is to teach people at the neighborhood level to own their own pond and to fish it. This is accomplished by

- generating employment for particular segments of a disadvantaged community
- capturing local/neighborhood spending to build local wealth
- inspiring self-help and cooperative group-oriented (social capital) assistance
- operating programs such as health, education, and nutrition for the public benefit
- providing an alternative or intermediate sector to create jobs in the local economy
- promoting democratic management and local ownership and control of enterprises

Nearly all of the activities discussed elsewhere in this book can be undertaken as community economic development initiatives. Around two decades ago, Teitz (1989) warned those who espoused neighborhood or community economic development that

> neighborhoods, by their very nature, are problematic as a target of economic development strategy, in so far as a strategy is intended to generate economic activity and employment directly within their boundaries. As the places where people live and work, neighborhoods reflect most clearly the conditions of life of their residents. Thus, they are a logical focus of advocacy and political mobilization. But the historic divorce of workplace from residents is now so far advanced in American cities that localized economic development efforts face great difficulties. (p. 112)

Fortunately, the tide is beginning to turn for the exodus of jobs and businesses from central cities across the nation. Over the last decade, there has been a "Back to the Downtown" movement occurring in our major cities, due to the rejection of suburban living by certain demographic groups (e.g., aging Baby Boomers, young professionals) as well as firms seeking to avoid the costs of urban sprawl (Birch, 2005). This *could* be a very positive trend for neighborhood revitalization and community economic development efforts overall. However, there are legitimate and growing concerns over how this Back to the Downtown movement contributes to growing income inequality and displacement of low-income residents due to gentrification. Thus, this major socioeconomic trend has the potential to overcome some of the inherent barriers to neighborhood or community economic development that Teitz (1989) identified by bringing economic activity back to central cities. However, unless the tools of community economic development can effectively be brought to bear on this new trend, the neighborhoods that were the focus of CED efforts may look and work much better for their new residents, but their efforts will have failed to improve the standard of living for the original disadvantaged residents. See Box 11.1 for CED principles that can guide neighborhood revitalization when brownfields are present.

Box 11.1	Brownfield Redevelopment Principles to Prevent Neighborhood Gentrification

Most older and poor neighborhoods have brownfield properties that are especially difficult to redevelop because they have known or expected environmental contamination. Prior to being redeveloped, these properties have to undergo assessment and cleanup of the environmental contamination, which increases their cost of redevelopment. There has been a range of public efforts at the national, state, and local levels to foster the cleanup and redevelopment of brownfields, whether in poor or prosperous neighborhoods. However, since these efforts began in the mid-1990s, the main brownfield redevelopment focus in both the public and private sectors has been on the most marketable and larger properties that are well located (i.e., not in the poorest neighborhoods). The rationale for the public-sector focus has been to maximize return on public investment, while the private sector logically and appropriately has sought to maximize profits.

The remaining brownfield inventory is increasingly composed of small and medium-sized sites, many of which would be considered marginal redevelopment prospects by the private sector due to their locations, limited end uses, and profit potentials. But neglecting their redevelopment stigmatizes and devalues surrounding nonbrownfield properties and acts as a barrier to neighborhood revitalization. The neighborhoods in which they are located are left further behind those being revitalized due to a proactive redevelopment climate catalyzed by major public initiatives such as the EPA's Brownfield Revitalization Act, as well as "back to the city" and urban sprawl containment (or Smart Growth) strategies. Thus, there is increasing concern over how brownfield redevelopment practices can contribute to growing urban income inequality and displacement of low-income residents from gentrification. The four principles below are proposed to ensure brownfield redevelopment policy and public funding do not help foster these undesirable trends:[1]

1. Focus on brownfields in neighborhoods with the worst health exposure and greatest need for economic development.

2. Require demographic and economic impact assessments of projects, as well as displacement projections and prevention/redress plans.

[1]See Leigh, Nancey Green. Testimony regarding "Revitalization of the Environmental Protection Agency's Brownfields Program." U.S. House of Representatives Committee on Transportation and Infrastructure, Subcommittee on Water Resources and Environment, February 14, 2008.

3. Emphasize a neighborhood approach in any provision for communitywide multipurpose grants for use for both assessment and cleanup on multiple sites.

4. Encourage the development of workforce housing on appropriate brownfield sites.

Following these principles may seem especially daunting in the aftermath of the Great Recession's devastating impacts on the real estate market. However, brownfields in the poorest neighborhoods are even less likely to be redeveloped now, when the overall market is depressed. An encouraging development that bears watching is the outcome of a new program called "Brownfields Area-Wide Planning Pilot Program." The U.S. EPA has given 23 grants to cities for piloting an areawide planning approach to community brownfield challenges in recognition "that revitalization of the area surrounding the brownfield site(s) is critical to the successful reuse of the property as assessment, cleanup, and redevelopment of an individual site" (U.S. EPA, n.d.).

This chapter will focus on organizational form and objectives rather than specific activities of community economic development. In this edition of *Planning Local Economic Development,* we are adding one new form to the five organizational forms we have previously discussed. The five are community development corporations, community cooperatives, local enterprise agencies, employee/worker ownerships, and community employment and training boards. The sixth addition, LEED-ND, can be distinguished from the other five forms because of its spatial orientation. They are compared in Table 11.1.

Table 11.1   Comparison of Organizational Forms of Community-Based Economic and Employment Development

Organizational	Objectives	Methods
Community development corporation	Build community-level institutions	Community organization and business formation
Community cooperative	Community/worker producer control	Collective business
Local enterprise agency	Unemployed/community business formation	Local resource mobilization

(Continued)

Table 11.1 (Continued)

Organizational	Objectives	Methods
Employee/worker ownership	Worker control	Worker finance
Community employment and training board	Human resource development	Training
LEED-ND	Mixed-income communities	Development projects

Community Development Corporations

The community development corporation (CDC) is an institutional form pioneered in the United States that has attracted the interest of European governments.

CDCs were conceived as part of the War on Poverty in 1966, when Congress authorized a demonstration program as an amendment to the Economic Opportunity Act. The legislation was vague, however, and the concept was still just beginning to take shape when the first CDCs started to receive federal funding in 1968. The early years of the CDC movement included a number of forays into ghetto development. Some basic principles that still guide community-based economic development were formulated then—community control, a comprehensive approach, a focus on business and economic development—but at that time no one knew how to apply them. Those early years also saw a number of failures, but even so, CDCs began to take hold.

They have gradually made the sometimes subtle transition from antipoverty agencies to economic development institutions. Their management and investment strategies have become more sophisticated. CDCs have expanded their resources, not so much through the original War on Poverty program or the later (now defunct) Community Services Administration as through other development programs, primarily in the federal government. To illustrate these changes, early CDCs concerned with community-control issues usually started and managed day-care centers, employment and training, and housing assistance as in-house enterprises.

Few early CDCs considered investing in start-up businesses and few CDCs now manage their own ventures (examples are real estate development and technical assistance efforts). Instead, CDCs tended to take minority equity and debt positions in proven (although often young) firms with experienced management. And, although CDCs still select projects in response to community priorities, they do so within the constraints of market feasibility.

CDC investments are risky, but in general they have become more successful with smaller investments. As a corollary to this trend, CDCs now work much more closely with the private sector, particularly small businesses and the financial community. Joint ventures with entrepreneurs, housing development syndications, and bank credit lines are now common CDC features.

The Senate Labor and Human Resources Committee, in assessing the effectiveness of various ways of delivering federal job training programs, concluded that community-based agencies performed exceptionally well as economic institutions. Avis Vidal of the Community Development Research Center at the New School in New York provided a detailed assessment of CDCs in 1995. At the time of her study in 1995, CDCs had produced more than 435,000 units of urban housing and 115,000 rural housing units since 1980 and acted to stabilize many of the nation's most seriously distressed neighborhoods by promoting and financing home and business ownership. Moreover, CDCs were considered cost effective, which encouraged the Ford Foundation to create the Local Initiatives Support Corporation (LISC). LISC has produced several hundred million dollars in real estate and economic development activity nationwide by leveraging public and private development dollars.

A long-term and comprehensive approach to development requires an institution that can develop and sustain a consistent but flexible strategy. CDCs are such organizations, and they provide full-time professional staffs and at least some planning capacity. Although some CDCs may rely heavily on community volunteers for help, most of their projects require professional and technical skills. The CDC staff must be competent enough to develop housing and businesses in distressed communities avoided by the private sector. This formidable task requires full-time energetic professionals. CDCs usually have in-house planning capacity to deal with the land-use and zoning issues as well as long-term land assembly and affordable housing development. Good CDCs develop strategies that are coordinated, comprehensive, feasible, and responsive to community needs. Such sophisticated planning allows CDCs to go head to head with better-financed organizations.

Institutional Advantages of CDCs

Given the difficulty of developing low-income areas, the notion that community-based organizations have been able to succeed where others have failed or simply stayed away may seem difficult to accept. After all, where there is a market, it should be adequately filled.

CDCs succeed because they consolidate issues and organize capital to deal with market failures in low-income areas. That is, CDCs re-establish the economic and social structure of low-income areas. Banks and other institutions try to work on the economic issues but may not take social barriers into consideration. Vidal (1992) concludes that CDCs "make a major impact on the problems of poor neighborhoods" (p. 19). The financial success of a CDC project is due to sensitivity to both political and business practices. This necessarily demands a comprehensive and coordinated strategy, incorporating social, economic, and physical planning. Because of their purpose, structure, and approach to economic development, CDCs combine characteristics that make them unique institutions. They

- use private development techniques for public purposes
- target benefits to communities and individuals in need
- mobilize local initiative to address local priorities
- take a long-term approach to development
- link planning to implementation
- link complementary projects within a comprehensive strategy
- understand and work with the processes of both the public and the private sectors
- legally can and in practice do attract both public and private resources in a variety of roles
- work directly with small businesses
- reinvest resources in the community
- have incentives to operate programs efficiently
- can transfer capacity among program activities

These characteristics are not, of course, limited to CDCs. Other institutions, including local governments, often perform some of these functions. Moreover, not all CDCs have the capacity to do all these things well. But CDCs are extremely flexible institutions. They can complement the activities of other local participants, develop their capacity through the assistance of these other institutions, and take increasing responsibility for development. In most communities, this process can be cooperative rather than competitive.

A city government, for example, may be able to use its powers of eminent domain to assemble land and its bonding authority to attract private capital for development, and then let a CDC develop and manage the project. In a rural employment training program, a local community college or the state's extension service might design a curriculum, while a CDC identifies and screens possible trainees and then places them with employers after the training is finished. States can contribute to these local partnerships by identifying roles for different organizations and by supporting innovative arrangements.

Challenges for Community Economic Development

Community economic development in organizations has not enjoyed enormous success in this new era of finance. The best example of this transition is the downfall of the once powerful Eastside Community Investment Inc. (ECI) of Indianapolis, Indiana. ECI was the poster child of community development corporations. In its heyday in the 1970s, it employed more than 100 people in a variety of community endeavors from housing to social services. ECI was a paragon of community activism and respect, one of the best examples of a community development corporation serving a distressed area of more than 28,000 residents. ECI had a housing corporation, a credit union, and health and community welfare services. It became a powerful community force, maintaining partnerships with Aetna Life and Casualty and Indiana National Bank with an available $1 million mortgage loan pool. As projects increased in size and offered opportunities to invest in housing and small business, ECI ran into a quagmire of financial red ink. In August 1997, ECI faltered and began to unravel (Johnson and Reingold, 2000).

Many community development corporations were founded and organized for social, not economic development, purposes. As a result, their staff may not have the necessary skills for managing complex economic projects. They also lack the oversight capacity of a sophisticated board of directors knowledgeable in business ventures. The internal dynamics of community development institutions focus on social over tough business decisions. Community development organizations may place emphasis on increasing staff over increasing economic returns. Furthermore, the multiple funding sources with different reporting requirements make the finances of community development organizations complicated, as well as difficult to monitor. Finally, community development corporations have no reserves or investment capital. As a result, any emergency can expose and unravel the entire fabric of the organization.

Community Reinvestment Programs

Community reinvestment is a social philosophy and a movement. Its aim is to replace capital that flows out of minority and disadvantaged communities by pressuring banks and other lending institutions to develop new lending practices for housing, businesses, and social institutions in low-income areas. The key to such reinvestment is the use of the Community Reinvestment Act originally authorized in 1977, which states in part that regulated financial institutions "have a continuing and affirmative obligation to help meet the credit needs of local communities [in] which they are chartered . . . consistent with safe and sound operation of such institutions" (quoted in Squires, 1992, p. 11). In 1994, to further address credit scarcity in poor communities, the Community Development Banking and Financial Institutions Act was passed. This provides for grants, loans, equity capital, and technical assistance to Community Development Finance Institutions (CDFIs).

Thus, community reinvestment straddles an ideological dilemma of finding good loans in impoverished neighborhoods. Proponents of this movement have helped to devise a number of coalitions across the nation designed to identify neighborhood goods, such as housing, and match them with qualified minority or community-based institutional borrowers. The community rein-vestment movement has had some impact on reducing redlining and other adverse lending practices by major financial institutions. For example, it has spawned a new finance industry that seeks low-income lending opportunities and has gained enormous impetus with the tightening of the community rein-vestment legislation in 1997. Banks seeking mergers must show that the mergers will not do harm to low-income areas and show a record of low-income com-munity investments. As a result, more capital is seeking low-income opportuni-ties than is available for the banks.

However, even its strongest proponents acknowledge that good invest-ment opportunities able to meet the test of the law are difficult to identify. Moreover, enormous racism and selectivity remain in lending practices in the financial community. One response to the lack of community-based financing in minority communities has been the emphasis on the creation of nontradi-tional lending institutions such as community credit unions. Another answer to this dilemma is the development of community development finance insti-tutions (CDFIs). Some CDFIs operate like traditional retail banks, while others are community development organizations or credit unions that provide busi-ness-, home-, or other forms of asset-backed lending. The major difference between CDFIs and other lenders is that they are actually involved with their borrowers. They provide technical assistance and identify other lending sources, such as government funds, to enhance the borrowers' opportunities for success.

Community Cooperatives

Until recently, cooperative ownership was largely restricted to primary indus-try. But interest has grown in this form because of its labor-intensive character and its democratic management potential. Further, the themes of community economic development "have a distinct affinity with the cooperative form" (Simon, 2001, p. 130). The primary foci of community cooperatives in the United States are job creation, housing, and credit.

Cooperatives are owned by their membership. According to the University of Wisconsin Center for Cooperatives (www.uwcc.wisc.edu), cooperatives have seven internationally recognized principles as the basis for doing business:

1. voluntary and open membership

2. democratic member control

3. members' economic participation

4. autonomy and independence

5. education, training, and information sharing

6. cooperation among cooperatives

7. concern for community

Several general situations give rise to the formation of community cooperatives, including:

- when a business owner wishes to sell to a community group in order to continue serving the community
- when a community service such as child care, elder care, or other care requires delivery
- when a group of skilled people who are underemployed or unemployed form an organization to sell their services collectively for community benefit

In each case, the steps for forming a cooperative are the same. First, a feasibility study needs to be conducted to ensure that the activity has real potential for success within a cooperative framework. Second, the organizational structure should be well thought out. Ownership shares, leadership, and similar matters need careful early discussion. Although there may be early enthusiasm for cooperative forms, this may quickly subside when people understand the system's rules. Finally, intensive training needs to be given to help the participants adapt to the new system.

Cooperatives require business plans as well as feasibility studies. Such work should at least provide answers to questions on the following topics:

Product Specification

- What evidence is there that a market exists for the product or service to be provided by the business?
- Are there similar products on the market or services available? If so, is their local business, with which you will be competing, offering the same product or service?

Workers

- Are the workers sufficiently trained in cooperative management?
- Is there a real balance of skills among the workforce? Cooperatives will not work if there are differential skill levels.

Premises, Equipment, and Materials

- Are there low-cost premises available for the initial startup?
- What transportation cost will be incurred in operating the venture?
- What are the sources of supply? Are they all under the cooperative's control? For example, is the cooperative selling products made by members or community groups?
- Can the cooperative obtain the necessary credit and access to capital to operate the facility?

Management Skills

Are there sufficient management skills in the group to provide for:

- designing the product or service
- organizing the production or distribution
- handling the banking and finance
- marketing

The cooperative is a recognized legal form, and in most states it has to be incorporated under the appropriate state statute to engage in business. Most states have statutes specifically governing cooperatives. Cooperatives can take advantage of a variety of public and private support, which includes favorable federal tax treatment, as well as access to credit from the National Cooperative Bank (Simon, 2001).

Local Enterprise Agencies

Local enterprise agencies (LEAs) are organizations dedicated to the creation of employment through the support and development of indigenous local enterprises, providing an intermediary link between public and private institutions and the community. They function primarily by facilitating access to capital and technical or professional assistance. LEAs are usually formed by a coalition of local business unions and government, along with community-based organizations. They facilitate nonprofit distribution that may or may not set up profit-making subsidiaries.

The primary functions of LEAs are to:

- provide extensive advice and services for small business entrepreneurs through a permanent organization
- provide complementary services that assist new businesses to get started by securing finance and technical assistance
- build confidence in the total community by forming new networks of professionals and grassroots groups
- improve local marketing capacity of new firms or existing firms

Employee/Worker Ownership

Employee/worker ownerships are a recent phenomenon. They are a potential response to pending firm closures. Workers and community groups become interested in assessing whether the companies can succeed if they are taken over by the workers. Not all company closures are due to failing business. Sometimes a company can be part of a larger portfolio of a diversified corporation that has realigned its strategic focus and the company does not fit with the new perspective. There are several legal structures that may be explored in this type of project. The two better-known examples are employee stock ownership and worker cooperatives.

Employee Stock Ownership Plans

Employee stock ownership plans (ESOPs) allow a company to establish a trust in order for it to be purchased. The trust acts as fiduciary agent for the firm's purchase using stock issued to the employees. Employees purchase shares through a combination of wage reductions, actual cash, and borrowing. Over the years of the plan, employees acquire vesting rights to their stock. All stock owned by an employee is resold to the company in the event that the employee leaves the firm or retires. The steps for forming an ESOP are as follows:

1. An employee corporation is formed.
2. The trust is formed and an ownership plan drafted.
3. ESOP borrows capital for equity contributions and operating capital.
4. Financial requirements are determined for the purchase of shares and to build equity accounts.
5. A debt service plan is organized.
6. The employee management structure is established.

State and federal laws govern the technical aspects of stock issues and trusts. These technicalities require close study by attorneys and other professionals because there are many potential pitfalls. Most ESOPs are likely to be in closely held rather than publicly held companies and provide an average of 10 to 40% of total company stock and limited voting rights, but the plans can be used to create majority employee-owned, democratically structured companies (Rosen, 1989, p. 258).

Worker Cooperatives

In worker cooperatives, the employees remain employees as such but are joint owners of the enterprise. Shares are issued to all of the employees, and these are reinvested for the firm's growth and development. Allocation of income at the end of the year is determined by weighted votes of employees, usually based on years of service. That is, an employee with 3 years of service has more votes than a new employee.

A worker cooperative differs from a conventional business, however, in that membership rights are personal rights, assigned to the people working in the company because they work there. In other words, the workers' voting and profit rights can never be bought. In a conventional business, by contrast, membership rights are transferable property rights attached to the shares of stock. The shares may be sold to any person who has the cash to buy them, and the person need not be connected with the business.

In worker cooperatives, the workers are the owners. The division of duties and responsibilities in such a system must be considered carefully. Not all employees may bring equal skills or talents to the firm. As a result, serious ruptures may occur in the democratic management process. Some members of the worker cooperative may not end up with a meaningful say in how firm development is carried out in their name. For this reason, staff development requires continual consideration.

LEED-ND

LEED for Neighborhood Development is a program created by the U.S. Green Building Council (USGBC). It extends the focus on creating green buildings that was the original motivation for the council's establishment. USGBC created the LEED (Leadership in Energy and Environmental Design) system to foster a more sustainable built environment by providing "building owners and operators with a framework for identifying and implementing practical and measurable green building design, construction, operations and maintenance solutions" (U.S. Green Building Council [USGBC], 2012). USGBC developed a rating system that measures how a building's location, construction, and operating systems can lower costs, reduce waste going to landfills, reduce greenhouse gas emissions, conserve energy and water, and increase the health and safety of its occupants. Buildings receive ratings ranging from Silver to Platinum based on the extent to which they achieve the criterion. The LEED system has different metrics for new construction versus existing building retrofitting.

Prior to the creation of LEED for Neighborhood Development (LEED-ND), the LEED system influenced developers to build or redevelop in a more sustainable way that benefited the building owners (in reduced operation costs and other financial impacts) and the building's occupants. LEED-rated buildings could appear in community neighborhoods needing new development, but their relationship to the neighborhood was not a consideration. Their presence could add to gentrification, the jobs–housing imbalance, or traffic and carbon emissions. The LEED-ND system creates higher expectations for the impacts of buildings and multiple building projects, specifically for their impacts on the surrounding community. It encourages building projects that protect and enhance health, the environment, and quality of life. The rating system defines the criteria for which points are given for projects that protect and enhance the overall health, natural environment, and quality of life in a community. It promotes the location and design of neighborhoods that reduce vehicle miles traveled (VMT) and create jobs and services that are accessible by foot or public transit.

In its rating system, LEED-ND specifies points for projects that create mixed-income communities. It specifically states its goal is "To promote socially equitable and engaging communities by enabling residents from a wide range of economic levels, household sizes, and age groups to live in a community"

(USGBC, 2012). While the way in which it seeks to create mixed-income communities is limited to requiring the building of housing for different income levels, this provision has the potential to make a significant contribution to community economic development through the provision of affordable housing in combination with its goal to reduce jobs–housing imbalances. LEED-ND is a notable effort that seeks to transform private development and was conceived by a private–public partnership of multiple organizations.

Figure 11.1   LEED for Neighborhood Development

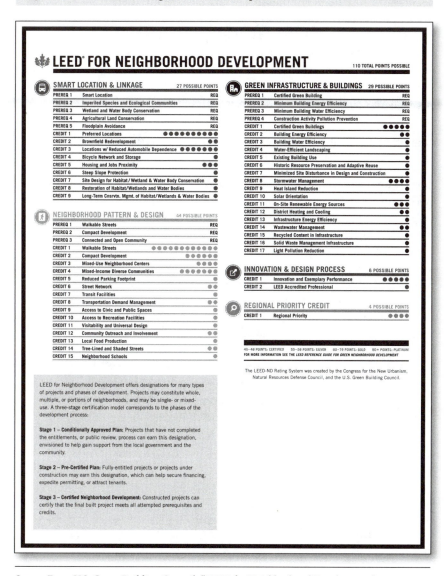

Source: From U.S. Green Building Council, "LEED for Neighborhood Development".

Targeting and Marketing Neighborhood/ Community Assets

Marketing a community is very much like marketing a product. Product and market research are employed to determine what type of assets a community has to offer, in what markets, and to what type(s) of clients. For maximum effectiveness, the community should be marketed only after determining the likely buyers of its resources—for example, tourism, where purchasers may be domestic or foreign. A community should develop knowledge of its marketing audience: What do they read? What appeals to them? How can they be reached? These questions are even more appropriate in industrial or commercial economic development. The market depends on who the community is trying to reach. This is true for individual projects, attraction efforts, and financial assistance for local projects. The fundamentals of target marketing are relatively straightforward. These are listed below.

Identification of the Community's Long-Term Goals

The level of long-term growth must be gauged with respect to overall population and/or jobs that a community is targeting. For example, to produce a job growth of 3% per year, an international audience may be the most likely target audience. Smaller, growing firms, however, may be more appropriate for a community that prefers more limited or controlled development.

A balance among different segments of industrial, commercial, and community-based activities may be desired as well. This balance determines what types of marketing efforts are undertaken and how vigorously they are pursued. In addition, knowledge of the existing infrastructure will influence the development alternatives examined. In fact, it may be impossible to select certain targets without a long-range infrastructure plan.

One of the best examples of how a community has organized and projected its resource base is the emergence of Emeryville, California, as the nation's premiere biotechnology center. Emeryville, with a population of fewer than 10,000, accomplished this by concentrating its infrastructure development on the requirements of the new biotech industries.

Marketing of the Community

Any marketing of the community must depict it as it is and the genuine opportunities it presents. Glossy brochures and rhetoric will not help market a community. Major manufacturing firms have their own in-house research staff, so they are not deceived by false advertising. Dissemination of misleading information will seriously damage an area's reputation.

The type of communication selected must appeal to the community's potential clients. If the prospective clients are Japanese businesses, information in one of the Japanese newspapers or magazines will reach this client base better than brochures written in English and hand-carried by the local mayor or community leader to the Japanese consulate.

Scientific or trade journals may be an even more important source for businesses than brochures or similar public relations efforts. If you want to get the attention of firms' managers, do it through the reading material of the senior executives. Whereas CEOs may read the *Wall Street Journal, The Economist,* or the *New York Times,* they seldom read brochures.

It is important to know the industry being recruited. Neighborhood or community leaders need to know some general details about the type of firm likely to visit the community. Many industrialists or would-be entrepreneurs have been discouraged by the seeming lack of interest in, or shallow responses of community leaders to, questions regarding the industry and its requirements.

Manufacturing firms are not the only focus of community and neighborhood marketing and recruiting efforts. Many communities feel that, to be competitive and perceived as offering a high quality of life, they need to offer strong services in the form of retail and health-care businesses. For example, communities that have been overlooked by some of the major retail chains have developed specific recruitment efforts aimed at them. They may also target the recruitment of medical and health-care professionals.

Incentives and Community Benefit Agreements

Incentives should be packaged to meet the needs of the firm or individual entrepreneur a community is trying to attract or encourage in the area. Financial incentives are seldom as important as a good business climate, strong retail potential, available research facilities, appropriate space at reasonable rates, adequate infrastructure, and a proactive local government with a flexible approach to incentives.

A community should list available assistance and resources as well as location information. Communities often publish promotional material with no information on who to contact for further details. As a result, they have missed sales simply because of poor communication. The entire community needs to be involved in promotion. (There are many stories about uncooperative staff giving a negative impression to visitors in casual conversations.)

At the same time, business being recruited to a community, or even just looking for a location to land, has come to see the offering of incentives as the norm rather than the exception. Many communities have found out the hard way that the incentives offered do not always warrant the benefits gained from the new business. The level of jobs promised may never materialize, or the jobs go to employees brought with the firm rather than to those in need in the community.

The burden on existing infrastructure—water, energy, and transportation—may degrade levels of service for the rest of the community. In recent years, the use of community benefit agreements has begun to proliferate. These are legally binding contracts negotiated by the community with the new business that can spell out who gets the jobs created, who pays for infrastructure, and other contributions the new business or development may make to improve the overall community.

The Community Prospectus: A Means of Communicating the Qualities of Your Community

Many communities invest in general promotional brochures. Although these may be helpful, they seldom attract a firm. Because targeted marketing requires establishing the specific feature identification required by an industry or certain type of firm, the best means of communicating to firms is through the community prospectus. This material acts much like a firm prospectus and allows the buyer to know what the community is offering and what opportunities are available.

The prospectus should describe the community assets and business opportunities in terms of industrial and market potentials, as well as community trends over the past few years and expected future trends in commercial and industrial opportunities. It should also relate any national economic or social trends that may affect a venture's potential in the community. Moreover, it should include a section on the community's research and development capacity, infrastructure plan, and financial assistance program.

The *research and development capacity* section is one of the most important components of any community prospectus. Access to higher education institutions, research laboratories, or facilities offering scientific knowledge and/or trained personnel is vital to almost all industries. It is important to describe the nature and extent of the scientific efforts in the area that relate to business, industrial, or agricultural products and services.

In addition, other private sector research or advanced facilities or equipment should be described as well as any major products, scientific breakthroughs, or well-known researchers resident in the area. Of course, very few communities have such resources within their boundaries, and most communities would benefit from projects that improve their research and development capacity in defined areas that complement their development strategies.

The *community infrastructure plan* section of the community prospectus should discuss the community physical infrastructure—location and buildings—along with specialized equipment and personnel (other than management) available to prospective businesses. It should describe what the community's industrial or retail/commercial space availability is in terms of specific venture requirements. For this to be effective, suitable building sites should already have been located and fully developed. If a site has been selected, describe it and how it meets the venture's needs, the businesses surrounding the site, whether the site and any buildings on it will be bought or leased, and the reasons behind these decisions.

The infrastructure discussion will cover slightly different topics, depending on whether the venture is manufacturing, retail, or service. Existing plans should be examined for the targeted businesses. Infrastructure descriptions for both retail and manufacturing should list the availability of water, power, and waste removal, as well as any environmental constraints and existing transportation systems. Telecommunications is an especially important infrastructure component and needs to be assessed carefully. Today, optic cable, international switching, and data-transmission facilities such as teleports are as important as water and sewerage capacity. Manufacturing discussions should also address the availability of industrial space at reasonable rates and whether facilities are available on a short- or long-term basis.

The description of human resource availability should include what kind of labor can be obtained locally for the type of venture sought. This section should also discuss the executive and managerial skills available in the area, as well as the general labor supply. If training is required, there needs to be a discussion on how it will occur and the associated costs.

The *financial program* section of the community prospectus is the last section because it is based on the information in the earlier sections. It should offer plans to improve the critical gaps in the community infrastructure as well as offer specific financial assistance for the desired type of firm. This section should, of course, make note of the financial programs available; these include initial financial assistance, venture capital, debt financing, and other specialized funding. Additional community funding or special arrangements for access to local capital should also be described.

Local Government's Role in Community Economic Development

Local governments can take an active role in stimulating and supporting community economic development by doing the following:

- developing revolving loan funds and similar financing as seed capital for community projects
- examining means to subcontract to community groups the delivery of community services or the operation of community facilities
- developing work spaces and facilities for community groups to commence enterprise activities
- identifying surplus or underutilized local government equipment that might be used by community groups
- establishing a network of people or service clubs that can provide technical assistance to community groups
- making community-based initiatives a component of the overall local economic development strategy
- helping communities negotiate community benefit agreements

Conclusion

As we stated at the start of this chapter, community economic development focuses on the neighborhood scale of socioeconomic transformation in a distressed locality. The need for effective community economic development has become even more acute due to the devastation the subprime mortgage crisis has wreaked on neighborhoods throughout America. Local economic developers are called upon to improve the capacity for these smaller geographic areas and their populations to withstand the buffeting of national and international economic trends as well as local restructuring.

Box 11.2   Example 11.1: Colorful Patchwork

One of the Tutwiler clinic's most successful efforts is the sale of brightly colored African-American quilts and quilted bags made by local women.

The project began in 1988—the brainchild of Sister Maureen Delaney, outreach director at the clinic. Sister Maureen is a community organizer from Oakland, California, who has been living in Tutwiler and working on outreach projects for five years.

Fifty local women are involved in the quilting effort, which allows them to earn money while contributing to the clinic. Prices range from $170 for a twin-sized quilt to $250 for a queen-sized model. Quilted bags—which have been sold at the Smithsonian Institution in Washington, D.C.—go for $20 each.

"The women get 70 percent of the price of the quilts," said Sister Maureen. "Nineteen percent goes toward buying material and eleven percent to supporting the outreach program."

"It lets me make a little money and I'm proud of that," said Lady B. Lloyd, who lost a leg to diabetes and pieces together quilt covers in her apartment across the street from the clinic. "I just love to do it. Most of the time I sit here all day by myself and I piece them together."

Williebelle Schegog, another Tutwiler resident, said she works on quilts from 9 a.m. to 3 p.m. every day except Saturday and Sunday. "Those are the Lord's days," she said.

"Quilting gives us something to do," added Alberta Mitchell, a member of the Tutwiler Improvement Association who also serves on the Community Education Center board.

Today, hundreds of mail orders are waiting to be filled, thanks to exposure the quilting program received on a CBS "60 Minutes" broadcast. There's a backlog of about nine months, according to Lucinda Berryhill, chairwoman of the Tallahatchie County School Board, and coordinator of literacy and quilting at the clinic.

The national television exposure also unleashed a flood of donations to the clinic's two Bargain Barn stores, which offer low-cost clothing and other useful items to area residents.

Source: Vanburen, M. P. 1993. "An Upbeat Note for the Mississippi Blues 'Hard Times Come Again No More.'" *International Journal of the W. K. Kellogg Foundation* 3(1). Reprinted with permission of the publisher, W. K. Kellogg Foundation.

Teaching Case 11.1

Workers as Owners

On a late autumn evening in northeast Franklin, a bookkeeper and a couple of stock clerks could be seen through the plate-glass windows of the ComUNITY Sporting Goods Store. For everyone else, work had ended. But for ComUNITY Sports' directors and stockholders, sitting on empty running shoe boxes and sports equipment crates, the day had only just begun. The president, Joe Offer, called the meeting to order, and soon the group was engrossed in a spirited debate on product mix. Some people advocated cutting the price of ski equipment early in order to stimulate sales in all of the city's ComUNITY Sports outlets. This had been a very successful tactic of the old management. Several people objected to this proposal simply because it was the old management's idea. "Who wants to be associated with a management that was forced into near bankruptcy on a nationwide sporting goods chain?" Another hot topic was corporate directors' liability. Both topics were being pursued in heated debate simultaneously as Joe Offer, the recently elected CEO and stores manager, called the meeting to order.

At this point, Jim Schader, then board secretary, spoke up. "Dun & Bradstreet's asking for details on our financial status," he said. "What's our policy on giving out this type of data to investment services?"

No policy existed, but there were plenty of opinions both on the point and at some distance from the actual task at hand. When no consensus was forthcoming, Offer finally expressed what turned out to be the majority view. "Our credit's good," he said, "and we will provide it because it will be good for us to cooperate early in order to get the best credit rating possible when we need it. We are directors and the only stockholders of the company."

And an unusual company it is. Until last year, the store in which this meeting was held and 10 others in the city of Franklin were combined with a chain of more than 200 discount sporting goods stores. The

(Continued)

(Continued)

company had prospered in the 1980s when discount consumerism was rampant, but the whole chain was in danger of collapsing by the time the employees made an offer to take over the entire West Coast division of the company and break it up into smaller city-based retail outlets separately managed by the workers at each store but under an umbrella corporate structure. Today, the ComUNITY Sports stores claim that weekly sales are 20% above those of other retail clothing and equipment chains; the Roslyn store sales are up 40%.

"It's *our* store," says Faith Mason, ski sales manager for all of the ComUNITY Sports stores. "We all feel that way about it. Owning the company gives us more incentive to make it a success. We're putting in about 80 hours a week—40 as workers, 40 as owners. And guess what? I actually *enjoy* coming to work. There will be more store systems like this one. It's a great program and too good an idea not to spread."

Yet support for employee ownership was not universal at the time it was proposed. In Franklin, for example, Cornell Young, a labor leader, encountered criticism when he first explored worker ownership a few years ago. "An executive at ComUNITY once told me it sounded like socialism to him," Young says, "but I said we just wanted to organize stores the way he and his friends had originally started back in the late '60s when they were radicals at Berkeley—everybody pays into a kitty, you elect some directors, you hire a manager. What's socialistic about that; that's exactly what they did before they joined the country club set."

Young has served for years as president of Local 357 of the United Retail Sales Union (URSU). The Local's membership peaked at about 9,000 in the mid-1970s, after which the depressed economy forced a string of sporting goods retail stores to close, which cost the union more than a quarter of its members. The crowning blow was when Pacific Tex, the conglomerate that spun off ComUNITY as part of its profit center in 1977, decided in 1981 and 1982 to shut down 14 of its West Coast area stores, idling nearly 400 URSU workers as well as members of a smaller textile union. The Pacific Tex had closed more than 150 stores in eight years—65% of its nationwide chain—and its losses in 1981 exceeded $30 million.

In many respects, it is a unique and unprecedented agreement. Workers obtain ownership of a segment of the company and the right to buy in the future as well as more authority and responsibility. It provides an avenue to learn management skills and provides a legal property claim; a right of first refusal to purchase stores from the company, so it cannot be bid up competitively and sold off to someone else. This arrangement creates an important source of worker-controlled capital—perhaps as much as $1.5 million a year at first, with more as time goes on—to finance incentives and investments in employee-owned enterprises.

Pacific Tex officials acknowledge that their main interest was and is in the stores they kept, not the ones they gave up. Without making judgments on the sales potential of the stores, they do characterize them as "experimental." According to one company official, the agreement reflects "a sharing of objectives with the union. U.S. business and communities have to find ways of working together and stop fighting with one another; that's the only way we can be internationally competitive."

Even while this experiment is underway, the directors of ComUNITY need to consider diversifying beyond sporting goods into men's and women's clothing lines imported from China. Since the union has gone on record as "Buy America," this is not an easy decision. But if a move is not made soon, the managers fear the ComUNITY experiment will disappear forever. This is a tough issue. The employer/owners feel that selling foreign goods will hurt local workers.

The board doesn't know how to raise this issue with the membership or the impact of failing to compete in a global marketing system.

The board has called you and your team as consultants and they want your advice on how to keep their experiment going.

Teaching Case 11.2

A Community Finds a Business

Lakes Alternative Energy Board (LAEB), a community development corporation, is composed of three community action agencies involved in alternative sources of energy. This partnership will simultaneously bring in revenue to the community, create jobs, and provide low-cost fuel to area residents.

LAEB serves the Lakes area, which is known for its high unemployment rate and high percentages of elderly residents and families with incomes below the poverty line. The area has been hit severely by the collapse of the two traditional sources of employment and revenue: the iron mines and the lumber industry. Fuel is also a primary concern in the region, with its 120-inch annual snowfall and temperatures below freezing for two months of the year. Fuel costs are high—many of the Lakes' elderly clients spend about half their income on fuel.

The first venture is the use of wood pellets as a fuel source, which will eventually lead to the building of a wood pellet-processing plant in one of the nine counties served by the four agencies. This mutually beneficial venture illustrates how community action agencies can turn their

(Continued)

(Continued)

nonmonetary assets into an effective base for the creation of community economic development projects.

Another project was to have been the construction of live-in demonstration models of energy-efficient houses: retrofitting existing housing, developing wood-based insulation materials, and producing low-cost stoves. At the time, though, the energy crunch was not a hot topic and the proposal was turned down.

LAEB has been incorporated by the three CAAs (community action agencies). It is investigating new, alternative energy sources with economic development potential.

The goals of LAEB included analyzing the use of wood refuse and small streams on farm property as an alternative fuel source, especially for low-income people; promoting the use of alternative fuel sources; and creating—and keeping—jobs in the wood industry through the private sector. The intent is to develop a low-cost fuel that can be used by both commercial and residential energy systems.

LAEB has stressed to Lakes residents that it is not in competition with the private sector; rather, it sees its function as a catalyst for local economic development. LAEB staff members define their role as helping private entrepreneurs get established in the alternative energy market. Possible spin-off ventures include maintaining storage facilities for bulk quantities of pellets, manufacturing the special stoves needed to burn the pellets, and running local dealerships to sell and service the stoves. LAEB also wants to establish a market for wood refuse that would generate income for loggers, truckers, and the struggling wood-processing plants in the area.

LAEB is attempting to involve all sectors of the community in its efforts. Representatives from the three community action agencies sit on the board, along with representatives from the lumber industry, local universities, the U.S. Forest Service, and cooperative extension services in each county, as well as low-income people from the area. There are also a number of technical advisory groups and committees set up to bring in authorities on various aspects of the lumber industry.

Once LAEB established its board and narrowed its focus to the development of wood pellets, it turned its attention to finding a private partner with the necessary experience to establish a pellet plant. Asperal, Inc., a wood pellet manufacturer in Minnesota, approached LAEB when it heard that the board had capital to lend to a private partner in exchange for establishing a pellet plant.

LAEB evaluated the quality of Asperal's pellets and its collateral and then negotiated a loan agreement with the company. In exchange for a low-interest loan, Asperal will work to establish a market for wood pellets in the Upper Peninsula. If successful, Asperal will begin building a pellet plant in one of the nine counties covered by LAEB.

Capitalizing on their status as nonprofit entities and their access to federal funds, the three community action agencies in LAEB used a government grant to cement a public–private partnership with Asperal. As the private partner, Asperal, Inc., benefits from the agencies' contacts in and knowledge of various sectors of their communities in gaining the support and cooperation of area residents. LAEB gains the business experience and technical knowledge of the private firm that will help ensure the venture's success.

The question before LAEB is what its next venture should be. The current energy crisis is over, and pellet sales will lag soon. How can all the energy and expertise be directed to creating jobs in the future?

Teaching Case 11.3

New Freedom House

New Freedom House was founded to set up a Native American jewelry distribution center on the Napahmoe Reservation in Taos, New Mexico. It markets products for four American Indian cooperatives—three that produce leathercrafts and one that makes garments. The cooperatives were the first ones established by the National Center for Native American Enterprise (NCNAE).

The initial distribution business via national sales catalog did well. People responded favorably to the products (design and quality), and the Christmas season brought substantial sales. After the holidays, however, sales slowed considerably. Freedom House responded by entering the walk-in retail business in Santa Fe, while continuing as a mail-order operation. The business also bought raw materials for all the worker cooperatives, many of which had been buying their supplies at excessive prices or were simply unable to purchase supplies in their local areas.

It was then, too, that NCNAE decided to turn over ownership of New Freedom House to the reservation tribes who supplied it with its merchandise and those who worked in the various cooperatives. The resulting cooperative would market goods for individual craft coops, buy their supplies, and have as members all those who worked in established cooperatives.

New Freedom House Cooperative (NFHC) is a two-tiered organization. The first consists of the "unit members," or unincorporated associations of

(Continued)

(Continued)

individuals organized on a cooperative basis who are engaged in the production and sale of handcrafted products. There are 13 unit members, all situated in Colorado and New Mexico, including, in addition to jewelry, several leather coops, a clothing coop, and a candle coop. Each unit member is entitled to elect one representative (usually its president) to NFHC's board of directors. The board elects officers, who in turn employ professional managers and a staff to operate the main office and warehouse.

Each unit member (workshop) is a separate entity, but all are organized on identical lines and their individual members sign identical Articles of Association. Any person may become a member of an association at any time by subscribing to its articles and paying dues. The members elect officers who function as a management committee. The number of partners ranges from 6 to approximately 25.

The By-Laws and Marketing Agreement signed by each unit member are the two basic governing instruments describing the various responsibilities of the members and the directors and officers.

Each worker's coop (unit member) is responsible for the production of particular items in the product line described in the Freedom House catalog. These products include suede handbags, leather belts, cufflinks, costume jewelry, dolls, stuffed animals and toys, children's clothing, canvas bags, candles, greeting cards, and numerous other items. Each workshop, moreover, is responsible for maintaining its own records of its total production and that of individual members. Every two weeks, an employee from the main office of New Freedom House collects the finished products and delivers raw materials and equipment that unit members have ordered.

Partial payment in the form of an advance is made for the products on the basis of a cost price that includes labor costs, costs of material, and overhead items for each unit member. The advance is distributed to workers on the basis of their weekly production.

After being collected from individual workshops, products are taken to the New Freedom House warehouse, where each item is tagged and inventoried by quality-control personnel. Any item not conforming to established standards is tagged for return to the particular workshop. After clearing quality control, all of the products in a particular category are pooled and placed in storage bins or on racks for distribution through retail outlets or mail-order sales on a national level. Proceeds from mail-order sales account for most Freedom House income. Mail-order catalogs are distributed to an extensive mailing list throughout the United States, Canada, and England. This list is constantly augmented by trading with other organizations and by leasing lists from direct mail brokerage services.

NCNAE has organized several urban-based organizations, including six retail outlets plus Graphic Arts Southwest, Southwest Media, and Flute

Publications. The latter are affiliated as craft workshops—that is, the publications and media workers are members of the NCNAE. Although their activities are conducted in an urban setting, their activities are directly related to the needs of the rural members.

New Freedom House has faced the future squarely, and the prospects are not good. The organization is large and too decentralized to compete with the better-capitalized mail-order firms tied in with the credit card companies. But New Freedom House has both a mission and a message. The board is now struggling with a proposal from a large New York mail-order firm to take over management and distribution of its products. Board President Chief Joseph reminds his fellow board members that neither the Anglos nor any other minorities were there when they needed them in the early days. Young Susan Windfall, another board member, says the chief's ideas are tired and racist. She believes it is time for Native Americans to show the way—and make big profits. Who is right? How would you go about setting up an agreement with an external retailer to work with the Native American community? Or would you reject the idea altogether and redesign the firm? If the latter decision were made, what would you do?

Community-based economic development and employment initiatives are important elements in a wider local economic development strategy. In general, these initiatives have strong social objectives underpinning economic ones. They are as much rooted in and motivated by needs (of groups, individuals, and localities) as they are in finding and exploiting economic opportunities. They offer a structure and resources to encourage economic activity at the neighborhood level. They provide access to job opportunities for local people who find entering the economic system difficult. (See Table 11.2 for a sampling of community-based employment development projects.)

Table 11.2   Community-Based Employment Development Project Idea Starters

Tool	Project Idea Starter
Employee/ ownership cooperatives	*Skilled trades cooperative:* A cooperative is formed of skilled people of various trades who offer advice on technical matters to local firms and provide a sales and repair service for all kinds of specialized equipment and machinery.
	Worker acquisition of existing firm: Industry workers agree to put up money of their own—and

(Continued)

(Continued)

Tool	Project Idea Starter
	accept a "readjustment in their pay"—in a bid to save their jobs and buy a sizable share in their former employer's business through the formation of a new company owned jointly by workers and perhaps a state equity bank (e.g., metalworkers with the blessing of a union and the support of a new equity bank). *Cooperative government projects bidding service:* People with expertise in various aspects of fabrication come together as a cooperative to bid collectively for contracts (government and other) that they do not have the capacity to bid for as individuals.
Community-based employment	*A home-energy auditing and retrofitting scheme:* The aim is to provide an energy auditing and efficiency test service to homeowners and prospective buyers to estimate energy costs and to provide quotes on retrofitting to reduce costs. The project also might supply a team of people capable of carrying out retrofitting activities.
Community-based service and employment development	*Recycling of waste as art and craft materials:* This project is to collect and redistribute industrial and other waste as art and craft materials from a shop/center that may be used by anyone in the community who pays a yearly subscription or a set fee per garbage-bagful. Also, lessons might be provided in making art and crafts with recycled materials.

The track record of community-based economic and employment development organizations has not always been good. Some of the reasons for this have been an imbalance in the mix of social and economic objectives, inadequate financing, and lack of skills and planning. Another major problem relates to the fundamental issue of ownership and control. In theory, community-based organizations for economic development and employment generation are democratically owned and controlled. In practice, however, problems have occurred when these organizations commence projects on a business basis. Finally, as Michael Teitz (1989) warns, these problems are mentioned here not to undermine the concept but to state the limitations clearly.

References and Suggested Readings

Birch, David. 1979. *The Job Generation Process.* Cambridge: MIT, Program on Neighborhood and Regional Change.

Birch, Eugenie L. 2005. *Who Lives Downtown?* Washington, DC: Brookings Institution.

Bradford, Calvin et al. n.d. *Structural Disinvestment: A Problem in Search of a Policy.* Unpublished mimeo. Evanston, IL: Northwestern University for Urban Affairs.

Carlson, David, and Arabella Martinez. 1988. *The Economics of Community Change.* Study funded by the Ford and Hewlett Foundations. Washington, DC: Center for Policy Development.

Center for Community Economic Development (CCED). 2008. *How Much is Enough in Your County? The 2008 California Family Economic Self-Sufficiency Standard.* Accessed June 2, 2008 from http://www.insightcced.org/index.php?page=cfess

Cummings, Scott, and Mark Glaser. 1983. An Examination of the Perceived Effectiveness of Community Development Corporations: A Pilot Study. *Journal of Urban Affairs* 5(4): 315–340.

Daniels, Belden, N. Barbe, and B. Siegel. 1981. Experience and Potentials for Community-Based Development. In *Expanding the Opportunity to Produce.* Washington, DC: Corporation for Enterprise Development.

Daniels, Belden, and Chris Tilly. 1981. Community Economic Development: Seven Guiding Principles. In *Resources.* Washington, DC: Congress for Community Economic Development.

Ferguson, Ronald F., and William T. Dickens, eds. 1999. *Urban Problems and Community Development,* Washington, DC: Brookings Institution.

Fuster, Stephen Collins. 1993. Colorful Patchwork. *WKKF International Journal* 3(1): n.p.

The Greenhouse Venture. 1989. *Economic Development and Law Report* 18(1): n.p.

Gurwitt, Rob. 1992. Neighborhoods and the Urban Crisis. *Governing* 5(13): 20.

Haberfeld, Steven. 1981. Economic Planning in Economically Distressed Communities: The Need to Take a Partisan Perspective. *Economic Development and Law Center Report,* December.

Hein, B. 1987. *Strategic Planning for Community Economic Development.* Ames: Iowa State University Extension.

Johnson, T., and M. Reingold. 2000. *Caution Signs for Community Development: Eastside Community Investment Inc. (ECI) of Indianapolis, Indiana.* Paper presented at the American Public Policy Analysis and Management Conference, Seattle, WA, April.

Kotler, Milton. 1971. The Politics of Community Economic Development. *Law and Contemporary Society* 36(1): 3–12.

National Cooperative Month Planning Committee. 2005. *Cooperative Businesses in the United States: A 2005 Snapshot.* Accessed April 10, 2008 from http://www.uwcc.wisc.edu

Parzen, Julia, and Michael Kieschnick. 1992. *Credit Where It's Due.* Philadelphia: Temple University Press.

Peirce, Neal, and Carol Steinbach. 1990. *Enterprising Communities.* Washington, DC: Council for Community-Based Development.

Rosen, Corey. 1989. Employee Ownership: Promises, Performance and Prospects. *Economic Development Quarterly* 3(3): 258–265.

Simon, William H. 2001. *The Community Economic Development Movement.* Durham, NC: Duke University Press.

Snipp, Matthew C. 1988. *Public Policy Impacts on American Indian Economic Development.* Albuquerque: University of New Mexico, Native American Studies Institute.

Squires, Gregory, ed. 1992. *From Redlining to Reinvestment.* Philadelphia: Temple University Press.

Teitz, Michael. 1989. Neighborhood Economics: Local Communities and Regional Markets. *Economic Development Quarterly* 3(2): 111–122.

U.S. EPA. n.d. Brownfields Area-Wide Pilot Planning Program. Accessed May 18, 2012, at http://www.epa.gov/brownfields/areawide_grants.htm.

U.S. Green Building Council (USGBC). 2012. What LEED Is. Accessed September 5, 2012, http://www.usgbc.org/DisplayPage.aspx?CMSPageID=1988.

Vidal, Avis. 1992. *Rebuilding Communities: A National Study of Urban Community Development Corporations.* New York: New School for Social Research, Graduate School of Management and Urban Policy.

——. 1995. Reintegrating Disadvantaged Communities Into the Fabric of Urban Life: The Role of Community Development. *Housing Policy Debate* 6(1): 169–250.

Yin, Robert, and Douglas Yates. 1975. *Street Level Governments.* Lexington, MA: Lexington.

12

Building the
Implementation Plan

The successful implementation of any economic development plan is dependent upon three key elements: Choosing the appropriate strategy, having the correct organizational structure, and garnering the necessary resources. The first element, choosing appropriate strategies, was the focus of Chapter 7 of this book. This chapter was followed by an exploration of common foci of economic development strategies: Locality Development (Chapter 8), Business Development (Chapter 9), and Human Resource Development (Chapter 10). In Chapter 12, we focus upon creating the necessary organization structure and identifying and deploying the necessary resources for successful plan implementation. With few, if any, exceptions, the necessary organization structure will be made up of private and public partners. Consistently critical resources for economic development plan implementation are financing and marketing.

The initiation of economic development planning is fundamentally an effort to influence the market economy. Further, the impetus for this effort is always because there are acknowledged deficiencies in the outcomes that the market economy has generated for a community overall and/or for certain segments of that community. While the public sector is always involved—directly or indirectly—in economic development plan implementation, the point of any such plan is to strengthen the private sector and the benefits this will generate for all of the community. Thus, local economic development plan implementation is invariably a mixture of public and private actions. For example, public provision of roads or mass transit and strong K–12 education systems are indirect but critical enablers for economic development. In response to market failures, the public sector needs to directly stimulate private capital formation and firm creation or location. In the next section, we discuss the use of public–private partnerships for implementing economic development plans or projects.

Public–Private Partnerships

Figure 12.1 is a stylized representation of public–private organizational relationships for plan or project implementation. The left side of the figure characterizes the public side of partnerships. It begins with a unit of local government (county or city level depending on the size of the area) responsible for economic development planning. The exact title of this unit varies across localities. Sometimes this entity is combined with a community development or other government department. Typically, the public economic development unit oversees planning, financing, and business and workforce development needs for strategic plans and specific projects. Some examples of public-sector activities it must engage in to realize plans and projects are creating land use and zoning supportive of economic development goals, identifying specific areas within the community that warrant designation as tax-increment finance districts or other types of economic zones because of their economic decline or underdevelopment, and providing an efficient permitting process for specific projects.

In one major city, Long Beach, California, the primary responsibility for economic development plan implementation falls to the Department of Community Development (CD) through the Economic Development Bureau (EDB), along with the Workforce Development Bureau and the Redevelopment Agency (RDA). But the City recognizes the success of its economic development planning requires an integrated and coordinated effort that leverages resources of other city departments as well as external partners. The key City departments include Planning & Building, Financial Management, Public Works, and our public safety departments, Fire and Police (City of Long Beach, 2007).

The right side of Figure 12.1 characterizes the private side of partnerships. Private partners can be in the for-profit or nonprofit sector. Included among for-profit–sector partners are trade and industry associations (e.g., chambers of commerce, a specific manufacturing association), banks, utilities, developers, and major locally headquartered companies. Nonprofit partners can include community development corporations, medical and educational institutions, and foundations, among others. When the focus is a specific project, private for-profit partners are looking for the best market opportunities, the highest and best use of land under consideration for development, and greatest profit-making opportunities.[i] Nonprofit partners typically are seeking to compensate for market failures and to address conditions in declining areas by taking on projects that are not in the best locations and for which high returns are not expected.

---

[i]"Highest and best use" of a piece of property generally means a use that is legal, reasonable, physically and financially feasible, and provides the greatest return.

Figure 12.1 Organizational Relationships for Project or Plan Implementation

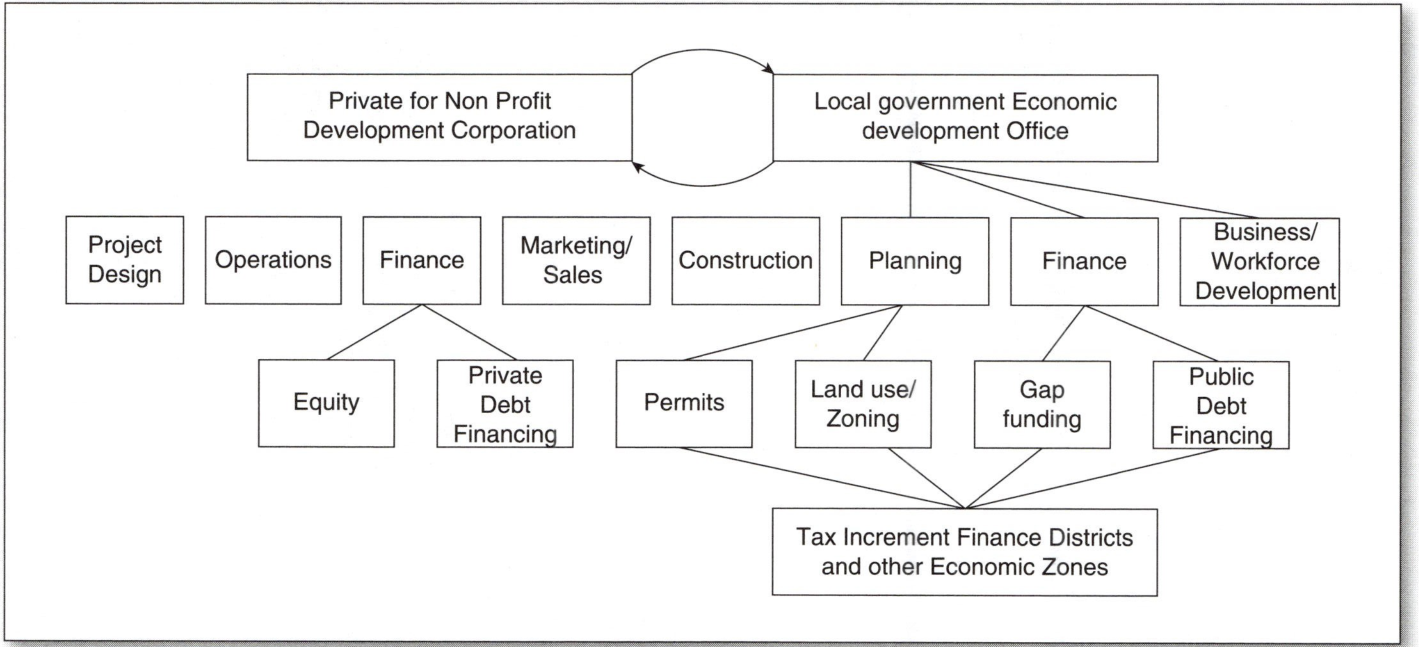

Project Design

Operations

Finance

Equity

Private Debt Financing

Marketing/Sales

Private for Non Profit Development Corporation

Construction

Permits

Planning

Land use/Zoning

Local government Economic development Office

Finance

Gap funding

Business/Workforce Development

Public Debt Financing

Tax Increment Finance Districts and other Economic Zones

Source: Adapted by Nancey Green Leigh from Figure 3.3 in Giles (2011).

Public–private partnerships can be complex and require considerable effort to create and sustain. The basic premise behind public–private partnerships is that of cooperation for implementing a plan of benefit to the larger community or of risk sharing for developing a specific project. A public–private partnership example of a project is one that uses the assets of the public sector—for example, a building, air rights, a change in zoning, low-interest loans—combined with tax benefits for private enterprise, ranging from credits for hiring local workers to tax relief such as land or sales tax deductions.

For specific projects, the private sector provides the design and development capacity along with cash or equity for financing. An example of a project is a parking structure used by the public for a fee combined with a movie theater that might be incorporated into the base of the same building operated by a private firm. The profit or income is split between the public and private parties in a variety of ways.

When public–private partnerships are focused on implementing a broader plan rather than a specific project, partners from both sides are often called upon to help market the community or a plan or both.

Marketing Community

Traditionally, communities do marketing for economic development to highlight their attractiveness to new employers and investors. However, there is increasing recognition that communities need to retain businesses and residents that have contributed to the economy. Thus, marketing is also necessary to ensure that a successful business seeking to expand will do so in the community, and a resident who is retiring considers the quality of life of the community attractive enough to retire in place.

While much of community marketing activity has focused on tourism and visitor services, community marketing is becoming increasingly sophisticated in seeking to position local assets in the global economy. Community marketing in today's environment is based on an inventory of local resources (human, cultural, natural, and built), opportunities, and options. Combined, these create a profile that helps the community determine the kinds of firms and institutions that "fit" best with its multidimensional resource base. Based on the profile, the community creates marketing messages for local and external consumption.

Communities have to develop a clear identity for their marketing to be successful. This identity needs to be authentic and capable of contributing to the base of the local economy. Over time, this identity may change in order to address long-term economic challenges the city has not been able to overcome, as well as to take advantage of emerging opportunities in the economy. For example, it was noted in the City of Long Beach's recent Economic Development Implementation Plan that "Long Beach has shed its skin numerous times. It has been a resort town, an oil town, a Navy town, an aerospace town" (p. 2). Long Beach's stated goal was to become a more diversified city, less susceptible to large economic shifts (City of Long Beach, 2007).

Components of Good Community Marketing Analysis and Designing a Marketing Plan

While each community has to develop interesting ways to present its assets, this presentation has to be based on real data for and indicators of the economic area that it represents. Typically, the local economy is part of a regional economic system or even a mega-region like Los Angeles, London, New York, or Shanghai, which requires setting the local economy (be it neighborhood, town, or city) within the larger regional context, even when local smaller-scale development is the goal. Below is a list of analysis steps that should be taken into consideration.

- *Market Area Context.* Determine what role the community has within the larger region and what resource(s) it contributes.
- *Local Market Capacity.* Determine the size of the local market area and its components with respect to demographic profile, met and unmet consumer demands, and product and service provision.
- *Resource Assessment.* Conduct a meaningful assessment of the strength, weaknesses, and resource potential of the focus area or local economy.
- *Market Scope and Penetration.* Determine the degree to which the local economy offers the ability to meet some market demands using its locational and related assets.
- *Niche Competitive Advantage.* Because globalization has reduced the comparative advantages of location and even fixed natural-resource assets, determine whether a combination of special attributes—cultural, social, educational, environmental, or equity performance that enhances community quality and stability—has the potential to create a marketing advantage for the local economy.
- *Cost Factors.* Determine what the key cost considerations are for firms or projects expressing interest in the local area or for which the community wants to compete.
- *Sustainability.* Determine what hard and soft infrastructure support the community can supply to firms that are part of the green economy.

Community (City or Neighborhood) Marketing Plan

No matter whether it is a firm, organization, city, or neighborhood, if there is an intention to compete, then there is a need to market and present. Many people confuse marketing with sales. Sales are the best indicator of good marketing. But marketing is the envelope that helps introduce the place or product. Good marketing presents the place or product in such a way that the consumer recalls it for the intrinsic reasons of quality and reliability. In too many cases, however, places substitute slogans for genuine market assessment and presentation. A good motto confirms the quality or other aspects of the product or place, but it is not a substitute for providing the services of goods. In this respect, communities have to present what they have and not what they would like to have. So it is not convincing to present a nice poster with an ocean background and attractive man or woman in swimwear for a desert community. However, many communities make the equivalent of such poor choices. They present what they think the consumer or the local leaders want the place to be rather than what it really is. Places like Washington, DC, can market themselves as "capital cities," but a small county seat would be foolish to use the same kind of presentation. Therefore, a city or community has to portray what is has and how it wants to position its attributes as the enabling factors for competing to serve, attract, or grow firms.

A basic checklist of requirements for designing a place-oriented marketing effort includes:

- *Identity*. Community has assessed its assets and come to a conclusion regarding the keys for its place identity—good transportation, strong universities, quality neighborhoods, specific firms, natural features or resources, and so forth.
- *Consolidated Presentation*. The most successful communities have a consortium of partner organizations that present the community through a coordinated, strategic message. These can include:

  o Site-selection consultants
  o Existing industry
  o Community stakeholders and leadership
  o State government
  o Legislative delegation
  o Greater-region development organizations
  o County commissioners
  o City council
  o Real estate community
  o Electric utility providers
  o Economic development organizations
  o Marketing mission and trade show contacts

- *Communications Infrastructure*. Communities have a layered communications infrastructure that includes person-to-person, print, and various forms of electronic media. Competitive communities have well-designed Web presences that prospective firms or residents can explore. These include all pertinent information about the community and use geographic information systems (GIS) as well as video to describe the community. Competitive communities

also explore additional ways to reach intended audiences such as holding conferences, seeking to place articles about the community in national and international media, and getting the city used as a set or backdrop for movies and
television.

Box 12.1 lists the marketing actions the county of Lancaster, South
Carolina, recently identified for its economic development plan implementation. Lancaster is relatively rural but in the sphere of influence of
Charlotte, North Carolina, and desires to create stronger economic development for itself.

Box 12.1   Marketing Tools for Communicating a Community's Assets to the Marketplace

- After identifying target sectors, develop specific marketing materials for the sectors.
- Develop a business/industrial park brochure profiling all business park locations.
- Produce a transportation network flyer or promotional piece for all target sectors that includes pictures, maps, and quotes from existing companies.
- Develop existing industry testimonials.
- Develop an incentive (state and local) overview for business retention and new firm recruitment.
- Develop a list of all local "certified" rail-served sites .
- Create a community profile providing a general overview and utilizing regional demographics facts such as:

  - Education
  - Labor force
  - Utilities
  - Quality of life
  - Cost of living

  - Transportation
  - Incentives
  - Sites/buildings
  - Major employers
  - Target industries/sectors

- Develop a professionally bound package of information materials.
- Develop a retiree recruitment marketing piece.
- Create an economic development website that provides information on available incentives, community demographics, and available buildings and sites.

Source: Adapted from Lancaster County, South Carolina. (2009). *Economic
Development Implementation Plan.* Accessed September 14, 2012, at http://
www.lancasterscworks.com/pdf/Strategic_Plan.pdf

Marketing can help to attract new business and residents to a community or retain residents and expand existing businesses. In many cases, however, communities find that it is necessary to help businesses and development projects obtain the financing they need to expand or locate to the community. This is most applicable when there is a market failure for the community or when the community is seeking to shift its economy to targeted growth sectors. The next sections present basic concepts of project financing that a serious student of economic development planning will explore further in classes on economic development finance.

Project Financing

Prior to securing the financing for an economic development project, the project idea must be determined to be viable within the environment it is designed to improve. Next, the project must be shaped to pass the viability test by building action plans specifying in some detail the project, outputs, resources, and support system requirements. For smaller, simpler, shorter-term projects, an action plan may itself be adequate to gain formal commitment for the project idea and thus claim materials, finance, and personnel to implement it.

As projects become larger, more complex, and longer term, however, action plans for the project design need to be fully detailed to claim resources. Detailed project plans are also required whenever a local government is considering acting on its own, or if projects are submitted that invite local government endorsement.

The preparation of a detailed project plan has four traditional basic tasks (items 1, 3, 4, and 5 below) to which we add a fifth (item 3). They are:

1. viability assessment
2. sustainability assessment
3. detailed feasibility studies
4. final design and business plan preparation
5. design of a monitoring and evaluation program

The main difference between the detailed project plan and the formerly described action plan is the degree of detail required. We will concentrate in this chapter on general standards for detailed project plans that can be adapted to any requirement.

Assessing Project Viability

Project development is the redefinition and determination of the potential of specific project ideas. During this stage, the decision must be made on whether to complete the planning phase and implement the project. In general, project development involves taking one or more attractive project ideas, shaping and specifying each precisely, and rejecting those that do not seem viable. To justify the project, the criterion of potential for economic development and employment has to be satisfied, at least preliminarily. In project development, viability is determined in relation to four interconnected bases: community, locational, commercial, and implementation (Malizia, 1985).

Community Viability

Because economic development is a community issue, the formulation and selection of local economic development projects constitute a community-wide political act. First, the local economic development process describes the necessary support base required to make a project viable. Then it decides whether the project has sufficient community support.

Caution is suggested when deciding whether a project has community viability. Many individuals and organizations may initially give casual support to project ideas but then withdraw their support when the project is likely to become a reality. To overcome this potential problem, local economic development planners should seek explicit oral commitments from other key actors. These informal commitments are required because to proceed on any other basis is far too cumbersome. Formal commitments are sought only after the project is found to be viable, an action plan assembled, and important actors and their roles identified.

Locational Viability

For the locational/market viability analysis, the resources required by the project need to be identified and their availability determined. How the proposal harmonizes with other existing or proposed projects needs to be considered.

Next, planners should identify potential customers for the product or service provided by the project and answer the following questions: Who are they? Where are they located? Why would they buy this product? How frequently? Planners then need to step back and consider market size and trends. They should determine whether the product is in a growth industry, whether the market area is growing, and what the expected size of the market is when operations begin. The next step is analyzing the competition. What are the strengths and weaknesses of the product relative to the competition? What is the market capture strategy—that is, what will be done to gain customers?

The answers to the above questions will provide two valuable pieces of information: (1) whether to proceed any further with the project, and (2) what should be addressed in a formal market study and marketing plan by consultants at a later stage of the economic development process. If the project appears to pass the test of locational/market viability, its economic/financial and operational viability then need to be considered.

Commercial Viability

Based on the answers to the questions asked in the market viability analysis, the community or other sponsor must estimate the revenue-raising potential of the project and judge the likelihood of the project recovering its costs. Knowing the level of risk to capital is a precondition to determining whether investors will be readily available and whether the project will have reinvestment opportunities. The economic viability studies should consider each of these aspects. They constitute the initial pieces of a project cost plan to be made in the next step of the local economic development process.

Implementation Viability

Implementation viability is determined by considering who in the community has the skills and capacity to undertake the task. There is no real point in embarking on projects if the skills to organize or manage the project are not present. In addition, the community has to consider how the services and goods are produced and the means of production, as well as whether the five Ms (materials, (hu)man power, markets, management, and money) can be satisfied in developing and operating the project. On completion of this task, the financial feasibility must be determined before the project is undertaken.

Sustainability Analysis

Sustainability analysis of projects and firms is an evolving field. It can broadly be construed to focus on social and environmental issues. With respect to social issues, a community that is providing financial and other support to a private development or firm will want to know how workers will be treated: for example, will they receive fair compensation packages? Will safety standards and rights be adhered to? With respect to environmental issues, will the development or firm seek to minimize its carbon footprint and the waste it generates? Will it follow green building standards? And will the managers of a development or firm also expect its suppliers to adhere to sustainable social and environmental practices?

Detailed Feasibility Analysis

The purpose of the detailed feasibility analysis is to identify the critical issues affecting each project's potential for success, to specify what conditions or requirements are necessary, and to evaluate the possibility of achieving these requirements. The information previously gathered for the project-viability analysis and the action plan forms the basis of the full-scale feasibility study. This study investigates in more depth any weaknesses identified in the earlier steps and does a more thorough analysis of each feasibility factor—especially the financial aspects. The research should result in an internal working document, which, in turn, forms the basis of the business plan. The business plan is a more formal document, designed for distribution outside the project planning committee. It incorporates much of the information in the feasibility study and also discusses how the conditions for success will be achieved *vis-à-vis* the operation of the business.

There is no standard format for a feasibility study, but there are a minimum of three special studies that should be undertaken:

1. market analysis

2. financial analysis

3. cost-benefit assessment

These studies should be undertaken for project startups, business expansions and acquisitions, and community development projects. Research and evaluation methods may differ somewhat in each case, however. The scope of each study will depend on the size and complexity of the prospective venture. If any major problems or weaknesses are identified, they must be examined thoroughly, increasing the study's length and complexity. Although the precise nature of each of these analyses will differ according to the venture under investigation, certain factors should be addressed in each of them. These will be discussed below, and sources for gathering information will be given throughout.

Market Analysis

At earlier stages in the planning process, we looked briefly at the overall market for a project's potential products or services. We also roughly defined the project's potential customers and estimated their numbers based on general research. The market analysis component of the feasibility study is more specific and detailed. It defines the project's primary and secondary markets and determines the total size and share of the market that the venture can be expected to capture. To do this, the market analysis must closely examine three factors: the project's product, the total potential market, and competition.

Products

The first step in assessing the feasibility of all possible projects is to specifically define the product or service, or the mixture of goods and services, that the activity or business will produce and/or sell. As discussed earlier, all other factors in the feasibility analysis will relate to this definition. If the venture will manufacture a product, this part of the analysis may include a technical study, covering such topics as:

1. crucial technical specifications, such as design, durability, and standardization

2. engineering requirements, such as equipment, tools, and work flow

3. product development, such as laboratory and field test results or plans

If the community does not have the capacity either to pay for or to carry out a technical product analysis, the venture is not a feasible one for that organization. If the venture will sell but not manufacture the product—as in retail or wholesale undertakings—the product analysis may consist of comparing products available to determine the type or model to be sold. At a minimum, the product or products to be sold should be described as specifically as possible.

Necessary or desirable location specifications may be part of this section for manufacturing, wholesale, and retail ventures. Site characteristics, such as proximity to raw material suppliers, customers, transportation, educational institutions, and other directly related resources, should be specified for manufacturing and wholesale projects. For retail ventures, store location is an important factor in the success of the business. The store location or possible locations will probably not be specified until the business plan is prepared. Retail store location will be addressed under market analysis, because location profoundly affects the market for most stores. For existing businesses, the feasibility study should review what its product and/or service has been. If any changes are to be made, these should be noted and explained.

Total Market

Having specified what products or services will be provided by the venture, the market analysis must answer the following two questions: Who will buy the venture's product or service? What are the characteristics of its potential customers? The answers to these questions will define the venture's primary market—those who will be its major purchasers or users—and its secondary markets—that is, its other potential customers. Trade journals and suppliers, community surveys, or surveys of local business may provide much of this information.

The geographic limitations on the venture's market must also be assessed. If it is a retail store, for example, it may be limited to a few blocks or the surrounding community. A manufacturing project may have a regional or perhaps even national market. Trade associations and other knowledgeable sources can help define the market area. Also, check with business schools, libraries, and the chamber of commerce.

Once the characteristics of potential customers and the geographic limitations have been outlined, the size of the total market can be estimated by determining how many people (or firms) with those characteristics are located within the specified geographic area. Population statistics (e.g., population census) and various business censuses (e.g., census of manufacturers) should be helpful sources for these figures. This information, along with the information gathered under the competition analysis, will allow the community to determine how many buyers in the market will become customers (the market share). Suppliers, trade associations, the chamber of commerce, state and federal agencies, and other business owners in the area can assist in making these projections.

It is important to remember that many factors affect the size of the total market and the size of the market share that the venture can expect to capture. There are many factors beyond the control of the community (e.g., demography, economic conditions, and competition). On the other hand, items like price, product, product mix, and location are within their control. Location has already been discussed, concerning its influence on a venture's potential market. The price of goods or services is another important element over which the community has little control. Even though the price must have, as its base, the cost of providing the good or performing the service, the price is also determined by what market the seller is targeting.

The venture can be designed to target customer groups in which the market analysis shows the greatest or most feasible demand. If, for example, the venture is based on expanding a nutrition program into general food services, it can investigate the size of several markets or market segments that exist for the same product. Examples would be senior citizen centers, childcare centers, and institutions such as schools, hospitals, and businesses. It can then determine whether enough demand exists in any of these segments alone or in several combinations to support the venture. (Remember that demand means not only need for the product or service but also the ability to pay for it.) The organization can then choose which market segments to target for the highest possibility of success.

Conducting the total market analysis, the organization should be asking what choices exist and which ones will make the venture the most feasible. Once this is determined, how much competition there is for that market should be researched.

Competition

When defining the competition, one must look not only at who sells the *same* product but also who sells substitute or alternative products. The local chamber of commerce and state and federal business censuses can help competitors and provide vital information about them. Ideally, the following information on each competitor should be compiled, if available:

- location
- products
- customers
- market share
- sales and market percentage
- competitive advantages
- analysis of how they compete
- growth potential
- community cultural dimensions

The significance of location depends on the type of business being analyzed. If the venture is a grocery store, it should probably not be located next door to its major competitor. Retail clothing stores, on the other hand, often benefit from being grouped near each other, as the group can attract more business than each store alone. The state development department, the chamber of commerce, and business schools and libraries should have information on the location needs of various businesses. Be careful not to eliminate competitors outside the venture's defined geographic market area. Customers may go out of their area to shop if their alternatives are limited or if the more distant store has better products or lower prices.

Under the heading of "Products," one should try to define what similar goods and/or services competitors sell. One should determine what kinds of customers competitors attract—for example, does one childcare center in the area attract mostly parents who have the time and inclination to volunteer? Does another serve single-parent families or families in which both parents work full time? What market segments are served by each competitor?

Competitors' market shares relate to how much, numerically, of the total market each has been able to capture—that is, the volume of the business. The market and sales percentages tell how significant the market share figures are. If a business serves 2,000 customers in a year, is this 5%, 10%, or 20% of the total market? Keep in mind that a single product or firm seldom captures a market.

Sales percentages can be determined by establishing how much consumers in the defined market spent on the product during a given period (total sales), and how much was spent buying the product from each competitor. The chamber of commerce, local business schools, and the library may have resources that specify these figures by individual firms.

Competitive advantages are the keys to a firm's success. How does each business attract its customers? Is it in a convenient location? Does it offer free parking or generous credit terms, free delivery, or installation? Are its prices lower, or does its product have a marketable difference in quality?

To determine the competitive advantages of different firms, try calling directly and take note of their advertising. What image are they projecting? What services do they offer? Learning about the competition is the first step in determining how the venture can compete. In addition to the kinds of advantages included in the questions above, a venture may also be able to capitalize on its relation to the community as a whole.

Under competitive advantages, one should also analyze how competitors may respond to the venture. Are they likely to cut prices, increase advertising, or expand certain product lines? How much additional risk do competitors' possible responses impose on the venture? What competitors do will probably relate to how they currently market themselves.

A competitor's growth potential does not necessarily mean the possibility of expansion in the physical size of the store or facility but its potential for increasing sales and market percentages. This can be assessed from an analysis of its competitive strategy or advantages and the projected growth of its market segments or buying power. If accessible, the growth patterns of the business over the past several years can also be analyzed.

The above information will provide a realistic assessment of the venture's total estimated market share. Once this has been determined, it is possible to project the sales volume, a critical element in its financial feasibility.

Financial Analysis

Numerous publications, such as Seidman's *Economic Development Finance* (2004) and Giles Bischak's *Fundamentals of Economic Development Finance* (2011), go into depth about different aspects of financial feasibility. White and Kotval's (2012), in *Financing Economic Development in the 21st Century*, also offer a useful compendium specifically addressing local economic development. Accountants may also be able to provide valuable assistance in understanding and completing various financial statements. We focus here on six important financial analysis tools:

1. estimates of initial financial needs

2. break-even approaches

3. financial sensitivity assessments

4. profit and loss presentations

5. financial cash flows

6. return-on-investment calculations

The first five of these tools are used to determine the financial profitability and debt service capacity of the project. The last tool is a measure of the project's return-on-investment capability, a measure often compared with that of other projects in investment decision making.

Each of these financial projections is sensitive to the assumptions and projections made under the other feasibility factors. For example, if the venture requires an engineer or manager (who will probably command a high salary), that salary requirement will increase the venture's startup and operating expenses. There may be many alternative ways of operating the business that could alter its financial standing. A business may, for example, have the choice of either manufacturing some parts itself or purchasing them. Financial feasibility could depend, to a large extent, on the alternatives selected for starting the undertaking. It may be beneficial to make several projections based on different alternatives so that they can be compared and the most feasible option chosen.

Estimating Initial Financial Requirements and Financial Sources

The first step in determining a venture's financing requirements is to calculate all the expenses to be incurred before the business brings in money to cover costs. This includes three categories of expenses: startup and initial operating costs and a reserve for unanticipated expenses. But the investors from whom funds are sought have to be considered as well. Good, straightforward financial presentations are excellent. However, some investors want to see other items, such as:

- Leverage—how will the startup capital be used to gain other resources from third parties—donors, government and the like? This needs to be built in to financial spreadsheets for the donor, lender, or investor.
- Return to community—a new criterion for many investors who realize that if the community is not part of the project, there may be costly delays. Projects that demonstrate community participation and sense of ownership are more likely to persevere, so the investor can be assured of realizing the anticipated return.
- Sustainability contributions and returns—how adoption of best practices for material and energy use as well as waste handling will contribute to the financial performance of the company while creating a lower environmental footprint and other benefits to the community.

Standard Financial Requirements

Startup expenses are the costs associated with developing and setting up the business. They include market research, technical feasibility studies, cost of hiring employees, purchasing equipment, deposits on premises, remodeling, and initial inventory. Startup costs also include the salary or living expenses of the people starting the business. Although some of these costs may be subsidized initially, all expenses should be recorded carefully so that the true costs can be calculated.

Initial operating expenses are the costs of running the business until it reaches the break-even point, where income equals expenses. These expenses include fixed costs—such as rent, insurance, and other payments that do not vary according to sales—and variable costs—expenses that do vary with regard to sales, such as advertising and wages. Precisely which costs are categorized as fixed or variable depends in part on the type of business.

A *reserve for contingencies* is required to cover unexpected contingencies and changes in the venture development plans. These costs are extremely variable—although, as a general rule, they are projected at 10% of total project cost. A worksheet that can be used to estimate the venture's financial requirements is set out in Table 12.1. It may be adapted to match the venture being started. The estimates for each expense category should be as detailed and accurate as possible, though startup costs can be filled in immediately. To estimate the initial operating expenses, however, the venture's break-even point must also be calculated.

Table 12.1   Opening Financial Requirements

Requirements	*Expense Approach*
Startup requirements	
Financial analysis	
Legal coasts	
Initial staffing	
Contractors (architects, engineers, etc.)	
Office (rent, purchase, use home or coffee shop)	
Refurbishments of home or facilities to operate enterprise—short term, long term	
New or used machinery	
Cost of products	
Marketing	
Environmental and waste handling fees Community contribution(s)	

(Continued)

Table 12.1 (Continued)

Requirements	Expense Approach
Borrowing costs	
Utilities options—generate energy and use recycled water	
Taxes or tax breaks	
Insurance	
Contingencies (at least 10% above total budget calculation	
Total	

Break-Even Analysis

The break-even analysis shows the relationship between total income and expenses at varying levels of production, sales, or provision of services. It indicates at what level, given certain conditions, sales will reach the break-even point. At that point, income exactly equals expenses. Prior to this, the venture operates at a loss and must be subsidized. Subsequently, it generates a profit.

A venture could have several different break-even points, depending on the conditions under which it is operated. Such conditions, for example, are the number of employees or whether the business has its own delivery truck or hires a deliverer. Changes in these factors can cause variations in expenses and income.

For the break-even analysis, expenses are calculated as total fixed costs plus total variable costs over a certain period (e.g., 1 month):

Total costs = Total fixed costs + Total variable costs

Income is calculated as the number of units sold (either products or services) multiplied by the price of the unit:

Total income = Number of units (products or services) sold × Price of 1 unit

Break-even analysis establishes whether the level of sales income will cover expenses. Once this is known, it is possible to calculate how long it will take to achieve the necessary sales level or whether it is possible for the venture to capture that particular amount of sales. This evaluation is made in conjunction with the information gathered in the market analysis. Based on how many months it will take to meet the projected break-even point, the operating expense portion of the initial financial requirements of Table 12.1 can be estimated.

Developing Financial Scenarios

Once all the project's initial financial requirements are known, the local development organization should develop a series of financial scenarios based on Figure 12.2. Each scenario should be developed using realistic projections of the costs involved. Several need to be constructed using best-case to worst-case

Figure 12.2   Finance Development Scenarios

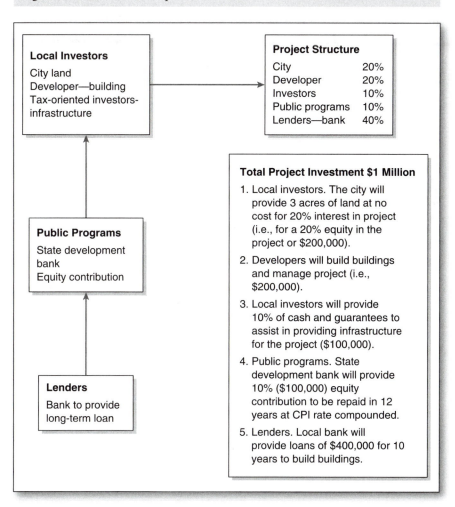

possibilities. Each component of the scenario should have a carefully developed narrative that explains how this form of funding can be obtained and the chances of obtaining it. In planning a new project, the necessary type of financing must be defined clearly. Failure to do so results not only in wasted time and effort but also in unnecessary confusion and, occasionally, failure.

From the community's point of view, a project's financing requirements are clearly defined by the purpose for which the funds will be used. The capital market institutions, however, define financing requirements by an entirely different set of criteria. To succeed in financing a project, financing needs must be defined using the criteria of both the project and the capital market.

The criteria used by lenders to analyze a financing package reflect six basic concerns:

Term. When and at what rate will the invested funds and interest be repaid? How does this correspond with the supplier's source of funds and stability?

Risk. What is the primary source of repayment and what is the probability that the invested funds will be repaid from this source? Is there a secondary source of repayment, and what is the probability that the funds will be repaid from that source if the primary source of payment fails to materialize?

Administrative cost. How much time and effort per dollar lent or invested will be required to ensure proper repayment and adequate control?

Return. What is the rate of return to the lender?

Community benefits. Will the investment result in the investor receiving additional deposits or make a contribution to new jobs, related business, goodwill in the community, or other tangible or intangible benefits?

Portfolio assessment and expertise. Banks, insurance companies, and other lenders specialize in different areas of expertise, such as home-loan banks or industrial banks, and tend to keep their money in those sectors. Does the investment fit the institution's geographic, financial, sustainability, and professional involvement?

As we show, this is an entirely different set of criteria than that used in defining earlier financial requirements; it will therefore generate very different definitions. The following example of the financing requirements for a hypothetical community business venture demonstrates the differences in definitions. A community wishes to fund the industrial estate discussed in the financial scenario. In a given project plan, it has been determined that approximately $2 million of finance will be required, to be used as follows:

1. Purchase property—1,000,000

2. Purchase equipment—$400,000

3. Carry receivables and inventory—$400,000

4. Early losses and contingency—$200,000

   Total—$2,000,000

When viewed by potential financiers, however, this same financing package will look quite different, as shown below:

1. Real estate loan, 20-year, minimal risk, low administrative cost, low return, no secondary benefits, good portfolio fit—$400,000

2. Secured equipment loan, 5-year, fair risk, fair yield, low administrative cost, will receive sustainability offsets, fair portfolio fit—$200,000

3. Accounts receivable factoring, annual renewal, acceptable risk, high administrative cost, high yield, no other benefits, good portfolio fit—$200,000

4. Required equity to secure above—$1,000,000

5. Additional required equity—$200,000

   Total—$2,000,000

To successfully prepare a realistic project plan, financial requirements need to be marketed. To avoid wasting valuable time and goodwill in locating the right financial sources, the project's financing must use the market's criteria.

Cash Flow Analysis

The Profit and Loss Statement

The venture's break-even point is determined by calculating its income and expense projections. These can be laid out graphically, in a quarterly time frame, on the venture's projected profit and loss (P&L) statement, sometimes referred to as an "income and expense statement." A sample P&L statement is provided in Table 12.2.

The P&L statement is a quarterly projection of operating expenses, combined with a quarterly projection of income (sales minus the cost of sales). Cost of sales includes the costs directly incurred by the business in producing the goods sold. In a manufacturing operation, this includes the cost of converting purchased materials into the finished product—raw materials, direct labor, equipment repairs, and so on. In a retail operation, costs of sales may simply include the purchase cost of the inventory that was sold. Trade journals and associations provide an average cost of sales for many industries.

These can be used for comparison or rough estimation but should be adjusted to reflect the venture's specific circumstances.

Table 12.2   Project Profit and Loss Statement

	1st Quarter	2nd Quarter	3rd Quarter	4th Quarter
Total net sales				
Cost of sales				
GROSS PROFIT				
Variable expenses				
Human resources				
Taxes				
Security				
Marketing				
Digital information and IT				
Legal Accounting				
Office supplies				
Telephone				
Utilities				
Miscellaneous				
Total variable expenses				
Fixed expenses				
Depreciation				
Insurance				
Rent				
Taxes and licenses				
Loan payments				
Total fixed expenses				
TOTAL EXPENSES				
NET PROFIT (LOSS) (before taxes)				

The P&L statement should be accompanied by a statement of the assumptions used in making the projections. This is especially important if several variations of the venture are being tested within the financial feasibility study. It is also a good idea to develop several P&L statements for each variation on the venture: an "upside" projection that shows what it will look like if every-thing goes perfectly, an expected statement based on reasonable assumptions and projections, and a "downside" statement that shows what it will look like if the venture runs into a lot of problems, or if circumstances vary a great deal in unexpected and negative ways. Once all the categories are filled in with pro-jected figures, the total expenses are subtracted from the gross profit (sales minus cost of sales). The resulting figure is the venture's projected monthly net profit before income taxes.

The Corporate Shift to Sustainability

A recent worldwide survey of 766 CEOs documents the increasing adop-tion of sustainability practices in firms (Lacey et al., 2010). The survey identi-fied three key drivers for the shift to sustainability: 72% of CEOs saw the incorporation of sustainability practices as a way to enhance the firm's brand or reputation, 44% saw it as an opportunity to grow revenue and reduce costs, and 31% saw it as a way to recruit and engage quality employees. Bob Willard has developed a number of tools to help firms analyze the business case for adopting sustainability, including spreadsheets that estimate the profitability gains when data for a specific company are entered. Figure 12.3 depicts

Figure 12.3   Sustainability Business Case

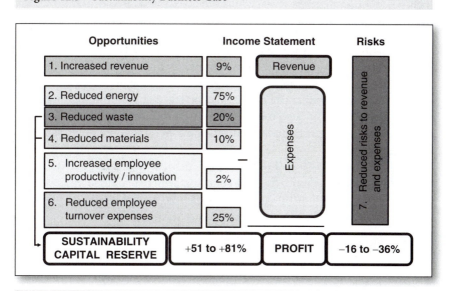

Source: Bob Willard, www.sustainabilityadvantage.com, 2012.

Willard's seven areas of concern to the firm, which can be mitigated through the adoption of sustainable practices: revenue generation, energy costs, waste generation, materials use, employee productivity and innovation, employee cost and turnover, and the risk of not meeting revenue and expense projections. Based on firm research, adoption of sustainability practices mitigates all seven areas of concern and can increase profits from 51% to 81% while reducing risk by 16% to 36%.

Traditional economic development implementation plans and specific analysis tools such as profit-and-loss statements are as applicable to sustainability-focused strategies as to traditional strategies. The need to make the business case for sustainability is imperative, and all the more so because of the deep recession that began in 2007 that has been followed by such a slow recovery. As more firm experience and data for those making the sustainability shift become available, however, economic developers are finding that making the case becomes a lot easier.

Project Sustainability

Project sustainability depends on how well the project does financially, as well as meeting the social and environmental needs of the community. Cash flows reflect one aspect of sustainability, along with the returns on investment for the project in both financial and social terms.

Cash Flow Projections

Cash flow projections are similar to P&L statements except that they deal with the cash a business will actually have on hand and the bills actually due each quarter rather than all of the income—some of which may be in the form of sales made on credit—and all of the expenses—some of which will not be paid during some months. The projected quarterly cash flow indicates whether the venture will have enough cash to pay its expenses each quarter or whether it will need short-term financing during some periods. A sample cash flow worksheet is provided in Table 12.3. "Cash flow cumulative" equals the cash flow quarterly for that quarter of the column plus the cash flow quarterly from the previous quarter. As with the P&L statement, you may want to make several projections based on how different circumstances, such as leasing or purchasing equipment, will affect the venture's projected cash flow.

The Projected Return-on-Investment Ratio

The return-on-investment (ROI) ratio estimates how much money a project will make compared with how much money was invested. It allows potential

Table 12.3   Cash Flow Projections

Startup Prior to Loan	1st Quarter	2nd Quarter	3rd Quarter	4th Quarter
Cash (beginning of month)				
Cash on hand				
Cash in bank				
Cash in investments				
Total cash				
Income (during month)				
Cash sales				
Credit sales payments				
Investment income				
Loans				
Other cash income				
Total income				
TOTAL CASH AND INCOME				
Expenses (during month)				
Inventory or new material				
Wages (including owner's)				
Taxes				
Equipment expense				
Transportation				
Loan repayment				
Other cash expenses				
TOTAL EXPENSES				
CASH FLOW (end of month)				
CASH FLOW CUMULATIVE (monthly)				

investors to compare whether the rate of return on one venture will be greater than the rate of return on the same money invested somewhere else. The ROI ratio is considered one of the best criteria of a venture's profitability and a key measure of management efficiency. Once the venture is operational, its actual ROI can be compared with industry averages as a measure of monitoring the venture's performance.

The ROI ratio is calculated by dividing net profits (before income taxes, if any) for a certain period by net worth at the end of the period. Projected net profit can be obtained from the P&L statement. *Net worth* is defined as the owner's equity, or the owner's investment; it is simply the business's assets minus liabilities. It does not include long-term debt, although in some cases it can include subordinated debt.

ROI is expressed as a percentage. As a simple example, if net profit before taxes for a 3-month period is $5,000 and net worth at the end of the period is $20,000, then the ROI ratio is 25%.

$$\frac{\$5,000}{\$20,000} = 25$$

In general, a ratio of between 14% and 25% is considered a desirable return for investment and possible future growth.

Table 12.4 Assessing Project Impacts

Direct Impacts	Possible Indirect Impacts	
Employment	*Employment*	*Income*
Construction	Multiplier effect creating other jobs	Multiplier effect
Permanent	Reduction in other jobs	
	Education and training	
Income	*Revenues*	*Land use*
Wages and salaries of employees	Sales	New developments around project such as housing and businesses
Low-income/ disadvantaged groups	Property tax	Increased property values

Direct Impacts	Possible Indirect Impacts	
Profits	Business permits and so on	Housing requirements
Land use	Service costs	Environmental/social costs
Changes in land values	Sewer	Transportation/traffic congestion
	Water and so on	Community amenity
	Schools	Increased air pollution damage and less "room" for additional industrial development because of air-quality standards
		Community social programs

Cost-Benefit Analysis

Cost-benefit analysis is a complex subject beyond the scope of this book. Thus, we will deal with it only in general terms. The following review of the basic notions of cost-benefit analysis should be supplemented by more extensive and detailed discussions.

A cost-benefit analysis examines a proposed project's net contribution to the local economy and community. It compares the local community's potential success at achieving fundamental objectives by pursuing a particular project against opportunities lost because resources were committed specifically to that project.

There are various techniques of cost-benefit analysis. The three most commonly used, however, are the net present value (npv), the cost-to-benefit ratio (c/b), and the internal rate of return (irr). Each of these techniques—and in fact the entire concept of cost-benefit analysis—has basic limitations. Before mentioning these limitations, however, the various techniques will be outlined briefly.

The first step in preparing the cost-benefit analysis is to estimate the project costs. These estimates should include all capital and operating costs calculated on a yearly basis for each of the years in which the project is expected to operate. The projected financial statement discussed in the preceding section will be a good starting point for identifying these costs. It must be appreciated, however, that these calculations reflect the project costs to its sponsor or operative entity, not the project's economic cost to the community. To determine the project's economic cost, changes must be made to the financial cost calculations. In determining economic costs only, those payments that reflect the actual use of a societal resource must be charged against the project. Payments that simply represent the transfer of control over resources from one segment of society to another should be deducted. These transfer payments include project costs such as taxes, loan repayments, and interest repayments on loans.

Sunken costs are defined as those that have been incurred on the project before the cost-benefit assessment was initiated. They should, of course, also be excluded from the cost of the project for the purpose of deciding whether to proceed with it. Only resource costs that can still be avoided are relevant. For example, the economic merit of a project designed to complete another project does not depend on the costs already incurred but only on the cost of completion.

The next step is to estimate the benefits generated by the project for each of the years for which it is expected to operate. These benefits will include revenues from the sale of the goods and/or services generated, and also money from the sale of any remaining equipment at the end of the project's lifetime. Contributions to society should also be added into the calculation of project benefits. To reflect these social contributions, the project's wage payments to previously unemployed workers and the price of its services must be weighed more heavily than their actual market value. This would signify in economic terms the project's contribution to the local economy and community. It must be noted that wages are counted as project costs; therefore, in charging costs to the project, the wages paid to previously unemployed people are reduced by an appropriate amount. The price of services, on the other hand, is counted as project revenues. Therefore, in assigning benefits to the project, the revenues gained from it are increased by an appropriate amount.

The process of identifying project costs and benefits is difficult. Table 12.4 presents an overview of the complexity of the issues described. The process of adjusting cost and benefit items to reflect the relevant community values and objectives is known as *shadow pricing*. How shadow prices are determined is a question best answered by an experienced cost-benefit analyst. Once the cost/revenue (benefit) items have been adjusted to reflect the relevant social or community values, we can proceed to calculate (1) the net present value (npv), (2) the benefit-to-cost ratio (b/c), and (3) the internal rate of return (irr).

The net present value (npv) is, quite simply, the amount remaining after subtracting the present value of all project costs from the present value of all project benefits. The key term is *present value*. This concept can be explained as follows: Because the project's operations occur in the future, it will incur costs and produce benefits at different points in time. Hence, it is necessary to express future costs and benefits in terms of their present worth—that is, in a chosen base year. This can be accomplished by using a social rate of discount, which is a specified percentage that devalues future project costs and benefits.

The benefit-to-cost (b/c) ratio is the present worth of all project benefits divided by the present worth of all project costs. The decision rule is simply that a project contributes to society if b/c is greater than 1. The internal rate of return (irr) is the discount rate that will make the project's net present value equal to zero—that is, the project's net present benefits equal to its net present costs over a given period of time.

There are limits to cost-benefit analysis. First, only those project impacts that can be quantified in economic terms can easily be incorporated into the analysis. Using cost-benefit analysis cannot adequately assess social projects, which may produce benefits such as teaching a community how to organize or instilling a sense of pride and self-worth in the community. Second, the definition of certain benefits must be conceived very narrowly. Finally, in determining weights by which to value a project's contribution to society, or in determining the social rate of discount, there is too much room for discretion and arbitrary decisions. Given this flexibility, a cost-benefit analysis can be manipulated to show a social profit.

Put in perspective, cost-benefit analysis allows one to compare competing projects and alternative approaches to the same project. It is not, however, a precise measure of its actual value to society. Because the analysis can consider only some of the social consequences of quantitative project measurement, many important "community spirit" and attitudinal values are lost. In most instances, therefore, it is necessary for the decision maker to take the calculations of cost-benefit as an approximate measure of the project's actual worth. To improve the cost-benefit assessment, the above calculations could be supplemented with a descriptive analysis of the project's nonquantifiable costs and benefits.

Organizational Design

In making a choice of organizational form for the project, a development organization should carefully consider a number of factors:

- economic development goals
- amount of control the organization wants over the project
- internal management and staff capacity
- impact of potential liability to the local development
- organization or government associated with the economic risk
- image in the community
- ability to obtain outside sources of public and private capital
- requirements of tax, securities, and business law

Some of the most common organizational forms are nonprofit-related in-house ventures, for-profit subsidiaries, joint ventures, and franchises. These forms will have different of tax, business, legal, community, and organizational factors. The local development organization should first decide on its goals for the venture and then work with a knowledgeable lawyer to find the most appropriate form to achieve those goals legally. Selecting the most appropriate legal structure for a project is not a one-time decision. As it grows and changes, both it and the local development organization may have different needs. The project's structure and its relationship to the local development organization can be altered to reflect the changed needs.

Using the Feasibility Study

Once feasibility studies are completed for each of the prospective projects, it is helpful to have each one reviewed by an independent expert and also by members of the local economic development advisory committee. The reviewers will provide different perspectives and valuable expertise. Their evaluations and recommendations for improvement will strengthen the feasibility study and also confirm that its findings are valid.

The reviewed feasibility studies should then be assessed by those responsible for determining whether to proceed with the venture. The evaluation of the feasibility studies should be spread over several meetings of the community or citizen group reviewing them. The first meeting could explain the function of the feasibility studies to the decision makers, as well as what they should be looking for in evaluating them. A second meeting could be used for the presentation and discussion of the results of the studies. A third meeting could be a community briefing session explaining the project's potential for the community and exploring other hidden costs and benefits. The last meeting would be for the final decision. Once a project has been selected, it is recommended that only one venture be started at a time. This will minimize risks to the implementing organization. The next step is the preparation of a business plan, if appropriate, or a project monitoring and evaluation program.

Business Plan Preparation

The venture's business plan will be closely related to its feasibility study, which will provide most of the data necessary to prepare the business plan. There are important differences between the two documents, however. The purpose of the feasibility study is to explore options for operating the venture in order to assess the possible success of the activity. The business plan will lay out, in detail, how the venture will operate and the assumptions upon which the operation is based. The feasibility study discusses different ways that the business might operate; the business plan describes the way that the business will operate. The business plan is a final check on the venture's feasibility. It is more detailed than the feasibility study and is often longer, especially if technical specifications are involved.

The format of the business plan is another variable. Like feasibility studies, business plans have no standard method. What the plan looks like depends on the type of business and how the plan will be used. Regardless of the format chosen, most business plans should discuss at least the following points:

- the industry and the business (including general industry trends and the history of the business, if applicable)
- the product and service that the business will sell
- the market (including market size, trends, competition, and market share projections)
- a marketing plan (including pricing, distribution, and promotion)
- prestartup and startup plans and schedules
- manufacturing/operating plans
- organization and management (including job descriptions, personnel needs, lines of authority, wages, and skills and experience of key personnel)
- community and sustainability benefits (including economic impacts, environmental, human development, and other social impacts)
- financial plans (including initial capitalization, proposed financing, and projected financial statements such as balance sheets, profit-and-loss statements, and cash-flow and break-even analyses)
- control and feedback systems (including monitoring plans)
- a discussion of critical risks and assumptions associated with the business and the business plan

Most of these issues were at least touched on in the feasibility study, although they are covered in greater depth and detail in the business plan. These basic topics can be covered in a variety of ways. What is important is that they be discussed somewhere in the plan. Seek advice from experts who can help decide what format to use and who understand the business project and the financing.

Monitoring and Evaluation

Project evaluation is important for economic development plan implementation or specific projects. It can lead to more efficient and effective projects as a result of systematic, careful analysis of project consequences and costs. It is an ongoing activity, beginning when a plan or project is in the design stage and continuing through implementation. It should also include a full review of the project once it becomes operational. In short, project evaluation begins right at the planning stage, and project evaluation procedures must be evident in the planning process itself. Indeed, the feasibility and business plan documents should include a separate section on the evaluation plan. This section should explicitly identify the following.

Criteria to be Used in Evaluation

For a project, if the main body of the feasibility document is done properly, evaluation criteria will naturally emerge out of the time schedule, cost and budget limits, and productivity output targets. Key result areas, specified in measurable terms where possible, will be the criteria for evaluation. This is as true of concrete technical projects as of social projects, though the latter are admittedly harder to quantify. The final benefits or effects the project intends to achieve, as defined by the project's both explicit and implicit objectives, should also be included among the evaluation criteria. These benefits may include such items as:

- a specified number of job opportunities for low-income members of the community
- opportunities for management skill development and job upgrading
- income redirection, given the flow of money in the community
- venture self-sufficiency
- facilitation of community development
- infrastructure development
- provision of quality goods and services
- community education opportunities
- community ownership, control, and decision-making opportunities

Strategic economic development plans for communities are also frequently evaluated by stated goals. For example, the city of Portland, Oregon, established goals for creating 10,000 jobs in four industries: clean technology, active wear, software, and advanced manufacturing in its 2009 Economic Development Strategy (Portland Economic Development Commission, 2009).

Evaluation Techniques

This section identifies the evaluation techniques to be used as well as the points in time when they are to be employed. In post-project evaluation, the evaluator's task is to measure if the planning stage did, in fact, reflect what actually occurred. This could mean a recomputation or remodification of costs and benefits in light of changing government priorities. The resulting figures would give developers a more realistic perspective of the project in relation to community objectives. Thus, this section should lay out the cost-benefit premise as the basis for future evaluations to be set.

Other approaches or evaluation techniques include the use of control groups for comparative analysis, baseline measures, sampling, and various data-gathering methods such as field surveys, questionnaires, and interviews. These techniques, again, largely occur at the beginning of a project if a study or research design is planned. If this type of study is done, an experimental test group of consumers and a control group may be determined. Furthermore, baseline measures such as size and number of jobs to be created can be set. Tests or interviews conducted can reveal certain critical aspects or situations prior to the start of the project.

At the time of post-project evaluation, the comparisons made would be the experimental group before and after the project, the control group before and after the project, and an evaluation of results based on the critical aspects studied. Other techniques used would be financially oriented, such as variance analysis, where a study of the budgeted versus actual financial performance is made. If the project did not utilize a budget, however, such analysis would be very difficult, if not impossible.

Time Schedules for Conducting the Evaluation

Aside from scheduling implementation, proposals should schedule evaluation so that it is not indefinitely postponed or indicate an acceptable lapse time in instances in which a project's desired results—especially social—are not evident immediately after project completion.

Budget for Evaluation

This section should include, aside from the total amount and the program breakdowns, the promised or possible sources of funding and the schedule of budget releases.

Organization and Staff Requirements for Evaluation

This section should outline the size of the evaluation team, its qualifications, the reporting relationships, and access to project information and staff.

Those responsible for post-project evaluation must, by definition, assume a comprehensive point of view. Whereas the project's components may be worked on individually during implementation, the evaluator looks at the project as a package. Success or failure is determined by the achievement of the whole venture measured against its objectives.

Often, a team of project evaluators is composed, at a minimum, of both a technical and a project-management expert. The group may consist of three to five individuals from various disciplines with recognized expertise in the line of the project. They are sometimes from universities or research agencies, as well as from various government offices. Their expertise and experience are of primary consideration in their selection, however, as the quality of the evaluation work will only be as good as the evaluators themselves.

Opinions differ on the relative merits and demerits of a preponderantly external evaluation team over an evaluation from within the project-operating agency. External teams have objectivity, possibly at the cost of lack of understanding, perspective, or access to background information, both hard and soft; internal teams enjoy familiarity and access at the expense of possible subjectivity.

Conclusion

As we noted at the outset of this chapter, initiation of economic development planning is fundamentally an effort to influence the market economy when there are acknowledged deficiencies in market outcomes for the community. The public sector is always involved—directly or indirectly—in economic development plan implementation for the purpose of strengthening the private sector and resulting benefits for all of the community. This chapter has focused on the mix of public and private sector partners, considerations, and tools for economic development plan and project implementation.

Significant attention has been given to marketing a community to achieve its economic development goals. This marketing is not just to outsiders but also to those within the community who make valuable economic contributions that the community does not want to lose but rather hopes to strengthen. Significant attention has also been given in this chapter to financing economic development projects and to their evaluation. A well-chosen project implemented through a strong public–private partnership can be a highly valuable catalyst for realizing the goals of a community's economic development plan. The chapter's overview of project viability and financial analysis was intended to give the reader a sense of the effort and complexity involved in creating and implementing an economic development project.

In contrast to the well-accepted steps for project development and analysis, the reader should be aware that the details of implementing an overall economic development plan will vary considerably depending on the size of the community (e.g., a small town or major city or county), the timeframe for the plan (e.g., 1 year or 5 years), and specific economic goals that are defined (e.g., target specific industry sectors, grow small business, increase the skills of the labor force). Local governments often hire outside expertise when implementing their economic development plans or projects. This expertise, however, augments but does not supplant the public–private partnership that is required for successful economic development implementation.

References and Suggested Readings

Berne, Robert, and Richard Schram. 1987. *The Financial Analysis of Governments.* Englewood Cliffs, NJ: Prentice Hall.

Bruggeman, William B., and Leo Stone. 1981. *Real Estate Finance.* Homewood, IL: Irwin.

City of Long Beach Economic Development Bureau. (2007). *Economic Development Implementation Plan,* 2007. Accessed September 13, 2012, at www.longbeach .gov/ecd

Giles, Susan, and Edward J. Blakely. 2001. *Fundamentals of Economic Development Finance.* Thousand Oaks, CA: Sage.

Giles Bischak, Susan, 2011. *Fundamentals of Economic Development Finance,* 2nd edition, Giles & Company Strategic Business Consultants.

Greenwood, William, S. Haberfeld, and L. Lee. 1978. *Organizing Producer Cooperatives.* Berkeley, CA: Economic Development and Law Center.

Hill, Edward, and Nell Ann Shelley. 1990. An Overview of Economic Development Finance. In *Financing Economic Development: An Institutional Response,* edited by Richard D. Bingham, E. Hill, and S. White. Newbury Park, CA: Sage.

Kidder, Peabody and Co. 1986. *Economic Development Finance.* New York: Author.

Lacey, Peter, Tim Cooper, Rob Hayward, and Lisa Neuberger. (2010). *A New Era of Sustainability: UN Global Compact and Accenture CEO Study.* Accessed September 17, 2012, at http://www.unglobalcompact.org/docs/news_events/8.1/ UNGC_Accenture_CEO_Study_2010.pdf

Lafer, Stefan. 1984. *Urban Redevelopment: An Introductory Guide.* Berkeley, CA: University Extension Publications.

Lancaster County, South Carolina. (2009). *Economic Development Implementation Plan.* Accessed September 14, 2012, at http://www.lancasterscworks.com/pdf/Strategic_ Plan.pdf

Lovelock, Chris, and Charles Weinberg. 1978. *Readings in Public and Non Profit Marketing.* Stanford, CA: Scientific Press.

Magee, Judith. 1978. *Down to Business: An Analysis of Small Scale Enterprise & Appropriate Technology.* Butte, MT: National Center for Appropriate Technology.

Malizia, Emil. 1985. *Local Economic Development: A Guide to Practice.* New York: Praeger.

Mancusco, Joseph R. 1983. *How to Prepare and Present a Business Plan.* New York: Prentice Hall.

Maryland Department of Economic & Community Development. 1984. *The Business Partnership in Maryland: Programs and Services for Maryland Business.* Annapolis, MD: Author.

McClain, Judy. 1992. Loan Funds Aid Rural Clinic. *Community Notes* (26): n.p.

Portland Economic Development Commission. (2009). *Economic Development Strategy,* 2009, http://pdxeconomicdevelopment.com/docs/Portland-Ec-Dev-Strategy.pdf

Presidential Task Force. 1982. *Investing in America: Initiatives for Community Economic Development.* Washington, DC: President's Task Force on Private Sector Initiatives.

Rados, David. 1981. *Marketing Non Profit Organizations.* Chicago: Auburn House.

Rolland, Keith. 1982. *A Survey of Church Alternative Investments.* New York: Interfaith Center for Corporate Responsibility.

Rondinelli, Dennis A., ed. 1979. *Planning Development Projects.* Stroudsburgh, PA: Dowden, Hutchinson and Ross.

Schaar, Marvin. 1980. *Cooperatives, Principles & Practices.* Madison, WI: Cooperative Extension.

Seidman, Karl F. (2004). *Economic Development Finance.* Thousand Oaks, CA: Sage.

Smith, Neville, and Murray Ainsworth. 1985. *Ideas Unlimited.* Sydney, Australia: Nelson.

White, Sammis B., and Zenia Z. Kotval. 2012. *Financing Economic Development in the 21st Century.* Armonk, NJ: M.E. Sharpe.

Willard, Bob. www.sustainabilityadvantage.com. Accessed May 3, 2012.

Zdenek, Robert. 1983. *Resources for Community-Based Economic Development.* Washington, DC: National Congress for Community Economic Development.

13

Institutional Approaches to Local Economic Development

I nstitutional approaches to, or structures for, local economic development have received considerable attention in recent years. One reason for this is that more local, regional, and state economic development institutions are being formed. The structure of the economic development program varies according to whether it is a state, substate, regional, or local city or countywide organization. In some instances, these organizations merely coordinate activities in the public or private sector, and in others the development organization is the de facto project developer. There needs to be a clear distinction between a plan for economic development and a plan for short-term measures, no matter how urgent, to meet immediate community needs. Planning for economic development intends to bring about a lasting and continuing change in the local economy so that it will better serve social objectives. Economic development is an institution-building process. As a result, it requires the establishment of *planning systems and institutions* that can manage the development process over extended periods of time. The planning process, not the plan or document, is significant.

An institution with specific responsibility to coordinate each step of the local economic development process is essential. The development strategy plan, as well as the process itself, requires fiscal resources, technical expertise, leadership, and imagination. Some type of fully staffed, locally based institution must be available to assist in identifying and mobilizing all these resources in order to carry out strategic planning. Matt Kane and Peggy Sand (1988) summarize the essential characteristics of an economic development organization:

> People and organizations with vested interests in an area's economic development must be drawn into the formation and policy processes for an economic development organization. Different stakeholders will have different goals

that must be made explicit and considered. The city government and private businesses certainly need to play a role. But so, too, do downtown and neighborhood representatives, labor unions, city residents, utility companies, environmentalists, other area governments, and officials from local universities. The list of stakeholders will vary from city to city. Some of these stakeholders may be important in setting general directions for an organization, while others may be needed for its day-to-day operations. A community's economic development organization may involve stakeholders in a formal or informal manner. But one way or another, involvement itself is important. Without it, an organization may find it lacks political support to rally the community behind its objectives and programs. (p. 22)

The planning model or approach is as important as the process. This chapter reviews the basic organizational requirements for economic development planning. In addition, case studies of various development organization types are presented.

Organizational Requirements for Local Development

There are several basic ingredients for any local/regional economic development organization. Table 13.1 describes these components and the activities associated with each of them.

The coordinating organization for economic development is best thought of as a set of functions within a structure rather than as a single institution performing all tasks itself. (That is, the activities associated with each of the columns in Table 13.1 can be performed by staffing the organization or by

Table 13.1   Components of Economic Development Organization

	Leadership Board Director	
Economic Analysis and Planning	*Marketing and Finance*	*Human and Community Resources*
Assessment	Promotion	Profiles
Forecasting	Project development	Education and training
Strategy	Financial planning	Community services
	Financial packaging	Regulation analysis
		Local government coordination

the staff of another existing organization.) For example, the board of directors' function might be performed by the existing city council or a subcommittee of the city council. Alternatively, a group of local governments across a region could form a combined board.

Similarly, the executive director might be a full-time position held by a second staff member of a local government or regional organization. Of course, a full-time professional director would be best. The marketing and finance functions, on the other hand, might be provided by the local chamber of commerce or a consortium of local businesses and financial organizations.

A local university or college may provide ongoing business and economic analysis, and the existing employment services agency might assist with human resource and community assessments.

Clearly, there is a wide range of effective organizational designs. The type of organizational form chosen depends on the size of the community and the level of sophistication of its institutions with respect to economic development. The specific form should be based on an analysis of the potential roles various institutions might play in the development strategy decided on by the community. Regardless of what form the development organization takes, the essential point is that it should have sufficient *authority* and *resources* to undertake at least the following activities:

- *research*—to provide background information on the area's needs
- *information provision*—on identified target activities
- *marketing*—customized according to specific development strategies
- *coordination of the activities of other groups*—important to the achievement of the overall development strategy

Funds should be balanced between those devoted to staffing and those provided to staff for work-related costs. Too much funding devoted to salaries can, for example, result in staff not carrying out important tasks because they cannot provide project funding. A well-developed local coordinating body for economic and employment development will have a clearly written definition of management and staff roles and responsibilities. The essential responsibility for overseeing the planning and venture selection process in the organization must be set forth clearly. The person in charge of analysis must be responsible for preparing and monitoring reports of analysis. Any new roles and responsibilities should always be explicitly identified and added to the workload of a particular staff member.

A well-developed local economic development organization also has strong financial planning controls and a forward-looking financial planning system. The financial system must not only be able to look back and describe what happened in the past—as is necessary in grant reporting—but also to look forward and make predictions so that the organization and its ventures can accommodate and react quickly to changes. The financial system should be structured so that overhead and administrative costs are not hidden but are allocated fairly and openly between the various programs. Strong financial controls enable the organization to keep accurate records of its finances and pinpoint trouble spots quickly.

The local economic development organization should also have a strong economic and employment planning component. This will enable the organization to look to the future and place current and short-term community interests and needs in the context of a long-term perspective on community revitalization and independence. The planning component also allows the organization to systematically increase the capacities of both the community and the organization for economic development activities. Effective targeted marketing programs for development activities are also crucial for success.

A well-developed organization will have a strong connection with the private sector and good relations with all the social groups within the community. This helps ensure that the organization meets the needs and expectations of these groups and enables the organization to make use of the community's resources to create healthy ventures. The support of the private sector is essential for obtaining business advice, financing, and also possible contracts. In addition, the support of the wider community can strengthen the organization's ability to obtain public and other grant funds and can demonstrate that the organization is involving the disadvantaged in the local development process. An appropriate legal structure should form the basis of a well-developed local economic development organization. Appropriate legal structures that reflect the needs and goals of the organization or venture are as simple as possible. This means that the economic development body has no external structure for its venture but houses it internally or that it sets up its venture as a separate subsidiary. Legal structures should allow the organization the amount of necessary control to monitor its investments effectively without interfering in their internal operations. Legal structure should follow function and therefore should be selected after the venture in order to ensure that the structure is appropriate.

Leveraging the nonmonetary resources (e.g., goodwill of the community and political connections) allows the well-developed local economic development organization to make the most of its resources. Indeed, the support and cooperation of local, state, and federal office holders is essential. The organization identifies and develops additional ventures through vertical and horizontal integration, such as starting a laundry to service an already operating nursing home. The organization may also spin off ventures, when appropriate, to free resources for the support of new ventures.

Public–Private Partnerships

The term *public–private partnership* has permanently entered the lexicon of local government. What is a public–private partnership? Why is it important to consider it as a component of economic development?

Public–private partnerships are not a new phenomenon. They are the legacy of more than 50 years of federal urban policies. In 1938, the federal government embarked on a set of housing assistance programs by chartering the Federal National Mortgage Association (FNMA), now commonly known as Fannie Mae, to create a secondary market for home mortgages. This program created a partnership between the public sector and the private market to produce housing in urban areas. The cities benefited from this national partnership. It was so effective that in the 1960s and 1970s, this concept was extended to rebuilding the inner cities through the Model Cities Program and later the Urban Development Action Grant (UDAG). UDAG was the most powerful stimulus for downtown restoration ever devised. Most of the nation's large cities cleared large portions of their downtowns to open them to revitalization projects crafted at the local level but supported through federal government transfers and loan guarantees. The UDAG program established the framework for local partnerships between government and local private sectors.

In the mid-1970s, local officials began experimenting with a new set of relationships with the private sector in order to complete the projects launched a decade or more earlier under more generous federal support. The lessons learned from UDAGs were adapted in the 1980s, when federal support was withdrawn at the height of local fiscal distress.

City officials became dealmakers by the late 1970s. These deals included the provision of essential infrastructure at little or no cost with promise of a return on the city's investment through a soft loan or a portion of the profits from the project. In many instances, cities built public garages for private developers or sold or leased back facilities to retailers. In essence, cities moved from their traditional role as regulator to one as coinvestor. "This new role marked a change," as Sagalyn (1990) says,

> in expectations about the public sector's separateness from the private sector.... These strategies placed a high premium on public entrepreneurship and private market feasibility.... And increasingly, in bargaining with developers, cities negotiated direct financial stakes in a project in the form of public profit-sharing arrangements, a practice very unlike the usual behavior of cities. (pp. 429–430)

As a result, most local governments entered the 1990s with considerable experience as entrepreneurs in the development process.

No matter what organizational structure is selected, public agencies and private firms have to enter into new relationships to make the development process work. This approach is much more than the public sector merely offering cooperation to the private sector to facilitate economic activities for private gain; it is also far more than occasional meetings between the municipal council and local business organizations, such as the chamber of commerce. Although these activities are important, and perhaps integral to good business–government relations, they do not constitute true partnerships among the sectors. Partnerships are shared commitments to pursue common economic objectives jointly determined by public, private, and community sectors and instituted as joint actions. Analysis of successful partnership efforts suggests the following guidelines:

1. *A positive civic culture that encourages citizen participation and is related to the long-term employment concerns of the community.* The goals for the development process must be shared among the community. Civic institutions that help create jobs and stimulate the economic base can form real partnerships, whereas self-serving business promotion or traditionally insular government—without a development role—cannot find any common ground for a partnership.

2. *A realistic and commonly accepted vision of the community based on the area's strengths and weaknesses as well as on a common conception of the area's potential.* This is the most important area for partnership formation. Without a common understanding of what the community has or what it can become, it is impossible to build a better community. Furthermore, unless there is a realistic vision of the area's potential, the community will never come together to achieve its goals.

3. *An effective civic organization that can blend the self-interest of members with the broader interests of the community.* Enlightened self-interest is undoubtedly the spark that lights the most action. If the interests of civic leaders, both individually and collectively, can be channeled through some structure in order to achieve what is in the common interest of the total community, the development process will work.

4. *A network of key groups and individuals that encourages communication among leaders and facilitates mediation of differences among competing interests.* This network builds respect and confidence in the community. It allows business, labor, and government to work out their differences in private rather than in public, thereby allowing the focus of public discussion to be on the areas of agreement rather than on the problems of poor relationships.

5. *The ability and desire to nurture civic entrepreneurship—that is, to encourage the risk takers and build their confidence.* Nothing is more damaging to the notion of economic development than communities that dismiss the work of effective people. It takes a few active and motivated persons and bold action to move an area or community into new job-creating ventures. If these people are not rewarded and encouraged, then the development process will stop and the community will suffer the loss.

6. *Continuity of policy, including the ability to adapt to changing circumstances and reduce uncertainty for business and individuals who want to take economic risks.* Too frequently, government, in the absence of any consistent goals, pursues ad hoc policies disruptive to the development process. There are steps that can be taken to minimize this. First, the community should work on a set of development policies that act as a frame for their actions in the development arena. For example, a community might adopt policies that promote labor-intensive developments. Subsequent projects, as well as regulations, have to be examined to see whether they fall within the framework. Second, local government and private enterprise, along with unions and community groups, should try to determine what kind of community they really want and build social and physical infrastructures accordingly.

These six guidelines form the basis for any organizational structure the community decides to adopt. Essentially, public–private partnerships are bridges of trust based on similar objectives but mindful of differences in roles.

Achieving public–private cooperation is the first step toward engaging in actual projects. The projects will follow easily if the structure is there to facilitate the relationships.

Finally, a key aspect of the well-developed local economic development organization is its aggressive identification of new areas for growth. For continuing success, the organization must constantly move forward, identifying new ventures and activities that will help it to meet its goals. Local government authorities and/or neighborhood associations must, in order to create new development initiatives, employ expert officers to act as project coordinators, economic development specialists, or persons working under similar titles. These individuals will in the following pages be referred to as economic development specialists.

The Economic Development Specialist

The appointment of a local economic development specialist to plan and/or direct the local development program has numerous benefits for the community, irrespective of whether a decision is made to form a new organization to guide the development process. This position helps bring both focus and commitment from the total community. The position also brings visibility for the community in wider economic and political circles. The duties of development officers vary according to the sophistication of the development system in a community. In some instances, development officers are executives who direct other specialized staff or large regional development organizations. However, most communities are likely to require an individual who can not only guide the development process but also accomplish the following tasks:

- *research*—to assess community economic and social needs
- *planning*—to organize people and information and set goals and priorities
- *management*—to develop and promote specific projects involving public–private partnerships
- *leadership*—to facilitate the effective functioning of the local development board or commission as well as lead staff

Institutional Approaches to Local Economic Development

As mentioned previously, the actual structure of a local development organization is dependent on community circumstances. It is, however, extremely important for everyone to understand the old management principle: "form must follow function." Too frequently, communities adopt a structure based on reading about the experiences of other places. The correct procedure is to design an institutional form that fits the political and economic situation. First, however, a community must appreciate that, regardless of the form the development organization takes, it is ultimately an "enterprise" and must have sufficient capacity to perform. There are two important characteristics that development organizations must possess:

1. *authority*—the legitimate power to act on behalf of the local government, community, unions, businesses, and other constituent groups

2. *resources*—staff, financial access, technical assistance, information, and other resources required by local economic and employment development projects and programs

For a development organization to be successful, it must be able to use a combination of authority and resources to facilitate work. If an organization exists in name only and has only nebulous coordinating responsibilities, it is unlikely to gain the respect of the business community. The community organization has the responsibility of specifying the limits of such authority at reasonable levels. The absence of delegated responsibility will mean that the organization cannot operate effectively and that the development officer spends too much time obtaining permission to function effectively.

A Typology of Development Organizations

There are three general types of development organization. First, there are *government or public* development organizations. These are components or complete delegate agencies of city or county government. Second, there are *private development associations,* which are sponsored by local/regional businesses and operate with the permission or endorsement of local government. These are private bodies usually affiliated with or a component of chambers of commerce, manufacturers, or other similar bodies. Finally, there are *local development corporations* that are a form of public–private partnership. They act as semi-independent bodies that coordinate and actually manage development projects for or with local government. These organizational approaches are seldom observed in their pure form; nevertheless, they will be described here as "archetypes." Each has its advantages and disadvantages.

A major advantage of the public agency is its connections to the political system; as such, it has access to the political resources of local as well as state and federal governments. Its chief disadvantage is the persistent delays of government bureaucracy. In local development planning, where responsiveness to the market and opportunity is essential, this may be a fatal flaw unless local government genuinely supports the agency through city council actions. There are other important advantages associated with public economic development organizations that IEDC's *Managing Economic Development Organizations* (2011) lists:

- use of finance tools to leverage private investment such as public grants and revenue sharing funds;
- municipal powers that can be utilized for economic development initiatives such as "taxing authority, eminent domain, ownership of land, rights of ways, zoning and regulatory powers, and the ability to construct and operate public facilities and services" (p. 90);
- use of other local government resources (planning, research, public works).

On the other hand, the disadvantages of public organizations for economic development include:

- economic influence is essentially limited to their political boundaries;
- ability to finance initiatives is subject to municipal debt limitations;
- may have prohibitions on lending money to the private sector; participating in profit-making activity; and building or operating non-public facilities;
- may be undermined by elected official turnover or weak commitment of officials;
- subject to private sector mistrust as well as public disclosure laws that "prevent private negotiations with relocating businesses or developers" (p. 91).

Private development organizations can act quickly, but they are bound by limited interests. Generally, they are concerned only with the promotion of existing private business and with the real estate and investment opportunities associated with new firms. Private organizations seldom involve themselves in wider employment and community welfare activities. Private groups, however, can function far more effectively than government bodies in economic sectors such as tourism and retail development. Private economic development organizations also have advantages and disadvantages (IEDC, 2011). Their key advantages include the ability to:

- make decisions quickly and not be accountable to a broad constituency
- raise funds, invest equity capital and make profits
- insulate individual investors from risk

Their key disadvantages are that they:

- lack municipal land powers such as eminent domain
- may have less public sector support
- may have to pay taxes on investment income
- requirement to be self-supporting may sometimes shift efforts away from economic development

Development corporations, or "joint power" organizations, that involve government as well as business and community are the most used form of organization because such organizations continue to enjoy government and private support. In some instances, however, the organization is given too little power or responsibility from either the private sector or government agencies. Key advantages of public–private economic development organizations include (IEDC, 2011):

- less subject to politicization of their work;
- can incur greater risk and make bolder decisions because their board is unpaid and unelected;
- augment government powers with "functions and powers of legal, private subsidiaries and affiliates" (p. 100);
- can draw on the expertise and resources of the public and private sector;
- protect decision makers from financial risk via incorporation; and
- can be self-supporting through assessing fees and dues.

Compared to solely public or private economic development organizations, the public–private form has one key disadvantage. While limited accountability to the public sector can create greater flexibility and provide access to more tools, it also can lead to eroded public support if the public–private economic development organization's goals are not perceived to serve the public interest appropriately.

When considering the three forms of economic development organizations (public, private, public/private), the following questions should be kept in mind: What role is the organization to perform? What resources are available for the organization? What are the capabilities, interests and needs of the locality?

Economic Development Agencies as Units of Local Government

Some local governments consider economic development a regular responsibility of government that should be incorporated into its organization structure. A development department is a very comprehensive organization, and the staffing required to run such an organization is effectively out of reach for most small local government authorities. Large cities have fully staffed economic development departments. This structure has the advantage of close communications, as shown in Figure 13.1.

Independent Private Development Agencies

This type of agency has existed for some time in various local government areas. In many instances, the tourism or retailer associations have evolved from more elaborated development bodies. The chamber of commerce or some existing business group usually acts as the nucleus for this organizational framework. These organizations are effective as lobbyists for local interests with the local government. They may also raise private funds and become involved in high-risk ventures because of their status. The major benefit to the community of such a body is that it puts peer pressure on businesspeople to get things done for the community. Some smaller communities have decided that this is the best approach because the local government can assist these organizations by providing land or facilities,

Figure 13.1   Model Structure of Development Organization That Is a Unit of Local Government

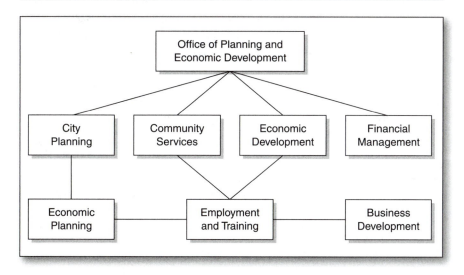

but it does not risk taxpayer revenue since it cannot (by law) be directly involved in deal making (see Figure 13.2).

Figure 13.2 Private Development Organization Model

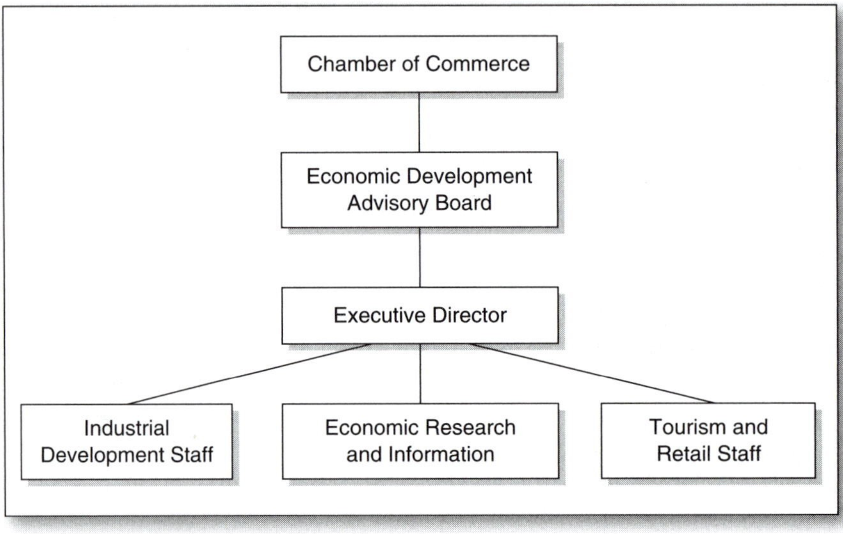

Economic Development Corporations

The economic development corporation is an excellent vehicle and should enjoy strong support from both the public and the private sectors, although there are instances where this support is lacking. Nonetheless, this institutional approach makes it possible to bring together the complete resources of the community if the public and private sectors have equal stake in the corporation.

The structure of a local development corporation can be very sophisticated or relatively simple. Many economic development corporations have moderately complicated structures. The most important feature of this institutional form is that it can perform all of the tasks local government delegates to it while acting as a private body. For example, it can:

- administer development funds from both public and private sources
- manage industrial estates or commercial facilities for the government
- operate parking facilities and other services as joint public–private ventures
- enter into contracts and borrow funds for various development projects
- engage in marketing and promotion activities
- provide a "one-stop" business service
- act as a small business assistance center
- provide marketing and technical assistance for local firms
- sponsor industrial and commercial attraction efforts

Clearly, a community development corporation is the most flexible structure for carrying out the multiple development tasks of dealing with poverty and social maladies in distressed communities. Nonetheless, we need to be mindful that

> we're not going to undo in ten years what it took 200 years to create. . . . If every CDC accomplished its goals, we would still not see the end of poverty. Poverty is the creation of the institutions we live in.. .CDC can be important to a larger agenda that addresses economic injustice. (Bauen and Reed, 1995, p. 15) (see Figure 13.3)

Figure 13.3   Local Development Corporation Model

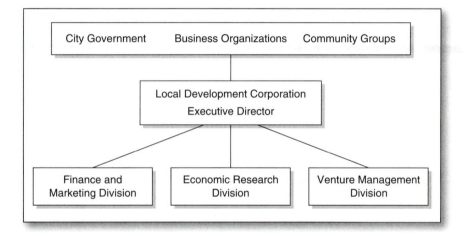

Summary of Institutional Approaches

Communities, regardless of their size, need to select an organizational form that meets their requirements. None of these forms is set in concrete: they can evolve over time, with components and functions being added or deleted as the need arises. There is no point in "reinventing the wheel," however. Adequate institutional development experience is available nationwide for communities to select a development framework to meet their needs. After the type of structure is selected, civic leaders can then tailor it to local circumstances.

Conclusion

Developing the correct organizational form is just as important as determining an economic development strategy. The form as well as the staffing will depend on the resources as well as the situation. Almost all economic development depends on public–private coordination and cooperation.

No matter what original forms of local economic development organization occur in a locality, it is likely that there will be pressures for them to change and adapt over time. In a 2012 report, "New Realities for Economic Development Organizations," Nourick (2012) observes: "EDOs of all sizes have been analyzing their strategic priorities and the practitioners' role in the community in order to be more effective and competitive in today's erratic economy" (p. 5).

In the aftermath of the Great Recession, economic development organizations have reduced funding from the traditional locally invested banks, utilities, and newspapers. They are turning to such disparate but locally vested entities such as hospitals, universities, cable companies, waste management companies, law firms, and auto dealerships (Nourick, 2012).

As public revenue has diminished, private funding of economic development has increased. The share of private-sector funding of economic development has grown from 30% in 1998 to 70% in 2011. As a consequence, economic development organizations must respond to increased pressure to track their performance in order to show what the return is to their investors. The trend toward private investor funding has also created greater pressure to demonstrate financial and organizational efficiency. This, in turn, is leading to more consolidations and mergers of economic development organizations (Nourick, 2012).

While more efficient use of resources is an important objective of economic development, a key question will be how well the multiple interests of local economic development (workers, firms, real estate, etc.) are met in the variations of consolidations and mergers that are taking shape.

References and Suggested Readings

Bauen, Rebecca, and Betsy Reed. 1995. Our Cities, Ourselves: The Community Movement in Adolescence. *Dollars and Sense* 197: 12–16.

Bradford, Calvin, et al. n.d. *Structural Disinvestment: A Problem in Search of a Policy.* Mimeo. Evanston, IL: Northwestern University for Urban Affairs.

Cummings, Scott, and Mark Glaser. 1983. An Examination of the Perceived Effectiveness of Community Development Corporations: A Pilot Study. *Journal of Urban Affairs* 5(4): 315–330.

Daniels, Belden, N. Barbe, and B. Siegle. 1981. Experience and Potentials for Community-Based Development. In *Expanding the Opportunity to Produce,* edited by R. Friedman, and W. Schweke. Washington, DC: Corporation for Enterprise Development.

Daniels, Belden, and Chris Tilly. 1981. Community Economic Development: Seven Guiding Principles. In *Resources,* edited by B. Daniels. Washington, DC: Congress for Community Economic Development.

Farr, Cheryl, ed. 1984. *Shaping the Local Economy: Current Perspectives on Economic Development.* Washington, DC: International City/County Management Association.

Gardner, Linda. 1978. *Community Economic Development Strategies: Vol. 1. Building the Base.* Berkeley, CA: National Economic Development and Law Center.

Haberfeld, Steven. 1981. Economic Planning in Economically Distressed Communities: The Need to Take a Partisan Perspective. *Economic Development and Law Center Report* (December).

Hein, B. 1987. *Strategic Planning for Community Economic Development.* Ames: Iowa State University Extension.

International Economic Development Council (IEDC). 2011. *Managing Economic Development Organizations* Training Manual, Washington, DC: Author.

Kane, Matt, and Peggy Sand. 1988. *Economic Development: What Works at the Local Level.* Washington, DC: National League of Cities.

Kotler, Milton. 1971. The Politics of Community Economic Development. *Law and Contemporary Society* 36(1): 3–12.

Nourick, Shari Alana. 2012. *New Realities for Economic Development Organizations.* Washington, DC: International Economic Development Council (IEDC).

Sagalyn, Lynne. 1990. Exploring the Improbable: Local Redevelopment in the Wake of Federal Cutbacks. *Journal of the American Planning Association* 56(4): 429–441.

Shanahan, Peter K. 1986. Economic Development at the Local Level: Public–Private Partnerships. *Australian Urban Studies* 13(4): n.p.

T.E.M. Associates, Inc. 1982. *Technical Assistance for the Revitalization of Communities.* Unpublished mimeo. Berkeley, CA: Author.

Weaver, Robert. 1991. Organizing and Staffing Economic Development Programs. In *Local Economic Development: Strategies for a Changing Economy,* edited by R. Scott Fosler. Washington, DC: International City/County Management Association.

Yin, Robert, and Douglas Yates. 1975. *Street Level Governments.* Lexington, MA: Lexington.

14

Local Economic Development Planning's Response to the Flatter and Climate-Challenged World

By now, it should be clear to students of local economic development planning that their field is complex and multifaceted. Local economic development may have been practiced in a simplistic manner in the past, but no locality can afford to make that mistake now nor hire local economic developers who do so. The ability of a local economy to thrive is contingent upon many factors, and those over which economic developers can and should have domain have been highlighted in this book. However, economic developers may also have a role to play in coordinating or facilitating responses to locality aspects that are not specifically their direct responsibility. For example, while disaster-management planning is not specifically the responsibility of the local economic developer, if such planning is not in place, all of the economic developer's and the locality's hard work can easily be wiped out through hurricanes, roaring fires, earthquakes or other natural disasters. Without excellent transportation systems (surface and air, private and public), efficient movement of goods and people cannot occur and economic development activity is stifled. Thus, economic developers often have to be advocates for transportation improvements. Likewise, they need to be advocates for an adequate supply of workforce housing in order to attract a competitive labor force. And they need to be advocates for quality health care and prekindergarten through high school education. These are essential building blocks for creating a quality labor force and a high quality of life that increases the community's attractiveness. In particular, a strong education system is a key requirement for economic development strategies that are focused on advanced technologies and processes.

412

In the final chapter of this book, we discuss technology and innovation economic development strategies that are an essential response to the flatter world, as well as economic development strategies necessary to cope with extreme weather events. We also discuss other essential strategies for protecting, growing, and even reinventing local economies.

Finding Solutions Through Technology and Innovation

It is important to note at the outset that, while technology and innovation are essential components of the response to climate change and maintaining competitiveness in a flatter world, they will by no means be the sole solution. Changes in lifestyle and ways of doing business that reduce dependence on carbon-based resources are required to minimize climate change and do not necessarily require new technological solutions. For example, it is essential to shift the predominant mode of transportation away from petroleum-fueled private automobiles and trucks by using existing mass transit technology and the lowest of technology (bicycles and feet!).

High technology became the "it" strategy of economic development during the final two decades of the 20th century and continues as the accepted economic engine for the 21st century but is now referred to by the more meaningful term *advanced technology*. The literature on attracting and retaining advanced technology firms reveals mixed results. The precise methods, as well as the factors that lead advanced-technology firms to select one community over another, are debated widely (Blakely and Nishikawa, 1992; Luger and Goldstein, 1991; Saxenian, 1987; Willoughby, 2000). Even after the dotcom bust of 2000, advanced-technology firms in the information sector remained the darlings of economic development specialists and local public officials. Public officials at every level continued to be enthusiastic in supporting efforts to attract, retain, or encourage new advanced/high-technology firms. Nearly every urban region in the Western world has a technology park and an advanced-technology strategy. Typically, these strategies use university resources and public facilities to create or incubate innovative firms with specialized technologies that can penetrate global markets. In the global economy with high firm mobility, localities have not abandoned firm-attraction strategies, especially of advanced-technology firms. However, they are also placing increasing emphasis on creating the conditions that will allow new advanced-technology firms to take root and make their corporate headquarters in the community à la Silicon Valley, the most powerful metaphor in high technology. In this region of California, just south of the San Francisco Bay Area, firms and multiple advanced-technology subsectors were not attracted but created.

In fact, most Western nations have embarked on advanced-technology strategies that emphasize both specific technologies and specific locations. For example, France, Sweden, Germany, Italy, and Japan have embarked on ambitious regional technology-development programs that pinpoint technologies as well as special human and physical infrastructure for specified localities. Within the United States, San Jose, Emeryville-Oakland, and San Diego in California; New York City; Cambridge, Massachusetts; Ogden, Utah; Austin, Texas; and the North Carolina Triangle are among the best-known and universally acknowledged technology success stories. The Japanese Technolopolis and Sophia Antipolis in France are the best examples of non-North American *techno-poles.* These special environments are the focus of many copycat policies aimed at stimulating new advanced-technology firms. However, Luger and Goldstein's observation back in 1991 still holds true:

> Research parks will be most successful in helping to stimulate economic development in regions that already are richly endowed with resources that attract highly educated scientists and engineers. This is not to say that regions with less rich endowments cannot have a high technology future, but more basic long-term investments in improving public higher education, environmental quality, and residential opportunities will be needed first. (pp. 183–184)

Empirical evidence has long suggested that advanced-technology development is nearly impossible to produce or purchase by traditional industrial incentives such as free land or low taxes (Luger and Goldstein, 1991). Rather, the evidence indicates that advanced technology firms are induced by the region's character. The economic development question is: Is it possible for a community that currently does not have the correct environment to create or stimulate one? In this chapter, we cannot answer this question categorically; however, we can suggest what communities will need at the various stages of technology development to examine and nurture their *innovation and technology development capacity* to start, retain, and sustain a high-technology firm environment.

The Technology Development Process

The range of support systems needed to encourage and foster advanced technology development are many and complex. Only a broad list of essential support structures is addressed in this chapter. The basic orientation we take is that the "soft infrastructure" (living amenities, cultural and educational institutions) sustains the "hard infrastructure" (money and physical) rather than the reverse. To plan for advanced technology, one must first understand how the technology process works. There are four stages, and the failure to provide the necessary supports at any one stage may ultimately inhibit the development of new products and industries.

High-Technology Regional Choice Model

The technology process is cyclical and interactive. Each stage in the process may revert back to or interact with a previous stage. For example, product failure spurs new research or a new phase of innovation. The process has its own support system requirements. In too many instances, the regional policy or program fails to recognize these distinct stages, and consequently fails to create the right environment at the right time. The basic infrastructure components for a technology-based economic development strategy can be described as follows:

1. *Research base.* Research identifies the basic scientific principles on which new technology industries or products are based. Research may be applied (designed to solve specific problems or have an application for a field of technology) or generic (nonspecific research in areas of continuing pertinence for a business enterprise). Targeted research may be market driven, guided by the knowledge of market requirements, or technology driven, guided by perceived capabilities of specific technology. Each field of research will also have its own peculiar support system. Most generic research is performed at national universities or laboratories, mainly with government funding. Most applied research is performed at large industrial labs. Many university communities have a set of research institutions with both the generic and applied/firm-based institutions. The communications or networks among research firms serve as the real incubators in economic development (Blakely and Nishikawa, 1992).

2. *Invention.* Inventions are products that may or may not arise directly from research. Often, they result from ideas that help to improve an operation's efficiency. In many cases, gadgets, devices, or programs are the result of invention. These are eventually developed and refined as new-technology products. A technology milieu creates an environment that stimulates more invention. Moreover, it is important to have in place organizations to assist in patent handling as well as creative financing in the community. It is no accident that places like Silicon Valley near San Francisco develop new firms. The San Francisco area has a very strong venture capital base and excellent legal services for scientists.

3. *Adaptation and development.* Adaptations resulting from research or invention modify or improve existing technology. Modifications of software, for example, improve the operation's efficiency.

   - The second stage in the process of technological development is product development. At this point, ideas, research principles, inventions, and adaptations are translated into an actual product. Prototype tests or models are built to evaluate the performance, application, and feasibility of developing the product to a commercial level. More detailed feasibility studies and some market research will be undertaken.

- Communities and regions can assist in the adaptation and development process by providing actual incubator facilities and creating technology or manufacturing zones so that firms can find suitable space for their initial operations.

4. *Innovation and dissemination.* The third stage in the process involves the commercialization of a new product or process. A company will decide to develop the product to manufacture or sell it. If it decides to manufacture, the firm may enter into joint venture or other production arrangements. Marketing, venture capital finance, and entrepreneurs will be important in the innovation and dissemination stage.

These first three stages in the technology process all represent investment costs. Through the manufacture or sale of new technology, a company should produce a return and recoup the cost of the product's creation. Production is the final stage of the process. Larger companies that have purchased or developed a high-tech product will manufacture and distribute it. Other companies will disseminate the production of components to subsidiaries to produce, for instance, chips and circuits. Constant marketing and monitoring of the product are essential during the production stage. Regular feedback to research and development and marketing is essential in order to continue to improve a product or terminate the production before it reaches the end of the technology life cycle.

To facilitate the development process, a community has to provide "places to meet." These places range from convention centers to restaurants and theater areas. This "soft infrastructure" can be as important as physical roads, sewers, and special industrial parks.

Regional/Community Support Systems for Advanced Technology

During each stage of the technological process, a complex range of support systems is required to ensure that the application of research or ideas is carried through to the production stage. Advanced technology development requires timely and totally integrated support systems. Advanced-technology firms have a complex and interrelated set of special requirements based on their stage of development as well as their size, technology base, and global market position.

In Table 14.1, support systems are depicted against the development stages discussed previously.

Table 14.1   Requirements for Industries by State of Technology Process

Requirement	Research	Development	Diffusion	Production
Information	Social interaction	Center/hotel	Innovation centers	Publication
Communication	Library			
Strategic relationship	Database		Information bureaus	Marketing
Human resources	Research scientists Inventors	Skilled technical staff	Entrepreneurs Venture capitalists	Management Skilled workforce
Education and research facilities	University research institute	Research labs	Conference facilities	Community college Technical institutes
Environmental quality	Quality living and working environment	Quality living and working environment	Quality living and working environment	Quality living and working environment
Government support	Government contracts for applied research Offsets	Joint ventures	Information support services	Offsets Export incentives
Finance	Research grants	Private investments and venture capital	Private investments and venture capital	Institution finance
Technology image	Quality residential areas	Reputation among luminaries	Clear identification with specialized tech firms	Top-quality companies
Enterprise facilities	Research institutes University and national labs	Incubator innovation Building centers Labs	Incubator innovation Building centers Labs	Technology, business, and quality industrial parks
Infrastructure	Basic infrastructure for research facilities	Research stations Testing areas	Research stations Testing areas	Fiber optics Airports Waste disposal

Fostering the Advanced-Technology Community

Creating an environment that maximizes information exchange, face-to-face communications, and the formation of strategic relationships is key to successful advanced technology development. These networks or channels of both information and exchange of capital and expertise form the nucleus for the other physical, social, economic, and environmental systems needed to support advanced technology industrial development.

Human Resources

Human resources, in terms of skills, know-how, and entrepreneurship, are essential for advanced-technology development. Most people involved in the research phase of development will have postbaccalaureate degrees, and often will have multidisciplinary skills.

Social skills in dealing effectively with people from a variety of cultures and foreign languages are essential in globally based enterprises. These skills develop as the result of peer group association and interaction during forums of scientific and social interest. One of the hallmarks of Silicon Valley has been the high level of social interaction that developed between scientists in one locality.

During the development and dissemination phase, the most important resource is the marketing department. Social entrepreneurial skills are an essential link between product development and production capital. Trained financial marketing depends on a human resource support system that can promote the products and bring in the venture capital. Special marketing, finance, and management skills are required in the final stage of the technology process, when a product is manufactured.

Advanced technology regions have been characterized by a high degree of employment mobility. This is partly due to the rapidly changing nature and high failure rates of technology enterprises. In addition, many individuals do not want to be bound to companies and prefer contractual or project-based employment. Most businesses look upon this favorably, as it reduces problems with staff retrenchments in economic downturns or at the end of technology life cycles. This mobility also encourages considerable interchanges of staff, and hence ideas, within companies and research centers, providing a convenient means for refresher courses.

Education and Research Facilities

Another important support system for advanced technology development is the presence of a university or technical institute of international standing that encompasses science and research. Evidence from studies carried out in the United States and elsewhere suggests that universities play a direct role in generating advanced-tech research. Further, their affiliated research institutes, often with a specialized focus, emphasize applied research and can be major catalysts for advanced technology development. Stanford Research Institute, for example, was one of the important ingredients in propelling the original high-tech development in Silicon Valley, California Such institutes might be privately or publicly funded, and may consist of one or more centers.

Just as important as these institutes are research laboratories and incubator establishments, which can be tied to major companies like Bell Laboratories and the Wang Research Institute. There is a tendency for major companies to form, or parcel out, work to subsidiary companies whose activities specifically involve research and development. Government research centers are also important in this process. Many are involved with generic or pure research.

Although universities, research institutes, and laboratories perform an important educational function in the process of technology development, strong support is essential at the secondary education level to provide future research scientists and innovators as well as technical workers. Students at high schools require strong basic math and science skills, computer literacy, and some training in research methods to gain employment in technology-based enterprises (Leigh and Walcott, 2003).

Environmental Quality and Community Amenities

The quality of the environment in which people would live and work can have a significant effect on whether an individual chooses to live in one locality or another. Experience throughout the world indicates that personnel involved in research and development choose to live in high-quality residential environments with good amenities as well as cultural, commercial, and educational facilities.

Business and Support Institutions

Although universities and research institutes play a significant role in promoting new advanced technology-based enterprises, major corporations and institutions that have research and development sections attached to their operations also can stimulate growth and clustering of technology industries. Many large American companies have defense contracts, which have been the principal stimulus behind numerous high-technology developments. Other companies in the pharmaceutical, medical, chemical, bio-and nanotechnology fields have generated spinoffs of advanced technology enterprises.

Many state and local governments recruit technology branch plants as the basis for forming a high-tech economic base under the (mistaken) belief that new firms will emerge from these branch operations and establish headquarters in their locality. Research indicates there is very little spinoff of new firms away from the research headquarters' locations (with the exception of software development). If a company moves its headquarters or a major division and product lines to a community, it usually continues to use its own internal support systems for servicing the branch operations.

However, a community that successfully implements a strategy of incubating or starting small tech firms may be able to create an agglomeration of technology industries within the region or locality. When this occurs, the multiplier effect of technology development is significant since R&D businesses pick up contracts from these larger companies.

Small companies are part of the technology life cycle of product development. Many never survive to grow into large firms, and instead become part of larger operations. There is a trend in recent years to establish innovation centers to encourage the development of small-scale businesses involved in advanced technology. Many of these have failed partly because they were too far removed from the major businesses they served. Innovation centers are more likely to succeed when located close to major users or developers of advanced-technology products and research institutions.

The importance of institutions as catalysts for advanced technology development has often been overlooked in the belief that the greatest spinoffs come from corporations. Medicine is one of the sciences in which research is expanding rapidly; hospitals are a base for much of that research. As hospitals become more specialized, there is a greater need for more precise instruments, drugs, vaccines, and equipment. Advanced technology firms have considerable opportunities to take advantage of these institutions' needs.

Government institutions that are catalysts for high-tech are telecommunications, government science laboratories, agriculture and marine research centers, defense, and administrative services. The last group is becoming increasingly dependent on substantial data storage and retrieval systems and processing. The obvious benefits of defense institutions are well documented, but the opportunities to develop advanced technology industries that serve the special requirements of other government institutions are numerous.

Enterprise or Incubator Facilities

Enterprise facilities describe the buildings, areas, or estates necessary to carry out business associated with high technology. Some of these would be developed as part of other support systems—for example, universities, research institutes, research laboratories, and innovation and conference centers.

There are four specialized development areas that can house new businesses: research and science parks, high-tech parks, business parks, and high-quality industrial estates. Their typical forms are described below.

Research park. A high-quality, low-density physical development in a park-like setting, where there is significant interaction between academics, researchers involved in research and product development, and commercial organizations and entrepreneurs.

Science park. An innovation center containing research and development enterprises that can also include light industrial production relating to scientific research and appropriate ancillary services.

Technology park. A collection of advanced technology industries concerned with both research and manufacturing, located in attractive, well-landscaped surroundings and situated within a reasonable service area of a scientific university or major institute.

Business park. A prestigious environment, suitable for a wide range of activities, including manufacturing, assembly, sales, and other office-based activities. There is no requirement for these parks to be close to academic institutions.

High-quality industrial park. These parks have attractive features for certain forms of contemporary light industry.

There are many benefits to be gained by new industries being located in specialized, well-marked facilities, namely, good services, shared facilities, a high-quality environment, and flexible planning conditions.

Advanced technology workers expect quality entertainment, dining, and retail outlets. These outlets are also important in developing associations between people involved in research and development and high-tech industries. These associations allow ideas to be expressed on an informal basis and help circulate knowledge.

Because many people involved in the fields of science, research, and development are generally highly paid, most of them expect higher levels of service and are prepared to pay for it. Their desire for expensive housing and quality schools is very attractive to communities seeking to raise their level of economic development.

Not all localities can expect to become centers of innovation and advanced technology development. However, every community can better prepare its human resources and incorporate new technologies such as advanced telecommunications into its public infrastructure. In so doing, it maximizes its ability to stay competitive in the new economy.

With broader acceptance of climate challenges and Smart Growth goals, we can expect the typical greenfield location and low-density development patterns of the four types described above to be altered in the future. Indeed, in the future, the most innovative research and business activities may be expected to seek out parks and facilities that meet the physical standards of sustainable development. For example, a June 2008 joint conference of the Association of University Research Parks (AURP) and BIO's Council of Biotechnology Centers featured a session titled "Innovation: Green From the Ground Up," which focused on creating LEED-certified green research parks (AURP, 2008). Further, Piedmont Triad Research Park (PTRP) in Winston-Salem, North Carolina, has adopted the LEED (which stands for Leadership in Energy and Environmental Design) rating system developed by the U.S. Green Building Council for the park's infrastructure and research centers. These standards require the use of construction materials that are renewable, do not harm the environment, and use less energy than those found in conventional construction. As quoted in the *Winston-Salem Journal*, the president of the research park, Doug Edgeton, observed:

> Sustainable-development practices are consistent with the mission and values of our tenant population. . . . Our effort to be better stewards of the environment and create a sustainable place further reinforces PTRP as a place where innovation lives. (quoted in Craver, 2008)

Globalization is rapidly changing the prospects for advanced-technology local economic development strategies in the United States and other advanced industrialized nations. The outsourcing of tech jobs to India and elsewhere that was discussed in the opening chapter of this book is a significant threat to these strategies. At the same time, "reshoring," or the bringing back of jobs to the United States, has been occurring in a number of firms because of dissatisfaction with outsourced performance or conditions becoming more competitive in the United States. What the long-term balance between outsourced or reshored (i.e., domestic) jobs will be is unknown, and so are the impacts on U.S. local economic development. However, what is clear is that strong school systems from prekindergarten through university are essential to maintain a competitive position in the global economy. The reason U.S. firms can outsource research and analytical jobs to India is because India has a large supply of well-educated research scientists and other professions who receive a fraction of the compensation of their U.S. counterparts. Of course, it is technology in the form of advanced communications and logistics systems that allows the export of some of the most advanced employment for developing technology and new innovations.

Advanced Manufacturing and Clean Technology

In recent years, advanced technology is increasingly being deployed to transform manufacturing and to shift all sectors of the economy to cleaner or greener production and processes. The federal government has taken concerted steps to promote advanced manufacturing, which it defines as

> a family of activities that (a) depend on the use and coordination of information, automation, computation, software, sensing, and networking, and/or (b) make use of cutting-edge materials and emerging capabilities enabled by the physical and biological sciences, for example nanotechnology, chemistry, and biology. This involves both new ways to manufacture existing products, and especially the manufacture of new products emerging from new advanced technologies. (www.manufacturing.gov)

The Obama administration believes "The nation's long-term ability to innovate and compete in the global economy greatly benefits from co-location of manufacturing and manufacturing-related R&D activities in the United States" (www.manufacturing.gov). This leadership at the national level can be seen as a clear rejection of the idea that advanced economies are postindustrial or service economies. Going back to the fundamentals for local economic development planning that contribute to stability and resiliency (the latter to be discussed in detail later in this chapter), an advanced economy should have a diverse composition of advanced industrial and service sectors.

To remain globally competitive, it will also be necessary for advanced manufacturing to contribute to the growing expectations of the international green economy. The U.S. Department of Commerce has a "sustainable manufacturing" program that encourages industrial processes and products that conserve natural resources and generate less pollution. The national network of Manufacturing Extension Partnerships helps smaller manufacturers with innovation and competiveness in emerging sustainable industries.

The Organisation for Economic Co-operation and Development (OECD), made up of 34 countries, including the United States, has developed a sustainable manufacturing index and guidebook to help firms become more sustainable. The index and guidebook are also useful to economic developers seeking to promote more sustainable production activity in their communities. There are 18 indicators identified that are grouped into three key areas of manufacturing: inputs, operations, and products (see Table 14.2).

The move toward the green economy will naturally have an impact on the workforce, and local economic development efforts are increasingly focusing on creating green jobs. The U.S. Department of Labor defines green jobs to be those "in businesses that produce goods or provide services that benefit the environment or conserve natural resources."

Manufacturing typically offers above-average pay and benefits to workers with a wide range of skills and job titles. This should particularly be the case for advanced manufacturing jobs. However, the U.S. industrial workforce has significant skill gaps and is also rapidly aging, making it difficult for employers

Table 14.2   Sustainable Manufacturing Indicators Specified by the OECD

Inputs	Operations	Products
Nonrenewable materials intensity	Water intensity	Recycled/reused content
Restricted substances intensity	Energy intensity	Recyclability
Recycled/reused content	Renewable proportion of energy	Renewable materials content
	Greenhouse gas intensity	Nonrenewable materials intensity
	Air releases intensity	
	Water releases intensity	
	Proportion of natural land	

Source: http://www.oecd.org/document/48/0,3746,en_21571361_47075996_47855728_1_1_1_1,00
.html

to fill jobs in emerging advanced and/or sustainable industries. Compounding the problem are surveys that found parents generally do not want their children working in manufacturing. Unless this is corrected through workforce strategies that promote manufacturing as a career option, local economic developers will have great difficulty helping their community either grow an advanced manufacturing firm from a local invention or attract one from elsewhere (Hoelzel and Leigh, 2012).

An additional critical challenge for local economic developers seeking to foster advanced and sustainable industry in their communities stems from what has often been a contentious relationship between industry and communities, as well as pressures to convert existing industrial land to residential and commercial uses. The negative image of industry held in many communities is largely associated with traditional industry, which, for good reason, was kept separate from residential and commercial development. Today's industry is cleaner and has a lighter imprint on the land, but attitudes and land use regulations are slow to take this into account. Consequently, opportunities for economic development are being missed. However, there are some forward-thinking cities in the United States (notably Brooklyn, San Francisco, Seattle, Chicago, Minneapolis, and Philadelphia) that are adopting proactive policies to retain industrial land that economic developers can learn from (Leigh and Hoelzel, 2012).

Resiliency in Local Economic Development

The economic and environmental crises of U.S. cities in recent years have generated a growing planning and policy focus on resiliency in economic development as well as other aspects of city systems. The increasing use of phrases such as *the resilient economy* or *resilient city* or *resilient region* may give the impression that this is a term and a movement that supercedes efforts to create the sustainable economy or city or region. We take the view that these are not competing terms or efforts; rather, resiliency is a framework nested within that of a larger framework of sustainability. That is, recalling the definition of sustainable local economic development upon which this book is based, we pursue SLED to preserve and raise the standard of living through a process of human and physical development based on principles of equity and sustainability. This requires achieving a minimum standard of living for all that increases over time while reducing inequality and fostering environmentally benign resource use and production. Resiliency has been defined as "the capacity of a region to respond effectively to a shock, such as the effects of realigning or declining industries, a national economic recession, or a natural disaster" (U.S. HUD, 2012). If the local economy or region is truly resilient, then its standard of living, levels of equality, and environmentally benign resource use and production will not be diminished by any major economic shock or extreme weather event.

In a major initiative focused on building resilient regions funded by the MacArthur Foundation, significant analyses have been made of the kinds of shock that can occur and how specific characteristics of regional or local economies affect their ability to recover. Hill and colleagues (2011) delineate three causes of economic shock. They can be due to (1) downturns in the national economy, (2) downturns in particular industries that constitute an important component of the local economy's export base, or (3) other external events (i.e., natural disaster, military base closure, exit of a major firm). Hill and colleagues define whether an economy demonstrates resilience or nonresilience to a shock as follows: "A region is *resilient* if, within four years of the onset of the downturn, its annual growth rate returns to the eight-year growth rate prior to the year the downturn occurred. If it does not do so within four years, we term it *non-resilient*" (p. 7).

Hill and company's analysis of metropolitan regional economies yielded a number of important findings for local economic development, four of which are highlighted here. First, while economies with a higher proportion of employment in durable goods manufacturing tend to experience more downturns and to be less shock resistant, they also demonstrate resilience more quickly. Second, economies are more shock resistant when they have greater numbers of major export industries, and when they have greater industrial diversity. Third, economies that are less shock resistant have lower education levels (high school degree or less). And fourth, economies with higher income inequality experience more downturns and take longer to recover.

In other research associated with the Building Resilient Regions initiative, Foster, author of Figure 14.1, developed a Resilience Capacity Index (RCI) that ranked 361 metro areas using 12 indicators in 3 capacity categories: regional economic, socio-demographic, and community connectivity. Of the three categories depicted in Figure 14.1, we will explore in more depth those under the regional economic capacity category: income equality, economic diversification, regional affordability, and business environment. Income equality is included in the index because regions that have more equal distribution of economic resources are hypothesized to respond more cohesively to shock (Cutter et al., 2010). Economic diversification is included because having economic activity spread more widely across industrial sectors means that business cycle impacts or industry shocks are lessened. The regional affordability indicator measures the proportion of an economy's households that pay more than 35% of their income on housing. Housing cost exceeding 35% of income is typically thought of as excessive (for example, homebuyers generally cannot obtain mortgages when payments would exceed 35% of their income) and suggests the household would have less spending and investment flexibility during

Figure 14.1   Resilience Capacity Index (RCI)

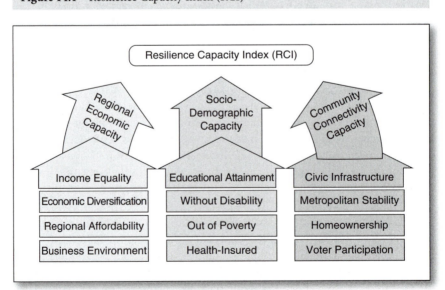

Source: Kathryn A. Foster, University at Buffalo Regional Institute and MacArthur Foundation Research Network on Building Resilient Regions. *Graphic design by Beuving Creative, Inc.*

a crisis. The business environment indicator seeks to capture how economically dynamic an economy is, with greater dynamism associated with factors such as higher proportions of small businesses, high levels of business churn (starts and stops), and residential high-speed Internet connections.

Having discussed economic development characteristics associated with resiliency, the next section focuses on what local economic development planning can due to promote resiliency after an environmental or economic crisis.

Local Economic Development Planning for Resiliency

A key role for economic developers is that of helping communities adjust to the economic changes that are causing or may cause serious structural damage to their underlying economic base. These changes may occur overnight or over a long period of time and result from industrial or corporate restructuring, new federal laws and regulations, reductions in defense expenditures, and depletion of natural resources or natural disasters. On top of this in the present era, local economies are still reeling from the unfortunate set of trends caused by institutional and international monetary missteps. For example, as was discussed previously in this book, the Federal Reserve's loosening of oversight and requirements for the home mortgage industry caused a subprime mortgage crisis that became international in scope while deeply affecting individual homeowners, local finance institutions, entire neighborhoods, and cities.

Because of the national dependency on oil to run the United States and other national economies, jumps in its price can raise the cost of doing business and moving goods and people in the economy to hardship levels in many communities. As petroleum is the basic input into the plastics and related industries, it is an essential input to much of what modern society consumes. Hence, unprecedented inflation in the basic consumer basket also began to accompany the subprime financial market collapse when fuel prices were also rising. While the rise in oil and gas prices has subsided, it should be a forewarning to many communities. Substantial increases in the cost of oil and gas threaten the middle-class lifestyle and create particular hardships for working-class families. Shifting to a greener, less petroleum-dependent economy now will ensure that the preview of what rapidly escalating prices can due to our national and local economies won't turn into a long-running nightmare.

If local communities have not already created a resiliency plan, let us hope the Great Recession and recent environmental disasters around the world will motivate them to do so, thereby helping to protect them from negative impacts of future economic and societal changes.

The Center for Community Enterprise (2001) defines a resilient community as one that "takes intentional action to enhance the personal and collective

capacity of its citizens to respond and influence the course of social and economic change" (p. 5). It has identified 23 characteristics of resilient communities that fall into four major categories: people, organizations, resources, and
community process (see Table 14.3).

Table 14.3   Characteristics of Resilient Communities

People
1. Leadership is representative of the community.
2. Elected community leadership is visionary, shares power, and builds consensus.
3. Community members are involved in significant community decisions.
4. The community feels a sense of pride.
5. People feel optimistic about the future of the community.
6. There is a spirit of mutual assistance and cooperation in the community.
7. People feel a sense of attachment to their community.
8. The community is self-reliant and looks to itself and its own resources to address major issues.
9. There is a strong belief in and support for education at all levels.
Organizations
10. There are a variety of community economic development (CED) organizations in the community such that the key CED functions are well served.
11. Organizations in the community have developed partnerships and collaborative working relationships.
Resources
12. Employment in the community is diversified beyond a single large employer.
13. Major employers in the community are locally owned.
14. The community has a strategy for increasing independent local ownership.
15. There is openness to alternative ways of earning a living and economic activity.
16. The community looks outside itself to seek and secure resources (skills, expertise, and finance) that will address identified areas of weakness.
17. The community is aware of its competitive position in the broader economy.

Community Process

18. The community has a community economic development plan that guides its development.

19. Citizens are involved in the creation and implementation of the community vision and goals.

20. There is ongoing action toward achieving the goals in the CED plan.

21. There is regular evaluation of progress toward the community's strategic goals.

22. Organizations use the CED plan to guide their actions.

23. The community adopts a development approach that encompasses all segments of the population.

Source: Reprinted with permission from Centre for Community Enterprise, The Community Resilience Project, http://www.globalfacilitators.org/VirtLib/Resilience/CommunityResilienceGuide .pdf

That local businesses have a great stake in creating community resiliency is persuasively argued by David Honour, editor of *Continuity Central* (see Box 14.1). Continuity planning is an activity in which businesses engage to enable the resumption of critical functions when a disaster or other disruption is experienced. Businesses should see community resiliency planning as an extension of their continuity planning because much of their success is dependent on a well-functioning community. Thus, businesses and local government and other economic development actors should view each other as important allies working together to create and implement community resiliency plans.

| Box 14.1 | Community Resilience: The Next Stage in Business Community Thinking? |

Companies and entities that are new to business continuity often focus their efforts solely within the boundaries of their organization. As their business continuity arrangements mature, their horizon expands to include supply chain vulnerabilities and any threats posed by the activities of other companies located close by. This is where many business continuity managers stop. But there is a further dimension to business continuity planning that the profession's innovators are starting to consider: the importance of community resilience.

(Continued)

(Continued)

No business exists in a vacuum; it has dependencies on its local community. Employees, suppliers, and customers may all come from the local area. The availability of all critical infrastructures is dependent on the local "last mile." If the community is impacted, then the business is also impacted. Good business continuity planning, therefore, needs to take into account dependencies in the local community and, for self-preservation rather than for altruistic reasons, needs to become involved in helping enhance the resilience of the local community.

There is a temptation for businesses to see community resilience as solely the role of the local authorities and emergency services. After all, these bodies have the statutory responsibility for emergency planning and disaster response. However, in a wide-area disaster, your company will be just one of many voices clamoring for help, and you will have no guarantee of assistance in time to meet your recovery time objectives. For an initial period, at least, communities often need to support themselves in times of disaster, and such self-help is much more likely to be effective if some level of planning has taken place.

The first step is to determine what makes up the local community for your organization. This will have different layers, each layer presenting different risk levels and therefore requiring more or less input and effort.

For example, if a business leases an office in a tenanted building in a business park on the outskirts of a town, it may have the following layers to its local community:

- The building layer: the community of other businesses that share the premises with it
- The business park layer: the community of other enterprises that are located in the immediate vicinity
- The surrounding suburb
- The town

The next step is to determine the stakeholders and community groups that you will need to work with within each layer.

After this, you can begin to take positive measures. These could include the following:

1. Working alongside local authority planners to support business continuity awareness raising and education among other businesses in the community

2. Creating a local business resilience group and inviting other local businesses to join. Joint activities could include:

   - Having regular forums to discuss business continuity and share ideas
   - Conducting tests and exercises

- Carrying out a community risk assessment and BIA. This may bring up new threats that you were previously unaware of
- Making a group subscription to work-area recovery space
- Agreeing to share a mobile recovery facility in the event of a disaster
- Jointly funding a business continuity consultant to provide services to the group members or to provide group training sessions
- On a more ambitious level, the local business resilience group could build and manage its own local recovery center
- The local business resilience group could also be an effective forum to liaise with local first responders about emergency credentialing, agreeing in advance which staff can enter a police cordon and providing appropriate ID and training for these people.
- The group could develop a joint local business continuity information and emergency communications portal. See http://www .continuitycentral.com/news03449.htm for an example of this from the United States.

3. Working with employees in their community setting—for example, making work-area recovery choices based on commuting zones rather than the main office location and enabling resilient home working to prevent transport disruptions from affecting business continuity. This could also include being aware of local incidents, which, while not impacting any company premises, have affected homes and communities of employees. Support could be offered to help with areas such as transport, child care, and rehousing to ensure the well-being of the employees and to enable a rapid return to productivity.

4. If you are a larger company, it may be appropriate to offer the services of your business continuity team as volunteers to support local authorities' business continuity planning activities. These are likely to be stretched for time and budget, and your support may be well received.

As well as making sense from a business continuity point of view, community resilience also fits well into the current trend for companies to take corporate social responsibility (CSR) seriously. CSR is a growing requirement of good reputation management and, in many countries, medium and large companies are now expected to have a CSR policy. To include community resilience activities within the remit of CSR could be a win-win situation, ensuring that the business is seen to have the community's needs at heart while at the same time bringing tangible benefits to the business itself.

Source: Adapted from "Community resilience: The next stage in business community thinking?" *Community Central,* June 2008. © Continuity Central Portal Publishing Ltd.

The 2005 devastation of New Orleans and the Gulf Coast by Hurricanes Katrina and Rita and the 2011 tornado-driven havoc that Joplin, Missouri, and many Midwestern and Southern communities experienced illustrate the difficulties and complexities of the disaster-recovery process. They also show how much better prepared for recovery communities could be by engaging in predisaster or resiliency planning. Plans need to be tailored to the nature of the disaster that one may reasonably foresee for a community—that is, a plan for a possible tornado in the Midwest may look very different than for a possible hurricane on the Gulf Coast. Further, there is a range of disasters for which the community should proactively plan to minimize impacts on economic development, for example, water shortages, company closings, or terrorist attacks.

The economic portion of the plan will also vary significantly from community to community, because it should be developed to address the specific needs of the local economy as defined by area businesses and infrastructure assets of critical importance to the economy. For example, by building into the local business retention and expansion database information about suppliers and distributors, the local economic development organization has the needed information to facilitate employers rebuilding these networks in the aftermath of a disaster.

Having the ability to do so brings to the forefront one of the key preparedness factors to facilitate recovery: availability of data and contact information. In addition to encouraging their local businesses to do so, part of disaster preparedness is the economic development organizations themselves backing up all data to a site outside of the immediate area—recommendations have been made for distances as far as 500 miles away, which can be accomplished by using an Internet "cloud" data-storage service—so that this information can be accessed in the immediate aftermath. Included in the economic development organization's off-site data backup should be local businesses' contact information, including phone, email, and physical addresses. Even when using a "cloud," redundancies in backup locations provide even greater protection.

Joplin, Missouri, was hit by an EF5 multiple-vortex tornado on May 22, 2011, with winds over 200 miles per hour. It left 161 dead and destroyed more than 7,000 homes and nearly 550 businesses as well as key institutions. A year after the tornado hit, 429 of the businesses that were either destroyed or damaged were up and running. The Joplin Area Chamber of Commerce partially attributes its community's successful reopening of about 80% of its businesses to the organizational continuity planning the Chamber engaged in prior to the May 22, 2011, tornado. Within 3 weeks of the tornado, the Chamber staff was able to make contact with all 530 employers by walking the streets (facilitated by added capacity from volunteers from other chambers in the region), which provided these businesses with a sense of someone being in charge of and committed to their individual business and overall community economic recovery, fueling the optimism needed to rebuild. Further, part of the Chamber's planning included designating emergency meeting locations, which it used along with SMS text messages to reconnect to employees and key local business owners. By being accessible to area businesses, the Chamber could be a source of providing reliable information regarding utilities, cleanup and rebuilding, and business services, which reinforced confidence for rebuilding. If the Chamber had not planned for its own organizational continuity, it may not have been as well positioned to facilitate that 80% rebuild rate.[1]

The impact of having a positive, unified voice of leadership for rebuilding can be highly effective, as Charleston, South Carolina, found in the aftermath of 1989's Hurricane Hugo. The decision by President Harry Lightsey to open the College of Charleston just 7 days after the hurricane was met with skepticism, but soon thereafter—and more than 20 years later—continues to be cited as having had an important positive psychological impact for rebuilding.[2]

The International Economic Development Council (IEDC) was an early entry in the growing awareness of predisaster planning, specifically with regard to planning for economic recovery, as it immediately stepped in to provide support to its members and peers in the Gulf Coast in 2005 (see www.restorey oureconomy.org). What began as a peer-to-peer volunteer effort evolved into a wider effort of educating economic development professionals regarding the importance of advancing disaster preparedness and postdisaster economic recovery planning. Additional organizations engaged in supporting predisaster planning activities include Community & Regional Resilience Institute (CARRI), the National Association of Development Organizations (NADO), Business Civic Leadership Center (BCLC), and the Association of Chamber of Commerce Executives.

IEDC's and its partners' efforts have resulted in the outline of a framework for predisaster planning. Not just the plan but the process itself should be tailored to the community and inclusive of all the relevant stakeholder groups for economic development, that is, representatives of local government, employers, business service providers, economic assets (for example, the local airport and prominent tourist destinations), infrastructure (roads, water, sewer, electric, telecommunications, etc.), workforce development (K–12 and higher education), hospitals and other large health care providers, and local lending institutions, foundations, and other organizations that can be a source of loans or grants for planning or recovering activities.

---

[1]Wellemeyer, Jonathan, International Economic Development Council. (2012). *Setting economic development priorities before and after a disaster: Joplin's experience.* http:// restoreyoureconomy.org/?p=1524.

[2]Graham, Mary, Senior Vice President of Public Policy, Charleston Metro Chamber of Commerce. *Community resilience and rapid recovery of the business sector.* Community & Regional Resilience Institute. Accessed March 12, 2012, from http://www.resilientus .org/library/Mary_Graham_1246387237.pdf.

As outlined by IEDC, the planning process for preparing for disaster is best focused on:

(1) Clarifying roles and responsibilities both in the planning and recovery phases

(2) Developing an understanding of economic assets and their potential vulnerabilities and strategic actions to shore up those vulnerabilities predisaster and address them postdisaster

(3) Writing a clear communications plan and contact information backed up in an Internet cloud or other off-site location

(4) Identifying and then making available a list of identified funding and support systems at the federal, state, regional, and local levels

(5) Integrating this plan with other relevant community plans and regularly revisiting and updating the plan, contact list, and funding and support system list. [3]

Through the restoreyoureconomy.org website, IEDC has also provided recommendations in the areas of engaging businesses in their own continuity or disaster-preparedness planning, building capacity to support recovery, developing business-recovery financing options, redevelopment planning (including land use and building code considerations), and workforce planning (including housing, training, retention, and transportation considerations). These activities could also be built into a predisaster planning process.

There are so many business recovery needs to address in predisaster planning—for example, capital, infrastructure, workforce, customers, technical assistance, and insurance—that the process can be overwhelming. With limited funding and time capacity to engage in proactive planning, it unfortunately often takes a disaster to motivate predisaster planning for the next one. An economic development organization can take the lead in encouraging preparedness by engaging in its own organizational continuity planning, like the Joplin Area Chamber, and by educating stakeholders and businesses about the much more substantial economic loss that can occur without the preparedness activities.

Conclusion: The Future of Local Economic Development Planning

As stated at the outset of this book, the United States is enmeshed in the global market system as leader, follower, and participant. Smart local economic and political decision makers are not surrendering their communities' fate to

---

[3]This bullet list is adapted from the International Economic Development Council manual *Economic Development Strategic Planning*, revised November 2011.

chance, the marketplace, or unsupportive federal policies. Growing concern over widening inequality and global warming that has accompanied past economic development is galvanizing those who seek sustainable economic development planning and bringing converts from those who have engaged in traditional economic development planning and practice.

The final section of this chapter and book discusses four local economic development strategies that local economic developers can pursue to foster structural change in practice. We call these the new fundamentals for local economic development planning: entrepreneurial, green, culturally adaptive, and knowledge based strategies.

Four Strategies to Foster Structural Change in Local Economic Development Planning and Practice

The four strategies to foster structural change can go a long way toward fostering the characteristics of resilient communities identified in Table 14.3.

The entrepreneurial strategy focuses on forming local businesses and job creation from within the local economy. It requires a critical mass of entrepreneurs, strong support networks, and a community ready for change, seeking innovation, and willing to take risks (Lichtenstein, Lyons, and Kutzhanova, 2004). The strategy relies on the creation of social and professional networks. These networks connect business owners with service providers as well as grant access to resources, materials, labor, financing, and new markets.

The second local economic development strategy is based on ecofriendliness or green development. There are a number of elements that can be found in the ecofriendly strategy, including green business, green building, waste management/ diversion business, brownfield redevelopment, greenspace development, ecotourism, and ecoindustrial development. These elements provide opportunities for new firm and employment creation, create demands for innovation, and use traditional marketing and recruitment skills aimed at attracting those who prioritize sustainability.

The third economic development strategy focuses on creating a culturally adaptive community. This type of community is one that sees its changing population as a source of assets to capitalize on, or seeks to use the arts and culture as an economic development tool. These scenarios are not mutually exclusive. Despite the lack of community support, high housing poverty, poor English skills, and underemployment, ethnic populations have managed to build businesses and communities throughout rural and urban America. They are becoming an essential part of rural communities and central cities, adding children to declining schools, businesses to decaying main streets, and arts to dying towns. The culturally adaptive strategy requires economic developers to tailor traditional small business development approaches to meet the needs of different groups. This can include providing translation of business support materials into appropriate languages, or linking ethnic and minority business to corporate networks that can buy their products or services. Providing targeted workshops, training, and venture capital are other fundamental steps.

The final economic development strategy is the knowledge-based strategy. This strategy prioritizes the development of human capital from early childhood education on, the creation of a skilled labor force, and the fostering of innovation and creativity to spur new businesses and sources of employment. Knowledge-based communities are defined by the specific resources at their disposal. These can include businesses or private sector community members, other community development organizations, as well as educational or research institutions, such as universities and colleges. Public–private partnerships are common. A distinguishing characteristic of knowledge-based communities is that they view the educational system not only as a vehicle for labor force development, but as one that can improve equity (School Communities That Work, 2002) and lead to "shared growth" where there is a "broad distribution of opportunities for meaningful participation in the economy and enjoyment of the benefits of an increased standard of living" (Schweke, 2004, p. 3).

In concluding this book, we cannot overemphasize that these are challenging but exciting times for local economic development planning and practice. Economic developers have a critical role to play in helping communities to respond to the flatter, climate-challenged world. Traditional economic development practice will not be adequate to create sustainable economic development and to counter widening trends of inequality. In order to serve their communities well, local economic developers will need a deep understanding of the major forces impacting local economies. Further, local economic developers must direct their efforts to helping communities implement innovative and thoughtful strategies for creating sustainable and resilient economies.

References and Suggested Readings

Association of University Research Parks (AURP). 2008. Accessed June 28, 2008 from http://www.aurp.net/bioparks2008/program/index.cfm

Berube, Alan. 2007. *MetroNation: Now U.S. Metropolitan Areas Fuel American Prosperity*, November 6. Accessed November 22, 2008 from http://www.brookings .edu/reports/2007/1106_metronation_berube.aspx

Blakely, Edward J., Brian Roberts, and Philip Manidis. 1988. Inducing High Tech: Principles of Designing Support Systems for the Formation and Attraction of

Advanced Technology Firms. *International Journal of Technology Management* 2(3–4): 337–356.

Blakely, Edward J., and Nancy Nishikawa. 1992. Inducing High Technology Firms: State Economic Development Strategies for Biotechnology. *Economic Development Quarterly* 6(3): 241–254.

Case, John. 1992. *From the Ground Up: The Resurgence of American Entrepreneurship.* New York: Simon & Schuster.

Centre for Community Enterprise. 2001. *The Community Resilience Manual, 2000.* Port Alberni, B.C.: CCE Publications. Accessed September 20, 2012, from http://www .globalfacilitators.org/VirtLib/Resilience/CommunityResilienceGuide.pdf

Craver, Richard. Research Park to Adopt Green Guidelines. *Winston-Salem Journal,* June 13, 2008. Accessed June 28, 2008 from http://www2.journalnow.com/con tent/ 2008/jun/13/research-park-to-adopt-green-guidelines.

Cutter, S., Burton, C. G., & Emrich, C. T. (2010). Disaster resilience indicators for benchmarking baseline conditions. *Journal of Homeland Security and Emergency Management, 7*(1), 1–22.

Estrin, Judy. 2009. *Closing the Innovation Gap.* New York: McGraw-Hill.

Friedmann, Thomas. 2008. *Hot, Flat, and Crowded.* New York: Farrar, Straus & Giroux.

Hill, Edward, Travis St. Clair, Howard Wial, Harold Wolman, Patricia Atkins, Pamela Blumenthal, Sarah Ficenec, and Alec Friedhoff. 2011. Economic Shocks and Regional Economic Resilience. Working Paper 2011-03. Berkeley: University of California, MacArthur Foundation Research Network on Building Reslilent Regions. http://igs.berkeley.edu/brr/workingpapers/2011-03-hill_et_al-conference_ economic_shocks_regional_economic_resilience.pdf

Hoelzel, Nathanael, and Nancey Green Leigh. 2012. Atlanta: How to Remake Cities as Places for Twenty-First Century Manufacturing. *Progressive Planning*, 35–39.

Leigh, Nancey Green, and Susan L. Walcott. 2003. Network Creation and Public Policy in Biosciences Technology: The Southeast Versus the Vanguard States. *Southeast Geographer* 41: 193–208.

Lichtenstein, Greg A., Thomas S. Lyons, and Nailya Kutzhanova. 2004. Building Entrepreneurial Communities: The Appropriate Role of Enterprise Development Activities. *Journal of the Community Development Society* 35: 5–24.

Luger, Michael I., and Harvey A. Goldstein. 1991. *Technology in the Garden: Research Parks and Regional Economic Development.* Chapel Hill: University of North Carolina Press.

Organisation for Economic Co-operation and Development (OECD). (2012). *Sustainable manufacturing toolkit.* Retrieved June 15, 2012, from http://www.oecd .org/dataoecd/55/60/48704993.pdf.

Rycroft, Robert W., and Don E. Kash. 1992. Technology Policy Requires Picking Winners. *Economic Development Quarterly* 6(3): 227–239.

Saxenian, AnnaLee. 1987. *The Cheshire Cat's Grin: Innovation, Regional Development, and the Cambridge Case.* Working Paper no. 497. Berkeley: University of California, Institute of Urban and Regional Development.

Saxenian, AnnaLee 1990. Regional Networks and the Resurgence of Silicon Valley. *California Management Review* 33(1): 89–112.

Schweke, William. 2004. *Smart Money: Education and Economic Development.* Washington, DC: Economic Policy Institute.

School Communities That Work. 2002. *School Communities That Work for Results and Equity.* Available from 895 Broadway, 5th Floor, New York, NY.

U.S. Department of Housing and Urban Development. (2012, Winter). Growing toward the future: Building capacity for local economic development. *Evidence Matters,* Accessed April 20, 2012, at http://www.huduser.org/portal/periodicals/em/winter12/highlight1.html.

Willoughby, Kelvin. 2000. *Building Internationally Competitive Technology Regions: The Industrial-Locational-Factors Approach and the Local-Technological-Milieux Approach.* Paper presented at the Management and Technology Program, College of Engineering and Applied Science, State University of New York at Stonybrook, December.

Index

About the Authors

Nancey Green Leigh is a professor and PhD program director in the School of City and Regional Planning at the Georgia Institute of Technology. Her economic development planning research and teaching focus on sustainable industrial systems for urban regions, spatial redevelopment, brownfields, employment, and economic justice. She is a former Woodrow Wilson Fellow and Regents Fellow of the University of California and past vice president of the Association of Collegiate Schools of Planning. In 2008, she was elected a Fellow of the American Institute of Certified Planners. In addition to *Planning Local Economic Development*, she is the author of *Stemming Middle-Class Decline: The Challenge to Economic Development Planning* (1994), coauthor of *Economic Revitalization: Cases and Strategies for City and Suburb* (2002), and has published more than 50 articles.

Edward J. Blakely, PhD, is a professor of urban policy in the United States Study Centre at the University of Sydney, Australia. He has held academic positions in teaching, research, academic administration, and economic development policy for more than 30 years, including Dean of the Robert J. Milano Graduate School of Management and Urban Policy and Dean of the University of Southern California School of Policy, Planning, and Development. He is a leading scholar and practitioner in the fields of planning and local economic development. Dr. Blakely served as a policy adviser to the mayor of Oakland and adviser to the Los Angeles Public School District. He was appointed by President Clinton as vice chair of the Presidio Trust, where he played a key role in the development of the former army base into a profitable civic facility. He has served on the board of directors of the American Planning Association, the Nature Conservancy, and the Fulbright Association. In January 2007, Dr. Blakely was appointed by the mayor of New Orleans to head the recovery effort following the devastation of Hurricane Katrina.